THE TAO OF COMPUTING

Henry M. Walker
Department of Mathematics and Computer Science
Grinnell College

JONES AND BARTLETT PUBLISHERS
Sudbury, Massachusetts
BOSTON TORONTO LONDON SINGAPORE

World Headquarters

Jones and Bartlett Publishers
40 Tall Pine Drive
Sudbury, MA 01776
978-443-5000
info@jbpub.com
www.jbpub.com

Jones and Bartlett Publishers
Canada
6339 Ormindale Way
Mississauga, ON
L5V 1J2
CANADA

Jones and Bartlett Publishers
International
Barb House, Barb Mews
London W6 7PA
UK

Jones and Bartlett's books and products are available through most bookstores and online booksellers. To contact Jones and Bartlett Publishers directly, call 800-832-0034, fax 978-443-8000, or visit our website at www.jbpub.com.

Substantial discounts on bulk quantities of Jones and Bartlett's publications are available to corporations, professional associations, and other qualified organizations. For details and specific discount information, contact the special sales department at Jones and Bartlett via the above contact information or send an email to specialsales@jbpub.com.

ISBN-13: 978-0-7637-2552-5
ISBN-10: 0-7637-2552-8

Walker, Henry M., 1947–
The tao of computing / Henry Walker.— 1st ed.
p. cm.
Includes bibliographical references and index.
ISBN 0-7637-2552-8 (pbk.)
1. Electronic data processing. 2. Computers. 3. Internet. I. Title.
QA76.W1855 2004
004—dc22

2004002152

Production Credits

Acquisitions Editor: Stephen Solomon
Production Manager: Amy Rose
Associate Production Editor: Renée Sekerak
Editorial Assistant: Caroline Senay
Marketing Manager: Matthew Bennett
Manufacturing Buyer: Therese Connell
Composition: Dartmouth Publishing, Inc.
Text and Cover Design: Anne Spencer
Printing and Binding: Replika Press Pvt Ltd.
Cover Printing: Replika Press Pvt Ltd.

6048

Printed in India
11 10 09 08 07 10 9 8 7 6 5 4 3 2

Dedication

To my wonderful family—my wife Terry and daughters Donna and Barbara—for their encouragement and support throughout my professional career, and particularly for their remarkable tolerance and understanding in the writing of this book.

Table of Contents

Part IV Web/Internet Questions

Part V Social/Ethical Questions

Preface

What should every citizen know about computers and computer technology? For better or worse, answers typically depend upon who is asked.

- Students commonly have a practical bent: How can one get the computer to perform specific tasks, why does a machine act the way it does, what is involved in getting computers to interact, and so on.
- Computing faculty typically emphasize the need to understand concepts and problem solving.
- The National Research Council (NRC) identifies appropriate general knowledge and skill as computer fluency, and summarizes its perspective in a 1999 report, *Being Fluent with Information Technology*.

On the surface, such perspectives may seem unrelated or contradictory. The practical details of interest to students may seem quite different from the high-level concepts and abstractions highlighted by faculty. Some textbooks written by faculty may do a fine job in covering foundational material, but often omit the practical issues that motivate students. Other books may describe pragmatic elements about how to run specific software (e.g., how one can utilize a bold type font in a word processing document), thus satisfying some students, but such books rarely provide adequate coverage of more general and lasting concepts.

Practical Questions with Thoughtful Answers

This book takes a different approach. The starting point is the observation that thoughtful answers to common, practical questions often require an understanding of ideas and principles. Simple, narrow, superficial answers can avoid deep issues, but these are rarely satisfying over the long run. Students want serious answers to their genuine questions, and such responses require the material that faculty wish to cover and the NRC has identified.

Question-Based

The second principle motivating this book is that students learn best when material connects with their experiences, backgrounds, and perspectives. To capture student interest, this book is organized around questions typically asked by general computer users. Common general questions provide the title and theme for each chapter, while more detailed questions provide a focus for each section within a chapter.

The style reflects the circumstances of a conversation. The reader has many questions about computing and information technology, and the book seeks to provide answers. Throughout, the starting place for discussion is a question—often a real question heard from a computer user or raised by actual students in class.

Computer Fluency

A third principle behind this book concerns the need to cover adequate material to allow readers to function effectively in today's computer-based society. Such background sometimes is described as *computer fluency*. More precisely, in 1999 a study group of the NRC produced the report *Being Fluent with Information Technology*, which addresses what every informed citizen should know about computers and technology. The report identifies ten high-level "intellectual capacities," ten "information technology concepts," and ten practical "information technology skills" that cover basic computer fluency.

Planning this book included a regular review of these areas, so that all fluency topics are addressed. The Appendix presents more detail of this coverage, with a table that maps fluency topics to chapters.

Of course, in some cases, faculty may wish to supplement this material with lab-based experiments and experiences. In such cases, this book provides appropriate background for the lecture/discussion component of a course, while a lab might use specific hardware/software manuals and exercises.

This Book as *The Tao of Computing*

"Tao" is a Chinese word meaning "the way," and many references to "Tao" are related to the ancient spiritual text *Tao Teh Ching*, or the *Way of Life*, according to Lao Tzu. *Tao Teh Ching* presents a humble, simple, clear, and elegant philosophy of life and behavior. The text consists of 81 short passages, many in blank verse; each passage provides insight for some component(s) of human living.

The Tao of Computing, of course, focuses on computer systems rather than spiritual philosophy. Within this focus, the book presents a clear and direct explanation of computer systems through a series of separate, but coordinated, answers to diverse questions.

Overall, this book seeks to unlock the mysteries of computers and provide a basis for further study and reflection, just as the *Tao Teh Ching* explains a path for the way of life.

Content Organization

Although practical questions of computer users may seem simple, these answers often draw upon important elements of computer design, software development and use, network connectivity, elements of the Internet, human–computer interactions, and applications. For efficiency in presentation, therefore, chapters are grouped into parts by broad subject (low-level issues, software design and problem solving, elements of networking, Web issues, and social and ethical matters). Within a part or chapter, material flows so that answers from early questions provide relevant background for later questions.

Terminology

One objective fact of life within computing is the use of technology to express ideas concisely. For example, computer terminology arises frequently in discussions of hardware and software, claims about new products and features, and projections for the future. Although general users need not know many of the more technical terms, they do need some basic vocabulary to understand what is said, and they need basic concepts and ideas to be able to evaluate claims (such as, is a new approach or product really revolutionary, or just a minor refinement?).

To establish this foundation, this book presents about a dozen basic terms in each chapter—not as isolated words, but as part of the natural flow of ideas. This inclusion of terminology complements the discussion of ideas and principles. At the end, readers should understand the important concepts and the words that support those ideas.

Other Pedagogical Features

Each chapter contains several additional features to promote learning and discussion:

- A summary at the end of each chapter highlights main concepts and ideas.
- Discussion questions raise ideas to promote productive group conversations. Some questions explore ideas presented within the chapter, others develop related ideas, and still others require personal reflection or research.
- Exercises reinforce topics within each chapter, emphasizing personal understanding and the application of ideas.

Credits to be specified in the Preface

Figures in this Book

Color versions of many pictures in this book are available on the World Wide Web at http://www.cs.grinnell.edu/~walker/fluency-book/. Some laboratory exercises also are available at this site.

Credits

Several passages in this book are edited versions of sections of *The Limits of Computing,* written by this author and published by Jones and Bartlett in 1994. Part of Chapter 11 is a revised version of material from *Abstract Data Types: Specifications, Implementations, and Applications* by Nell Dale and this author, published by Jones and Bartlett in 1996.

The author gratefully acknowledges the permissions received from individuals and publishers for the following figures and passages.

Chapter 1

Figure 1.4 comes from Figure1: B. Burgess et al., "The PowerPC 603 Microprocessor," *Communications of the ACM*, V. 37:5, June, 1994. p. 35. (c) 2002 ACM, Inc. Reprinted by permission.

Figure 1.5a was taken for this book by Ed Dudak, Physics Technical Assistant at Grinnell College.

Chapter 2

Figure 2.1 was developed for this book by Fredrick C. Hagemeister, Curricular Technology Specialist for the Sciences at Grinnell College.

Figures 2.4 through 2.8 are pictures in the public domain. Figure 2.4 was taken by C. Clark, NOAA Photo Library, NOAA Central Library; OAR/ERL/National Severe Storms Laboratory (NSSL). Figures 2.5 and 2.8 were photographed by John and Karen Hollingsworth, U.S. Fish and Wildlife Service. Figure 2.6 was taken by Joseph O'Brien, plant pathologist, Forest Health Protection Unit, U.S. Forest Service. Figure 2.7 is the Food Guide Pyramid from the U. S. Department of Agriculture (USDA) and the U. S. Department of Health and Human Services (DHHS).

Chapter 7

"A Dead Fish" is taken from Dennie and Cynthia L. Van Tassel, *The Compleat Computer*, *Second Edition*, Science Research Associates, Inc., 1983, p. 22. Reprinted by permission of the authors.

"Piano Sale" is also taken from Dennie and Cynthia L. Van Tassel, *The Compleat Computer*, *Second Edition*, Science Research Associates, Inc., 1983, p. 233. Reprinted by permission of the authors.

Chapter 13

Figure 13.3 reflects a view of a Grinnell College Mail Services page. This image appears courtesy of Grinnell College.

The picture of the first multimedia message in sidebar figure 1 is a personal photograph of Nathaniel Borenstein who has its distribution rights. The picture appears with his permission.

Chapter 15

Material from Kevin Engel's *The Strategic Guide to Quality Information in Biology, Chemistry, Computer Science, Medicine, Physics, and Psychology* appears with the author's permission.

Acknowledgments

Some questions used here derive from the author's conversations and correspondence with members of the Special Interest Group in Computer Science Education (SIGCSE), of the Association for Computing Machinery (ACM). Over the years, the author has benefited greatly from his association with that organization and with the many conversations he has had with its members.

The author is grateful for the encouragement and professional assistance provided by Jones and Bartlett Publishers, particularly that of former Editor-in-Chief Michael Stranz, Editorial Assistant Caroline Senay, and Prodution Manager Amy Rose. Special thanks to Theresa DiDonato, who provided wonderful feedback on the first full draft of this manuscript. The finished book is substantially improved by her insights and suggestions.

Many thanks to Fred Hagemeister, Instructional Technology Specialist at Grinnell College, for his technical review and suggestions regarding graphical formats and image representations. Thanks also to Todd Coleman, another Instructional Technology Specialist at Grinnell, for his help in developing images for examples on the same material. Similarly, Dan Keller was most helpful in gathering cables and preparing equipment for the author's pictures of various pieces of hardware.

Special thanks also to the Academic Support Assistants for the Science Division at Grinnell College who have helped with many components of manuscript preparation. Mary Heitsman deserves particular credit for her efforts in typing and preparing the book's index; Stephanie Peterson helped with questions and mechanics related to image processing; and Karen Thomson has contributed to many aspects of documentation preparation for many years. Additional thanks to Ed Dudak, Physics Technical Assistant, for his help in producing Figure 1.5a.

The author greatly appreciates the support of Grinnell College throughout this project, particularly its Senior Leave program. Special thanks to Grinnell's Committee for the Support of Faculty Scholarship and Dean James Swartz for their naming the author as Frank and Roberta Furbush Faculty Scholar in Mathematics and Computer Science for 2002–2003. Such scholar programs come about through the progressive thinking of interested contributors, and the author is particularly grateful to the Furbush family for the establishment and support of this grant program.

Finally, the author thanks his wife Terry and daughters, Donna and Barbara, for their encouragement and support throughout his professional career. Book development requires a focus. In writing, the world can seem wonderful when directions are clear and words flow, but an author can be grumpy and worse when progress seems slow. Terry, Donna, and Barbara demonstrate remarkable tolerance, understanding, and support throughout all these times; this book is dedicated to them.

Part I
Low-level Questions

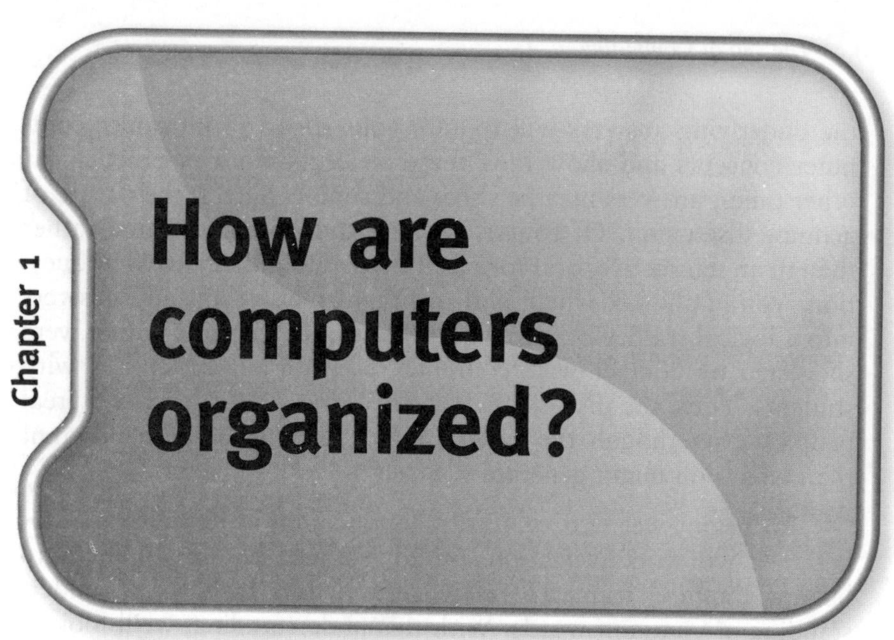

Chapter 1

How are computers organized?

COMPUTERS PERVADE many of our everyday activities. We use a computer when we withdraw money from an ATM, make purchases with a credit card, and check our voicemail. In the world around us, computers assist people in guiding airplanes, designing cars, stocking store shelves, and maintaining school records. We use computers to communicate with e-mail, to find information through the World Wide Web, and to type papers. We may hear people blame the computer for errors, delays, or foolishness.

In much of our contact with computers, we simply may follow directions or accept whatever we encounter. However, from time to time, we also may wonder how all of this technology works. For example, when we insert disks into disk drives or drag our mouse over icons displayed on our monitor screen, how does a computer know what to do?

Over the years, your experience likely has generated many questions regarding computers. You also may have overheard others talking or heard various claims or read advertisements, but wondered what they were talking about or whether their claims were actually true. The purpose of this book is to address your questions. Think of sitting down with a tutor/friend for a series of conversations. You ask questions, and your friend supplies the answers. Sometimes your questions may seem simple, but the answers actually require considerable background. At such times, your tutor/friend may need to provide more information than you expected. Often, the underlying answers will require your friend to introduce computer concepts and show how these concepts work in practice. At other times, answers may be short and simple. Such is the nature of genuine discussion. Of course, because this book is printed rather than in an interactive, oral format, I needed to anticipate what questions you might ask when, and to organize questions and answers into a logical framework. In what follows, the questions often were suggested by contact with computer users or during classes with students. Thus, the discussions aim to address real concerns by real people—even though the ordering of questions may be different than what you might generate yourself.

To begin, we need to clarify some common terminology. For better or worse, conversations on any subject require all parties to have a common frame of reference, and this includes an understanding of common words. With this understanding, we'll look at computers from the most basic level: their organization.

What is meant by "computer programs," "software," "data," "computer applications," and "processing," and how do they differ?

Each of these terms arises frequently in conversations about computing, so it is particularly helpful to understand these words at an early stage.

For a computer to perform any work, it needs instructions to follow. Contrary to popular images from science-fiction movies, such as C3PO in *Star Wars* or David in *A.I.*, a computer has no insight or intuition. Instead, it must be told how to accomplish every task, and these instructions must be given in great detail. These instructions are called **programs**; a program is simply a detailed sequence of instructions that tells a computer how to perform a task. As an example, when we use a computer to help type a paper, the computer utilizes a program that contains instructions to place words on a screen and to move the cursor from one line to another.

In contrast, **data** are the pieces of information that are handled according to the instructions in a program. As you will see in Chapter 2, data may appear in a variety of types, including numbers, characters, and graphical images. To continue the document-typing example, the characters typed by a user constitute one type of data. When the user types on a keyboard, the user is entering data. Additional information has no inherent meaning to a user, a program, such as Microsoft Word or StarOffice, may include instructions about how to interpret that information. Other data might include font descriptions that give information about the form of each character—perhaps in normal appearance, italics, or bold. As this example illustrates, data may come from either of two initial sources: the user or the application itself. To explain these sources further, data coming from a user consists of information exactly as typed. Application data includes data supplied by a program. This might include information about initial fonts or spacing in a document. If the user specifies what type of font to use, then obviously that information has the user as its source. However, if the user does not supply that information, then the program must make some choices regarding font and margins, and that default information may be added to information supplied by the user. As it runs, a program also generates additional data to create the desired final results.

Combining these ideas, **processing** is the term used when a computer follows programs in working with data. Thus, an application that allows us to type and format documents is sometimes called a word-processing program, because the application contains a range of instructions to format our data as we designate.

Interestingly, over the years the distinction between a program and application data has blurred somewhat. Often in early computer work, special application data were written directly into a program. A program was written specifically for a certain task. For example, the act of processing text might have involved the use of only one type font, and its details were an explicit part of the program. Further, the length of a line on the page might have been specified as 80 characters. Other type fonts and font sizes were not available, so there was no need for a program to accommodate other possibilities.

However, as applications have evolved, they have become more flexible. To accommodate various alternatives (for example, different type fonts), various details are now stored as data. Program instructions continue to tell the computer what to do, but processing may be adjusted according to the data actually encountered. Thus, in today's environment, a **computer application** includes both the program(s) and the application data that it relies upon. When such an application is purchased or installed, it typically contains several files, including both the programs and the special application data. For example, when you download and install Adobe Acrobat Reader (to read PDF files from the World Wide Web), you download the basic viewing software, plus quite a variety of special-purpose programs to handle such tasks as working with Web browsers, sending e-mail, interacting with movies, reviewing spelling, and using security options in electronic commerce. Such packages are common when an application includes many functions, each of which comes with one or more files.

Although the notions of programs, data, processing, and computer applications are reasonably precise, the term **software** is somewhat ambiguous. Often, software refers to programs—the instructions that tell a computer what to do step-by-step. In the early days of computing, *software* usually had this limited meaning. However, as programs have evolved to rely on behind-the-scenes application data, the term *software* now may also refer to the entire computer application.

How do computers work?

This is one of those short, simple-sounding questions that requires an extremely long answer. Consider the next few paragraphs as a first, preliminary answer; consider the entire book as a more complete response.

Conceptually, computers may be considered as simple, elegant machines, despite the web of wires and circuits you might see if you open up the body of your computer. When computers perform a task or process information, they rely on only a few fundamental parts of their system. The connections among those components are simple, and data flow easily among the various pieces.

In practice, this simple picture of a computer is complicated by the need to address serious constraints, such as cost and speed. To be useful, a computer must be affordable; expensive technology might allow the construction of fancy or powerful computers, but such machines would not be helpful if they cost too much. Similarly, computers must work fast enough to meet our needs. We may not care if computers take a few minutes to print our papers, but we would not use them if the printing took weeks or months.

Real machines employ a large range of technological tricks to gain high speed and capability at a relatively low cost. Although this technology improves performance for many applications, the resulting computers no longer achieve conceptual simplicity and elegance. For example, as we will explain in more detail in Chapter 2, the technology for storing information within a computer usually either facilitates fast processing or holds large quantities of data—but not both. Thus, real computers combine technologies for data storage; this hybrid approach accommodates reasonably large collections of information, but also has inherent processing delays. Such trade-offs are a constant challenge to computer developers, and sometimes simplicity is sacrificed for the sake of performance.

To further address this basic question of how computers work, the next questions and answers discuss a conceptual view of computers by looking at their most simple and basic structure. Later questions and answers review various technological additions that have been made to improve the cost and speed of computers.

What are the main components inside a machine?

Whenever you use a computer, the results you see come from a collaboration of many behind-the-scenes pieces. For example, when you open or save a document, you may hear the whirring sound of a disk drive used for long-term storage. Other pieces generally are quiet in their operation, but their contributions are essential in getting work done.

The basic operation of a simple computer involves only three components:

- The **Central Processing Unit** (CPU), which directs all operations in the computer and performs the processing steps for the data
- **Main memory**, which holds the data during most of the processing
- **Input/Output** (I/O) devices, such as keyboards, monitors, printers, and disks, which allow data to move in and out of main memory

Example: To clarify how these basic components interact, consider an application that adds two numbers entered at a keyboard and displays both numbers and their sum on our computer monitor.

Both our keyboard and our monitor are I/O devices. To get our numbers into the machine,

1. We type a number at our keyboard.
2. The number is placed in temporary storage in the keyboard.
3. The keyboard notifies the CPU that a piece of data is present.
4. Being the coordinating guru, the CPU issues a command telling the keyboard to store the value at a designated place in main memory (our first number in location A and our second number in location B).
5. The CPU tells either main memory or our keyboard to send the values to our monitor, so we can see what we have typed.

Although the work requires several small steps, the approach uses an I/O device (the keyboard) to move our values into the computer. The next task in our calculator example involves processing our data, and all such processing is done in the CPU itself. In order to perform such processing within the CPU, data must be stored in special, high-capability storage locations called **registers**. Although details vary somewhat from machine to machine, data processing generally follows these small steps:

6. Load our first value (from location A in main memory) into a CPU register.
7. Load the second value (from location B) into another CPU register.
8. Add the two values now in the CPU with the result going to a CPU register.
9. The CPU tells main memory to place the sum at a designated location (e.g., at location C).

With addition completed and the desired result in main memory, a final step moves the answer to a place we can see it:

10. The CPU tells main memory to send the sum (from location C) to the monitor for display.

Although this outline of work is tedious to write (and read), these steps emphasize the division of labor in a simple computer. Except for the physical operation of input (typing) or output (forming characters on the screen or on paper), the CPU controls every activity. Further, the CPU does the actual data processing (e.g., addition). To support such processing, main memory holds data both before and after the CPU does the actual work.

Finally, input devices (e.g., a keyboard) gather data, notify the CPU when data are available, and provide that data for transfer to main memory. Similarly, output devices (e.g., a monitor) display or save data, obtained from main memory, as directed by the CPU. Schematically, this entire processing of entering, adding, and displaying numbers is shown in Figure 1.1.

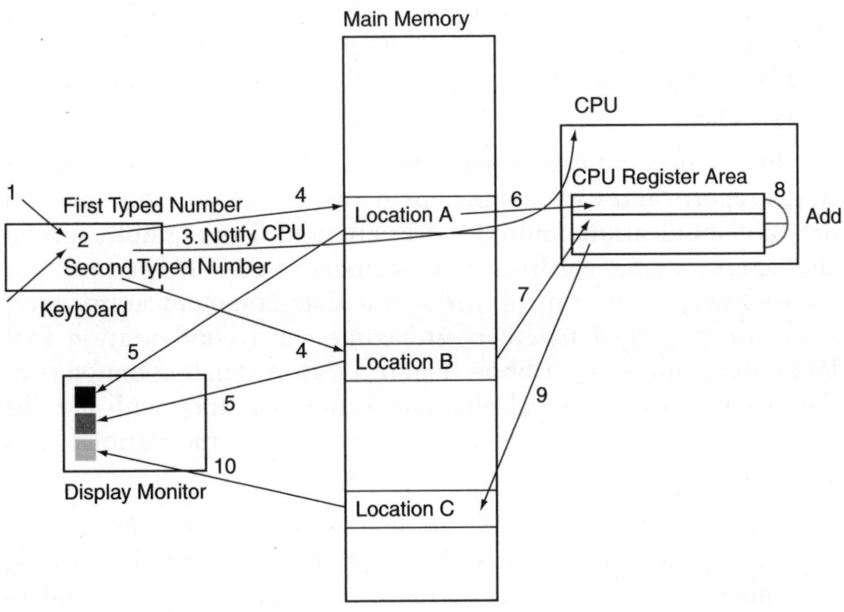

Figure 1.1
Reading, adding, and displaying numbers.

How are components connected within a computer?

As the addition example suggests, each component of a computer has circuitry to perform a specific task. Often this circuitry is produced as a single electrical entity, called a **chip**. These individual components built from chips need to communicate on at least two levels:

1. All components must be able to send signals or status reports to the CPU and receive commands from it.
2. Data must be able to move between components.

Through this process, one can think of a signal or status report to the CPU as being analogous to raising your hand in class when you want to participate in a discussion or ask a question. In the case of a keyboard, the signal or status report may indicate that the user has typed something—perhaps after a long wait. For a printer, the signal may indicate that the paper has moved to the right place for actual printing to occur. Another type of signal or status report might indicate that the printer is out of paper. The details of signals or status reports can be tricky, but the idea is fairly simple.

In practice, individual wires may be adequate to handle simple status reports and CPU commands. However, to promote speed in data communication, multiple wires are used. For example, several characters may be sent from main memory to the CPU at once. For convenience, both control wires and data-communication wires often are packaged together—sometimes in a configuration that looks something like a ribbon (Figure 1.2a). Another common configuration involves several plug connections or slots, with parallel wires connecting the respective connections of the various slots (Figure 1.2b).

Another practical consideration is how to make the physical connection between the parts of a computer. For example, initially, one might consider connecting the CPU to main memory and to each I/O device by a separate wire ribbon. However, even with only a few such devices, the collection of such ribbons would become

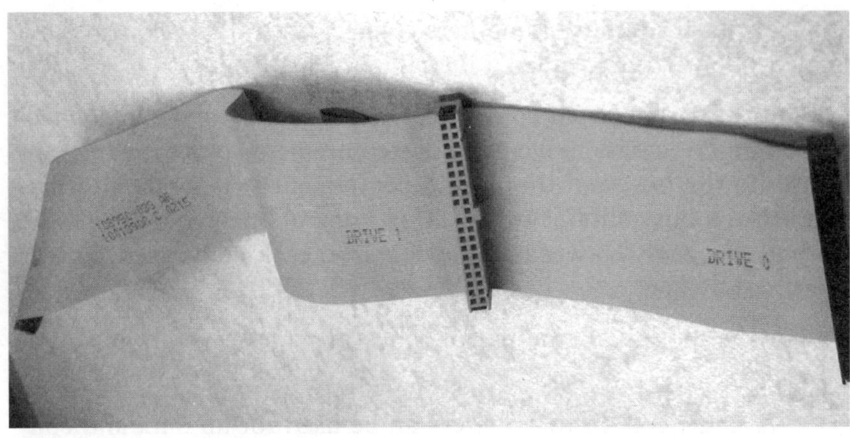

Figure 1.2a
A ribbon of parallel wires, with a connector at one end.

Figure 1.2b
Expansion slots, connected by parallel wires.

unwieldy. Instead, most computers connect several components to a single ribbon of wire, called a **bus**. (Figure 1.3.)

Utilizing a bus, each component requires only a single connection point. For a data movement, one component copies the relevant data onto the bus, and the second component stores this information. Also, a bus contains wires, called **control lines**, to facilitate the sending of signals between components, so each component knows what to do when.

For the most part, the use of a bus provides several important benefits:

- A single collection of wires can be used for all data and control communication.
- Each component connected to a bus need know only how to interpret its own commands and how to move data to and from the bus.
- Numerous components can be combined in the same machine with minimal interference.
- New components can be added to a machine over time—as long as there is a place to connect them on the bus.

As an aside, note that the ability to add new components to a bus comes into play when considering the upgrading of a current machine

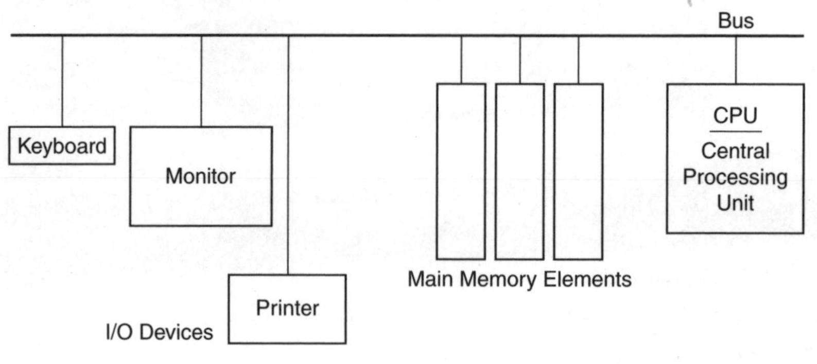

Figure 1.3
Diagram of multiple components connected via a bus.

or the purchase of a new one. Many computers come with expansion slots. Often, **expansion slots** represent additional connecting places to an internal bus, allowing connections for future components. When a computer has such connections available, adding new capabilities can be easy—perhaps as simple as just plugging in the new hardware. However, when all bus connections are already in use, there may be no free connecting points, making expansion difficult or impossible.

Therefore, when purchasing a machine, a buyer may want to consider what expansion is possible. Typically, one can expect new devices and capabilities to enter the market over the lifetime of a computer. These can be added to an existing machine if it has some appropriate free expansion slots—perhaps extending the useful lifetime of an existing machine.

With so few main components, what do the other hardware elements do?

Although the basic CPU-memory-I/O-bus model is sufficient to run most computer programs, the applications may run very slowly. In many cases, this poor performance has three basic causes:

1. The movement of data from one location (such as main memory) to another (such as the CPU) takes time.
2. Connection of components with a single bus limits data movements to one at a time.
3. The CPU coordinates all activities and performs all processing, so any processing must wait until the CPU can monitor or handle it.

Latency: All activities within a computer take some time to complete. For example, the CPU may request a piece of data from main memory, but it takes time for main memory to retrieve that information and make it available on the bus. As a different example, the addition of two numbers within the CPU requires time. We might think of these time delays as being insignificant by themselves—and they may be in some circumstances—but in other cases, such delays combine to consume considerable amounts of time. More generally, any work within a computer takes some time, and this time delay is called **latency**.

When considering the numerous data movements required for most processing and how to increase computer performance, three approaches may come to mind. The first is obvious: Developers of computer equipment work to reduce latency in the various components. For example, main memory is accessed frequently during most processing. Thus, speeding up how quickly memory stores and retrieves information (reducing latency) would likely have a significant effect in making overall processing go faster. Computer equipment is sometimes called **hardware**, and hardware developers constantly seek ways to reduce the time it takes to move data and process information.

As a second approach, one might try to increase the amount of memory (the number of registers) within a CPU, so there is less need to move data repeatedly between main memory and the CPU. Unfortunately, providing full processing capabilities to memory locations in the main part of a CPU is quite expensive and technologically complex. For example, even as sophisticated a processor as the Pentium CPU chip has under 40 full-capability storage locations. (Technically, a complex CPU like the Pentium has different types of registers for various specialized tasks, so a count of registers depends on which tasks you want to include. For the Pentium, most register counts would be 8, 16, 24, or 32.) Some other types of processors (called **Reduced Instruction Set Computers** or **RISC** processors) can achieve as many as 64 or so such storage locations, but even then the numbers are rather modest.

A third approach (actually the second realistic approach) to increasing computer performance builds on the observation that although processing may require much data over time, relatively few items are usually needed at any given moment. The idea is to keep current data very close to the CPU, where it can be recalled quickly when needed. Such high-speed memory near the CPU is called **cache**. Cache normally is rather small, but quite effective. (If you have worked with a Web browser, you might have encountered the notion of cache for keeping track of recent Web pages. Although that disk cache follows a similar philosophy as cache for high-speed memory, the discussion here involves different technology than a Web cache.)

The idea of main-memory cache is that the first time a piece of data is needed for processing, that information must come from main memory—but a copy is placed in cache. When the same information is needed the next time, it may be retrieved from the relatively fast cache rather than the fairly slow main memory. As this scheme may suggest, cache can work only when coupled with an effective bookkeeping system, so the location of a piece of data (in cache or main memory) can be identified quickly. Without good bookkeeping, identifying the location of data could take as long as getting the information directly from main memory—thus undermining any advantage cache might have. In practice, such matters can be handled well most of the time, and a CPU will usually find most of the data it needs in cache memory. Thus, one section of a Pentium IV chip includes a cache memory containing a few thousand data items. Although data still must move between cache and a Pentium's full-capability registers, the availability of the high-speed cache is very effective in allowing the Pentium to process information efficiently.

Busses: Conceivably, increasing the number of busses in a computer would improve the computer's performance by allowing several pieces of data to move between components at the same time. Unfortunately, connecting all components together with multiple busses is quite difficult technically, because activity along one bus might need to be coordinated with other activity along another bus. Thus, few computers use multiple busses to connect large numbers of components.

However, hardware designers may use specialized busses to connect a few (two or three) isolated components. This works particularly well if those elements are close to each other—perhaps parts of the same chip. For example, busses within the Pentium connect the full-capability registers with high-speed cache. This enables data to move between the cache and registers without interfering with data transfer between other components over a primary bus, such as might be needed between an I/O device and main memory.

Moving Work Outside the CPU: Although a CPU serves as the coordinator of all work in a computer, common tasks sometimes are delegated to specialized components. The idea is that when the CPU decides that a task is required, a separate component could be instructed to perform that work rather than require the CPU do it. For coordination, a component usually signals when the task is done by sending a signal, called an **interrupt**, back to the CPU. This entire approach is similar to the way a site manager may assign skilled workers at a construction site. At the start of a day, one electrician may be asked to install wiring in a room, a plumber might run a pipe to a drain, and a wall finisher might install sheetrock in a room. At various times in the day, each worker may report that the required task is done, and the manager then assigns the next job for that specialty.

For example, to print, the CPU may tell a processing chip located in an I/O device that data in a specified area of main memory should be printed on a designated printer. This separate I/O chip then can handle the details of moving the data to the printer, and the printer can follow the steps required to shape the relevant characters or graphical elements on the paper. When the printing job is complete, the separate I/O chip generates an interrupt, indicating the work is done. Thus, instead of taking time to interact with the printer and move data, the CPU simply issues one command to the I/O chip and then moves on to other tasks. The CPU decides what documents are printed when, but the mechanics are off-loaded to other components.

The CPU also delegates tasks to processing chips located in I/O devices when reading from the keyboard, moving data between main memory and a disk, and interacting with outside computer networks. In this way, the CPU saves its own time for processing of other data.

What does the "brain" of a computer look like?

The "brain" of a computer is the CPU. As we have already noted, in real computers, the modern CPU chip is a combination of several smaller components; typically registers, circuitry for various processing tasks (e.g., addition of numbers), and cache are packaged together within a single chip.

To see just how this works, consider an early PowerPC chip, the 603, built through a combined effort of Motorola and IBM. The actual chip is built on a wafer of silicon and measures just 7.4 by 11.5 millimeters. Circuits etched within the chip involve some 1.6 million transistors. Although such circuits are much too small for an unaided eye to distinguish, Figure 1.4 shows a greatly enlarged picture of the basic PowerPC 603 circuitry.

Although many details of this CPU chip are well beyond the scope of this book, we can relate many of the main sections of the chip to the basic components already discussed.

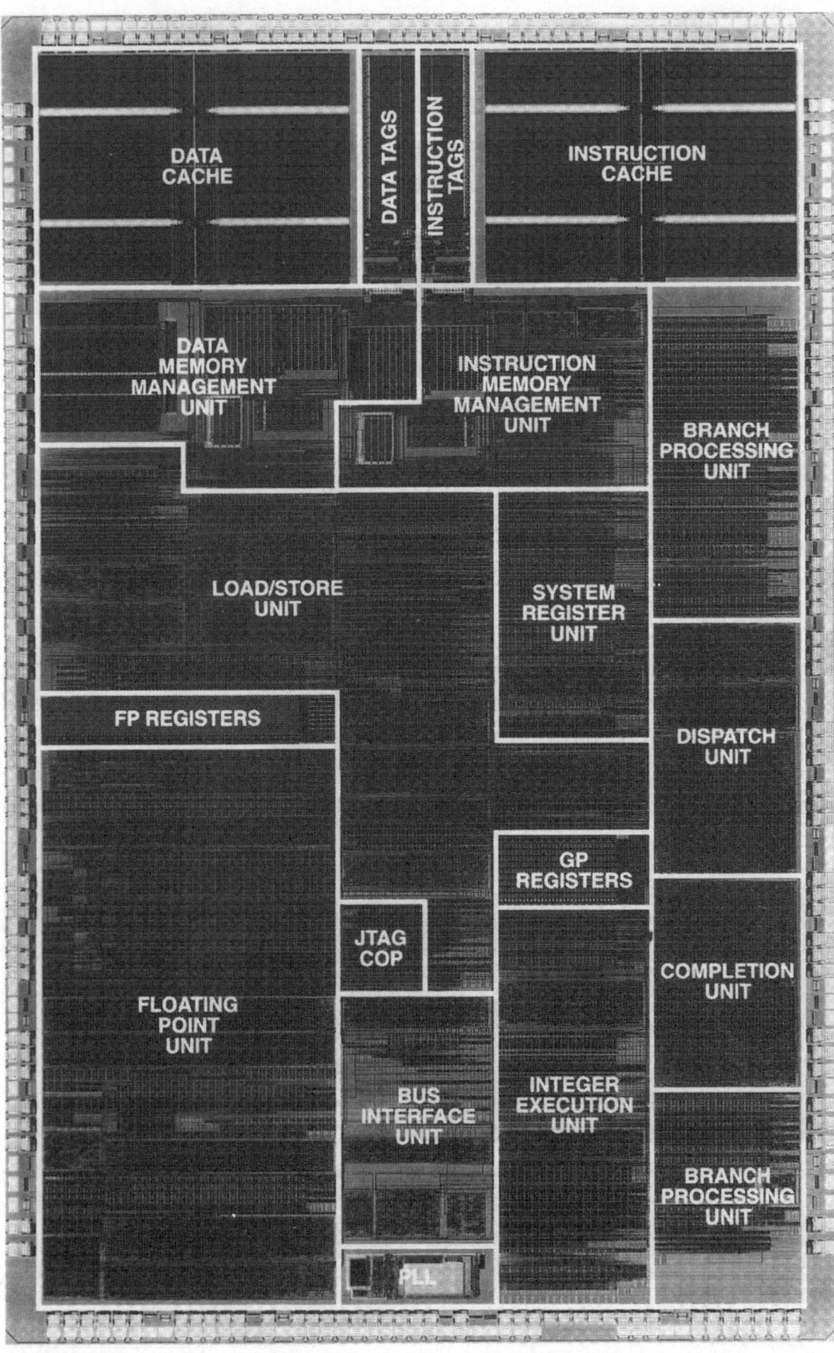

Figure 1.4
The PowerPC 603 microprocessor.

First, conceptually, information is divided into three basic types: instructions telling the computer what to do, general data (normally integers without decimal points), and real (or floating-point) numbers with decimal points. As Figure 1.4 suggests, the floating-point (FP) registers are the full-capacity storage locations for real numbers, and the general-purpose (GP) registers hold other data. The chip contains special circuitry associated with each type of register to perform basic operations, such as addition and multiplication. As the names suggest, a Floating Point Unit contains the basic circuitry for such capabilities as arithmetic operations and the comparison of floating-point numbers, while the Integer Execution Unit performs the analogous functions for integers and other data. Other, more specialized processing operations are handled by circuits on the right side of the CPU chip, including the Branch Processing Units, the Dispatch and Completion Units, and the System Register Unit. (Unfortunately, details of these specialized operations and Units are beyond the scope of this text.)

The PowerPC CPU chip contains a small, but high-speed, cache for both data and instructions. Movement of data is initiated by the Load/Store Unit which determines what information will be needed next. The Data and Instruction Memory Management Units determine whether the desired information is already in cache. (The various tag fields help in this determination.) If the needed information is already located in cache, it can be obtained quickly and directly from the appropriate location on the chip. If not, the Bus Interface Unit can be used to interact with the bus and main memory.

The outside edge of the chip contains about 240 small rectangular pieces. These serve as the locations to make electrical connections with the chip. However, because the entire chip is well under a half-inch square, making such connections directly would be a significant practical challenge. As a result, most chips are housed within a relatively large **chip casing** that connects the chip itself to wires or pins that are of a manageable size. In the case of the PowerPC 603, a typical casing is shown in Figure 1.5a. The corresponding casing for a Pentium CPU chip is shown in Figure 1.5b.

For each example, the casing secures connecting wires to the actual chip in a fixed and workable configuration. The result still is not huge (measuring only ¾ inch or so on a side), but the wire con-

Figure 1.5a
A ceramic casing for the PowerPC 603.

Figure 1.5b
A ceramic casing for the Pentium chip.

nectors are much easier to handle than the extremely small pad areas on the chip itself.

How does this description of components relate to what I can actually see within a computer?

As with CPU chips, many components within real computers may be combined in several ways. First, a single chip may contain several logically separate pieces, as illustrated with the PowerPC 603. These chips then are placed in chip casings to facilitate making connections. Looking within a computer, one can see several of these chip casings, with the chips themselves embedded inside.

Next, collections of chips often are combined onto flat plastic **cards**, with the chips connected by thin, flat wires. Cards are large enough that they can be handled fairly easily. (Note, however, that chip circuitry works with low voltages and very low electric current. Static electricity in one's fingers may be sufficient to disrupt chip circuits, and one must be very careful in handling cards.)

Figure 1.6 shows a card from a computer manufactured by Compaq, containing a Pentium chip. The Pentium chip casing is the relatively large square region toward the left middle. This shape corresponds to Figure 1.5b, although lighting may make the shading look somewhat different.

In this machine, main memory is made up of eight chips arranged in an almost horizontal row on a card toward the top of the figure. This memory card is plugged into a slot and held in place by white clips at the left and right. Looking more closely, this machine has room for three of these main memory cards, with three sets of corresponding white clips. The visible memory card is in the first slot. The second (empty) slot is mostly obscured in the figure by the existing memory card, but we can see many of the connections on the third (also empty) memory-expansion slot.

Also on this card, the large, square, black component toward the middle right is an I/O component used to display graphical output. In several areas, you also can see many small wires running from one component to another. These represent part of an on-card bus—that is, a bus with wires etched directly on the card. In Figure 1.6, you can see several sets of what seem to be parallel lines—particularly

Figure 1.6
A Compaq card containing a Pentium chip.

just above and to the right of the CPU chip. These lines actually are wires, and the combination of lines represents one or more busses. Finally, the many round objects are electrical components known as capacitors, used to store electrical charges.

Turning from the basic hardware to the makeup of an overall computer, consider Figure 1.7. As this figure shows, the largest parts of a computer involve a structural framework to hold the various components. For example, one section may hold a disk or CD unit. Another section provides several slots, often connected by a bus, for cards holding the CPU or main memory. (In some cases, more memory can be added just by plugging another card into a free slot.) A third section holds an electrical transformer, so that electricity coming from a wall plug can be converted into the form needed by the components (typically low-voltage DC rather than high-voltage AC current). Laptop computers also will contain one or more batteries to provide electrical power even if the computer is not plugged in.

Looking specifically at Figure 1.7, first note that space typically separates the various components. Not only does this allow servicing of components, but also allows air to circulate. With electricity being used throughout the machine, heat is generated. Dissipation of

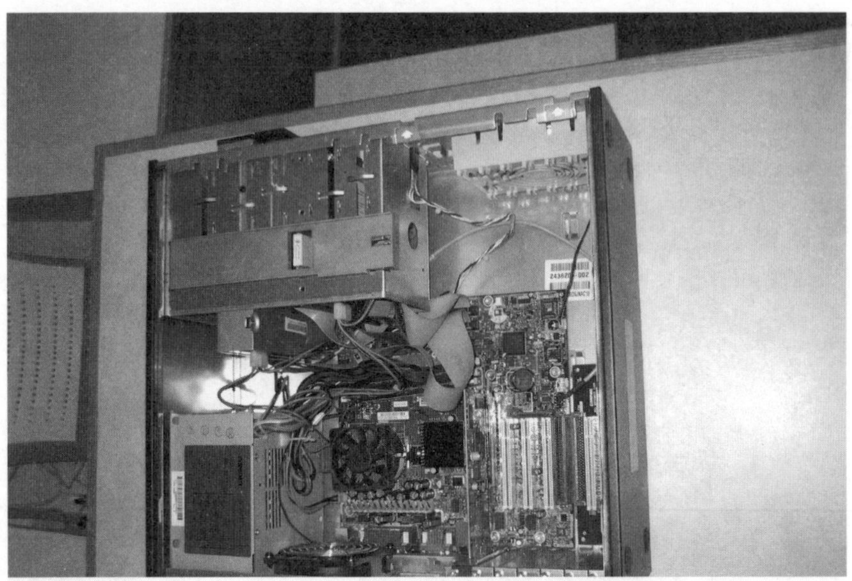

Figure 1.7
A Compaq desktop computer.

this heat is vital, because chips and other components tend to malfunction (or even melt) when subjected to excessive heat. The space that separates the parts of the computer helps the computer stay cool by promoting air flow.

Within the figure, the CPU card of Figure 1.6 appears toward the bottom middle. The card looks somewhat different than before, however, because a fan is mounted directly over the Pentium to promote air flow and heat dissipation. Another fan can be seen mounted on the side of the cabinet, below the Pentium card in the figure.

At the top left of the figure, the cabinet has room for several disk or CD drives. These mount facing outward, with electrical connections on the inside. Wire ribbons connect to some of these I/O devices.

This machine also has several expansion slots on the lower right of the figure, and wires behind the card form a bus to connect these slots. A separate card is plugged into the first slot, and the other slots are empty.

Finally, the lower left of the figure shows a transformer/power supply that provides power appropriately to the various other components.

Overall, the internals of real computers provide a clean and logical layout of the various components discussed in this chapter.

What is a "virtual machine"?

Although much of this chapter has focused on hardware, in practice, few users need to worry much about many hardware details. For example, cache memory and movement of data along the bus go on behind the scenes, without user involvement.

This observation may seem reasonably obvious, but it raises an important computing principle. Each user interacts with certain elements of a computer, according to her or his needs and according to the nature of the task at hand. A hardware engineer, for example, may focus on hardware details and the inner workings of the computer. In contrast, a person preparing a paper for her American Literature class will think in terms of word-processing software. Text is entered into a window that appears on a screen; the user works with the software to select a type font and size; page margins are set, perhaps looking at a ruler; and so on. For this application, the user thinks in terms of a screen—probably with buttons and displays and images.

These two examples, work by a hardware designer and work by a student, highlight that different people view computers in different ways. The nature of the interaction depends on the task at hand, and the computer may take on a rather different look and feel from one task to another. In the computer world, the work environment for a specific task is called a **virtual machine**. A virtual machine provides an interface, a collection of capabilities, and a way of thinking about the task at hand. Some virtual machines may emphasize textual or numeric information; others may utilize graphics and images. Typically, a virtual machine appears self-contained to the user of an application, but behind the scenes work at one level is built upon underlying levels of activity.

As we will see in coming chapters, computers often organize activity into a series of layers. Each layer has its own functionality, and each represents the user with a different virtual machine. At the hardware level, this chapter had outlined elements of circuitry organized into chips and components, connected by busses, and so on. Work at this level emphasizes electrical activities and detailed instructions to carry out basic operations. Applications, such as word processors, spreadsheets, and Internet browsers, represent high-level virtual machines. As the book progresses, we will look at these various high-level applications again. We also will have occasion to explore some intermediate-level virtual machines.

Summary

Computers contain several primary components: the central processing unit (CPU), main memory, and input/output (I/O) devices. These are connected by wires, often called busses. Within a computer, many circuits are combined into chips, and chips in turn are placed on cards. You can see the cards and chips when you look inside modern computers.

Latency measures the time required to accomplish a task, such as the movement of data from one place to another. Performance within computers can be improved in several ways, such as:

- Several pieces of data may move from place to place in parallel.
- Small, high-speed memory (cache memory) may store frequently used information.
- Processors other than the CPU may handle specialized processing tasks, informing the CPU through interrupts when the tasks are done.

Information within computers can be divided into three general categories: instructions, general data, and real (or floating-point) numbers. CPUs are divided into pieces, each of which usually handles a specific type of information.

Although circuitry handles low-level tasks within a computer, processing involves various levels of abstraction; work at high levels can build upon tasks done at lower levels. The virtual machine that users see, perhaps with windows and buttons for a word-processing application, provides a functional environment that builds on low-level operations that are available from more primitive levels.

Terminology from This Chapter

bus
cache memory
card
chip
chip casing
computer applications
control line
CPU
data
expansion slot
hardware
I/O devices
latency
main memory
processing
program
register
software
virtual machine

Discussion Questions

1. In a barber shop or hair salon with just one barber or stylist, customers come in the door, take a seat in a waiting room until called, move to the barber/stylist chair for their haircuts, go to the cash register (also in the waiting room) to pay, and then leave through the door.

   a. To what extent does the above flow correspond to processing in a simple computer? (If the barber or stylist plays the role of a CPU, what roles correspond to the door, the customers, and the waiting room?)

   b. Does anything in the barber shop or salon correspond to cache memory? Why or why not?

   c. Suppose the salon has a greeter/cashier as well as a stylist. Does this second position correspond with anything within a computer? Explain your answer.

2. Consider the following model related to a student preparing one or more papers. The student finds appropriate books for her work in the library, but does all of her reading and writing in her dorm room. The dorm room has a desk and a small bookcase. The desk has room for only two books, in addition to the word processor where she writes her papers. The bookcase has room for eight books. Due to fire regulations and a general tendency for neatness, the student never uses the floor or other places in her room to store books from the library.

   a. Suppose the student is working on a small paper for which she wants to use two books from the library. Write an outline of the steps she would follow in using the books. For example, she would need to check the books, and use them at her desk.

b. Suppose the student is working on a paper of moderate size, for which she wants to use seven books from the library. Again, write an outline of what steps she might follow in using the books. Remember that only two books can be open on her desk at one time.

c. Suppose the student wants to consult 12 books for a large paper. Again, write an outline of what steps she might follow. Even using both her desk and her bookshelf, her dorm room can store only 10 books.

d. Suppose the student wishes to work on all three papers, for parts a, b, and c at once. After doing some work on one paper, she wants to put it aside and think about it while she works on the other papers. Again, outline how she might proceed in using the books while she makes progress on the three papers.

e. Compare the work of the student in parts a through d with the workings of a computer. To what extent does the model of student activity have an analog to the CPU, registers, cache memory, or main memory? Are there any ways in which this analogy breaks down? Explain your answer.

3. When a customer calls a service technician regarding a problem with a television set, the technician travels to the customer's home. The technician keeps a collection of commonly used tools in her truck, and uses these as needed in troubleshooting the problem. Often, the technician can fix the problem during the initial call. However, sometimes the technician must take the television set to the shop for more extensive repairs. And sometimes the technician must order parts from a factory or warehouse before the problem can be fixed. To what extent does this hierarchy of equipment and service (house, tools in truck, equipment in shop, parts from a warehouse) correspond to the storage of data within a computer? Explain any similarities and clarify any differences.

4. Check the warranty requirements regarding a computer that is available to you. If not prohibited by the warranty or by school/company policy, remove the outside cover of a computer. Looking inside, try to locate the CPU, main memory, expansion slots, etc. What other components can you identify?

5. Technological considerations typically limit how much circuitry can be jammed into a single chip. Thus, if one part of a chip is enlarged to increase its capacity, then another part often must be decreased with corresponding loss of function. Looking at the PowerPC 603 CPU chip in Figure 1.4, estimate what fraction of the chip is devoted to each of the main components:

   a. operation processing

   b. identifying and locating information

   c. cache

   d. interactions with the bus

   Then determine the relative sizes of the different sections of this CPU chip.

Exercises

1. Using your own words, give a careful definition for each of the words or phrases identifed in the summary "Terminology from This Chapter."

2. This chapter introduces basic concepts of hardware and software.

   a. Give a careful definition of these two terms. Be sure that your definitions clarify how these two ideas differ.

   b. Consider "hardware," "software," and "other" as three main categories for topics discussed in this chapter. Then place each of the other words or phrases listed in the summary "Terminology from This Chapter" under its appropriate category. Briefly justify your classification.

3. In cities, busses transport people, with specified stops along a fixed route. Consider the extent to which busses within a computer fill a similar role. How are the two types of busses similar? Are there differences? Explain.

4. Make a field trip to a computer store to inquire about the availability of expansion slots within computers. What can

you say about the availability of such slots? Do such slots come at an additional cost? Explain your conclusions.

5. The text indicates that the actual PowerPC 603 chip is just 7.4 millimeters by 11.5 millimeters, although the picture of this chip is magnified significantly in Figure 1.4. Use a ruler to determine the approximate size of a connection area on Figure 1.4, and then scale the dimensions down to the actual chip size to estimate the actual size for an actual connection to the chip.
6. A chip contains many electrical circuits and components. One such component is called a transistor—a type of switch to turn a circuit on and off. The text notes that the PowerPC 603 chip contains about 1.6 million transistors. Estimate the size of one transistor, ignoring other electrical components on the chip.

Chapter 2

How are data represented in a computer (and who cares)?

WHEN WE USE computer applications, we interact with the computer at the user level, normally focusing surprisingly little attention on the technology that allows us to accomplish our work at hand. For example, when browsing the Internet, we likely think about the topic we are researching and the information on the screen rather than the servers and networks that make our communication possible. When writing using word processors, we concentrate on the content we want to convey and consider the application's role only in such matters as type font, type size, and page layout. As the user, we work with what we "see"; rarely do we stop and think about how the computer processes and organizes our data so that we can see them. Because the machine handles so many behind-the-scenes tasks, we can easily ignore the technical details of how data are represented and stored. We let the machine make the technical decisions, and our work can progress smoothly. The computer's technical decisions about data representation, however, can affect our work in several ways. It is to our advantage to understand how the storage of information impacts:

- The accuracy of our results
- The speed of processing
- The range of alphabets available to us
- The size of the files we must store

- The appearance of the graphics we see on the screen or printed on a page
- The time it takes for materials to download on the Internet

An awareness of data representation and its consequences can guide us as we develop our own materials and as we use the materials of others.

Why should I care about the way data are represented inside computers?

You scanned an image of your cats, Shamrock and Muffin, and put it on the Web, and now you want to print out a copy. Because you're also burning a CD, sending messages to your friends, and watching a soccer game via Web cam, you have a lot of applications open and running. As you try to print the image, you encounter two problems: First, your computer is taking a very long time to open the image on your Web site, and second, the printed image doesn't look nearly as good as the one on the Web. To help your situation, it would be useful for you to have a better understanding of how the image you're working with is stored and how the computer is working to process your information. For many applications, processing within a computer involves tradeoffs among speed, accuracy, capability, and size. For example:

- If you were using your computer to perform large calculations, you could achieve limited accuracy (think about how rounding numbers sacrifices the accuracy of a calculation, but on a larger scale) relatively quickly and use relatively little storage space, but greater accuracy may require considerably more time and/or space.
- Some word-processing applications increase their speed or their demands for storage by compressing the size of the data they store, limiting the range of characters in which they allow data to appear. Restricting data to the simple Roman alphabet with relatively few punctuation marks, for instance, prevents the use of additional symbols (e.g., the Greek letter ∂) that can be cumbersome or impossible. Such issues vanish with other storage approaches, but these may require much more space and more time for processing.

- The way computers store images can change to suit the needs of users. Pictures stored in a small file save space but may look fuzzy or blurred; those stored in an intermediate-sized file may display well on a computer monitor, but appear grainy or fuzzy when printed. Pictures stored in a large-sized format may display nicely on paper, but may consume considerable space and require much time to move between machines (e.g., download over the Internet).

As these examples suggest, computer applications often must find an appropriate balance between speed and accuracy and between size and usability when they store data. The basic questions they face involve how much accuracy is really required, how quickly results are needed, and how much flexibility is appropriate. In simple applications, the best tradeoff solutions may be obvious, or any choice may work well. In other cases, however, data management decisions can have a significant impact on the application's effectiveness and the user's satisfaction. The important decisions often depend upon matters of data representation, so a basic understanding of representation issues can have a direct effect on our applications.

Before I address your detailed questions about data storage, we need a common understanding of some of the technical details involved in data representation.

Why do computers work in binary?

The simplest and cheapest electrical circuits involve elementary on/off switches. When you flick a light switch on or off, electricity flows or it does not; a voltage is present or it is not. If we interpret the presence of voltage as the digit 1 and the lack of voltage as the digit 0, then having a light on can be represented as a 1, and having it off, a 0. In mathematics, numbers formed out of only the digits 0 and 1 are called **binary numbers**. The reasonably natural relationship between circuitry and binary numbers has made binary numbers an effective way to store data in computers.

To expand upon this idea somewhat, some early computers were actually based on the decimal system (which is based on the 10 digits, (0 through 9). In such a system, one might think of a 9-volt charge as corresponding to the digit 9, an 8-volt charge to the digit 8, and so forth, with a 0-volt charge representing the digit 0. Although a decimal system may work fine for a computer conceptually, in practice it has several problems. First, considerable circuitry is needed to distinguish one voltage from another. Second, circuits typically yield some voltage loss in various components, so voltages of 6.6 or 7.3 volts might reasonably occur. In a decimal-based computer, the interpretation of such intermediate voltages adds considerable complexity to circuits. Such complexity affects costs and reliability, so decimal-based machines can be relatively difficult and costly to design and maintain.

In a typical binary machine, a common convention is that any voltage from 0 to 1.3 volts is interpreted as the digit 0, while voltages above 1.7 volts represent the digit 1. Having a range of voltages allows circuits to accommodate variations of voltage that naturally may arise. (Circuits are designed to avoid voltages between 1.3 and 1.7 volts, so such voltages may be considered errors.) With no other choices regarding possible digit values, processing can utilize simple and cheap on/off circuits.

Technically, a single 0 or 1 is called a **bit** of information. Such a data element is sufficient to hold the answer to a yes/no or true/false question, but a single bit is inadequate to store more general information. Thus, in a binary system, several bits typically are grouped together in various size units, so that they can hold greater information. A particularly common grouping involves 8 bits and is called a **byte**.

To see how natural numbers, the integers starting with 0 and going higher, can be stored in a byte, consider the following numbering scheme. (If you know about the binary system, this will seem quite familiar.) Note that there are eight columns, or place values, because this is an 8-bit number. The placement of each 0 and 1 influences their value. To convert a binary number into a decimal number, start at the right of a sequence of 0's and 1's, and label the digits with a power of 2. Then add the labels corresponding to where the digit 1 appears in the sequence. Here is an example:

8-bit number:		0	1	0	0	1	1	0	1
		↑	↑	↑	↑	↑	↑	↑	↑
Label:		128	64	32	16	8	4	2	1
(or power of 2):		2^7	2^6	2^5	2^4	2^3	2^2	2^1	2^0
Number's value: 77	=		64		+	8 +	4	+	1

In this system, 00000000 represents the decimal number 0; 00000001 represents the decimal number 1; 00000010 represents the decimal number 2; and so forth. Following this pattern, the largest number would be 11111111 or 128 + 64 + . . . + 2 + 1 or 255. Altogether, this approach allows us to store the integers 0 through 255, inclusive, for an 8-bit number or byte, and we can conclude that one byte of data can take on 256 different values. Of course, this range is adequate for some data storage purposes in computers, but not for others. The 8-bit number with a range of 256 alternatives will arise several times later in this chapter and throughout the book.

? Why should I care about the way data are represented inside computers?

At a very simple mechanical level, we can easily conclude that, of course, there are limits on the size of numbers that machines can store! Because the main memory of any computer is finite, a computer has storage limitations. We cannot store numbers of unbounded size (e.g., integers with arbitrarily large numbers of digits) in a finite space.

How, then, can we describe the limits we have on the numbers we can store? Unfortunately, although this question is easy to ask, the answer is fairly complex. There are two main approaches to data storage:

1. *Fixed-size-storage approach:* Computers allocate a specified amount of space for a number; the maximum size of an integer or a real number is predetermined by the computer's circuitry.
2. *Variable-size-storage approach:* Space is allocated to numbers as needed; small integers take up rather little space, whereas very large integers require much more space.

Fixed-size Storage Approach: In the fixed-size storage approach, a standard format and storage size are used for all integers or for real numbers. (More about this format shortly.) Typically, the predetermined format and size can accommodate the data for common applications, and the hardware circuitry in fixed-point storage systems can perform frequent operations (such as addition, subtraction, and multiplication). With such built-in functionality, the capabilities of the CPU, main memory, and bus can be coordinated, and processing is fast and convenient—as long as the applications do not require values beyond the limits presented by the storage size and format. Computers that use the fixed-size storage approach allocate a predetermined number of bits for each integer or each real number. We already have noted that 8 bits or a byte can be used to represent integers from 0 through 255, and computers often have special circuitry to handle such numbers. However, most applications require significantly larger integers, so computers usually support larger groupings of bits as well. One of these larger groups of bits is called a **word** of storage, but the size of a word varies from one computer to another. As the cost of memory has decreased and as technology has allowed more processing capacity to be included on CPU chips, the number of bits available for an integer has increased.

For example, in the 1970s and 1980s, memory was relatively small and expensive. Thus, many machines allocated 2 bytes (16 bits) for integers. Following the same analysis used for 1-byte numbers, these 2-byte integers could represent numbers from 0 up to 65,535 ($= 2^{16} - 1$). Alternatively, this same amount of storage could be split between positive and negative integers, in which case the range went from −32,768 up to 32,767. To optimize processing of such numbers, memory storage locations and CPU registers each contained 16 bits, and busses contained 16 parallel data wires, so all bits in an integer could be moved from place to place concurrently. Larger machines in that period may have utilized 32 bits for integers (or even 48 or 60 bits), but such machines were quite expensive.

As technology has progressed, however, 32 bits for integers has become common. The transition from 16 bits to 32 bits actually involved two basic phases. First, CPU registers and CPU processing circuitry expanded to 32 bits to allow fast operations on these large numbers. In this phase, busses and, perhaps, main memory still were organized around 16-bit integers, so movement of data from main memory to the CPU required two steps. (First half of the data were moved, then the second half.) Once data finally got into the CPU, processing could proceed quickly, but getting data there was slow. Technology took another step forward, however, and soon busses and main memory expanded to 32 bits as well, allowing an entire integer to move from one place to another in a single step.

Today, most computers with fixed-storage allocation allow integers to be at least 32 bits. Thus, integers can range from 0 to 4,294,967,295 ($= 2^{32} - 1$) or from $-2,147,483,648$ to 2,147,483,647. In practice, this amount of storage is adequate for many applications.

The storage of real numbers (e.g., decimals) is somewhat more challenging. Conceptually, we can add a period (which for a binary number is called a radix point or binary point, rather than a decimal point), with subsequent digits representing powers of two with negative exponents. That is, digits to the left of the binary point are labeled with non-negative powers of two, whereas digits to the right are labeled with negative powers. As before, I'll illustrate the idea with an example.

Example: Determine the Decimal Value of the Binary Number 100.1101

Again, we label each digit with a power of 2:

8-bit number:		1	0	0	.	1	1	0	1
		↑	↑	↑	↑	↑	↑	↑	↑
Label:		4	2	1	point	½	¼	⅛	1/16
(or power of 2):		2^2	2^1	2^0		2^{-1}	2^{-2}	2^{-3}	2^{-4}
Number's value:	=	4		+		½ + ¼		+	1/16
	or	4		+		8/16 + 4/16		+	1/16
	or	4 13/16							

Because 13/16 may be written as the decimal 0.8125, we conclude that the binary number 100.1101 corresponds to the decimal number 4.8125.

Although such data conversions may be tedious, with adequate practice and a table of powers of two for consultation, they become fairly easy (see the end-of-chapter exercises for practice). Simply converting these numbers to binary, however, does not completely resolve the question of how real numbers should be stored within a computer. The difficulty centers on knowing how many digits to allow both before the binary point and after. For example, sometimes we may want to store extremely large numbers (e.g., 2^{20}), whereas other times an application may require many very small numbers (e.g., 2^{-20}). As a compromise, the storage of real numbers in fixed-storage systems involves keeping track of both a specified number of significant digits and the power of two used for the first label (the digit furthest to the left). For example, if storage kept track of six significant binary digits, then we might store 100110 in our example, as well as the exponent 2 for the first digit's label. In this case, the final digit (representing 1/16) would not fit in the storage space available, and thus would be lost—compromising accuracy. For the six significant binary digits, we have only six binary digits of accuracy, and the seventh digit is lost. Storing data in this way, therefore, can potentially have a serious impact on accuracy.

In this example, think about starting with the stored digits 100110, and then having the binary point "float" over the digits according to the stored exponent. Although this imagery may seem peculiar, it does explain (at least partially) why real numbers in computers are usually called **floating-point numbers**. Floating-point numbers are any numbers with a decimal point or radix point.

For technical convenience, actual computers make some adjustments in both the digits stored and the exponent, but the basic idea is just as described. In common modern standards, either 32 bits or 64 bits are used for floating-point numbers, as follows:

32 bits (or single-precision floating-point numbers):

1 bit for a + or − sign

23 bits for the digits of the number

8 bits for the exponent

64 bits (or double-precision floating-point numbers):

1 bit for a + or − sign

52 bits for the digits of the number

11 bits for the exponent

As a technical detail, these floating-point numbers do not store a number's first nonzero digit, because that digit will always be 1. Thus, single-precision and double-precision numbers represent 24 binary bits and 52 binary bits of accuracy, respectively. Inaccuracies in the representation of numbers would appear first in the 25th or 53rd binary digit, respectively.

Comparing binary accuracy to decimal accuracy requires a bit more mathematics than we have space for here, but the following can give an idea.

Consider what is required to write the decimal number near 1000:

- In decimal notation, we write 10^3 for 1000, using just beyond 3 decimal digits.
- In binary notation, we write 2^{10} for 1024, using just under 10 binary digits.

Thus, roughly speaking, what we can express in 10 binary digits, we can express in 3 decimal digits. Extending this same idea further, what we can express in 20 binary digits, we can express in 6 decimal digits. Altogether, every three or four binary digits correspond roughly to another decimal digit. Putting this together, 24 binary digits then express about the same level of numbers as 7 decimal digits.

Although the formal mathematics requires considerably more analysis, this basic idea can be applied to show that the 23 bits of single-precision numbers correspond to about 7 decimal digits of accuracy, and the 52 bits of double-precision numbers correspond to about 16 decimal digits of accuracy.

This discussion clearly has been somewhat technical, but the main point is that storing real numbers allows only limited accuracy. We may enter a number with 20 decimal places into a computer, but only about 7 digits will be stored accurately if single-precision numbers are used behind the scenes. In case this seems of only abstract significance, consider the following case study.

Example: Designing Aircraft

In the design of one company's aircraft, one step required the computation of the sine of a 20-digit number. In this computation, the normal approach is to subtract multiples of π to obtain a result between 0 and 2π and then apply the sine function. In this particular case, however, the computer used for the computation stored only 20 digits of accuracy. Thus, after the initial subtraction, no digits of accuracy remained. The result of the subtraction was completely meaningless; the sine function was applied to an essentially random number, and the result was used to design aircraft. Unfortunately, the engineers did not analyze this computation carefully for many years, and instead felt confident in using the computed results in the design of the aircraft. The serious implications of such mistakes could have been avoided by paying more attention to the storage of these numbers and the nature of their computations.*

* From *The Limits of Computing*, p. 100. For more information, see *Software Engineering Notes*, Volume 11, Number 5, October 1986, p. 9.

Variable-size Storage Approach: Without a constrained format or size for the numbers that make up its data, the variable-storage approach must rely on combinations of hardware operations rather than depending on its hardware circuitry directly. Although more flexible than fixed storage, this typically makes processing slow and cumbersome. On the other hand, flexible storage possibilities may allow computation with numbers of substantially greater size or accuracy. The fixed-size storage approach for floating-point numbers, as previously described, has the advantage of efficiency, because number formats and sizes are predetermined, and circuitry can be created to perform common operations. Thus, arithmetic can be quite fast, although sometimes accuracy suffers. The variable-size storage approach, on the other hand, avoids some problems of accuracy by asking the computer to allocate space as needed to accommodate numbers. This is not unlike the familiar approach people follow when writing numbers on paper. When we write the number 14., we leave room for only two digits (plus a decimal point). However, we must leave room for 11 digits (plus a decimal point) when we write the number 3.1415926535. Numbers with many digits may require considerable space on a piece of paper, whereas numbers with few digits can be quite compact. The variable-size storage approach in computers follows a similar method, where numbers are provided as much space as they require and are stored one digit at a time or, perhaps, as a sequence of a few digits grouped together.

Although variable-size storage allows a wide range of numbers to be stored accurately, this advantage comes at the cost of speed. Circuitry alone cannot anticipate all combinations of large and small numbers and plan for them. Instead, processing is done digit by digit (or a few digits at a time), just as we might perform addition or multiplication. Such work is much slower than the corresponding work for fixed-size numbers. For some types of applications, the gain in accuracy may adequately compensate for any reduction in processing time. However, when variable-size numbers have many digits, extensive processing may require unacceptably long delays to produce results.

In practice, the fixed-size approach is much more common than the variable-size approach.

Can a finite computer store real numbers with an infinite number of decimal places?

Although the variable-size storage approach may allow many digits of accuracy within a computation, a finite computer can store only a finite amount of data. Thus, a machine cannot directly store numbers with an infinite number of decimal places.

In some cases, this problem can be resolved through cleverness with either the fixed-size storage or variable-size storage approach. As a decimal example, consider the fraction ⅓. As a decimal, this is equivalent to the infinite sequence 0.3333333333. . . , and there is no way to store an infinite number of 3's. On the other hand, we could store the fraction's numerator and denominator separately—storage of the 1 and the 3 would take only a small amount of space each. Further, with this storage of fractions, arithmetic operations are straightforward, although finding common denominators can be a little tedious. In simple applications, this approach can work well and give the appearance of handling numbers with an infinite number of decimal places.

However, in this fractional approach, arithmetic operations often yield progressively larger denominators—even if fractions are regularly reduced to lowest terms. Thus, storage of numerators and denominators in a fixed-size format often is not practical, and the variable-size storage may require considerable processing for even simple operations. Overall, storage of fractions through separate numerators and denominators can be useful in some applications, but it comes at a cost in speed. With the practical difficulties of storage and speed, a fractional approach is rarely used in extensive processing. Instead, digits beyond what can be stored are either discarded or rounded, with discarding being the more common alternative. In either case, accuracy is compromised.

The problem of real numbers with an infinite number of decimal places is compounded by the fact that not all such numbers can be written as fractions. For example, the mathematical number π cannot be written as a fraction; there is no ongoing pattern of digits, and no abbreviated storage will suffice. The only way to store π is to store all of its digits, and that infinite sequence cannot be done in any finite computer.

Can storage of data affect the accuracy of results?

The previous discussion leads us to the unfortunate conclusion that not all numbers can be stored with complete accuracy within a computer. In a fixed-size storage approach, accuracy is lost beyond a predetermined number of digits of accuracy. In a variable-size storage approach, infinite sequences (such as 0.333333333 . . .) must be stopped somewhere, losing accuracy. Even with a fractional approach, numbers such as π cannot be stored with complete accuracy. The term **representational error** is used to describe any difference between a desired number and the actual number stored. Any scheme for the representation of real numbers will introduce representational errors—at least in some cases.

A second type of error, called **roundoff error**, arises through arithmetic operations with either the fixed-size or variable-size approach. As a simple decimal example, suppose an application divides the exact number 1.0 by the exact number 3.0. Although the theoretical result should be 0.33333333 . . . , storage constraints limit the number stored to a finite number of digits. For example, if 10 digits are stored, then 1.0 divided by 3.0 yields the result 0.3333333333—close, but it is off by a little more than 0.00000000003. This discrepancy is roundoff error. To continue our example, if the result now is multiplied by 3.0, the result would be 0.9999999999, not the 1.0 we might hope for. Of course, if the original numbers 1.0 and 3.0 contained some errors as well, then any error in the result could be compounded.

Together, representational errors and roundoff errors sometimes can combine over many operations to yield very large errors over time. A wonderful example of this comes from the Vancouver Stock Exchange.

Example: The Vancouver Stock Exchange Index

Between 1981 and 1983, the Vancouver Stock Exchange Index was computed with each trade of stock. The computation used four decimal places in the computation, but the result was then truncated (not rounded) to three places of accuracy. This computation was then repeated with each of the approximately 3000 trades that occurred daily. As a result of the truncation of the calculation to three decimal places, the index lost about 1 point a day, or about 20 points per month. Thus, to correct this consistent numerical error, the index was recomputed and corrected over the weekend of November 26, 1983. Specifically, when trading concluded on November 25, the Vancouver Stock Exchange Index was quoted as 524.811; the corrected figure used to open on Monday morning was 1098.892. The correction for 22 months of compounded error caused the Index to increase by 574.081 over a weekend without any changes in stock prices. In this example, computations began with correct data, but subsequent processing introduced a significant error in the result.**

** From *The Limits of Computing*, pp. 100–101.

As this example suggests, the storage and processing of floating-point numbers often are subject to numerical error. As a practical matter, this means that we may need to be careful in interpreting results from computers. For example, some analysis of accuracy may be appropriate before giving great significance to computer-generated answers, especially if decisions must be based on many digits of accuracy.

How does a computer know to use a Roman alphabet for English, but other alphabets for Russian, Greek, or other languages?

In the early days of electronic computing (perhaps the 1900s through 1970 or even 1980), much of the experimentation with and development of technology occurred in America and Great Britain. In these environments, researchers typically used English as their primary (or only) language, and therefore developed text-based systems for computers with a 26-letter Roman alphabet in mind. Other computer development occurred in Europe, but most of these people also used a Roman alphabet. Further, because most hardware came from U.S. manufacturers, researchers in non-European countries often began with equipment based on the Roman alphabet and basic English punctuation.

With the domination of English for communication, the challenge for early computer manufacturers was to find a reasonable way to represent English letters, digits, and punctuation so that they could be interpreted electronically. Although these characters certainly are not numbers, the basic approach was to represent each as a sequence of zeros and ones, as bits, so that the computer could interpret them. Several variations were developed, but 7-bit or 8-bit codes were commonly used, so each character was stored as 1 byte of data. After all, 1 byte can hold 256 different bit sequences, and this number is adequate for listing all uppercase letters, lowercase letters, digits, and basic punctuation.

Details of coding are not particularly important as long as a coding system contains an agreement about which sequence of bits represents which character. Two common encodings for the Roman alphabet soon emerged. Large computers typically used the **Extended Binary Coded Decimal Interchange Code (EBCDIC)**, particularly when punch cards were common for data storage, whereas small machines often used the **American Standard Code for Information Interchange (ASCII)**. See the sidebars on EBCDIC and ASCII for some historical background on the development of each of these coding systems.

ASCII

ASCII is a 7-bit code that was developed as part of an effort to facilitate the sending and receiving of information electronically. Much of the early work on ASCII came from a group at IBM, headed by Robert W. Bemer. An early paper describing the work was published in 1960. Bemer and his group worked to create both a draft coding system and equipment to communicate with it. In May 1961, this work led to a proposal to the American National Standards Institute (ANSI). ANSI, in turn, proposed a national standard in 1963, and a final ANSI Standard X3.4 for ASCII was established in 1968. During this process, considerable work was done to ensure that the ASCII ANSI Standard would be compatible with the international standards. Early computers often used teletypes, a form of electrified typewriters, for input and output, so care also was taken that the ASCII coding system would be compatible with the idiosyncrasies of teletypes.

Over the years, several national variants of ASCII have emerged to meet the needs of various languages. The International Organization for Standardization (ISO) now defines a family of 8-bit coding standards based on ASCII for various alphabets. In such 8-bit codes, the original 7-bit coding usually is extended by adding a 0 bit at the front, and newly added characters have an 8-bit code that begins with a 1. For example, ISO Latin 1 uses the traditional ASCII for its first 128 characters, and then fills out the remaining 128 characters with letters containing various accents and other letters needed for Western European alphabets.

EBCDIC

Although IBM cooperated in the development of the ASCII code, it focused much of its attention and energy on the development and use of EBCDIC. At this time, many companies used punch cards to store much of their data, so one of the design features of EBCDIC was to allow an efficient translation between the data saved in a punch-card format and data stored within a computer in EBCDIC. Although EBCDIC is often mentioned as a single coding system, in fact, several variations evolved; for example, IBM worked extensively within the international community, and so it developed some 57 different national EBCDIC character sets to complement its marketing efforts.

EBCDIC was an 8-bit code, built upon an earlier 6-bit code (Binary Coded Decimal Interchange Code) that had been used on early IBM computers. EBCDIC was used extensively with the popular IBM System/360 machines of the 1960s, and this helped motivate EBCDIC's continued use for many years. IBM continued to rely on EBCDIC for its computers until 1981, when it released the IBM PC. The IBM PC computer and operating system made full use of ASCII instead.

To illustrate these codings, Table 2-1 gives the 8-bit encodings for selected letters, digits, and punctuation.

Table 2-1 EBCDIC and ASCII Codings for Several Characters

Character	EBCDIC Encoding	ASCII Encoding
A	11000001	01000001
B	11000010	01000010
C	11000011	01000011
a	10000001	01100001
b	10000010	01100010
c	10000011	01100011
0	11110000	00110000
1	11110001	00110001
2	11110010	00110011
, (comma)	01101011	00101100
- (dash, hyphen)	01100000	00100101
. (period)	01001011	00101110
[(left brace)	not available	01011011
] (right brace)	not available	01011101

Although each approach demonstrates internal consistency in the ways uppercase letters, lowercase letters, and digits are coded, the actual bit patterns are essentially arbitrary. For example, the EBCDIC encodings for uppercase letters represent larger integers than the EBCDIC encodings for lowercase letters ("A" is represented by 11000001, and "a" is represented by 10000001). However, the situation is exactly opposite for ASCII encodings ("A" is denoted by 01000001, and "a" is denoted by 01100001).

Over time, ASCII has become more common than EBCDIC, but ASCII character encodings are still based on the Roman alphabet—using just 7 or 8 bits (256 combinations) to represent characters. In more recent years, especially with the expansion of international communication and the advent of the Internet, demand has grown to accommodate different alphabets and characters. Essentially, this is done in one of two ways. The first approach continues to use a small number of bits (often 8 bits) to store a character, but allows those bits to be interpreted according to alternative alphabets. The ISO has adopted encodings for various character sets. Thus, standard ISO-8859-1 specifies a standard coding for a Western (Roman) alphabet; standard ISO-8859-7 provides a standard for Greek; and standard ISO-2022-CN specifies Simplified Chinese.

With these various standards as options, a computer application must be told which to use. For example, in writing materials for display on the World Wide Web, Web designers are expected to specify in an early part of the code for any page which alphabet the browser should use when it displays the page. The encoding being used for a specific Web page or application is called a **character set**. Thus, when you look at the source code of a Web page displayed in a browser, check for information beginning with the word "META" and try to find the statement "charset= . . ." to determine the alphabet and encoding used. (To see the code for a Web site, use the menus on your browser to view the "source" of a page.) If the META data are omitted, then the browser is forced to pick what encoding to try and often defaults to a Roman alphabet. Because browsers may make bad choices without guidance, the World Wide

Web Consortium requires META data, although in practice this is omitted from many Web pages.

The second approach that is commonly used to represent the characters in a wide variety of languages involves using many more bits per character than the eight used in the ISO character-set standards just described. For example, the Java programming language utilizes the **Unicode Character encoding system,** which uses 16 bits (2 bytes) for each character. Because 16 bits allows 65,536 different combinations of bits, Unicode offers sufficient options for encoding characters from many alphabets in the same coding system. For example, Table 2-2 shows several characters for non-Roman alphabets and their Unicode equivalents. The space for each letter now requires 2 bytes—twice the space required for ASCII characters, but this extra space provides many more alternatives.

Table 2-2 Selected Non-Roman Characters and Their Unicode Equivalents

Alphabetic Script	Character	Unicode Equivalent
English	A	0041
Russian	Я	042F
Thai	ฉ	0E09
Cherokee	Ꮺ	13EA
Letterlike Symbols	℞	211E
Arrows	⇌	21CC
Braille	⠯	282F
Chinese/Japanese/Korean Common	㑟	345F

How are images created on a computer monitor or on paper with a printer?

A picture on a computer is organized as a collection of dots, called **pixels**, placed close together. When you look at a picture on your monitor, the pixels are typically small enough and close enough together so that you do not see them as separate pieces of information; rather, you see only the picture that they create together. Human vision is remarkable in its ability to perform this integration of picture components! For example, a typical Web image contains 72 dots per inch, making the image easy for the browser to upload and of a decent quality to view. A printer may distinguish 300 or more dots per inch, which allows for fairly high-quality printed images. This number of **dots per inch** (**dpi**) or **"bits" per inch** (**bpi**) is called the **resolution** of the image. Generally, pictures with a few dots per inch appear coarse or fuzzy, whereas pictures with many dots can look reasonably crisp and clear. Professional printers and publishers may use 600 or even 1200 bpi printers when they print their books and images, so that their materials will look particularly sharp and professional.

Computers break down images into pixels, because information for each dot or pixel can be stored separately, making it easier for the computer to process. For a simple black and white picture, for example, the storage of each pixel might use a single bit: a 1 might indicate that the pixel should be white, and a 0 might indicate that the pixel should be black. More commonly, rather than storing one bit for each pixel, computers store 8 bits, or a byte. This makes a range of gray colors possible, and a byte of data is stored for each pixel. In this case, 00000000 would represent a very black color, 01111111 an intermediate gray, and 11111111 completely white. Such a system is called a **gray scale**.

Using a gray scale for a 3 × 5" picture to be printed using a 300 bpi printer, 1 byte would be needed for each pixel, and the overall picture would be 900 by 1500 pixels. Thus, the overall picture would require 900 times 1500, or 1,350,000 bytes of storage, if stored byte-by-byte.

In a color picture, a similar approach is followed, except that color is broken up into its red, green, and blue components, and

1 byte is used to store the intensity of each of these colors. Thus, each pixel has 3 bytes of information: one for red, one for green, and one for blue. A pure red pixel would have intensity 11111111 for red, and 00000000 for both green and blue. Because the color white contains a full measure of red, green, and blue, the code for a white pixel would have intensity 11111111 for all three hues. In contrast, black is the absence of color, so a black pixel's code would specify 00000000 for red, green, and blue.

This use of pixels and red/green/blue intensities to store image information yields what is called a **digital picture.** In **digital technology**, a wide range of color intensities is possible for any pixel (256 possible reds, 256 greens, and 256 blues), but this range is not infinite. In contrast, a painter mixing paint has complete control of the combinations and hues of each color she or he creates, allowing a much fuller range of possibilities. Also, the painter need not worry about dots, but applies the paint continuously over the canvas or paper. The physical approach of using the paint itself without restriction is called **analog technology**, and is different both conceptually and practically from the digital technology used with bits and bytes in a computer.

A color picture uses 3 bytes of color information for each pixel, so a full picture would require three times the storage of a full black and white picture (with shading). For the 3 × 5" image stored at 300 bpi, this yields a requirement for 4,050,000 bytes of storage—about 4 megabytes.

The pixel-by-pixel storage of all color information provides complete detail about every aspect of a picture, and this collection of information is called a **bit map.** Typically, a full file for a bit map of one picture would include a header (with some type, format, and size information), general information (such as width, height, and resolution), and the image information of 3 bytes per pixel. On many computer systems, this material is labeled as a simple version of a ".BMP" file. Unfortunately, as our computation indicates, storage of all color information in such a file yields rather large files—even for relatively small pictures—taking up considerable space if they are stored or requiring significant time to download (particularly if one's Internet connection is fairly slow).

Because bit maps require large amounts of data, various approaches have been developed to reduce the amount of data actually stored. The idea is that image information will be stored in some compressed format in such a way that the computer can compute the full bit map based on the compressed data.

What are some of the approaches used to store images in a reasonably compressed way?

Several different schemes are used for the compression of images, and some approaches may utilize a combination of these schemes.

Color Tables: Although a color picture requires 3 bytes of information for each pixel, few pictures actually contain millions of different colors. Instead, one could define a table of colors actually used, and then specify colors based on that table. This table of colors is called a **color table**. For example, if an image contained only 100 different colors, then a table would have 100 distinct entries, with each entry having a red, blue, and green value for that color. The color of each pixel in the actual picture then could be specified by indicating which table entry contained the appropriate color.

A file for an image using this scheme, therefore, would have to contain the image information as well as a color table that has 3 bytes per entry. The image data, however, would be composed only of table indices. In our example where an image contains only 100 colors, the numbers for up to 100 colors could be stored as 8-bit entries in a table, so pixel information would require just 1 byte rather than 3 (plus the original table). If the picture is large, the size of the color table itself may be insignificant compared to bit-by-bit specification of the image according to colors in the table. Overall, this approach could cut file size by approximately one-third.

Font Tables: Graphical information often involves text, so display information for a specific type font can be stored in a table to help conserve storage space. This table of font information is a **font table**. One entry in the table might indicate the details for displaying the letter "A" in a particular font, another entry would specify the letter "B", and so on. When a font table is used, an image containing letters would only need to indicate the name of each letter and where to place it on a display. The table would define its font. Although this yields no savings in space if a letter is used only once, such a system can be effective if letters appear multiple times. Also, for standard fonts, tables might be stored permanently within a printer or display. In such cases, an image or text file would not need to contain the font table at all, because the font table would already be in the application that would be working with the file. Only references to the font table would be needed for complete image processing.

Shape Tables: Generalizing on the idea of color and font tables, one might store information about common shapes (e.g., circles, rectangles, ovals, lines) in a table called a **shape table**. As with font tables, collecting such shape information in one place saves little space if an image uses each shape only once. However, if the same shapes are used repeatedly in a picture, then use of a table allows each shape to be defined just once, and each instance of the shape in the picture can be indicated just by giving the table entry plus the location where the shape appears.

Shapes and Colors: When fonts or shapes are defined in tables, it is possible to designate one color for each occurrence of a letter or shape. If, for example, you want circles along a horizontal line in your image to appear in the colors of the rainbow, you can refer to both a shape table and a color table for each circle. As long as the computer knows the location of each circle, it can fill in the rest of the shape and color information by consulting the tables. This approach requires rather little information to draw many geometric elements and, thus, potentially condenses your image's file size. In this setting, a full recording of a letter or shape might involve the shape (from a font or shape table), a location, and a color (either using red-green-blue intensities or specifying an entry in a color table).

Drawing Commands: In describing the shape of an object in a shape table, one approach is to store a pixel-by-pixel description of the object. Although this can work well, such descriptions can require considerable storage, and the shapes themselves may not scale to a larger size very well. Thus, as an alternative approach, a picture might instead be constructed by drawing it using basic commands, just as an artist draws a picture or paints a scene using a pencil or brush and some basic movements. For example, one could draw a house by sketching various elements (walls, doors, windows), adding color by instructing "this wall should be tan," and so on. Further, individual elements, such as a wall, door, or window, could be drawn by starting at one place, moving up, then to the right, then down, and then back to the start.

Data Averaging or Sampling: Rather than store information for each pixel in a picture, you can condense the size of an image file by selecting a smaller collection of information to store. As a simple (but not very good) example, you could choose to store only every other pixel in an image. Because only half the pixel information would be stored, the size of the image file would be cut in half from the original. However, when you decide to display the full picture, your computer would be forced to fill in the missing data. One possibility your computer may take would be to assume that the color at one pixel was just the same as the one just before it. Effectively this would display each stored pixel over two parts of the reconstituted image. Your computer might instead decide to compute the average color numbers of neighboring stored pixels to determine the value to be displayed at a nonstored position. In general, selection of only certain pixels to store is called **sampling**. Reconstruction of pictures by averaging is called **data averaging**.

With any such sampling or averaging approach, the resulting picture cannot be as sharp as the original, because some information has been lost. The resulting picture still might be recognizable; it might even seem quite acceptable for many purposes. However, it will have lost some crispness and clarity from the original. As averaging or sampling increases, picture quality can be expected to deteriorate further.

Voice Sampling

Although this notion of sampling may seem like an impractical and unrealistic option for condensing space, it should be noted that this process is common in another context: voice communications over the telephone. To be more precise, when you speak, you create sound waves that are picked up by the telephone's microphone; when you listen, you hear sound waves created by a speaker. These are analog signals, and ordinary telephones may communicate directly with analog signals. At some stage in communications, however, these analog signals may be converted to a digital format and converted back later. In this digital format, sampling can be used extensively.

To analyze our talking, we could consider our speech as producing an infinite series of values concerning pitch and volume. Rather than transmitting this continuous stream of speech, telephones typically sample speech about 8000 times per second, using 8 bits of information for each sample. This produces 64,000 bits of information per second, rather than the infinite stream of communications from the person talking. Although the details are technically complex, the bottom line is that telephone systems can reconstruct voice patterns quite well by sampling, rather than transmitting the continuous (and infinite) speech patterns of a speaker.

Data Compression: All of the approaches described so far to specify image information yield a file or collection of information about colors. What, then, is the most efficient way to store this information? The simplest approach, of course, is just to store each piece of data. And, if the data are sufficiently varied, then this might be best. However, often we can take advantage of special characteristics of the data to help us store image information more efficiently. Various approaches for storing images compactly are examples of **data compression.** Here are a couple of simple approaches that are adapted for use in actual fax machines.

The data for each color in an image might be specified in relation to the color's frequency. Suppose, for simplicity, that each pixel on a text document is white, gray, or black, and that the background of the page is white. As we scan along a line, we would first see white, then parts of a letter, then more white, another letter, and so on. Breaking down what we see into colored pieces, we have a block of white, a block of black or gray, another block of white, more black or gray, an so on. Our next step is to encode the colors, and because white appears most often, we will choose a short code in binary. Let's choose the single digit 1. Black and gray appear less often, so we choose two-digit codes for these: 00 for black and 01 for gray. Note that although the number of binary digits varies from one color to the next, when we read the code, we will automatically know each pixel's color. If the first digit is 1, it's the color white. If the first digit is 0, then the pixel is either black or gray (it cannot be white), and we must look at the second bit to determine which color we have. This example illustrates how we can code colors based on their frequency, with the most common colors having a short code and less common colors having a longer code. (A common technique for determining such codes is called the **Huffman algorithm**, and such codes are used very commonly in data compression.)

Once a color is identified in our line of information, we could repeat the color code for each matching pixel on the line. As noted, however, we can expect a block of pixels of one color and then a block of the next. Because most colors come in blocks, we can save space by combining a count with the color, rather than repeating the color information for each pixel. For example, if the color gray occurs for 50 pixels in a row, we could say "50 gray" rather than "gray, gray, gray, . . . , gray" 50 times. As with determining codes, the details require care, but this approach can provide considerable space savings without losing any information regarding a specific image. It allows image data to be compressed greatly, and this approach motivates the detailed mechanisms for fax machines. Fax machines process a page by scanning one line after another, and this approach to data compression allows an efficient transmission of the images.

I have encountered ".gif", ".ps", and ".jpg" image files when surfing the Web. How do these image files work?

GIF is an abbreviation for Graphics Interchange Format and specifies a particular file format copyrighted by CompuServe Incorporated. Several variations are possible, but a picture stored in a .gif format basically uses one or more color tables, where each table is limited to 256 colors. Although .gif files also can take advantage of predefined font tables, the main usage of .gif files arises in pictures containing relatively few colors. When pictures contain direct colors without a great deal of shading, the abbreviation of colors through a color table such as that used for .gif files can be particularly effective.

Images can also be saved as **PostScript** files or ".ps" files, a framework based on drawing commands. For example, the "moveto" command traces a line from a current position to a specified new one, and the "arc" command draws an arc (including a circle), given its center, radius, and so on. To supplement these basic commands, PostScript also allows general shapes to be defined and then used in multiple places. Thus, fonts for characters can be defined once (like font tables, but with drawing instructions), remembered, and then used as often as desired. This format is particularly useful when a picture can be rendered efficiently as a drawing or when the image contains many of the same elements (e.g., text using the same fonts).

.jpg or **JPEG** files, created by the Joint Photographic Experts Group (and hence the acronym), are based largely on what people actually see. It turns out, for example, that human vision relates more to luminance than specific color, and the **JPEG** approach takes this into account. The specifics are quite complex, but the idea is to divide a picture into blocks of 8 by 8 pixels. These blocks are then processed using such ideas as data averaging and sampling according to how much detail and clarity a user specifies. These abbreviated files then are made even smaller using data compression. If the user wants a high-quality image, then the 8 by 8 blocks maintain much of their content, and relatively little compression can take place. If a relatively low-quality image is acceptable, then information (particularly about color) may be discarded in order to produce rather small files. When using the JPEG format, the creator of an image must determine how much detail and clarity are needed, and instruct the image processor accordingly. Normally, such decisions rely upon finding an appropriate balance between image quality and file size.

Because JPEG files involve adjustments of a picture based on computations, picture quality usually deteriorates each time a picture is processed and saved. This quality is not true of the GIF or PostScript formats. On the other hand, using the JPEG file format can result in remarkable reductions in file size.

Do these differences among various file formats really matter?

As noted in the previous section, each file format has particular advantages and disadvantages, which in turn affect when you would want to choose one format over another. Let's look at each in turn.

The GIF format is based on storing up to 256 colors in a color table. This produces crisp, clean pictures unless an image contains considerable shading with many colors. In such cases, shades of color may be adjusted to fit within the 256 limit, and coloring may be lost. Because each pixel is stored separated, .gif files may not scale well. Further, large images have many pixels, and a .gif file may not contain enough information when a picture is expanded in size.

The PostScript format is based on drawing an image and works well when shapes are used. Because pictures are drawn, images saved in PostScript formats often scale up in size well. On the other hand, if shapes are sufficiently irregular, drawing can be difficult; at the extreme, each pixel might need to be drawn separately. This can result in large files in certain circumstances.

The JPEG format processes pixel information in 8 by 8 blocks, according to the level of compression specified by a user. Although this can result in quite small files, the quality of an image can suffer if its compressed file becomes too small. Often its loss of quality involves subtle changes in color or sharpness.

What are the tradeoffs in handling pictures and other graphical applications?

Much of this discussion of file formats and storage mechanisms may seem rather abstract, so let's consider three examples.

Example: Text

Figure 2.1 shows a picture of a page of text. As this picture indicates, the page of text could be stored in several formats: HTML (designed for text in Web pages), PostScript, GIF, JPEG, or TIFF (approximately a bitmap format). With PostScript, the file could assume that either the printer already has font information (no font need be embedded) or that the printer will need font information for printing (font will need to be embedded). JPEG files allow varying qualities, so this version would allow a medium level of clarity and precision.

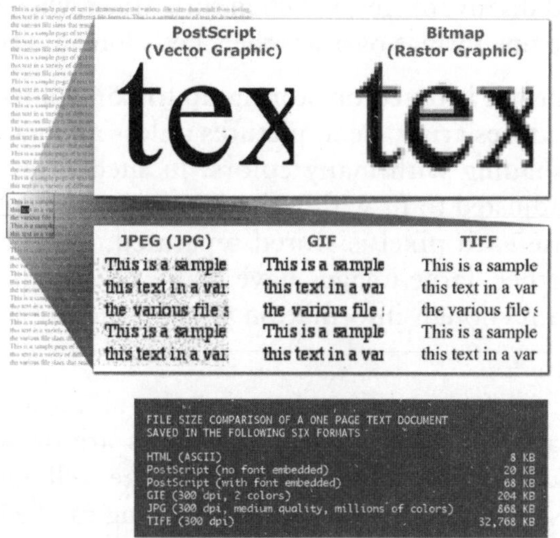

FILE SIZE COMPARISON OF A ONE PAGE TEXT DOCUMENT SAVED IN THE FOLLOWING SIX FORMATS

HTML (ASCII)	8 KB
PostScript (no font embedded)	20 KB
PostScript (with font embedded)	68 KB
GIF (300 dpi, 2 colors)	204 KB
JPG (300 dpi, medium quality, millions of colors)	868 KB
TIFF (300 dpi)	32,768 KB

Figure 2.1
A textual image.

Because this material is black-and-white text, color is not much of an issue. However, the various formats yield very different size files. HTML is designed for text on the Web, so its format is the smallest (but it cannot handle fancier graphics directly). PostScript is the next smallest. Comparing the two versions, information about how to draw fonts takes up about 48,000 bytes of information, a little more than twice the space required to place those fonts to obtain the page of text. Further, because PostScript shows how to draw fonts, the image information scales well; zooming in on the text produces crisp, clear text. Such a file format obviously works very well for this type of textual material.

The GIF format for this picture is somewhat simplified, because only two colors are needed to display text (black and white). A JPEG format of medium quality still divides the image into blocks of 8 pixels by 8 pixels, and processes using some averaging and sampling. Although the GIF format handles the two colors somewhat better, both .gif and .jpg files are fairly large. Further, because both GIF and JPEG are based on a specific image and its pixels, neither format scales well. If pixel information must be expanded to produce an image of several times the size, the resulting image often seems rather fuzzy.

Example: Foliage

Next, consider a picture of foliage in the backyard of a house. Figure 2.2a shows the original picture taken by a digital camera. This original picture is large and in color: In JPEG format, as it comes out of the camera, the file requires 1,124,557 bytes (about 1.1 megabytes). This takes some time to download on the World Wide Web, so it needs to be condensed to be practical. For this example, the original picture was stored as a 4 × 3" picture, using the 72 pixels per inch used by Web browsers. The results, in GIF and JPEG formats, are shown in Figures 2.2b and 2.2c.

Color versions of these pictures may be found at
http://www.cs.grinnell.edu/~walker/fluency-book/index.shtml

(High resolution was used for the JPEG format, so the file size would be about the same for .gif and .jpg files—about 59–60 kilobytes.) Both sizes are in range of what can be handled reasonably well by browsers in Web-based applications. However, the .gif file is sharper and crisper, because it maintains a record of the specific colors and pixels. When the number of colors is controlled (the original photo for this example contained mostly shades of green, and this rendition contains shades of gray), then the GIF format can work well.

Figure 2.2a
Foliage: original version (1,124,557 bytes).

Figure 2.2b
Medium resolution in GIF format (59,001 bytes).

Figure 2.2c
High resolution in JPEG format (60,668 bytes).

A PostScript version of the foliage file also was created in the writing of this chapter. However, that file was about 12 megabytes in size, about 12 times larger than the original. PostScript often does not work well for pictures when the images begin in another format.

Example: Library Shelves

The original picture of these library shelves is shown in Figure 2.3a, with the revised GIF and JPEG formats in Figures 2.3b and 2.3c, respectively.

As with Figure 2.2, color versions of these pictures may be found at http://www.cs.grinnell.edu/~walker/fluency-book/index.shtml

Again, medium-resolution GIF and high-resolution JPEG formats were chosen because as storage files they were approximately the same size. In this case, the revised .jpg file again is slightly less crisp in the foreground, and the colors for that region also are somewhat truer in the gif file. However, the colors blend together somewhat in the back shelf on the .gif file, while that shelf on the jpeg file retains shading better.

Figure 2.3a
Library shelves: original version (868,551 bytes).

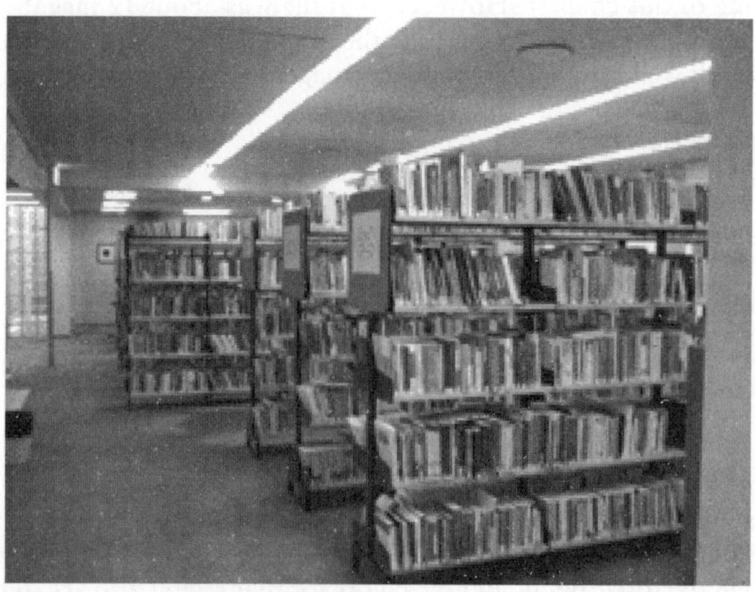

Figure 2.3b
Medium resolution in GIF format (50,790 bytes).

Figure 2.3c
High resolution in JPEG format (47,301 bytes).

Summary

Although we may not pay much attention to how data are represented in various applications, the details matter.

- Numeric integers may be constrained in size.
- Real or floating-point numbers may have limited accuracy.
- Computations with numbers may produce roundoff errors, further affecting accuracy.
- Data storage may affect what characters and languages we can use conveniently in our applications.
- Pictures are displayed pixel by pixel, so storage considerations can affect file size and image quality.

Altogether, how data are represented can have serious implications in the applications that we use, and we need to be aware of how storage details might effect our applications.

Terminology from This Chapter

analog technology	data averaging	Huffman algorithm
ASCII	data compression	JPEG or JPG
binary number	data sampling	PostScript
bit	digital technology	representational error
bit map	dots per inch	resolution
bits per inch (bpi)	EBCDIC	roundoff error
byte	floating-point number	shape table
character set (character encoding system)	font table	Unicode
color table	GIF	word
	gray scale	

Discussion Questions

1. The decimal number 1/10 translates in binary to the infinite value 0.000110001100011 . . ., so the decimal 1/10 cannot be stored exactly in either the fixed-size or variable-size approach for floating-point numbers. Similarly, the decimal number 1/100 cannot be stored exactly and must involve some representational error.

   a. A bank computer could store account balances in either dollars or cents. (Thus, $1.23 could be stored either as the floating-point number 1.23 or as the integer 123.) Discuss the relative merits of each approach, and find at least one advantage of each approach.

   b. When interest is computed for a bank account, the result will rarely translate to an exact number of pennies. Rather, the interest will have to be translated to a penny amount. If the interest is always truncated or rounded down to the nearest cent, discuss what should be done with the rest. (This will be a trivial amount for each account, but could add up if a bank has thousands or millions of accounts.) If the interest is rounded to the nearest cent, then sometimes the bank would pay a fraction too much interest to an account. Again, this is trivial for a single account, but the possibility arises that the bank could pay this overage thousands or millions of times. Discuss the relative merits of rounding down (truncating) or rounding to the nearest cent from the standpoint of both the bank and the customer.

2. Display the Web page http://www.cs.grinnell.edu/~walker/ in your browser, and then display its source.

   a. Find the line specifying the META data used, and determine what character encoding is being used.

   b. Use your browser menu options to change the encoding used, and describe what happens.

   c. Find a page on the Web that does not have a META data specifier, and try to determine what alphabet or character set your browser uses.

3. This chapter describes several common techniques for reducing the size of files that store graphical images: color tables, font tables, shape tables, drawing commands, data averaging and sampling, and data compression. The chapter also discusses three file formats: GIF, PostScript, and JPEG. Generate a table, with file formats across the top and size reduction techniques down the side. Then fill in the table to indicate which techniques are used with which formats.

4. Consider the pictures given in Figures 2.4 and 2.5. In each case, determine which file format(s) might be used most effectively for the storage of the image.

Figure 2.4
Multiple cloud-to-ground and cloud-to-cloud lightning strikes during nighttime. Observed during night-time thunderstorm. http://www.photolib.noaa.gov/nsll/nssl0010.htm
Credit: C. Clark, NOAA Photo Library, NOAA Central Library; OAR/ERL/National Severe Storms Laboratory (NSSL) in public domain: http://www.photolib.noaa.gov/aboutimages.html

Figure 2.5
Bond Swamp National Wildlife Refuge, Georgia. http://images.fws.gov/default.cfm?fuseaction=records.display&CFID=3034979&CFTOKEN=61422747&id=5936A895%2DE2F9%2D425D%2DB5225B1D5334696B
Credit: John and Karen Hollingsworth, U.S. Fish and Wildlife Service in public domain: http://images.fws.gov/default.cfm?CFID=3034751&CFTOKEN=64693326

Exercises

1. This chapter identifies basic elements of data storage, considers three main types of data—numbers, text, and images; and describes several techniques for data compression.

   a. Using "basic elements," "numbers," "text," "images," and "techniques" as headings, please categorize each word or phrase identified in the summary "Terminology from This Chapter" under the appropriate heading.

   b. Give definitions for each word or phrase that you have listed under "basic elements," "numbers," or "text."

   c. Identify the idea behind the various types of images and techniques, but do not try to describe all of the technical details.

2. Compute the decimal values of the following binary numbers:

   a. integer: 1011

   b. integer: 1010101

   c. integer: 10101010

d. floating-point number: 11.01

e. floating-point number: 1010.101

3. Rather than using the binary system for real numbers, this problem uses the more familiar decimal system. Throughout, assume numbers are stored in the format described in the text with significant digits and an exponent (power of 10). Also, assume that a system can maintain seven decimal digits; if a computation yields a result requiring more than seven digits, the number will have to be rounded or truncated (your choice, but you must be consistent).

a. Explain how the number 12,345,670 could be stored correctly in this system.

b. Suppose 1 is added to 12,345,670. What is the resulting number actually stored as? Does your answer depend on whether the result is rounded or truncated?

c. Suppose 1000 is added to 12,345,670. Again, indicate the resulting number stored, and comment on whether rounding or truncation matter.

d. Suppose the number 1 is added to itself 1000 times. Indicate the result obtained, either with rounding or truncating.

Now consider the sum

1 + 1 + . . . + 1 + 12,345,670

where there are 1000 1's at the start.

e. What is the result if addition proceeds from left to right (the 1's are added first)? Does your answer depend on whether addition uses rounding or truncation to seven significant digits?

f. What is the result if addition proceeds from right to left (the first addition is 1 + 12,345,670)? Again, does your answer depend on whether addition uses rounding or truncation to seven significant digits?

g. Addition is said to be associative if numbers can be added in any order to get the same result, and much mathematics depends on the associativity of arithmetic operations. Using your results in this problem, can you say anything about the associativity of addition for floating-point numbers in computers? Explain briefly.

4. Consider the pictures given in Figures 2.6 and 2.7. Suppose each picture was stored in GIF, PostScript, and JPEG formats with "medium" resolution. For each file, which file do you think would be largest? Smallest? Briefly justify your answer.

Figure 2.6
Armillaria spp. http://www.na.fs.fed.us/spfo/for_images/scan2.jpg
Credit: Joseph O'Brien, plant pathologist, Forest Health Protection Unit, U.S. Forest Service

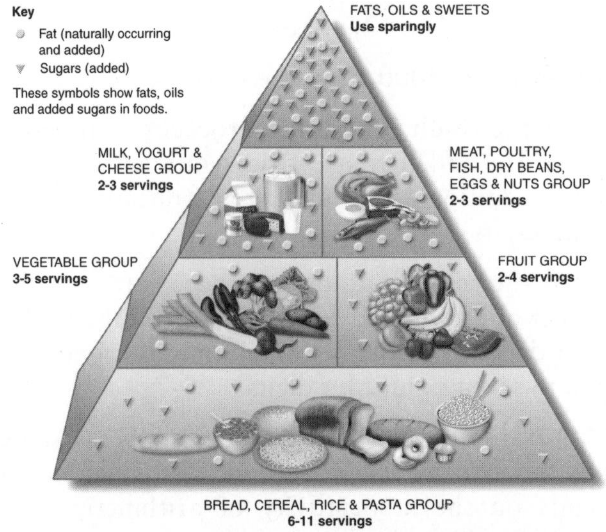

Figure 2.7
Food guide pyramid. http://www.usda.gov/cnpp/images/pymid.gif
Credit: U.S. Department of Agriculture (USDA) and the U.S. Department of Health and Human Services (DHHS)

5. Suppose you wanted to place Figure 2.8 on a Web page or in an e-mail. For efficiency in data storage and transmission, you decide to limit its size to about 50,000 bytes (about the same size as the pictures in Figures 2.3b and 2.3c). What file formats might you consider for this figure? Explain your answer.

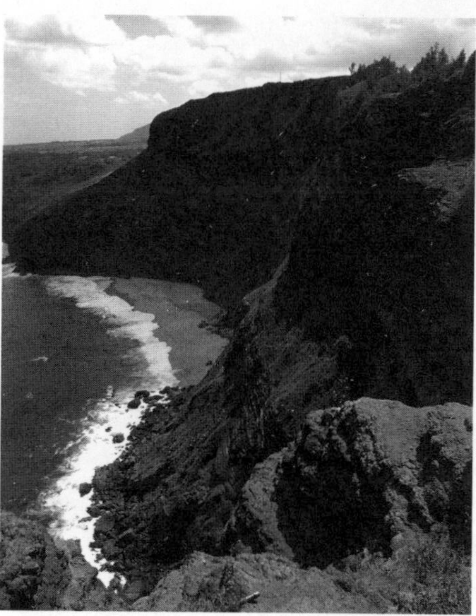

Figure 2.8
Kilauea Point National Wildlife Refuge, Hawaii. http://images.fws.gov/default.cfm?fuseaction=records.display&CFID=3034751&CFTOKEN=64693326&id=F3A4C76F%2D4FF0%2D4D3A%2DAEC021EAF451FA01
Credit: John and Karen Hollingsworth, U.S. Fish and Wildlife Service in public domain: http://images.fws.gov/default.cfm?CFID=3034751&CFTOKEN=64693326

Chapter 3

Where are programs and data stored?

AS WITH THE representation of data, many applications make the details of program and data storage transparent to users as they run programs. Thus, when running a program, we rarely worry about where the program was stored, how main memory is allocated for our work, or how data move into main memory or the CPU. Similarly, when we save a file from a word processor, spreadsheet, database, or Web browser, we normally do not think much about where on the disk the material is stored or, when we open a file, how the machine knows where to look for it. However, it is natural to wonder how these materials are stored and retrieved. Sometimes a basic understanding of such matters can guide us in getting work done efficiently. Also, such background leads to a consideration of viruses—undesired programs that often are obtained as parts of another stored program or data file. This chapter reviews some basics of program storage, data storage, and viruses and considers how we can use this knowledge in our regular use of computers.

What kinds of memory are there?

Chapter 1 began an answer to this question by describing basic functions of the CPU and its registers, cache memory, main memory, and I/O devices—all connected by a bus. Addressing this question here allows us to consider four additional elements of a computer's memory:

- Types of main memory (RAM and ROM)
- Transitory versus permanent memory
- Files and their organization
- Virtual memory and its relationship to files and main memory

When we are finished, we will have the hierarchical view of computer storage that is shown in Figure 3.1. (Although Figure 3.1 serves as a nice summary to this section of the chapter, you may have to keep reading to learn what all of the terms there mean; please be patient as you read ahead!)

Types of Main Memory: As we begin our consideration of computer storage, we need to consider a computer's main memory a bit more carefully. When considering main memory, most of it, called **random access memory (RAM)**, functions as described in Chapter 1. Instructions from computer programs and data are stored and retrieved in various locations as needed, and this space is reused as our work moves from one application to another.

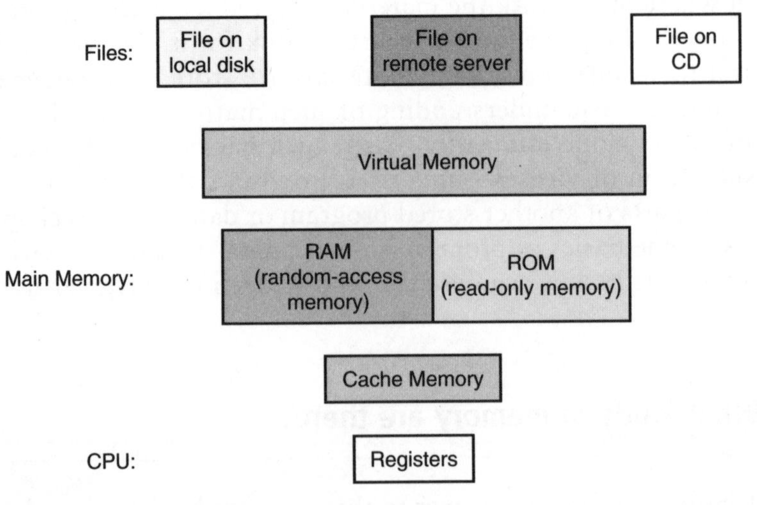

Figure 3.1
A hierarchical view of computer storage.

However, a small area of a computer's main memory may be predetermined for special purposes. For example, when a computer first starts up, the computer must have preliminary instructions to get started. Also, it may be convenient for certain functions to be wired directly into a section of main memory. This predetermined memory is called **read-only memory (ROM)**, and its contents are built in when a chip is manufactured; instructions can be obtained from it, but the space cannot be recycled for other uses.

A computer owner might encounter ROM when an added capability requires the owner to plug a special chip application directly into the machine. Historically, computer software, such as packages to interpret new computer languages, sometimes was distributed using ROM technology. After buying the new feature, the computer user opened the machine's cabinet and physically plugged in the ROM chip.

Today, modern applications for general-purpose computers typically come on a CD or disk that is not part of main memory, and usage of ROM is more specialized. One area of application may be the distribution of operating systems or games for small, specialized computers. The upgrading of the small computer or the playing of a new game may require the user to plug a chip into the machine.

A second common use of ROM technology arises behind the scenes, and a user may not be directly aware of it. For example, operating systems, such as Linux, Macintosh OS X, or Windows, are large programs that are stored on disks or CDs. Although these provide many services, they require a computer to read the disk or CD. However, when you first turn on a machine, the computer has little knowledge of what to do. It has not had time to read information from a disk, and it needs instruction on how to read a disk! Thus, startup instructions are preprogrammed in ROM. These instructions may include testing some hardware and interacting with a disk to load the basic elements of Linux, OS X, or Windows. Such work is possible because the instructions are preprogrammed. Capabilities may be limited (you do not see a fancy window-based interface when you first turn on a computer), but the instructions in ROM allow the computer to start.

Transitory versus Permanent Memory: Although main (RAM) memory, cache, and CPU registers handle data relatively quickly, they cannot remember what they have stored when the power is turned off. These are examples of **transitory memory**, which does not retain data values after processing is completed or when electric power is discontinued. Data held in RAM or the CPU is not retained from one run of a program to the next, so this type of memory cannot be used for long-term storage of information.

In contrast, data stored on disks, tapes, and CDs can be retained and retrieved over long periods of time—at least with reasonable care—and these storage media are called **permanent memory**. Even though this name suggests unlimited storage times, one must be a bit careful. Disks and tapes can be erased by magnetic fields—be careful to not carry them in a case that also contains a refrigerator magnet. Tapes can become brittle and break or distort when subjected to heat. CDs can become scratched. And, for any of these media, it would be unwise to tack them to a bulletin board in a lost-and-found area. However, with reasonable care and handling, disks, tapes, and CDs will hold data for many years without trouble.

Files and Their Organization: From the discussion in Chapter 2 of how various types of data are stored, we know that all information for any application is stored within a computer as a sequence of electrical voltages, which correspond to a series of 0's and 1's. At this basic level, work for any application has a similar look, and binary information for an application typically is stored as a logical collection, called a **file**. According to the needs of the application, such a file may range from only a few bytes to many thousands of bytes. Thus, conceptually, a file is simply a sequence of bits stored on a permanent memory device, such as a disk, tape, or CD.

When using tapes to store data from memory, computers normally begin reading the tape at one end and continue reading until the other end. With this simple approach for processing, file handling is fairly straightforward. To store a file on a tape, the tape first is examined until empty space is found. Then, the computer writes a file header, including a file designator or a name provided by the user, and the file material itself. To retrieve the file, the computer reads the tape from the beginning, until the start of the file is found. Then the material is retrieved in sequence. Although the examination of tapes from their beginning can take some time, such storage and retrieval is quite simple to implement.

Although information could, in principle, be stored on disks in much the same way as on tapes, such a linear organization does not take advantage of the special capabilities of disks and is not very efficient. Instead, it is helpful to be able to split large files into several pieces. File storage then requires two main tasks: locating where a file begins and determining where subsequent pieces might be found. To understand how these tasks are managed, we first need to consider some basics of disk storage. Figure 3.2 shows a typical organization of a basic disk.

As Figure 3.2 suggests, a disk is logically organized into a series of concurrent rings, called **tracks**, and each track is logically subdivided into pieces, called **sectors**. (Different disks may have different numbers of tracks or sectors, but the basic approach applies to any disk storage.) File storage proceeds by allocating a series of sectors for each file.

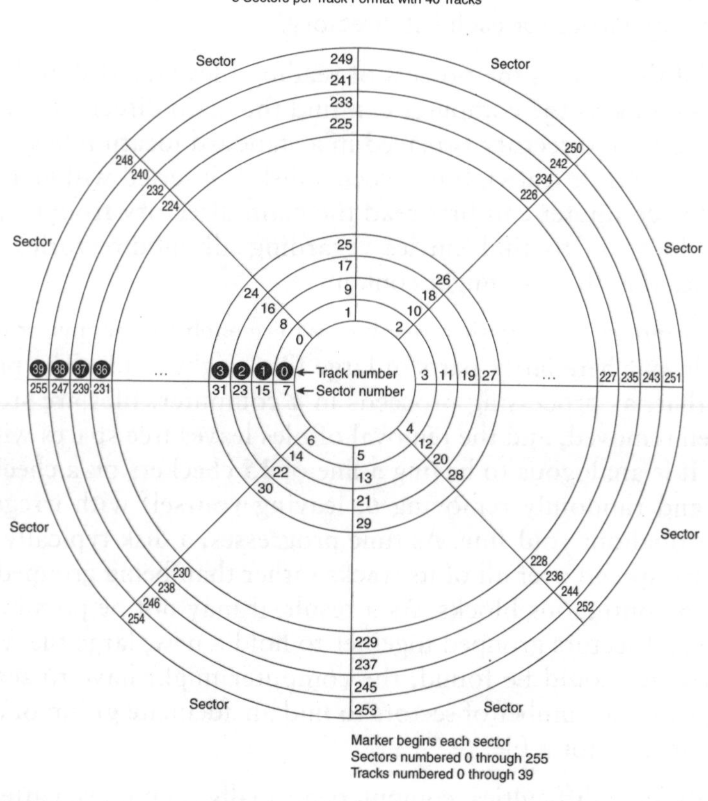

Figure 3.2
A typical disk organization.

To keep track of what file begins where, the computer maintains a table for each disk. The table contains an entry for each file; the entry contains such information as the name of the file, its length, and the track and sector at which it begins. Such a table is called a **directory** or a **folder**. With such a directory, the retrieval of file information proceeds in two steps: First, the computer consults the directory to determine the starting location of the file, and second, the computer begins reading the file at the designated track and sector on the disk. When saving a new file, the computer finds free space, makes a directory entry indicating this starting location, and then stores the file in the identified location.

If there are many files, storing them all in a single directory may be cumbersome, and subdirectories may be utilized. In such a case, file entries will be stored in tables for subdirectories, subdirectories will be stored in their own track and sector, and a main directory will contain entries for each subdirectory.

All of this allows the process of reading files on a disk to begin nicely, as long as the computer can find the main directory for the disk. The main directory is placed in a standard location (e.g., sector 0 of the inside track); thus, when a disk is inserted within a machine, the computer can first read the main directory from its prescribed location to find entries regarding all subdirectories and other files that the disk might contain.

Although this discussion resolves where each file begins, it does not address where latter parts of large files might reside. The problem is that, as processing proceeds in a computer, files are stored and then removed, and the removal of files leaves free spaces within a disk. It is analogous to having a line of 15 checkers on a checkerboard and randomly removing 6, leaving yourself with irregular gaps throughout your line. As time progresses, a disk typically has free space spread over all of its tracks rather than being grouped together in contiguous blocks. As a result, it may not be possible to find several sectors grouped together to hold a new, large file. Even if such space could be found, the computer might have to search through a large number of sectors to find an adequate group of contiguous sectors for a file.

With these difficulties, computers normally do not even attempt to find contiguous space when storing files. Instead, when storing data for a file, a computer finds a sequence of available sectors—

whereever they may be. The location of the first sector is recorded in the appropriate directory, as we have seen. Then, for each sector, the computer records the location of the sector that contains the next file data.

With this bookkeeping, retrieval of a file begins by consulting a directory to determine the track and sector for the initial file data. Once that material is obtained, the computer determines the location of the sector where the file data continue. Once material from that second sector is read, the computer again identifies where it should go next. This continues until the end of the file is found. Although file data may be found physically anywhere on a disk, retrieval proceeds sequentially—one sector at a time.

For a CD, storage can proceed in much the same way as a disk, except that, for traditional CD storage, once a CD is prepared with data, then the data are fixed. (The jargon is that a CD is burned with its data.) As with a disk, a CD may contain multiple files, indexed by multiple directories or folders, and the location of the main directory is determined by convention. However, because files normally are just added to CDs and not deleted, CDs do not have the problem that files are located on sectors that can be scattered around. Instead, files can be stored in sequential portions of a CD.

On a personal level, you may have experienced the differences in organization of files on tapes and CDs when listing to audio. Music on audiotapes is stored sequentially. Thus, you have to rewind and fast-forward to find a song; you are never quite sure where a song begins, and you are using sequential access to find it. In contrast, a CD maintains a directory of songs. Thus, you can hit rewind once, and the CD player automatically knows where the previous song begins by consulting the directory. Similar comments apply to playing videotapes in contrast to DVDs.

Virtual Memory and Its Relationship to Files and Main Memory: When we discussed main memory and CPU registers in Chapter 1, we noted that the CPU does the actual processing, so that data must be moved to the CPU in order for work to be accomplished. However, the CPU contains very little storage space, and main memory provides significantly more storage. CPU registers are fast, but main memory provides bulk storage for applications during processing. Also, to improve performance, computers utilize cache memory between the CPU registers and main memory. Cache memory is slower than direct storage in CPU registers, but faster than storage in main memory. Because processing typically uses relatively small amounts of data at a time, current data can be stored in cache for relatively fast access.

The relationship between main memory and file storage on tapes, disks, and CDs is similar. Access to data on tapes, disks, and CDs is slow, because these media require physical activity to store and retrieve data. For example, to obtain data from a tape, the tape is moved along a device (sometimes called a **read head**) that senses electronic signals on the tape. Similarly, placing data on a tape requires the tape to move over a device (called a **write head**) that places charges on the tape. Sometimes the same device is used for both reading and writing, in which case it is called a **read/write head**. Disks and CDs must spin around until relevant data can be detected by read/write heads. For disks, those read/write heads also must move inward or outward from track to track to reach the appropriate sector. All of this activity requires something to move physically, and such motion consumes much more time than activities requiring only electrical processing. On the other hand, tapes, disks, and CDs have some great advantages: storage is permanent, the devices are relatively inexpensive, and storage capacity is much greater than that found in main memory.

Coupled with this contrast between main memory and file storage, computer applications have expanded dramatically in size over the years, and many applications now require huge amounts of space when they run. Thus, even as technology advances have allowed memories to have relatively large capacities (at least in relationship to the past), the demands of applications have increased even faster. For example, crisp and clear graphical images often consume thousands of bytes (or kilobytes) of storage, and such images are now used commonly in both word-processing documents and Web applications.

Unfortunately, as you have seen in Chapter 1, the CPU controls all processing in a computer and handles many specific tasks. Thus, in order to run at all, instructions from computer programs and applications must be placed in the CPU during program execution to guide the computer in its processing, in the same way that data must move to and from CPU registers for processing. Because the CPU is loaded from main memory, main memory must hold program instructions and data to allow processing to occur.

When the program and data are stored initially in files, one organization of storage involves three basic steps:

1. Move the full application program and initial data from the files to main memory.
2. Move program instructions and data between main memory and the CPU as needed while the program runs.
3. Move final data from main memory back to relevant files.

In this process, steps 1 and 3 might be relatively slow, but processing in step 2 might be reasonably efficient. Although moving material between memory and the CPU as needed could work, it would limit programs and data (combined) to a size that would fit in main memory all at once. Such a limitation would not be a problem for some applications, but it would constrain others severely. Further, if a machine were configured to run several programs concurrently (e.g., print from one application while working on another), then all the programs and data sets would be needed in main memory at once. (More about the handling of concurrent processing in the next chapter.) Altogether, the requirement that an entire application (program and data) fit in main memory at once turns out to be severe, and one that the designers of computer systems want to avoid.

The solution to this problem is to use main memory as cache for files, just as cache memory itself acts as high-speed temporary storage for the CPU. To be more specific, a computing environment considers space for running programs and their data at a logical level as being very large. Such logical space is called **virtual memory**, and is designed to be large enough to store all programs and data for the several computer applications and activities that might be running at once. In this context, the term *virtual memory* deserves some comment. To a computing practitioner, the term is meant to suggest that a program may be considered as a large (perhaps limitless) expanse of continuous storage. That is, in solving large or complex problems, programmers prefer to think of a program and data as being together in one section of memory; conceptually, virtual memory should be as large as needed. In practice, such a block of space may involve a larger physical size than is actually available through main memory technology. Thus, in practice, virtual memory typically is located physically on a large section of a disk within the computer. Because the processing of programs may access this material frequently, virtual memory usually is placed on a disk with relatively fast access times, such as a hard disk, rather than a relatively slow floppy disk or removable disk.

With this virtual memory, pieces in actual use (called **pages**) are loaded into main memory, just as the most recently used program instructions and data from main memory are loaded into cache and retrieved. During execution, moderate-sized pieces of the application first move from virtual memory (on a disk) to main memory, and then smaller pieces move to cache and the CPU as needed. When program execution moves from one part of the program or one part of data to another, the pieces in main memory and cache can be updated appropriately. Schematically, this organization of memory is shown in Figure 3.3.

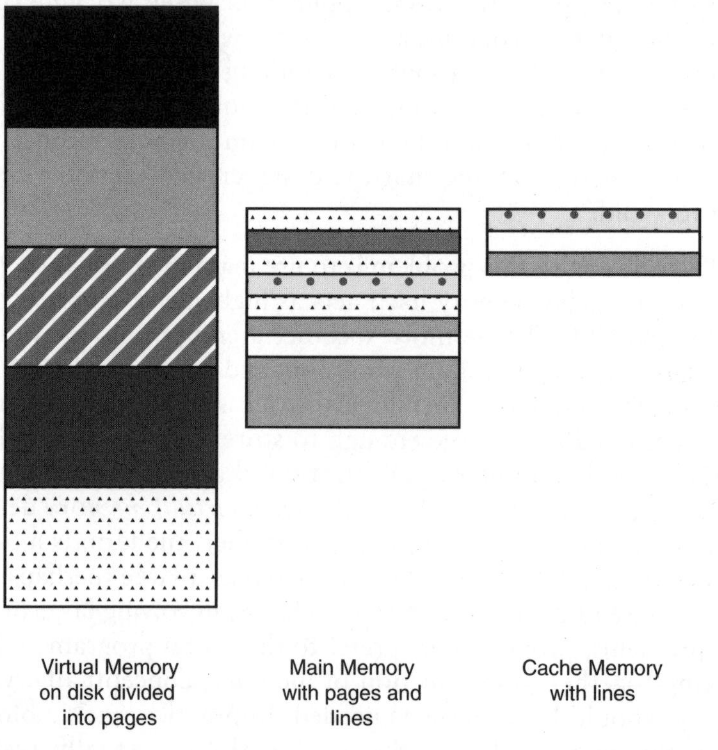

Figure 3.3
Levels of computer memory.

As this figure suggests, virtual memory is much larger than main memory, and main memory is again much larger than cache. In the figure, virtual memory is divided into five pages, which are the same size as the large blocks in main memory. This main memory in the figure is large enough for just two pages, and currently the pages with light shading and with dots are loaded into main memory. (Think of any of the shaded colors as part of the shaded page, and any of the dotted areas as being part of the dotted page.)

In considering cache, pieces of memory are called lines (rather than pages). The small shaded or dotted blocks or lines within main memory are the same size as the pieces within cache, and the cache in the figure is large enough to hold three lines. Currently, two lines of the lightly shaded page and one line of the dotted page are loaded into cache.

When do data move from one type of memory to another?

With various parts of a computer application involving files, virtual memory, main memory (RAM or ROM), cache, and CPU registers, this question is natural! It can be hard to figure out just what happens when an application runs. To understand this better, let's follow the basic flow of information for an application, such as editing an existing document with a word processor.

To begin, we click on a document, or we type the names of the program and document in a window. This tells the computer that processing is to begin. Some main steps follow:

1. The word-processing application is copied (probably from CD or disk) to the disk area for virtual memory. A working copy of the entire application now resides in virtual memory, and the computer tries to start the program.
2. While running, the program will require the computer to follow some instructions from the program—perhaps to open an editing environment on the screen with appropriate buttons and windows. The computer realizes these instructions are not yet in main memory, so the first section of the program is copied from virtual memory into main memory.
3. As an individual instruction is needed by the CPU for processing, a copy of the instruction is placed in cache memory.

4. As initial processing proceeds, the CPU needs to retrieve one instruction after another, but the CPU does not remember where these instructions are found. Thus, at each step, the CPU asks the high-speed cache for the next instructions. If the instructions are not in cache, the CPU consults main memory; if the instructions are not there either, then another section (page) of the program is loaded from virtual memory into main memory.

5. Once initial windows are drawn on the screen, the word-processing package identifies the document to be edited and realizes that the first part of the document should be retrieved for display in an editing window. To retrieve this part of the document, the computer first copies part of the document file to virtual memory. This version of the document stored in virtual memory may become a working copy of the original document.

6. The computer then copies the needed section of the working copy from virtual memory into main memory, and pieces are brought into the CPU and cache as the display is needed.

Suppose now that the user wants to edit text at the bottom of the document, so he or she uses the arrow keys to move methodically down the document to the end. At this stage, processing changes from the initial display to the constant redisplay of additional document material, based on instructions that correspond to the arrow keys. Here are the main steps for this work:

7. Use of the arrow keys probably involves different instructions from the opening of windows, so the CPU needs the arrow-handling part of the program. Upon checking cache and main memory, the computer realizes this material is needed from virtual memory. This part of the program then is copied, first to main memory (likely as one intermediate-sized section) and then to cache (in small pieces) as needed. If space in main memory is limited, then the instructions for the arrow handling may replace the startup instructions that are no longer needed.

8. As the program gets to new parts of the document, they, too, will move to virtual memory, main memory, and cache as needed for the display. While the virtual memory may retain

the full document already displayed, main memory may contain only the current or recently displayed pieces.

As editing of the document proceeds, the computer will have to work to keep cache, main memory, and virtual memory consistent, so that any changes made in one small section (perhaps in cache) are also made in main memory and virtual memory.

When, later on, an updated document is saved, processing again moves to a new part of the program. Some main steps in the saving process are as follows:

9. The "save" part of the program is identified in virtual memory, copied as a section to main memory, and then placed in cache in pieces as needed.
10. The updated document from virtual memory is copied back to a regular file on a disk or other medium.

As this outline suggests, virtual memory contains the entire program and data for an application as it runs; main memory contains sections of the program and data set used recently; and cache contains the most recent materials used in processing by the CPU. Movement of program sections and data to the main memory and to cache occur on an "as-needed" basis, and materials are not copied until they are actually needed for processing.

How much memory is enough?

This question arises frequently when people are considering the purchase of a computer. Unfortunately, the only safe answer is something like "it depends on what you plan to do." Large software applications and applications that utilize graphics or sound may make heavy demands on main memory. Most application packages make recommendations regarding an appropriate minimum size for main memory; however, such minimums may not be reliable guides for purchasers of new equipment for at least three reasons:

1. New versions of software may be larger and require more memory than previous versions, so when you upgrade your

software, more of your computer's memory will be used for the same software.

2. New software, unplanned at the purchase time of your computer but desired as your needs or experience changes, may require significant amounts of main memory.
3. Software may run on machines with only moderate amounts of memory, but performance may be sluggish. If you have only the minimum amount of memory, you may be sacrificing performance.

The first two of these reasons have the common theme that memory demands of application software have expanded dramatically over the years. Modest applications that once ran in only a few thousand bytes of memory (e.g., a few kilobytes) now have new features and graphical capabilities that may require millions of bytes of memory (e.g., megabytes). Of course, a potential computer owner may believe that she or he will not need to purchase new software or new versions of old software, so there is no need to plan for additional capacity. In practice, however, such intentions often are impractical. New versions of software may correct errors that were uncovered in previous versions. Even if the original software has adequate capability, reliability, and performance, the owner may want to share documents or application files with others (e.g., professional colleagues, friends, or family) and receive materials from them. If those people have new versions of software, old versions may be unable to read or otherwise handle what the new versions produce. Compatibility of versions can be a problem, forcing adoption of new versions to allow sharing—even when the current software seems to work fine.

To give some idea about how the size of software packages increase, let's consider an example: the Microsoft operating system. Originally, it ran with a simple textual interface, without windows or a mouse, and computers ran in isolation, with no connection to a network or other machines. Over time, Microsoft has added many features and capabilities. Although these may have made computers easier to work with, they also have expanded the size of the operating system software and often required more memory. For technical reasons, measuring program size can be somewhat tricky (e.g., just what do you count). Also, units of measure change over time (usually with the unit getting larger as time progresses).

However, Table 3-1 can give some idea of how the size of programs increases over time.

The third reason mentioned earlier, that the speed of software is sacrificed when a computer has only the minimum amount of memory needed, is connected to the need to move materials between virtual memory (on a disk) and main memory. Disk access requires the physical movement of disks and read/write heads, so large amounts of data transfer can take a long time. Ideally, one would like material to flow from virtual memory to main memory just once—when the program section or data are first needed. However, if main memory is too small, then current sections may continually replace previous ones. The result can be constant movement of materials between disk and main memory—a situation sometimes called **thrashing**. On personal machines, one sometimes can hear constant disk activity, well beyond the loading of initial materials. When this circumstance arises, a larger memory often can make a substantial difference. With more memory available, more of a program and its data can reside in memory before a new request for information from virtual memory requires something to be replaced. When performance seems particularly slow, a computer owner may want to investigate whether the addition of main

Table 3-3 Growth in the Size of an Operating System over Time

Date	Product	Approximate Length
August 1981	MS-DOS	4000 lines of (assembly language) code
March 1983	MS-DOS 2.0	20,000 lines of code
August 1993	Windows NT 3.1	6,000,000 lines of code
September 1994	Windows NT 3.5	9,000,000 lines of code
August 1996	Windows NT 4.0	16,000,000 lines of code
February 2000	Windows 2000	18,000,000 lines of code
2000	Windows NT 5.0	20,000,000–29,000,000 lines of code (depending on source used)
2001	Windows 2000	35,000,000 lines of code
2002	Windows XP	40,000,000 lines of code

memory could make a significant difference. Sometimes this type of upgrade in equipment can provide a relatively inexpensive alternative to obtain acceptable performance rather than purchasing new equipment.

Putting these ideas together, here are two common guidelines for purchasing main memory for a computer:

1. Review the minimum memory size recommended for the programs you will use, and try to move up a level or two in the memory you purchase for your computer to anticipate future needs.
2. Consider purchasing as much memory as you can, while staying within your budget.

Because these guidelines proceed according to different criteria, they may yield different conclusions. The point of each is that, over time, applications consistently demand more and more memory, so any purchaser should anticipate that future needs will be more than what one can foresee at present.

What is the difference between deleting a file and erasing it?

In many computer systems, **deletion of a file** involves two steps: The computer

1. removes the record of the file from the corresponding directory, and
2. marks that the various sectors of the file (previously in use) are now free.

Erasure of a file involves three steps: The computer

1. writes over all information in the various sectors containing file data,
2. removes the record of the file from the corresponding directory, and
3. marks that the various sectors of the file (previously in use) are now free.

As this description indicates, erasure involves an initial step not present for simple file deletion, but thereafter the two processes are the same.

In deleting a file, the space is no longer allocated for file use, and that space is recycled for use by another application.

However, when a file is only deleted, the actual data from that file are still physically present on the disk. This means that, at least in principle, the old data might be accessible to a new application that happened to reuse this space. This deletion process is quite analogous to the disposal of papers by placing them in a wastepaper basket or trash bin. Although the material is gone from the standpoint of the original user, the information might be accessible to a nosy neighbor who is willing to take time going through the trash.

Erasure of the file, on the other hand, physically removes the information (analogous to the use of a shredder in our paper analogy), so a nosy neighbor cannot make use of the old information, even if she or he might find an old disk.

What does it mean to "defragment" a disk, and should I care?

As noted during the discussion of file storage on disks, information is divided into pieces, which are stored in tracks and sectors throughout a disk. When processing disk data, the disk must spin so that the relevant sector may pass under the read/write head. However, when the pieces are widely scattered, the read/write head must move considerable distances (e.g., between the center of the disk and the outside edge) to get to the required sector. Such moves can take considerable time, producing noise on the disk drive somewhat akin to what one hears during thrashing. In the terminology of computing, we say that files whose pieces are spread over much of a disk are **fragmented**. When a disk contains many fragmented files, we say the disk is **badly fragmented**.

At the other extreme, an ideal placement of files on a disk occurs when sectors of a file are located on contiguous sectors. Such a contiguous arrangement allows for easy file access, primarily through only an initial movement of the read/write head. Once the head is appropriately positioned, reading and writing of the file can occur by allowing the disk to rotate. Such processing can be particularly smooth and efficient.

When a disk is highly fragmented, therefore, one might want to reorganize where material is stored on the disk to obtain a contiguous arrangement of file sections. Such a process is called **defragmenting a disk,** and this task typically can be performed by various utility programs. It should be noted that the defragmenting process can take considerable time for a highly fragmented disk for at least two reasons:

1. Modern disks have large capacities, with the ability to store many files and a large number of tracks and sectors. Thus, defragmentation may require the analysis and movement of large amounts of data.
2. When moving sectors of one file together, some pieces of other files may have to be moved out of the way first. Overall, data may have to be moved several times before a final, satisfactory arrangement is found.

Complete disk defragmentation may consume a lot of time if a disk has become highly fragmented or disorganized. The amount of time needed to complete the defragmentation may even range up to several hours, so this is a process that some folks prefer to run overnight, when the machine is not being used for other purposes. After the deframenting work is completed, disk access can proceed relatively efficiently, sometimes making a noticeable difference in performance.

What is a computer virus, and how does one work?

A **computer virus** is an unwanted or unanticipated program, often designed to damage a computer or degrade its performance. A relatively benign virus might pop up a window on a computer screen, displaying a surprise message. More destructive viruses might erase files, change data, send many e-mail messages, or degrade computer performance (perhaps by consuming much CPU time).

Viruses are programs, so they perform their work when the CPU runs them. Because a virus does unwanted work, a user would be unlikely to consciously ask the CPU to run a virus. Instead, viruses normally come packaged as a behind-the-scenes part of something else, and when the other item is activated by the computer, the virus also is activated. Here are some possible scenarios in which a user might accidentally encounter a virus and its work:

- A virus can be received as an e-mail attachment. In the form of an attachment, the virus is harmless, because e-mail will just treat it as data. However, if the user opens the attachment, and if the user's e-mail handler allows the execution of opened attachments, then the act of opening the attachment instructs the computer to run the program, allowing the virus to begin its processing.
- A virus can insert itself into another program. (In this case, the virus is said to have infected the other program.) When the user runs the other program, the virus also is activated.
- A virus can be part of the formatting instructions for a word-processing file or part of a computation for a spreadsheet. In this case, the virus is part of the user's data file for an application, and the virus is activated when the infected part of the data is accessed.
- A virus can also be embedded as a program within a Web page. As we will see in later chapters, a Web browser can be set to run programs. Often, programs running on a Web page are useful. For example, they may be intended to display some helpful material or to analyze data as they are typed into the Web page. However, browser-based programs can also open and be destructive, in which case they would be classified as viruses. (In principle, a browser is supposed to prevent various undesirable activities from taking place, but errors in the browser program itself might allow other, less-desirable activities to take place.)
- A virus can be inserted into a disk, in a place that is routinely activated when a computer first starts up. In this case, starting the computer would also execute the virus.

Although many of these scenarios seem to involve rare events, like receiving an infected e-mail, opening a Web page that contains a virus, or reading an infected disk, a virus often includes a component that helps it expand the number of files it infects. For example, the running of a virus could include its making one or more copies of itself, perhaps inserting itself into new or existing files or sending itself to other users or other computers. Thus, if a virus gets established anywhere in a computer, running it once may create many additional copies—increasing the chance that it may be run again. When a virus regenerates, it spreads.

Because any virus takes up space and utilizes CPU resources—at least from time to time—any virus interferes with processing. If the virus also modifies or deletes files, then it also may have destructive effects.

How can a virus be detected?

The list of entry points for a virus, given in the previous section, indicates that viruses may come to a computer in many ways: on an infected disk, within an infected program, included in a data file (e.g., a word-processing document or spreadsheet), as an e-mail attachment, through a Web browser, or over the Internet. With so many potential sources, and with sources arriving in a binary format that is awkward for humans to read, it is impractical for a user to physically scan every file that comes into a machine and expect to weed out the viruses.

A user can, however, ask a utility program, called an **anti-virus program**, to perform this scanning. Typically, an anti-virus program contains information about known viruses, and compares each file entering a computer against those known viruses. Thus, when a new disk is placed into a computer, the anti-virus program immediately reads every file for signs that it might be a virus. Often the computer is set up so that disk files cannot be accessed until this virus scan takes place. If no viruses are found, then normal processing can continue. However, if a virus is identified, then either the complete file will be deleted or the anti-virus program will be instructed to remove that virus program from the file (if such removal seems possible).

In this identification of viruses, note that the anti-virus programs normally compare new files with information about known viruses. However, because various misguided folks create new viruses regularly, the information for the anti-virus programs must be updated frequently. Details on how this is done will depend upon the anti-virus software installed on a specific machine. For any such protection, however, a user must be proactive in getting such upgrades on a very regular basis.

How can I protect myself against computer viruses?

The basic rules for virus protection involve scanning all files before they are installed on a computer and not running or even viewing unknown materials. Here are some more specific suggestions:

- Be sure anti-virus software is running on your computer, and keep the virus information up to date.
- Do not download software from the Web or copy software from someone else (even a friend) without first having the software checked for a virus.
- Be cautious before you allow your Web browser to run programs behind the scenes.
- Do not open an e-mail attachment unless you really know what it is.
- Do not run a macro for a word-processing package or spreadsheet unless you know its source and know it to be reliable.
- If your computer is connected to the Web, install and utilize a firewall on your computer (to be described in Chapter 10).

As this list suggests, the keys to protection against viruses include constant vigilance and skepticism. Viruses can infect any source they have contact with, so it is possible they are present in the software you buy or the e-mail you receive from friends. Protection means scanning everything and taking little for granted.

Summary

Memory within a computer may be classified in several ways. Most main memory consists of random access memory (RAM), which is transitory; read-only memory (ROM) and files are permanent.

Information in files may be stored on disks or CDs either contiguously or in blocks; in either case, directories identify the locations of the various parts of the material.

Conceptually, instructions and data are stored in virtual memory while a program runs, but this space may be larger than can physically fit within a computer's main memory. Thus, pages of virtual memory are brought into main memory as needed during program execution. Similarly, parts of main memory being used most frequently are usually placed in cache memory for fast retrieval. Actual processing occurs in the CPU, which contains only a few storage locations, called registers. Data move between virtual memory and main memory, between main memory and cache, and between cache and registers according to the demands of processing, and considerable behind-the-scenes work is involved in keeping all types of memory up to date.

Over the years, programs, operating systems, and data sets have become progressively larger, and this has placed increasing demands on computer memories.

During processing, data may become scattered throughout disks, and defragmenting a disk can bring related pieces close together to aid performance.

Computer viruses are unwanted or unanticipated programs, often designed to damage a computer or degrade its performance. Viruses can enter a computer in many ways, and the best defenses include constant care and vigilence. Anti-virus programs can help identify viruses before they can be run on your computers.

■ Terminology from This Chapter

anti-virus program
deleting a file
disk fragmentation
disk directory
disk sector
disk track
erasing a file
file
page
permanent memory
RAM
ROM
thrashing
transitory memory
virtual memory
virus

Discussion Questions

1. Although disks, tapes, and CDs will hold data for an indefinite length of time, retrieval of the data on these media requires functioning players. However, past generations have stored music on phonograph records and on 8-track tapes—both of which were considered "permanent storage" in their day—and now it can be difficult to find machines to handle either of these technologies. Similarly, old computer disks may have been 5¼" in diameter, rather than the 3.5" that have dominated the market in recent years. Also, within the realm of computer tapes, technologies have evolved over time, and some tapes from even just a few years ago may be unreadable on modern tape drives.

a. Consider what "permanent" storage of electronic documents might mean in an environment where technology changes every few years.

b. With the cost of binding and storage of paper-based journals, there is strong incentive for libraries to turn to electronic formats for these works. However, libraries also seek to maintain runs of journals indefinitely—over decades and longer. Discuss issues of electronic storage for "archival copies" of journals and other materials.

c. If you have reasonable access to a librarian, ask her or him how your library views electronic archives for journals.

2. Consider the situation in which an individual removes a file and then, in a panic, decides she or he wants that information back.

a. Might this retrieval be possible if the file was deleted (but not erased)? Explain.

b. Might this retrieval be possible if the file was erased? Explain.

c. If your answer to part a or b was "yes," would retrieval be possible in all cases or just in some cases? Explain.

3. Sometimes a problem arises with just a small section of a disk (e.g., with one sector).
   a. Identify a circumstance under which trouble with a single sector could affect reading of all files on the disk.
   b. Identify a circumstance under which trouble with a single sector could affect the reading of some files, but not others.
   c. Identify two circumstances under which trouble with a single sector could affect reading just the very last part of a file.
   d. Could trouble with a single sector affect the reading of all data in a single file? Explain.
4. ROM, or read-only memory, is prepared at time of manufacture, so it contains specific data or program information. While ROM cannot be changed, a computer can read and use the information. Sometimes one hears stories of write-only memory (WOM). The idea would be that a computer could send data to WOM, but this information then could not be retrieved. Explain why WOM is not considered useful and thus is not be manufactured or used.
5. Some have defined a weed, in gardening, as any plant that is growing in a place it is not wanted. Discuss how a virus in a computing environment is similar or different from a weed in an agricultural environment. (Find at least two similarities and at least two differences.)
6. The Association for Computing Machinery (ACM) is the largest professional society for the computing community. The ACM home page is www.acm.org.
   a. Using the search capability from this Web page, locate the ACM Code of Ethics. Does this Code of Ethics mention the development of virus programs? If so, what does it say?
   b. Review the application form for ACM professional membership and for ACM student membership. To what extent does ACM membership commit an individual to acting responsibly (e.g., not developing computer viruses)?
7. Consider the following scenario (based on actual cases): An individual discovers a way to circumvent a computer's secu-

rity system and writes a virus to exploit this weakness. The individual then releases this virus to "friends," causing the staff of a local computer center several hours of work as they clean files and check that any damage has been corrected. Now suppose the individual is caught in either of the following ways:

- The individual comes forward soon after the initial infection to reveal the details of the virus.
- The individual is identified through careful detective work of the computer center staff.

In either circumstance, the development of a virus is against computer center rules, and the director wants to prosecute. However, the individual claims the development of the virus was a good thing, because it did nothing harmful and highlighted security weaknesses before real trouble could occur.

a. Do you think the director is right in wanting to prosecute?

b. What do you think about the individual's claim that writing the virus actually was a public service?

c. Does your answer to a or b depend on how the individual was caught? Explain.

Exercises

1. Two key concepts introduced in this chapter are "permanent memory" and "transitory memory."

a. Give a careful definition of each of these terms.

b. Now consider the words or phrases identified in "Terminology from this Chapter." Use "permanent memory," "transitory memory," and "other topics" as main categories, and organize the other words or phrases into these categories. Explain why each term belongs in its category.

c. In part b, can you find any unifying theme for the terms in the "other topics" category? Explain.

d. Give careful definitions of each of the terms listed in "Terminology from this Chapter." Be sure your definitions distinguish between similar, but different, concepts.

2. The chapter noted that when storing a file on a disk, a directory contains an entry that indicates both the starting point of the file (track and sector) and the file's length. Also, corresponding to each sector for the file, the computer stores the location of the next sector. When reaching the last sector for the file, there is no next sector, so suppose that the computer records instead that this is the last sector. Discuss how this arrangement allows the computer to check that files may be stored using a correct structure.

3. Some utilities perform a series of checks to help determine if the directories and files are structured correctly. Identify a few (at least two) tests that such utilities might perform.

4. According to the chapter, RAM is an example of transitory main memory. Is ROM an example of transitory main memory or permanent main memory? Briefly explain your answer.

5. Suppose that a power malfunction occurs at exactly the time that a file is being saved, thereby preventing some or all elements of a file from being saved correctly. Explain how each of the following circumstances might arise.

   a. The first part of a file has been saved correctly, but the second half contains junk (nothing related to what was in the original file).

   b. Two files start differently, as they are supposed to, but they are identical after a certain point; that is, they refer to identical sectors after their initial differences.

   c. A file repeats itself over and over, after a certain point.

   d. The file has disappeared completely.

6. Explain why defragmenting a disk can improve a computer's performance considerably, but defragmenting the disk a second time—immediately after the first defragmentation—has no further effect.

7. Suppose you open an attachment in an e-mail message. Nothing seems to happen for awhile, but then a peculiar picture appears on your computer screen. Some time later, you learn that one of your friends received a message from you with an attachment having the same effect.

a. Do you think the attachment you received was a virus? Why or why not?

b. If you discover a friend sent you a virus, what do you suggest is the most appropriate response?

c. If you learn you sent others a virus, what is your best course of action?

8. The chapter indicates that the storage of files on CDs normally can be contiguous. Files are inserted, but not deleted, so that disks fill up from one track to the next. Although this is the traditional means for storing data on CDs, new technology allows files to be deleted as well.

a. If a CD is non-rewriteable, explain why files can always be stored sequentially.

b. If files are always inserted starting at one end of a disk and progressing toward the other end, explain why the files can be sequential.

c. If files can be deleted from a directory, but not erased from the disk itself, describe how file storage could be contiguous.

d. If files can be deleted and that space reused later, explain why fragmentation might be possible.

e. Investigate CD technology that allows you to delete files from a CD as well as to insert them. For example, you might find information about Adeptec's DirectCD, more recently marketed by Roxio, Inc., under the name Drag-to-Disc. To what extent might fragmentation arise when files are deleted with this technology? Does the answer depend upon whether the disk is rewriteable or not? Explain your answer.

Chapter 4

What is an operating system and what does it do?

WHEN DISCUSSING COMPUTERS, we often hear comments such as "I use a Windows machine," "I like Linux," "My Macintosh runs OS X," or "Windows XP seems more reliable than Windows NT." Similarly, various computer users or salespeople may tout the advantages of Windows XP, Windows NT, Linux, or Mac OS X. Unfortunately, such statements often dwell on esoteric details, reflect subjective personal preferences, or involve lengthy technical discussions.

For the general computer user, discussing details about operating systems may seem obtuse and obscure. Every computer seems to have a Windows, Linux, Macintosh, or other operating system, but why do operating systems exist at all, and how are they similar or different from each other? This chapter addresses such basic questions and leaves the lengthy technical discussions and opinions for others at another time.

What is an "operating system"?

Operating systems have evolved over several decades, so it is helpful to take a historical perspective when trying to understand them. We have already noted that a computer functions by following detailed instructions. In the early days of computers, every user had to supply absolutely every detail of information that a computer would need to run. If a program was to read data from a keyboard, then the user's program had to include instructions about how that reading was to take place. If the program needed to store or retrieve data on a disk, then the program needed to include instructions about where to find the disk's directory, how to read the directory's entry for the desired file, where to locate the specific file (e.g., track and sector numbers), and so on. If the program was to print output, then the program had to include all of the detailed instructions for interacting with the printer. In order to handle a range of I/O devices, a user might have to supply hundreds of detailed instructions for even a very simple program. For example, a program to convert a temperature in Fahrenheit to the corresponding temperature in Celsius might require 200–300 instructions. In all of this work, the mathematical formula [Celsius = (5/9)*(Fahrenheit − 32)] would require under 20 instructions; the remainder of the instructions would dictate how the computer should handle input and output.

In reviewing programs like converting Fahrenheit to Celsius, it did not take long for early computer scientists to realize that much of the I/O handling was standard across programs—many programs were doing the same basic tasks. To improve the efficiency of writing program instructions early computer scientists decided to duplicate the common instructions and include this package in each program. With this approach, each program might be large, with all instructions for I/O as well as instructions for the specific application, but a user only had to develop the special instructions for her or his application.

Another common set of instructions within a typical program had the task of transitioning from the running of one program to the running of the next. If each program had to be completely self-sufficient, then initial work would be required to prepare the computer for running each successive program. For example, the computer would have to be told how to read the instructions for the forthcoming program before it could transition to it. This initial work was required for each program.

Computer scientists soon realized that the transition process could be streamlined if the end of one task could include the preparatory work for the next. Then, when one program was complete, the next user would not have to tell the computer how to read the next program. This preparatory work was not strictly part of individual applications; automating the program-to-program transitions helped all users. For example, when I wrote my first programs in the 1960s, I was expected to end each program with a particular program instruction that invoked the right transition code. With this instruction, the next program could be read easily. But if I omitted this instruction, the next user had to restart the computer before his or her program could be read.

The pooling of instructions for common tasks and transitions gave rise to the first operating systems. Over time, this collection of common activities has expanded considerably, but the perspective remains the same. An **operating system** is a program, or collection of programs, containing instructions for coordinating computer usage among users and for handling common tasks. Although details vary from system to system, today's operating systems normally facilitate the following general tasks:

- Details of input and output
- Administration of a system to allow multiple users to work concurrently
- Allocation (and deallocation) of main memory for different users
- Sharing of resources (e.g., files, printers) among several users or machines
- Communication among users and among machines
- Mechanisms for protection and security of programs and information

To clarify this list somewhat, consider a typical initial interaction we might have with a computer. After turning on the machine, a window appears on many computers asking us to log on with our username and password. Assuming we provide correct information, we then see a display of various directories, files, or applications. If our computer does not require us to log in, we might see this display immediately. Up until this point, all of our interaction has been with the operating system. One of the first goals of an operating system, therefore, is to keep track of authorized users. Thus, it is responsible for providing places to type name and password information, for checking the correctness of this material, and for displaying our working environment.

When we view the collection of directories and materials that appears on our screen, many computers allow us to use the mouse to designate which application we wish to run. The operating system then locates the relevant programs and data for that application and provides the program with a way to display information in windows. If we subsequently run a second application, then the operating system keeps track of both programs and their data. For example, the operating system allocates some virtual memory to each application, determines which parts of that material should be loaded into main memory, and schedules work so that progress can be made on both applications. Similarly, if we use the mouse to click on one application and then on the other, the operating system keeps track of which program to highlight at each moment. If we type data, the operating system decides which program should receive the data we provide.

Similarly, if we tell one program to print results, then the operating system interacts with the printer and coordinates the printing together with the currently running applications. Of course, specific functions of our applications are handled by those individual programs, but the operating system helps provide coordination and handles various behind-the-scenes tasks.

Why are there different operating systems?

The list of tasks handled by an operating system is reasonably long, so it is hardly surprising to learn that these tasks can be done in more than one way. As an analogy, consider the choices we have in purchasing a car. If our goal is to move a family with several children and their belongings, we might purchase a minivan. If our goal is speed—with the need for few passengers—we might consider a sports car. If our goal is economy, we might want a compact car with high gas mileage. If we want to consume a lot of gas and hog the road, we might buy an SUV. Each of these vehicles meets basic transportation goals, but different types of cars reflect different priorities and perspectives.

The development of operating systems similarly reflects different approaches to the coordination and streamlining of computer tasks. For example, the first versions of Unix (from which the Linux operating system developed) were designed at Bell Laboratories, the primary research organization of AT&T, to assist researchers in their work. The idea was to provide a common environment for simple, effective, and efficient processing on many types of computers. In this environment, researchers needed to be able to share information and combine various programs into larger tasks. In achieving this work environment (or virtual machine), Unix emphasized terse, powerful commands based on textual input. In contrast, the first versions of the Macintosh operating system emphasized a graphics-based virtual machine, containing pictures of files and programs. Rather than typing text to combine commands on a single line, Macintosh users took advantage of a mouse to issue simple commands to start various applications.

With different design objectives, operating systems developed in different directions, with different strengths and capabilities. Even with their different initial perspectives, however, the operating systems have not stayed static. Rather, each operating system has evolved in remarkable ways, and capabilities from one system have been adapted for another. For example, as computer users grew to appreciate the graphical interfaces on the Macintosh and other systems, both Microsoft and Unix found ways to incorporate those features into their own products. Today, operating systems may have some common capabilities, but behind the scenes they achieve those features differently.

Altogether, the varying needs and priorities of users have prompted multiple approaches for handling common computing tasks, and these perspectives have led to different operating systems.

What is "multitasking," and does this idea affect me?

Most computers have only one CPU, so they can do only one thing at a time. Historically, a computer would first work on one task until it was done before moving on to another task. As an example in a reasonably modern context, if you were editing a document using a word processor, then no other work could be done on your computer at the same time. When you wanted to print the document, then printing was the only task allowed. This meant that you could not continue to work on the document while you were printing it. When the CPU was devoted to printing, it could not also handle other processing requests. Such an environment is said to support single tasking, and this approach was widespread in early computers.

Although single tasking is conceptually simple, in practice it leaves the CPU idle at times. For example, printing requires paper to move through a printer, and the single-tasking CPU has to wait for the paper movement. Similarly, the CPU can execute program instructions much faster than a typist can type, so the CPU that utilizes single tasking is idle if it has to wait for information from a typist. In general, I/O devices usually involve some mechanical activity and thus work much more slowly than an electricity-based CPU. In single-tasking computers, therefore, the CPU generally has to wait for information from I/O devices.

Rather than waste CPU capabilities, **multitasking** allows a computer to coordinate the processing of several tasks at once. For example, while the CPU waits for I/O for one task, it might make progress on the work for another task. Similarly, if several user tasks require computational work, the CPU may take turns. It makes some progress on a first task, then on a second, then on a third, and so on, until each desired task has had some attention. This may finish some work, but additional work may remain. So, in a second round, the CPU may go back to the first task for some additional work, and then continue processing on the second and later tasks. In a third round, again the CPU gives each task additional attention.

Overall, with the CPU's activity split among several projects, the progress on any one project may be slower than if that task received exclusive CPU attention. However, because a CPU works quickly, a user may not notice any slowdown for relatively simple tasks. For example, because interactions with a printer and editing a document are each relatively straightforward, a multitasking environment would allow each to take place at the same time. (In both cases, the limiting factors are likely to be the movement of paper through the printer and the speed at which a typist can enter data, and the CPU is likely to be able to do all required processing for either of these tasks while it is waiting for action from the other.)

On the other hand, even a multitasking environment can proceed only as fast as its CPU allows. Thus, if a user is doing an extensive computation in a spreadsheet and also editing a large document (that requires extensive virtual memory), then the user may notice a significant deterioration in speed from the norm in both applications.

For the most part, we can appreciate multitasking, because it allows us to shift our attention from one task to another or from one window to another. However, because all of our work competes for

CPU time and other resources, some processing tasks may take a long time in a multitasking environment—longer than if the CPU could devote all its attention to the task, as with single tasking.

Why do operating systems worry about coordinating different programs or users? Can't they just work separately?

Within the technical community, this question can be answered by noting that coordination is necessary when different programs or users need to share common resources. In case you find that answer unduly formal or abstract, however, let's consider three examples.

Printing Example

Suppose we are developing two documents at the same time. Perhaps one document is our written research report to be handed to an instructor or customer, whereas the second represents the slides we will use in an oral presentation. For our research report we may use a word-processor application, and for our slides we may use a slide application, such as PowerPoint or Keynote. Each application would have its own separate window. Because both documents relate to the same research project, we want both windows open at the same time. This allows us to refer to one document while we write or edit the other.

When we have reasonable drafts ready, we decide to print both documents. To print, we go to each document window, select the "print" option, and instruct the computer to perform the printing operation. We request two copies of the first document, the research report, by choosing the print option twice for that material, and then we print the slides. If we make these requests within a short period of time, the request to print the slides might be sent to the CPU while the first copy of the first document is still printing, and the second copy has not yet been started. The computer now has some choices to make; one printing task has started, and two more are pending.

Without coordination, each of these printing requests would have to work independently. The result could be chaos. During the printing of the first document, the printer might be asked to print the second copy as well. The result could be a jumble, with one copy interspersed with the second. When the request for the second copy arrived, parts of it might appear on top of the two previous copies. Such independent actions clearly are not acceptable.

Instead, the operating system keeps track of all requests that have been made for printing. Work then proceeds on the first request, and the other printing tasks are postponed. When the first copy has been printed, the operating system can review what additional printing requests are pending, choose one, and start that print job. When that is done, the operating system can go on to the third request. Altogether, different users or programs may make requests to print, but the operating system has the final say on which request is fulfilled and when. In the terminology of computing, a printer is considered a computing resource, and the operating system is responsible for controlling which user or task has access to what resource and when.

Memory Example

Consider again the printing example, but this time from the standpoint of main memory. As we know from Chapter 1, working with each of the two document windows will require that some parts of the programs and some data be stored in main memory. Each document window corresponds to a running program, and each document contains information; the CPU will get its instructions and data for each document from main memory. For both programs to run and appear on the screen, parts of main memory will have to be allocated to the first window, and parts to the second.

Again, such memory allocation requires coordination. Not only must the operating system allocate different parts of memory to different tasks, but also these allocations must be remembered and utilized so that the material for one document is not confused with that of the other. To avoid errors, such allocation requires careful bookkeeping and administration.

Bank/File Example

Consider the processing involved within a bank for a deposit or withdrawal. Typically, account information is stored on a file—perhaps on a disk. To be specific, the processing of the withdrawal of $50 from a checking account (initial balance $600) can use these steps:

1. Determine old balance ($600) in the account.
2. Deduct the $50 withdrawal.
3. Record the new balance ($550) in the account.

This outline works quite well until both a husband and wife are on business in separate cities and each decides to withdraw $50 from different branches of the bank at the same time. If these transactions are processed in parallel, the following steps might occur concurrently:

Processing Husband's Request	**Processing Wife's Request**
1. Determine old balance ($600).	**1.** Determine old balance ($600).
2. Deduct the $50 withdrawal.	**2.** Deduct the $50 withdrawal.
3. Record the new balance ($550).	**3.** Record the new balance ($550).

In this case, because the two requests were processed at the same time, work started on each request with the same balance ($600), and the final balance given for each request was the same ($550). Thus, each person received $50, for a total of $100, but only $50 was deducted from the account.

This simple example is typical of the troubles that can arise when multiple transactions are to be processed at the same time. For each transaction, work may be straightforward, but complications can arise when several tasks occur simultaneously. In the banking example, there was no way to anticipate which spouse would make the withdrawal request first. Thus, the banks (and their programmers) could not anticipate what sequence to follow in the processing; indeed, it may happen that different sequences would need to be followed on different days.

To generalize somewhat, we can consider printers, main memory, and files as resources within a computer system. Our examples of printing, memory, and banking then illustrate circumstances in which several tasks seek to utilize common resources at the same time. In such cases, it may be necessary to place constraints upon allocation of these resources—when and how data are accessed and what processing is done when and where. Once these constraints are determined, the operating system is responsible for coordinating transactions and enforcing constraints.

To accomplish this coordination, the operating system has final control over the allocation of resources. When a task wants access to memory, when a user wants to print, or when several users want to work with the same file(s), programs translate such desires into requests to the operating system. The operating system may allocate the resources and allow the tasks to proceed; however, the operating system also may deny or postpone the requests. If both spouses request bank withdrawals, then the operating system requires one to wait until the other is done.

What do you mean by "booting" the computer?

Sometimes, if a computer is not working the way one would like, you might want to kick it. With a laptop computer, the temptation might be particularly strong. However, this is not what is normally meant by booting a computer.

Rather, **booting a computer** refers to starting it up and allowing the operating system to set itself up so that it can appropriately coordinate users and processing tasks. Booting a computer also may include starting utility programs to handle various administrative tasks.

To expand somewhat, an operating system typically must maintain several tables to keep track of

- What data are where in main memory
- What disk(s) or CD(s) are in place
- What connections there might be to external devices (e.g., printers, the Internet)
- What users have logged on
- What programs currently are running

Also, the operating system may start several behind-the-scenes programs to handle specialized tasks, such as monitoring e-mail, coordinating printing requests, playing music, or responding to requests from other machines over a network.

Because a computer user expects these services and activities to function smoothly when called upon, the startup of a computer must include relevant preparation for these demands. This preparation is part of the process called "booting a computer."

On some computers, it is worthwhile to note that the operating system reports what services it is starting during the boot process;

lists of services appear briefly on the screen to keep the user informed. Although users may not care about the details, scanning the list can provide some insight about the numerous tasks that are performed during this initialization period. (Flashing messages on the screen also can distract the user during this boot period. Without messages, the user may become restless, waiting for the computer to become ready for use. Further, with nothing to do, the user may become dissatisfied with the slowness of the computer. The user may even wonder if the computer is doing anything at all—perhaps the computer is malfunctioning! With the display of status reports, users realize that something is happening, and they are likely to be more patient. Software developers have learned this tendency and may display messages to boost user satisfaction or to mask slow performance.)

What is a "reboot," and why might it be necessary?

Rebooting a computer involves stopping all current processing on the machine and restarting it. After a reboot, the computer should be in exactly the same state as if it were just turned on; that is, all standard tables in the operating system are created and initialized, behind-the-scenes utility programs are started, and the computer is ready for users to log on and work.

As a computer operates, one would expect the operating system to maintain its internal tables, to keep track of the various activities under way, to allocate and deallocate main memory as needed, and to otherwise allow processing to continue smoothly. When programs and the operating system run as planned, it should never be necessary to reboot the machine, or to turn it off and start again. Rebooting should not be considered a normal operation.

However, sometimes things go wrong. Computer programs, such as operating systems, may contain errors—as described in the next chapter. Similarly, hardware may malfunction or a power supply may be lost. With any of these circumstances, even a momentary lapse in processing or a single mistake in an instruction could interfere with one of the coordination tasks of the operating system. When system tables contain incorrect status information or when coordination breaks down, then this behind-the-scenes activity must be restored to normal. Sometimes this can be accomplished efficiently with a reboot.

For example, in working with materials from the World Wide Web, I periodically have found the screen or browser to apparently freeze or lock when particular pages are loaded. In such cases, the computer does not respond to commands; even the mouse pointer on the screen does not seem to move when the physical mouse is moved by hand. In such cases, the computer does not seem to respond to pushing any keys, and normal actions do not remedy the situation. With normal activities worthless, the only alternative seems to involve drastic action; rebooting the machine can be a constructive alternative.

Why do so many people and companies use Windows?

Although the answer to this question could include advertising, subjective personal preferences, and a discussion of technical capabilities, let's instead look at this question from a historical perspective.

Back in the 1970s, most serious computers were large and expensive—often designed to handle data processing needs for large companies. By the late 1970s and early 1980s, however, progress in technology prompted the appearance of a number of smaller machines, later called personal computers, designed for use by individuals in their own offices. Unfortunately, these machines were largely incompatible. Each hardware manufacturer determined its own specifications (CPU, bus characteristics, main memory details). Further, several different operating systems were in common use. Programs designed for one machine frequently could not run on computers built by other companies, files from one system could not be shared easily with others, and each system had its own strengths and weaknesses—often based on proprietary hardware and software.

Through the 1970s, IBM focused its attention and energy on large corporate computers, and it enjoyed a strong reputation in that market. However, by the late 1970s, IBM decided it also needed to compete with its own small personal computers. And, rather than keep its hardware specifications proprietary, it shared them freely. As a result, other companies could imitate its hardware (producing IBM-compatible computers), and application developers could write software to run on any of this family's compatible machines. With IBM's stature in the computer field, the market enthusiastically embraced this open view of hardware, and IBM's reputation assured that IBM captured a reasonable percentage of the personal-computer market.

Of course, any computer hardware requires an operating system. Rather than write its own, however, IBM decided to utilize one available from Bill Gates and collaborators (i.e., Microsoft). Thus, in August 1981, Microsoft released MS-DOS 1.0, the first operating system for the IBM personal computer. Subsequently, new developments by IBM were accompanied by corresponding expansions of the Microsoft operating system. For example, Microsoft released DOS 2.0 in 1983, when IBM developed a hard disk for its personal computers.

Microsoft also became very effective in expanding the capabilities of its operating systems in response to developments in the computing field. For example, in the 1980s, Apple produced a very effective, easy-to-use graphical interface for its Macintosh computers. By 1990, Microsoft had developed Windows 3.0—its own version of a **graphical user interface** (**GUI**).

Within the marketplace, the combination of compatible models of hardware (IBM compatibles) and a uniform operating system (Microsoft DOS and then Windows) solved many previous problems. Users could share data files from one computer to another; developers could write applications that would reliably run on many brands of computers, producing a remarkable range of programs for the market; competition in the market kept costs under control; and users could mix hardware and software to meet their specific needs.

Altogether, Microsoft with IBM was extremely creative in unifying much of the personal-computing market, and Microsoft aggressively promoted and developed its operating system and software. The fractured markets of the 1970s have given way to the more uniform environments of the 2000s, in which compatibility and sharing are vital components of a computing network. Microsoft's early role with IBM certainly is an important element in its dominance today.

Why can't a Windows machine read a Macintosh or Linux disk, but many Macintosh and Linux machines can read a Windows disk?

Already we have observed that the purpose of an operating system is to streamline the running of applications for users and to coordinate the running of programs. Because this work has many different components, alternative strategies have emerged to accomplish it, each with its own priorities and perspectives. For example, Microsoft Windows, Macintosh OS 9.0, and Linux follow their own approaches to each of the many tasks that operating systems oversee. (Technically, in early 2000, Apple made a fundamental shift in its Macintosh operating system when it released OS X. Version 9 used its own approach to disk formatting, whereas Macintosh OS X became Unix/Linux based. New Macintosh operating systems largely are compatible with Linux, whereas previous versions of the Macintosh and Linux operating systems followed a different approach.)

These differences extend to the conventions regarding the location and format of disks and their directories. In particular, each operating system follows its own convention about which sector(s) are used for the main directory and what the format of a file entry is in that directory. Thus, to read a directory, an operating system goes to the appropriate sector, reads a sequence of bits and bytes of data, and interprets those data based on the conventions for that format. To read a different disk format, the operating system would have to go to a different sector, and/or the bits and bytes read would have to be interpreted in a different way.

In normal processing, an operating system would expect a disk to conform to its specific format conventions. Thus, a Windows machine would expect a disk to follow its format, a Macintosh would expect a disk in Macintosh format, and a Linux or Unix machine would expect a disk in that format. When a disk of another format is used, therefore, an operating system cannot follow its normal approach to make sense of the data. For this reason, the Windows operating system is unable to read a Macintosh or Linux disk.

In the case of a Macintosh or Linux machine, the same initial confusion arises when a Windows disk is inserted. However, with the widespread use of Windows, developers of Macintosh and Linux decided that it would be useful for their machines to be able to share disks with Windows users. Thus, when a Windows disk is inserted into a Macintosh or Linux computer, the operating system realizes that the format does not correspond to normal conventions and then shifts modes to try reading the file in a Windows format. This second effort allows Macintosh and Linux machines to read Windows disks.

Which operating system is best?

The three most common operating systems for personal computers today are Windows (by Microsoft), Macintosh OS X (by Apple), and Linux (by Linus Torvalds and a world-wide confederation of developers). Through various historical events, each of these has specific objectives and strengths, and each has both a strong cadre of advocates and another strong group of critics. Here are a few highlights of recent arguments:

- Over the years, Microsoft has been extremely aggressive in marketing, so that various versions of Microsoft Windows now are used on a large fraction of individual workstations. Such widespread use has allowed users of systems to share their materials (programs, data) easily.
- Macintosh operating systems have consistently emphasized a simple, clean, and powerful graphical interface. Apple's operating systems have allowed users, even beginning users, to easily perform valuable tasks, such as editing text, pictures, and sound.
- Unix and Linux tout their reliability and ability to link complex processing tasks, with new graphical interfaces simplifying interactions with users.

Proponents on each side could expand on these comments at great length (just ask them!). Each of these operating systems has its own strengths and advantages, and the choice of one over another depends on what a user wants to do and with whom that user wants to interact.

Why does my diskette work at home but not in the computer lab at school, or at work?

Disks may fail to work for several reasons. The previous section suggests one such reason. If your home machine uses a Macintosh or Linux operating system, then a disk for that machine would normally be formatted for that system. If the computers at school or work used the Windows operating system, then the disk format would not match the conventions for Windows, and the disk would be unreadable. (Of course, the disk would work fine again when you brought it home.)

A second potential reason could involve transportation. A disk that used to work at home but won't work at school may have been damaged in transit. For example, on the way to school or work, the disk might have been placed near a magnetic field. (Perhaps the disk was placed next to several credit cards with magnetic strips.) Or, your disk could have been left on your car's dashboard in the hot afternoon sun, or squashed in your backpack. If the disk was damaged, then it will not work at school, and it will not work at home either. Of course, you cannot check that when you are at school, and should therefore investigate possible other causes for its malfunctioning.

A third potential reason that the disk won't work is more subtle. The reading and writing of material on disks depends on a specific configuration of tracks and sectors. Some disks are identified as "**double density**," in which case the tracks and sectors might be packed together more closely than for "**single density**." Similarly, some disks are "**single sided**," whereas others are "**double sided**." That is, data may be stored on just one side of some disks, but data may be placed on both sides of other disks. Both double-density and double-sided formats provide mechanisms to store more information on a disk than would be possible with the traditional single-sided, single-density format.

In reading and writing data on double-density disks, the disk drive itself must be able to distinguish tracks that are close to each other. For double-sided disks, the disk drive must be equipped with read/write heads that can access both sides of the disk. In each case, trouble would arise if data were stored in a double-density or double-sided format but the disk drive was not capable of handling that format. (As a practical matter, drives that are sophisticated enough to read double-density normally can also read single-density. Similarly, drives for double-sided disks also can read single-sided ones.) If your disk drive at home uses a compressed format but the computers at school or work do not, then your diskette at home would not work there. Today, most computers with removable disks can read double-sided, double-density diskettes.

The fourth potential reason involves a partial hardware malfunction. A disk drive requires the precise movement of read/write heads to specific track locations. If a read/write head were to overshoot slightly, it might read or write from the space between tracks. If it were to overshoot a bit more, it might have moved to the location of the next track. Thus, the read/write heads must consistently move to exactly the correct location—within reasonably tight tolerances.

As a disk functions over time, it is not unknown for this read/write head movement to come out of alignment slightly. In this case, a write operation would still place data on the disk, and a read operation would still retrieve it appropriately. However, misalignment means that the location of the data would not be quite right—perhaps the data would be stored on the space between where the tracks should be rather than on the desired track itself. If the same read/write head were used for reading and writing, any such misalignment would be the same for both reading and writing, and the operations would appear to work fine. However, if the disk were moved to a new machine and the data were not exactly where they should be, the reading operation would fail. Of course, it could be that the home machine's disk drive works fine, and the one in the lab is misaligned. This could be checked by trying to use the disk on other lab machines. When a disk from home fails in several lab machines, then it may be time for the servicing or replacement of a home disk drive.

Summary

Operating systems handle common tasks and administrative functions that allow users to run computers with relative ease. Such tasks include identifying one user from another, keeping track of distinct requests (e.g., associating typing in a window with the correct processing), scheduling and coordinating processing, allocating resources (e.g., files, printers, memory), handling files, and communicating with other machines. When these tasks are performed centrally, individual users need not worry about doing these tasks themselves.

Multitasking allows computers to split their processing time and resources among several processes or users. Processing requires coordination when computers work on several tasks at the same time.

When starting a computer, the operating system must prepare for its role of coordination; this process is called *booting*. *Rebooting* involves shutting a computer down and starting it again. Although rebooting should be needed rarely, if ever, it sometimes provides a convenient way to recover and move forward when malfunctions arise in processing.

Because the oversight and administration of computers can be done in many ways, different operating systems have developed, including Microsoft Windows, Linux, and Macintosh OS X. For historical reasons, many people and companies use Microsoft Windows, but various operating systems have their strengths and proponents. With different mechanisms for handling administrative tasks, different operating systems may not work in compatible ways; activities that work well on one system may not work on another, and disks may be readable only on some systems.

■ Terminology from This Chapter

booting a computer
double-density disk
double-sided disk
graphical user interface (GUI)
multi-tasking
operating system
rebooting a computer
single-density disk

■ Discussion Questions

1. Could a single-tasking machine allow a user to listen to music, print a document, and read e-mail at the same time? Explain why or why not.
2. As noted in the chapter, three operating systems dominate desktop and laptop computers: Microsoft Windows, Macintosh OS X, and Unix/Linux. Each of these operating systems has its own strong advocates, and each has its critics.
   a. Choose one operating system to investigate. Then organize a class or group debate on whether this operating system should be the one installed in all labs and classes at your school. For example, the group in favor of using that operating system would promote its relative strengths and be able to defend it against possible claims of weakness.

b. Divide the class or discussion group into three teams, each of which is to serve as a proponent for one of the three dominant operating systems. Then conduct a round-robin debate or group argument, in which each group promotes the thesis that its operating system should be installed in all labs and classes at your school.

3. Both the U.S. Justice Department and several states took Microsoft to court, alleging monopolistic practices.

a. Investigate the nature of these cases, and determine their current status.

b. Review the claims and counterclaims of these cases. To what extent do you believe the claims were valid?

c. Based on your readings of the cases, do you agree with the outcomes and settlements? Explain.

4. During an evening at home, a student listens to music, reads an assignment, writes a short paper, answers several telephone calls, eats a snack (while reading and writing), and plans a weekend shopping trip to a nearby mall.

a. To what extent does the activity of the student represent multitasking?

b. How might the evening's schedule change if the student was limited to single tasking?

5. IBM's hardware philosophy of the 1980s for personal computers is sometimes called an open hardware approach. A company shares its basic specifications, allowing others to copy some basic elements and capture some of the market.

a. Why do you think a company might believe that an open hardware approach would be in its best interests?

b. Investigate the development of the personal computer market in the 1980s to determine the extent to which this open hardware approach helped IBM meet its objectives during that period.

6. Developers of the Linux operating system now follow an "open source" policy that is analogous to IBM's "open hardware" approach of the 1980s.

a. Investigate how this policy works today in practice.

b. Who actually controls Linux and its development?

c. To what extent is an open source policy commercially viable? Explain your answer.

Exercises

1. a. Give a careful definition of each of the words or phrases listed in the "Terminology from This Chapter."

   b. In reviewing these terms, which seem related specifically to operating systems, and which seem related to other elements of a computer? Briefly explain your answer.

2. One computer system displays a picture of a mailbox on a corner of the screen. When the user receives new e-mail, the mailbox display turns red and updates a count of the number of unread e-mail messages received. After a couple of minutes, the mailbox returns to a white color—regardless of whether the new message was read or not. This same scenario regarding mail holds whether or not the user is engaged in other work, such as editing documents.

   a. Does this description contain sufficient information to determine whether the operating system supports multitasking? Explain.

   b. What, if any, changes would be required in the above description if the system allowed only single tasking? Explain.

3. The transfer of money from a checking account to a savings account might follow these steps:

   a. Determine the initial balance for the checking account.

   b. Determine the initial balance for the savings account.

   c. Deduct the amount to be transferred from the checking account.

   d. Add the amount to be transferred to the savings account.

   e. Record the new balance for the savings account.

   f. Record the new balance for the checking account.

The transfer of money from savings to checking would be analogous (with the words *checking* and *savings* swapped in steps a through f)

Suppose a couple has a checking account with an initial balance of \$500 and a savings account with an initial balance of \$1000. Suppose further that the husband decides to transfer \$50 from savings to checking, while the wife decides to transfer \$50 from checking to savings.

a. If the husband goes first, and then the wife goes second—starting after the husband finishes—trace the above steps to show that each account ends with the same amount it started with; that is, the transactions of the husband and wife effectively have canceled each other out.

b. Suppose the husband and wife initiate their transactions at exactly the same time. Identify a sequence of events that would show \$450 in checking and \$950 in savings at the end—effectively losing \$100 of the couple's money. (Because this outcome is not considered appropriate, this scenario provides another example of why coordination may be needed for independent programs.)

4. Some people describe Microsoft as being extremely innovative, whereas others claim Microsoft is primarily just a good marketing company. Conduct some research to find arguments on both sides of this topic. Review the two points of view, and then state and justify your own conclusion.

5. Consider a laboratory setting in a school, in which students work independently on their own work. Throughout the lab, an instructor circulates from student to student, responding to questions and providing help when asked. To what extent might the instructor's activity in this lab be considered multitasking? Identify at least two elements that seem consistent with the idea of multitasking and at least two elements that seem different.

Part II
Software/Problem-Solving Questions

Chapter 5

How are software packages developed?

PEOPLE USE COMPUTERS because they help solve problems. What do you use a computer for? To access e-mail? To type out your history paper? To keep track of the transactions in your checking account? In each of these cases, the computer solves a problem for you: It figures out how to connect to the Internet, determines how to communicate with your keyboard and display what you type, records deposits and checks written, and maintains your running account balance. These computer solutions do not develop spontaneously from primordial elements. (At least, no one has witnessed such solutions springing into existence from nothing and lived to report the event.) Rather, they emerge from a coordinated effort between hardware and software. Computer solutions result from the building of appropriate equipment (hardware), the development of logical techniques (called algorithms) that specify how the problem can be solved, and the translation of these techniques into software. The process of problem solving and developing software requires considerable time and effort, and is the focus of this chapter

What are the main steps in software project development?

Software sometimes begins with a fuzzy idea or vision related to the solution to a problem. We may recognize a problem and have a general sense that a computer might help in the solution. For example, farmers of large farms pay considerable attention to what fertilizer is needed on what parts of their fields. Applying too much fertilizer may contribute to the pollution of ground water, as well as costing money for little gain. Applying too little fertilizer reduces crop size, generating less income. To address this situation, farmers often take soil samples from various parts of their fields and perform tests to determine the optimal amount of fertilizer to be applied in each area. Unfortunately, the desired quantity of fertilizer often differs from one part of a field to another, and it is impractical to manually adjust the amount of fertilizer dispersed from the spreader while a tractor moves through a field. (The farmer would have to stop the tractor, make an adjustment, drive a bit more, make another adjustment, and so on.) Such a situation led to the vision that a computer might use a Global Positioning System (GPS) to keep track of the tractor's location in the field and make adjustments as the farmer drives. As you might expect, development of such a system required working through many details, such as determining specific needs, practical constraints, and numerous elements of farming equipment. Even with such complexity, modern systems are available to control fertilizer application based on this broad vision.

At other times, we may believe that there is a market for a new software package that would perform a particular task and want to create it. For example, when computers were just coming into people's homes, most people maintained records of their bank accounts manually on paper. For a checking account, an individual would record deposits, withdrawals, and any fees as they occurred. With each transaction, the individual would add or subtract the relevant amount to obtain a new bank balance, and this running balance was compared with a statement received monthly from the bank. Although the process was supposed to be fairly straightforward, transactions sometimes were forgotten or misrecorded, and arithmetic errors were not uncommon. Locating such problems often required considerable time and effort. Because computers seemed to be effective in storing and retrieving information and in doing arithmetic, it seemed likely that the computer might be helpful in this record-keeping effort. After identifying the basic problem of maintaining account records, the program developers had to consider just what functionality users might want, what types of input and display would be most helpful, what legal constraints or accounting standards might apply, and so forth. The idea of a software package required considerable discussion and clarification before developers could settle on just what the package should do. Some time later, developers realized that the details of check writing might be useful in helping folks fill out their annual income tax forms (at least in the United States). Again, an initial vision required considerable refinement and clarification before developers could produce a home-finance package that could handle both bank accounts and tax statements in ways that users would find helpful and easy to use.

In most cases, the process of moving from the initial idea to a finished product that meets the needs of various people is rarely trivial. Significant work is required to precisely define the problem, clarify what capabilities might be needed to help solve it, determine mechanisms to achieve the desired capabilities, translate the solutions into programs that a computer can interpret, and perform checks that the software does what is intended. Clearly, many steps (and people) are involved in the process of developing software.

Problem solving by creating software frequently proceeds according to the following basic steps—each of which will be defined and explained shortly: writing specifications, developing algorithms, coding algorithms, testing and running programs, and maintaining programs.

Writing Specifications: A **specification** of a problem is the careful statement of what problem is to be solved. In most mathematics, science, and engineering courses, this specification is complete in every assignment; students are told precisely what work is to be done. Unfortunately, however, even in such settings as a controlled classroom environment, it sometimes happens that the statement of a problem is flawed. The statement, for example, may be ambiguous or contradictory. (Some faculty members have been known to state that each of their assignments actually has two parts: the first consists of determining what the question is supposed to be asking, and the second involves answering the corrected problem.)

In less-controlled environments, the careful specification of a problem may take considerable work. For example, consider the traffic lights in a reasonably large city. Lights at each intersection may be red, amber, or green in each direction, and a timing device or controller changes the lights from one color to the next after a prescribed time interval. In this setting, an overall goal might be to determine when lights should change color and to coordinate the color changes at various intersections in such a way as to allow traffic to flow most efficiently. Here the intuitive idea may seem clear: Traffic should move smoothly from one place to another with little delay. But, how does one decide when traffic is moving smoothly? If most traffic is traveling out of town during the evening rush hour, how much should that traffic be delayed so that a single motorist can go in another direction? Is traffic delay measured as an overall average, or is there a maximum amount of delay that is acceptable at any intersection? Even if traffic does not seem to be badly congested, how would one know if another traffic light pattern would allow motorists to travel faster to their desired destinations? Any formal specification will need to address many questions of this type; otherwise, it will be impossible to determine whether a proposed solution is satisfactory or not. Overall, specifications must indicate exactly what issues are to be addressed and how potential solutions will be evaluated.

Developing Algorithms: Once a problem is carefully specified, techniques or formulae can be developed to solve the problem. The careful statement of these appropriate techniques is called an **algorithm** and the process of developing algorithms is called the **design phase** of problem solving. A careful statement of the algorithms and any related material is called a **design** for a solution. Consider baking a pie: You have the ingredients and tools, but need a clearly written, precise, step-by-step recipe, or algorithm, so that you can accomplish your goals. In an academic setting, algorithmic techniques are often discussed in class meetings or in course reading. Sometimes, a specific algorithm is even stated as part of the problem (e.g., "use Newton's Method to approximate the square root of 2 to three decimal places"). In other settings, the choice of algorithm is not always clear, and, in some cases, new algorithms may need to be discovered in order to solve a problem.

In evaluating a potential algorithm, a highly desirable characteristic is that the algorithm produces correct results. However, in many cases, an algorithm with solely that quality still may not be acceptable. For example, one solution to the problem "Predict the Dow Jones Average for next Thursday" is "Wait until next Friday," but this approach is not sufficiently timely. Similarly, one solution to the question "Find the call number of Walker's text *Introduction to Computing and Computer Science*" would be "Transport 100,000 people to the Library of Congress and have them search all of the shelves until the book is found." Such an approach would probably answer the question reasonably quickly, but it might use more resources than appropriate. These examples suggest that algorithms must not only produce correct answers, but also obtain those results in a timely manner using resources that are appropriate and available for the job.

Coding Algorithms: Once an algorithm is chosen, it must be written in a form that a computer can interpret. Computers work by following instructions that they are given, and any algorithm must be translated into a form that uses only the special instructions that the computer can follow. This translation process is called **coding** or **programming**, and the end of this coding is a computer program. (In the movie *2001*, the computer Hal responds to instructions given in English and to visual commands. Such understanding is commonly seen in movies. Realistically, however, computer understanding of natural language is still far from being realized, and the goal of much research in computer science is to be able to allow the automatic translation of speech or vision into a form that can be used by computers.) At a basic level, all information and instructions inside computers must be in a very primitive form, and considerable work is usually necessary to translate algorithms from English or another form understandable to people into a form a computer can interpret. We will discuss algorithms in more detail in Chapter 7.

Testing and Running Programs: After an algorithm has been translated into a form a computer can use, one would hope that the program could be used to solve the specific problem it was designed to solve. If data from the specified problem were entered into the computer, the computer should produce the desired results. This step comprises the running of a program.

Although the initial running of a program has been known to produce helpful and correct results, it is usually the case that errors will occur somewhere in the problem-solving process. Specifications may be incomplete or inaccurate, algorithms may contain flaws, or the coding processing may be incorrect. Edsger Dijkstra, a very distinguished computer scientist, has observed that in most disciplines such difficulties are called errors or mistakes, but that in computing this terminology is usually softened, and flaws are called **bugs**.* (It seems that people are often more willing to tolerate errors in computer programs than in other products, but more on this in later chapters.)

---

*Edsger Dijkstra, "On the Cruelty of Really Teaching Computing Science," *Communications of the ACM*, Volume 32, Number 12, December 1989, p. 1402.

Unfortunately, errors or bugs arise frequently in many programs, particularly in large ones, and the next step of program development involves finding errors and correcting them. It can be very dangerous to rely on the output of a program until you are confident that the results are correct. Thus, programs are usually run with special data, the results of which are known ahead of time. This **testing** allows the results from a program to be compared with the previously known results to determine if errors are present. When errors are found, it is necessary to find the cause of each error and to correct it; this process is called **debugging**. When working on large projects, this process of testing and debugging can take considerable time and effort.

Maintaining Programs: At the beginning of this section, it was observed that, in giving assignments, an instructor sometimes will need to clarify or expand the statement of the problem, so that students understand what they need to do. In addition (although it may be hard to believe), teachers have been known to change their minds about an assignment. In such cases, students may try to revise any work they have already done in order to meet the new specifications of the problem, but, if the problem has changed too much, the entire assignment may need to be done over.

This same situation commonly arises in working with complex problems that computers may help solve. For example, changes in tax laws or accounting procedures may require different calculations or records to be processed. Companies producing computer programs that calculate state and federal income taxes must stay up to date and release new versions each year to ensure that the programs are making the current computations. Further, as people gain experience with a computer program, they may suggest ways the program might be changed to make it more useful. Feedback forms or customer surveys are often used to solicit input on how a program can be improved.

More generally, programs may need to be changed to accommodate new or changed circumstances or to correct errors that may not have been found during testing. With short programs, such work can often be accomplished simply by rewriting the algorithm or code, but, in more complex settings, rewriting is simply too time-consuming and expensive. Thus, old programs are frequently reworked to meet the revised specifications; this process is called **maintenance**. For large projects, this maintenance effort may extend for many years, and it may require a considerable investment in equipment, people, and time. In many cases, developers of programs will anticipate the need for maintenance, and algorithms and programming techniques will be used that may simplify the task. Throughout this maintenance activity, changes in one part of a program or the correction of some errors may introduce other errors. Thus, testing must continue throughout any maintenance work.

How do developers decide what capabilities to put in their software?

To be useful, a computer program must meet a user's real needs. This may seem both easy and obvious, but in practice, the identification of user needs and wishes can be far from straightforward.

How are the users' needs determined?

A natural starting point to discover user needs is to explicitly ask potential users what they want. If you envision selling your software to a general target audience, then you need to investigate just what needs that audience might have. Such a study is called **market analysis**. For example, you might develop a customer survey, asking potential customers what features they would like in a program. You might observe people at work to determine just what they do so you know what to automate. You might talk to managers or experts in the field to clarify relevant or useful elements. Similarly, if you were developing software for a specific client, you might interview that customer at length—perhaps talking both to management and to workers in the field to understand what they currently do, how various departments work together, and how a new system might streamline or integrate various functions.

Although asking the potential audience or client what is desired or needed is an important step, the process of identifying capabilities for software often requires further analysis. For example, even if a customer is highly motivated to answer your questions, the responses may provide only partial guidance for at least three reasons:

1. A user often is aware only of her or his current life circumstances, and their feedback may take advantage of unstated assumptions and informal practices.

2. If the application is new, the user likely thinks in terms of present practice and may not be able to envision a system that is dramatically different.

3. User needs often change as users become more sophisticated, businesses grow, and laws change.

Let's consider an application that highlights each of these difficulties in writing complete specifications.

Word-Processing Example

If your entire experience with writing involved only the use of a pencil on paper, you would never have had the experience of a system checking your work for spelling or grammar. Similarly, if you had needed to break a word over two lines, you always would have done your own word division and hyphenation. Further, you likely would not have thought about multiple type fonts and type sizes. In describing your needs for word-processing software, chances are that you would unlikely be able to think of all the features that now are common in such software. That does not mean you wouldn't want them; however, they would be out of your realm of experience, and even a truly innovative person would likely think of just some of them. And, if you did not think of the features, you could not tell a developer you wanted them.

Extending this example, suppose you were an experienced author, journalist, or publisher with extensive experience in writing and publishing printed works produced with the traditional typesetting process. In this case, you would be familiar with page layouts, type fonts and sizes, spacing and paragraphing, tables, and lists. Your experience also would include editing of the manuscript using special symbols (called proofreaders' marks), the manual setting of type, multiple rounds of proofreading, and the separate (manual) compilation of the table of contents and index. With such background, you might want a software package to automate the familiar tasks you regularly did (layouts, fonts, spacing), but, given your experiences, you might ask for a mechanism to incorporate the same proofreaders' marks that you use into the process. You might not think that another process (e.g., comments or annotations) could be used in place of proofreaders' marks, and it might not occur to you that software might be able to generate the table of contents or index automatically.

Remember also that we tend to project our most current experiences in our opinions, even if we do so unintentionally. Your initial consideration of what you need in a word-processing program, therefore, might take for granted that you would be writing in your native language (e.g., English). This need, however, could change. You might, at a later date, either because of a class or a trip, find it necessary to write in a language (e.g., Russian or Chinese) that uses a different alphabet or in a language (e.g., Hebrew) that reads from right to left rather than left to right. Over time, moreover, your vision might also deteriorate, and your needs would change to include wanting material on your screen to appear at a larger size. With such changes in circumstances, the software you initially described would no longer meet your current needs. Your new needs would require a change in specifications.

Prototypes: Users typically have only an imprecise notion of what they want, and because users' needs evolve and change, software developers may utilize a variety of techniques to refine programs as they are being created and maintained. One such approach is the use of **prototypes**—mock-ups of possible user interfaces, reports, and capabilities. A prototype presents a sample user window, output, or feature that can be reviewed by users. The prototype may not perform all desired tasks—for example, it may contain only places for users to input data or sample output formats. Data entered may not actually be processed, outputs may contain sample data only, and any processing may be slow or simplified. Even with such limitations, however, a user can experience a design to determine what seems helpful, what adjustments might be appropriate, and what new or different features should be considered.

For example, in a prototype of a word-processing package, the user might view a window that displays a box indicating the current type font and another box for the size of the font. Buttons might specify bold or italics or underlining. Such a window allows the potential user to comment on the layout of the word-processing screen, the way various features might be used, and the range of current features. Multiple prototypes might provide alternative layouts so users could comment on the relative merits of different layouts. However, in a prototype, the software might support only one type font, without the actual option for bold, italics, or underlining. One prototype for a word-processing package might place boxes and buttons on the top, while another might place a different collection of boxes and icons on the side, and a third might split these elements along the top and bottom.

A prototype normally does not have full functionality; rather, it provides insight regarding what would be most useful to include in the real application. Sometimes, several prototypes for an application might be developed to ascertain what alternatives have greatest appeal or usefulness. Thus, prototypes can help guide the design process. Because prototypes have limited functionality, they may be produced quickly and cheaply, allowing several alternatives to be tested before committing much time and effort on a final system.

Extreme versus Classical Programming: In classical program development, the steps of specification, algorithm development, coding, and testing follow in sequence—with the expectation that each stage largely will be finalized before going to the next step. Thus, considerable time is spent initially in performing market analysis, surveying potential clients, developing prototypes, and so on, in order to refine detailed specifications. The program specifications then are mostly fixed before the design can start. Carefully developing the specifications allows the design phase to have a complete outline of just what is required and what is not required. With that knowledge, designers can select algorithms and data storage that take maximum advantage of the details of the problem. Later, design is similarly fixed, so coding and testing also can depend on a full understanding of those decisions and framework.

Although this classical development cycle can be effective, each step typically takes considerable time, and the first version of a product becomes available only well after the customer or client first had the idea for the project. Often this time may extend a year or more from the initial conception of a system to the first release of software to the client. Unfortunately, in the intervening time, circumstances sometimes change. The original specifications may no longer address current needs, and the resulting software may not be as helpful as originally anticipated.

To address the long times generally needed during the classical development cycle, a relatively recent approach has been to recognize that needs change continuously, to develop software in small increments, and to release new versions of software frequently. One approach for rapid software development sometimes is called **extreme programming** or **agile programming**. Although this methodology has many interrelated characteristics, an important component involves viewing each version of a software package as another prototype. With each release, the customer(s) can evaluate current functionality, determine what changes are desired, and identify new features to be added. Of course, a first streamlined version of software may take a few months to appear, as it must contain some minimal functionality, but this can be significantly shorter than the time for a full-functionality version. After this first version/prototype, subsequent versions may appear every few weeks, in each case adding functionality and adjusting capabilities based on user feedback.

Whether following the traditional approach to specifications or a more streamlined approach, the selection of capabilities for software normally is user-driven. A developer tries to determine what customers want and then produces software to meet those needs.

If development is user-driven, why are there features I don't use or even want?

Ideally, computer software evolves in perfect response to customer wishes and needs. In practice, however, the "features" of software do not always match the actual needs or wishes of individuals. Try to think of a feature that a computer that you work with has that you don't like or use. For example, a word-processing program may persistently "correct" your work, when you actually mean precisely what you've written. This discrepancy between the ideal and practice can arise in several ways. Here are a few potential causes:

- Needs and interests of people differ. Thus, when software is to serve a large number of people, the features wanted by some may be different from those desired by others. In this case, some people may like automatic correction of a word-processing document, whereas others may not.
- Even if everyone agreed that automatic correction was desirable, the notion of what is correct and what is not may depend upon context. For example, in Chapter 1 of this book, we used CPU as an abbreviation for the central processing unit. In the context of computing and Chapter 1, CPU was a correct spelling. However, in another context, the same sequence of letters might reflect a spelling error.
- In a competitive environment, developers of one software package often want their software to be seen as superior to that of others. Thus, the developers may include capabilities found in other packages, and they may add their own enhancements to obtain what they hope will be a competitive edge. They may worry that their product may seem inferior or outdated if others' can do something their software does not do. Although this perspective may add many capabilities, it does not follow that all users will find these additions helpful or desirable.
- Software developers may adopt a perspective that, over time, customers will appreciate a feature—even if they do not currently think they want or need it. Such a perspective might be viewed positively (the developers are anticipating future user

needs and desires) or negatively (the developers are paternalistically dictating what customers should want).

Why are software packages and operating systems changed or updated so often?

If you own your computer or have a friend who owns one, think about the last update made to the operating system. What new features did you notice? How important were these features to you? Did you feel that the new version outdated your older version too quickly? Or, were you holding your breath for the next edition's release? When considering changes in software, an important initial observation is that different people view rates of change in different ways. For example, a developer who wants to publicize new or enhanced features on a regular basis may seek to release new versions of software every few weeks or months. Publicity that highlights new, innovative capabilities can support an image that the developer's package represents the leading edge of technology, which in turn will encourage sales. Certainly, if your product has the latest features and outperforms the competition, users will be inclined to buy your product over your competitors'. Generally, computer technology changes rapidly, and the competitive advantage goes to the companies that utilize innovative ideas quickly. In the computer world, technology that is one or two years old probably has been surpassed in important ways in capacity, capability, or speed. The degree to which the latest packages actually improve on today's technology, however, is often exaggerated in advertising, as you'll learn in the next chapter. Still, the developers benefit from promoting changes and new features when seeking to draw in new customers, and are likely to advocate for a product that changes frequently.

On the other hand, users of technology likely appreciate stability in a product. If a software package meets their main needs, users may have little motivation to change. Whereas a developer might want to release a new version every three months, users generally would prefer a longer schedule; even a new version every two years may seem too frequent an update! A change in software requires time and expense for purchasing, installing the software, and retraining. Such an investment may be worthwhile if the new version resolves serious deficiencies, but minor changes may have relatively little benefit from the users' perspective. For the user, there may be a considerable advantage if technology does not change for a period of several years.

In short, change occurring "so often" may have a different meaning for developers and users.

But why should software change at all?

Just as with the discussion of automatic correction within word-processing software, why software changes involves both ideal circumstances and practical realities. For example, a software developer may be following the model of extreme programming—making small, incremental planned releases of software, whereby each version responds to customer feedback obtained from the previous version. In this model, clients form a vital part of the development team, and software adapts quickly in accordance to client needs and reactions. Particularly when developers are working for an individual client (who pays the bills), frequent system changes and package updates may be an expected part of the development process. Neither developers nor clients expect the current version of software to be final; rather, software is viewed as an emerging and steadily improving entity.

Software is also understood to be in a continuously fluid state in the more traditional development process for large projects that involve multiple teams, each of which focuses on one component or piece of the overall software package. In this context, each team may spend considerable time developing or revising specifications, refining algorithms, coding changes, and testing; the time frame for each part of the software may be several months or even a few years, as teams conduct market surveys, develop prototypes, and the like. However, when several teams work independently, new versions from various teams may become available at different times. To an end user, the application may seem to change every few months, but in reality each part may change only once a year or so.

On the practical side, software may change rapidly to react to market forces or to correct errors. As already noted, developers generally gain a competitive advantage by having cutting-edge software that addresses user needs better than their competitors. To see how this might affect the updating of software, suppose that, as a developer, you plan to make half a dozen important improvements over the coming year. In a nonrushed environment, you might plan all updates so they will be ready for a significant upgrade in a year's time; a user's software might remain the same for a full year—providing stability—and the new features can be developed, integrated into the new version, and tested in a careful and methodical way. And, with no competitors, such a process might be wonderful.

However, if after a few months a competitor releases a new version of their software with some of your planned new features, then your current software may seem antiquated to potential new buyers, and you might lose sales. As a response, you might decide to release new versions of software every time work on each of the new features is complete. With half a dozen improvements planned for the year, this might create six newly released versions of your software over the year rather than one at the end. The result would be many more updates than you had initially intended, but you would not be at a disadvantage relative to your competitors.

Market forces also can encourage developers to reduce the time they spend on testing programs before they are released. If your competitors introduce software with new features, delays in getting your own software to the marketplace may put you at a disadvantage in the market and reduce your sales. As a response, you may decide to run basic tests on your new versions of software, but choose to omit comprehensive tests that would consume several weeks or months. You note that the tests of the new features show that they seem to be working adequately, and you know the old features worked fine in previous testing. It would take considerable time to test that the new capabilities do not interfere with the code that handled the previous features, so you may opt to omit those tests in the interests of beating the competition.

Unfortunately, we users know that the quick release of software can mean that the software contains errors undetected in testing. If serious errors are discovered after the new version is released to the public, then as a developer you might have to develop and distribute a quick fix—again increasing the frequency of software upgrades.

And, of course, none of the previous technical discussion takes sales of new versions into account. Sometimes, once a user purchases one version of a software package, then the user is entitled to free upgrades—perhaps for a year or more. In other cases, the user may be required to purchase upgrades. In the latter situation, a developer may have particular incentive to generate new versions frequently, because each new release represents another opportunity for additional revenue and profit.

 Why does most software contain errors (bugs)?

As we have just seen, some errors in software may be the result of difficulties that were not discovered in testing. A mistake was made in the development of the program, but that problem was not revealed by comprehensive testing. Software errors, however, are not composed solely of overlooked mistakes.

 What kinds of coding mistakes pass through testing?

The correctness of programs requires a remarkable degree of completeness and accuracy. Unfortunately, unforeseen problems can arise well beyond the testing phase of software development. Here are two illustrative examples:

WWMCCS Example

The World Wide Military Command and Control System is a computer network designed to provide communications for the military both in peace and during emergencies. In November 1978, a power failure disrupted communications between Florida and Washington, D.C. When power was restored, the Washington computer was unable to re-establish communications with the Florida machine. In reviewing the specifications, it seems that mechanisms were available for connecting new machines to the existing systems; additional computers could "log on" to the network. No one, however, had anticipated the need for an existing computer to log on to the system a second time, and this omission prevented the computers from re-establishing communications in a normal manner following the blackout.*

* From *The Limits of Computing*, p. 97. For more information, see William Broad, "Computers and the U.S. Military Don't Mix," *Science*, Volume 207, March 14, 1980, p. 1183, and quoted in *Software Engineering Notes*, Volume 11, Number 5, October 1986, p. 17.

Mariner 1 Example

The July 22, 1962, launch of the Mariner 1 space probe to Venus gives a particularly good illustration of how a seemingly trivial typographical error can have dramatic consequences in computer programs. The program controlling that rocket should have contained the line

```
Do 3 I = 1, 3
```

instructing the computer to repeat a particular sequence of instructions several times. Instead, the comma was replaced by a period:

```
Do 3 I = 1.3
```

which assigned the value 1.3 to a variable called Do3I. As a result, the probe veered off course shortly after launch and had to be destroyed by mission control officers. Here a simple typographical error caused the loss of an $18.5 million probe and launch vehicle. Unfortunately, when programs are tens of thousands of lines long, finding a mistake in a single character is extremely difficult, if not impossible.**

** From page 103 of *The Limits of Computing*. That reference cites *Annals of the History of Computing*, Volume 6, Number 1, 1984, p. 6, reported in *Software Engineering Notes*, Volume 8, Number 5, October 1983, p. 4, with further editorial comment in Volume 11, Number 5, October 1985, p. 17.

If the code for individual parts of the program is correct, what can go wrong?

Even if code is correct for distinct aspects of a program, different parts of a program sometimes interact in unexpected ways. For example, suppose a program is constructed for a school so that only people in a Treasurer's Office or Financial Aid Office are allowed to access a student's account to view financial information, while only those in the Registrar's Office or Student Counseling Office can access accounts to view grade information. In this case, a common processing approach might be to check a user's privileges at the beginning of a session, and then remember that information for future use. For the most part, such a system could work without difficulty. For each user, an initial check is made, and access is allowed or denied appropriately. However, suppose someone from the Treasurer's Office updates a student's financial account, recording that a payment was made. That worker now has some privileges because she or he is already in the system. If the program were not sufficiently careful, the program might also allow access to the student's grade information rather than limiting access to only the financial information. Such access should be denied, and in a direct test the person from the Treasurer's Office would not be able to view the grade data. However, trouble might arise from a sequence of events. Because the person from the Treasurer's Office had made changes to the account and then tried to access the student's grades, she or he was able to circumvent the security that regulates access. Although this example may be relatively easy to anticipate and check, computer programs often have dozens, hundreds, or even thousands of interacting components. By themselves, each may function smoothly, but certain sequences of events may disrupt that normal processing, producing errors.

What if all the interacting components of a program are error-free? What else can cause errors?

A third type of difficulty may arise when several programs are running on a system or when several users access the system at the same time. For example, recall that in Chapter 4, a husband and wife decided to withdraw $50 from different branches of the bank at the same time. In most cases, the processing for withdrawals would yield the correct result, and $100 would be deducted from the couple's bank account. However, Chapter 4 also identified a special sequence of events that resulted in the couple's two requests yielding incorrect balance updates; only $50 was removed from their account. In cases where an unusual sequence of events produces inaccurate results, programs could be tested at length over a long period of time, and the special sequence might never appear during testing. The error, however, could arise unexpectedly at any time during actual use. When that precise sequence of events does happen and problems occur, the root of the problem is particularly difficult to track down and resolve. We will return to this general topic in Chapter 9, when we address questions on networking and distributed systems.

Altogether, although some types of problems can be found easily during testing, others slip through, and some arise only with certain sequences of events. Extensive testing can help check scenarios that might arise when a single user runs the software. However, interactions of multiple users create additional problems that may or may not become apparent through normal testing.

What is a programmer? Do they work in isolation?

The term *programmer* sometimes is used in a narrow context, and sometimes the context is much broader. In the narrow sense, a **programmer** is a person who translates algorithms into computer programs. That is, the programmer takes the design developed by others and writes it in a careful and precise format that can be interpreted by a computer. In this work, the programmer must be fluent in a specific language available to the computer's environment, and the programmer must be able to write detailed instructions in that language.

Although this term sometimes has this restricted meaning, the term **programmer** also is used at times to refer to someone engaged in the general algorithm development and coding endeavor. In this broader context, part of the programmer's task likely involves some coding of detailed instructions in a specific language. However, other parts of the programmer's job may involve the development of specifications, designs, algorithms, and testing. In this sense, "programmer" may mean any problem solver who does coding—at least from time to time.

A popular myth about software developers is that they work by themselves, often in windowless cubicles, interacting only with the computer in front of them. Although such a viewpoint may correctly describe some programmers (especially in the early days of computer development), this perspective largely is not true today. Rather, because software is successful only when it meets customer needs, today's programmers must be able to interact effectively with clients. Programmers must be able to listen effectively as customers talk about an application, and programmers must be able to ask insightful questions to clarify needs.

Further, most serious software developed today is far too large and complex to be developed by a single individual working alone. Rather, computer programs are developed by teams of people. Each team member has an important role, and the success of the entire enterprise requires that programmers coordinate their efforts. One person working in isolation may produce interesting material, but that person's work may not fit into an overall product without significant communication, coordination, and effort.

To highlight this point further, for several years, I organized panels of people from the computer industry to explain to educators what high-technology companies wanted in prospective employees. Altogether, over three dozen industry professionals gave their views on the most important qualities for those entering the computing profession. Remarkably, every industry professional gave the same two traits as being most important:

- Programmers must have excellent communication skills.
- Programmers must be able to work in teams effectively.

The computing industry professionals differed regarding which of these qualities was most important and which was second, but every professional listed these as their top two traits. Specific technical skills never ranked higher than third. This reality may be rather different than the stereotype of the isolated, nonverbal programmer.

How do I know if it is wise to upgrade my software? Sometimes it seems to be helpful; sometimes things get worse.

A common traditional saying states, "If it isn't broken, don't fix it." The idea is that there is no point in tinkering with something that works fine as it is.

For software, that question translates to "When should I consider my software broken?" Normally, software upgrades either fix known errors, provide additional capabilities, enhance performance, or involve some combination of these. As an individual user, therefore, an upgrade seems appropriate if the previous version contains errors that you find troublesome, if you would like to take advantage of new features, or if you find your current work takes too long. Conversely, if the new version contains features you neither want nor need, then you might question the advisability of upgrading your software. Of course, to know what the upgrade contains, you will first have to do some research and read about it. It can be very difficult to know whether or not an upgrade is appropriate; you might want to consult reviews or colleagues before changing your software.

Also, if you do not have a strong need to upgrade immediately, you might want to postpone an upgrade until a time of relatively low activity or stress. For example, if you are writing a thesis for a class, studying for final exams, or working on your financials in preparation for filing income tax returns that are due shortly, then this probably is not a good time to change your computer system. An upgrade at this time might be helpful in some ways, but you might be in serious trouble if something were to go wrong.

In cases where you are working as part of a larger group—in a class at school or with a department at work—the notion of "broken software" needs to be expanded to include problems sharing material with your peers. For example, if the school or company upgrades its software, then your old files might not work properly on the revised system. If the materials are for your use only, then you might get along fine with the previous version and not care about using them at school or work. However, if your materials are to be shared, then an upgrade may be needed. In this case, because of the incompatibility of your files, your old version is essentially "broken," and the upgrade provides a crucial fix.

As a final observation, when connected to a network, some of today's software may automatically check with a central server on the World Wide Web to determine whether new versions are available. In some cases, the software may report periodically about what is available and ask you when or if you want to upgrade. In other cases, software licensing may allow the vendor to download upgrades automatically—without the need for your authorization.

In this latter case, you may not have a choice concerning software upgrades, and you will need to hope that the new versions work properly with the other software on your machine.

Summary

The software development process typically begins with a general idea or vision related to a problem. Subsequent work involves writing specifications, developing algorithms, coding those algorithms, testing programs, and correcting errors (debugging). Various development methodologies organize these phases of development in different ways.

Developers identify users' needs in many ways, including market analysis, surveys, anticipation of future needs, and prototypes. Often, developers hope to address the needs of multiple constituencies, and specific features may or may not be helpful to all individual users.

After programs are written, a maintenance phase involves correcting errors, adding or modifying features, and adapting to new business conditions. Even if software works well, new or different capabilities may be required as users gain experience with the product and as business or legal circumstances change.

Although the term *programmer* sometimes is used narrowly to mean the writer of computer programs from known algorithms, at other times, programmer often refers to an individual engaged in a wide range of activities from writing specifications through algorithm and program development to testing and maintenance. Today, programmers usually interact with colleagues and clients; they rarely work in isolation. Communication skills and the ability to work in groups are just as important as technical skills for programmers.

Much software is complex and requires many components to interact in specific ways. Testing can uncover many errors in software, but tests may not reveal subtle problems that might arise in special circumstances. When software is particularly large and complex, the correction of some errors may introduce new ones, and it is not always clear when specific errors should be corrected. Often, you are well advised not to upgrade software on your computer, because new versions may contain unneeded features while introducing the potential for new errors. You may need to weigh likely benefits and risks of new software before purchasing or installing it.

Terminology from This Chapter

bug	extreme programming	programmer
coding	maintenance	prototype
debugging	programming	specifications
design		testing

Discussion Questions

1. Although much of this chapter deals specifically with the development of software, many of the points made here apply to problem solving more broadly. Identify several problem-solving themes developed here for computing that apply in science and technology more generally.

2. Working in pairs, have one person describe in complete detail an algorithm to make a peanut butter and jelly sandwich, while the other person carries out the algorithm. Materials on hand at the start should include a (clean) knife and spoon, an (unopened) loaf of bread, and (unopened) jars of peanut butter and jelly.

   In performing the algorithm, the second person should not try to be difficult, but should seek not to make assumptions either. For example, the second person should not expand the statement, "insert the knife into the peanut butter jar to get a tablespoon full of peanut butter" by opening the jar. Similarly, in response to the statement, "spread the jelly on a slice of bread," the second person should not assume that the bread should be positioned horizontally or that jelly should be on the top surface of the bread.

   This question may provide insight on the difficulties of giving complete and accurate directions for solving problems. The writing of computer programs consistently requires such complete and accurate directions.

3. What assumptions do you make about the reliability of the software that you use?

4. What would happen if you knew that the software upon which you were currently depending malfunctioned 5% of the time? Would you behave differently?

5. Consider each of the following reports regarding early versions of the F-16 fighter plane. In each case, speculate about what stage of the software development cycle (specifications, algorithm design, coding) might have generated the difficulty, and explain your answer.

   a. The F-16 fighter plane uses a computer to help control the raising and lowering of its landing gear, and the hardware and software have worked effectively in accomplishing this task. In an early version, however, the assumption was made that the plane would always be flying whenever the request was issued to raise the wheels. Unfortunately, violation of this unwritten assumption early in the testing of the plane caused significant damage. (Since that time, a new procedure, weight-on-wheels has been added to check this assumption.)*

   b. Control of the F-16 is under the direction of a computer so that the technologically advanced machine will be able to respond immediately to situations it encounters while flying. In an early version of the plane, however, the navigation system did not distinguish between the northern hemisphere and the southern hemisphere, and the plane would have flipped over when it crossed the equator.**

6. Suppose you rely on a software package to do various computations as part of your work. This question encourages discussion regarding legal liabilities involving software updates.

   a. If you know your current software sometimes generates an error and you learn that this problem is fixed in a new version, do you think you should be legally liable for damages if you do not upgrade your software as soon as possible?

   b. Suppose it seems your current software handles processing correctly. A new version of the software comes out,

---

*From *The Limits of Computing*, pp. 17–18. Other problems with the F-16 are reported in *Software Engineering Notes*, October 1986, p. 6.

**From *The Limits of Computing*, p. 20. This story was reported in a letter by Earl Boebert in *Software Engineering Notes*, Volume 6, Number 2, April 1980, p. 5.

apparently with some nice features, so you upgrade. Some time later, you discover that the new version contains a previously unreported error, making your recent work wrong. Whom do you believe should be legally liable for any damages arising from your incorrect work?

c. Does your answer to part b change if the software downloads upgrades automatically—without asking you first?

d. In part c, does your answer change if your license agreement for your original software explicitly states that the software vendor is not liable for damages? Discuss how such licensing terms might muddy liability rules.

Exercises

1. a. Of the terms listed as "Terminology from This Chapter," identify those that relate to steps involved in using a computer to help solve a problem. That is, indicate the names of the steps that are typically followed in problem solving using a computer.

b. Give a careful definition of each of the terms in part a.

c. Suppose you are asked to cook a dinner for a group of friends. For each of the steps in parts a (or b), indicate if the step also would have a counterpart in your planning and cooking the dinner. In each case, explain your conclusion.

d. Define any other "Terminology from This Chapter" not covered in part b.

e. Do the terms of part d have any counterpart in cooking the dinner for your friends?

2. Consider a problem that you recently encountered. If you have used computers recently, choose a problem for which the computer was part of the solution. Otherwise, choose a problem from a field of science, engineering, or mathematics (e.g., a physics, chemistry, mathematics, or computer science problem).

a. How aware were you of the problem-solving process in approaching the problem?

b. Relate the steps involved in specification, algorithm development, coding (if done as part of your solution), and testing.

c. To what extent were you involved in each step?

3. Consider the activities surrounding the solving of problems in a class setting, in which students complete assignments given by an instructor.

a. In a class, how are specifications for problems determined?

b. How does the statement, "Students attempt to solve the problems given, perhaps using techniques presented by the instructor or in the text," relate to the steps involving specifications, design, coding, testing, and maintenance?

c. Describe the roles of the students, the instructor, and the book in determining algorithms.

d. Where or how might maintenance be considered within a typical class?

4. Computer users often ask, "Why can't programmers get software right the first time?" Various parts of this chapter provide elements of an answer. Synthesize the points given here to formulate a careful answer to this question.

5. In mathematics, a positive integer larger than 1 is said to be *prime* if it is evenly divisible only by 1 and itself. Thus, 7 is prime, because its only factors are 1 and 7. On the other hand, 6 is not prime, because 2 and 3 also are factors.

Now consider an algorithm that declares a number is prime if it is 2 or if it is odd and larger than 1. Otherwise, the number is declared to be not a prime.

a. Identify five cases where the algorithm is correct.

b. Can you identify an infinite number of cases where this algorithm gives the correct answer?

c. Identify five cases where the algorithm produces the wrong conclusion.

d. Can you identify an infinite number of cases for which this algorithm gives an incorrect result?

e. Now suppose this algorithm were made into a computer program. From your answers to parts a through d, how might you choose test data to show that the program did not always produce correct answers?

f. Now suppose a program has produced correct answers for thousands of different test cases. To what extent can you conclude the program is correct? Do your answers to this problem provide any insights about testing and program correctness?

Chapter 6

What should I know about the sizes and speeds of computers?

The following true/false quiz highlights several issues related to the size and speed of computers. Before reading the chapter, make your guess about each of the following four statements:

1. True or false: The size of computer memory chips has doubled about every 18 months since 1965.
2. True or false: The size of disk memory has grown by about 50% every year or so since 1982.
3. True or false: The capacities of central processing units (CPUs) within a computer have a long record of doubling about every 18 months.
4. True or false: With the size and speed of computers increasing so quickly, and with the cost of computers decreasing regularly, computers should be able to solve most any problem within a few years.

We'll get to the answers to these true/false questions before long, but first, let's consider images that are common in the popular press. Various sources seem to reinforce the perception that statement 4 is true—even if some of the details in statements 1, 2, and 3 may not be. But are these perceptions correct?

Advertising and news reports commonly publicize new and improved products. In the field of technology, such publicity often touts faster computers with more storage capacity and expanded software packages with new features. We regularly hear about experimental products that perform impressively well on small collections of data and extremely well in situations where options are limited. Various reports and claims then suggest that before long the products will work in more extensive circumstances. Soon the reports have us believing that new computers can process much more data and solve many new problems based on major advances in technology.

Such reports and claims abound, with new ones appearing regularly, and we need to greet each of them with some skepticism. It may indeed be true that new technology represents a breakthrough, or that some promising research will lead to remarkable new products fairly soon; however, recent history also demonstrates that many reports are wildly optimistic. New work may include a modest step forward (or maybe not), but a small adjustment of previous technology rarely should be considered a breakthrough. We also must be aware that marketers want to present products in ways to maximize sales, and researchers are searching for additional funding. Therefore, we need to weed through overestimates and exaggerations to discover the true degree to which new developments will impact the world of computing. This chapter will explore some common questions that will help you critically evaluate claims and reports before accepting them.

How fast does technology really evolve?

Computer technology has progressed at a remarkably fast and sustained pace for decades. For example, the size of computer memory chips has doubled about every 18 months since 1965 or so. Back in 1965, Gordon Moore, a co-founder of Intel and then chairman of its board of directors, observed that the industry was developing a new generation of computer chips every three years or so, and the number of transistors on chips increased by a factor of four with each generation. A four-fold increase in 3 years corresponds to a doubling in about 18 months. Although originally just an observation, this rate of increase has continued with remarkable consistency in the ensuing years, and this ongoing rate of advancement for chip technology is now called **Moore's Law.**

Because Moore's Law is based only on observation, it is not a scientific law at all. However, the capacity of transistors within chips has followed this pattern for nearly 40 years, and Moore's Law is a widely cited measure of advancement in the computer field.

The size of computer memories is dependent largely on the number of transistors available on chips, so one consequence of Moore's Law is that computer memories have indeed doubled about every 18 months since 1965. Statement 1 in the opening quiz is true.

Similarly, disk technology continues to progress rapidly. In his 1999 book, *Structured Computer Organization*, Fourth Edition, for example, Andrew Tanenbaum notes that "Measuring disk improvement is trickier, . . . but almost any metric will show that capacities have increased by at least 50 percent per year [since 1982]" (p. 26). Thus, statement 2 in the opening quiz also is true.

Likewise, the capacity of a central processing unit (CPU) chip depends very much on the number of transistors. Applying Moore's Law to CPUs, statement 3 in the opening quiz is true. Interestingly, a similar trend generally applies to the speed of CPUs as well as to their capacity, as shown in Table 6.1. From Chapter 1, we know that clock speed is only one factor in determining how much work a CPU can do within a given amount of time. Table 6.1 therefore can give only a partial idea of computing power and speed. Regardless of the details, the increases noted represent huge increases in computing capability in relatively short amounts of time. The statistics come largely from Intel (http://www.intel.com/research/silicon/mooreslaw.htm) and from Andrew Tanenbaum (as cited earlier).

Table 6.1 Chips Produced by Intel

Chip	Year Introduced	Transistors	Speed (in MHz)
4004	1971	2,250	0.108
8008	1972	2,500	0.108
8080	1974	5,000	2
8086	1978	29,000	5–10
80286	1982	134,000	8–12
80386	1985	275,000	16–33
80486	1989	1,180,000	25–100
Pentium	1993	3,100,000	60–233
Pentium II	1997	7,500,000	233–400
Pentium III	1999	24,000,000	750–1,000
Pentium 4	2000	42,000,000	1,200–1,400

With statements 1, 2, and 3 of the opening true/false quiz being true, it may be easy to believe that statement 4 must be true as well. After all, if computing technology continues to improve at a rapid rate, it can solve many more problems—right?

Before you get carried away, consider the following illustrative fable.

A Fable: A King Meets the Combinatorial Explosion

Once upon a time, a king needed a great task performed. In response, a clever young man named Paul agreed to do the work, if the amount of payment was adequate. When the king asked Paul about his requirements for compensation, Paul responded that the king might choose between two options:

Option 1. Payment could consist of one-fifth of the crops produced in the kingdom for each of the following five years, or

Option 2. Payment could be made as follows:

- One kernel of corn would be given for the first square of a chess board.
- Two kernels of corn would be paid for the second square.
- Four kernels (twice the previous amount) would be paid for the third square.
- Eight kernels (again twice the previous) would be paid for the fourth square.
- This counting would continue, with successive doubling for each square, until payment was made for each square of a chess board.

When the king considered these choices, the first option seemed justified for the great service required, but the king liked the sound of the second option better. After all, the king reasoned, how could a few kernels of corn compare to a full fifth of the crops harvested for each of five years, as offered in Option 1? With this, the king contracted with Paul for the work using Option 2 as the form of payment.

A year went by, Paul completed the work, and it was time for payment. The king ordered baskets of grain to be brought, and the process was begun of counting kernels of corn. For the first row of the chess board (eight squares), the payment involved $1 + 2 + 2^2 + 2^3 + 2^4 + 2^5 + 2^6 + 2^7$ or $1 + 2 + 4 + 8 + 16 + 32 + 64 + 128 = 255$ kernels of corn, much less than a bushel. (The USDA and the University of Illinois have developed a measure, called the Corn Yield Calculator, to determine quantities of corn. According to this measure, a bushel averages 72,800 kernels of corn.)

For the next row, the payment was

$$2^8 + 2^9 + 2^{10} + 2^{11} + 2^{12} + 2^{13} + 2^{14} + 2^{15}$$

or 65,280 corn kernels. Since a bushel of corn typically contains about 72,800 kernels, this payment was still less than a bushel of corn.

With the next row, however, the king became uneasy. The payment for this row was

$$2^{16} + 2^{17} + 2^{18} + 2^{19} + 2^{20} + 2^{21} + 2^{22} + 2^{23}$$

or 963,040 corn kernels, which is about 13-¼ bushels. Although this amount was still relatively small, the numbers were getting larger, and only three of the eight rows of the board had been considered.

During the counting for the next row, the king thought ahead to the last (64th) square. Following the pattern he now understood, this last square alone would cost 2^{63} kernels of corn—roughly 8×10^{18} kernels or about 110,000 billion bushels! The obligation could never be met. With a staggering debt, the king abdicated his throne, and the mathematically sophisticated Paul became monarch of the kingdom.*

* To put this number in perspective, the world's annual production for corn in the mid-1980s was roughly 17.7 billion bushels a year. Thus, even in modern times, it would take roughly 6,215 years for the world to grow enough corn for payment for this last square. Paul's entire payment would take about twice this long, or about 12,430 years, using modern technology.

What made Paul's Option 2 payments so huge?

In reviewing the fable, the key to the huge payments involves the doubling of the kernels of corn for each square. If, instead, the number of kernels was increased by two for each square, then the payments would have been much more modest.

- Square 1 requires 1 kernel.
- Square 2 requires 3 kernels.
- Square 3 requires 5 kernels.
- Square 4 requires 7 kernels.
- Square i requires $2i - 1$ kernels.
- Square 64 requires 127 kernels.

Overall, this amounts to

$$1 + 3 + 5 + \ldots + 127 = 4096$$

kernels of corn (about 0.056 bushels). Such an amount is quite small indeed. The difficulty with the payment in the fable, therefore, is not that the payment increased for each square; rather, it is that the huge numbers came about because payments doubled.

How would other payment schemes affect the overall size of payments? For example, what would happen if payments depended upon a power of the number of squares considered? Suppose the number of kernels was determined as the second power (the square) of the number of the board square considered. In this case, the payments would proceed as follows:

- Square 1 requires $1^2 = 1$ kernel.
- Square 2 requires $2^2 = 4$ kernels.
- Square 3 requires $3^2 = 9$ kernels.
- Square 4 requires $4^2 = 16$ kernels.
- Square i requires i^2 kernels.
- Square 64 requires $64^2 = 4096$ kernels.

Here, the payments are increasing considerably faster than when they increase by only two for each square, but the total ($1 + 4 + 9 + 16 + \ldots + 4096 = 89{,}440$ kernels) (about 1.2 bushels) is still manageable.

Although these alternate formulae yield significantly smaller payments of corn for Paul, other formulae can give much bigger results. For example,

1. Start with 1 kernel for square 1.

- For square 2, multiply the amount from square 1 by 2.
- For square 3, multiply the amount from square 2 by 3.
- For square 4, multiply the amount from square 3 by 4.
- For square i, multiply the amount from square $i - 1$ by 1.

Note: Here, one can show that the payment for square i is $i \times (i - 1) \times (i - 2) \times \ldots \times 2 \times 1$. This number is sometimes called i factorial, and is written $i!$.

2. For square 1, pay 1^1 kernels.

- For square 2, pay 2^2 kernels.
- For square 3, pay 3^3 kernels.
- For square i, pay i^i kernels.

Each of these formulae produces much larger payments than were required of the king in Option 2. (If you're feeling ambitious, try determining the size of the payments due in each case for the first row of squares on a chessboard.)

Now that we know that the formula used for successive squares influences the end result, what role does the size of the chessboard play? For example, suppose a board had 20 or 50 or 100 squares. What payments would the king have owed Paul? (You will explore these computations in the end-of-chapter exercises.)

How does this fable relate to computers?

Although it may seem a bit corny to consider such kernels in a textbook about computing, similar issues arise in analyzing various solutions to problems. In this fable, a plan for payment was chosen that could never practically be completed. Similar difficulties arise in many situations where computers are used as part of a proposed solution to a problem. In computing applications, however, it is often hard to appreciate the amount of work or the number of resources required to do a task, because computers seem to work at such tremendous speeds and they can store such vast amounts of data. For example, it can be hard to comprehend the significance of such measures as a million (10^6) instructions per second (MIPS) or storage for 10^9 characters (a gigabyte).

In computing and mathematics, the term **combinatorial explosion** is used to describe the situation when the work (or space) required to solve a problem increases by a factor of two or three or more for each successive value of n. Paul's original payment scheme (doubling the number of corn kernels for each square) is one example of the combinatorial explosion. The two alternatives just given provide further examples.

Although I have already noted that computer technology continues to evolve at a rapid pace, this fable reminds us that some problems require a remarkable level of resources. Even with extremely fast computer speeds and large capacities, some problems require more resources than computers have now or may ever have in our lifetimes. With advancing technology, we may take for granted the amount of computing power at our disposal, and this can cause us to overestimate the ability of computers to solve a problem efficiently. So, when we look at new technology, we need to consider how well it will work when dealing with huge amounts of information given that, in combinatorial explosive situations, the computer may need to process enormous amounts of information. Paul's scheme causes a problem for the king when it mathematically explodes—so, too, do problems cause difficulty for computers when the amount of processing required for a solution becomes entrapped within the combinatorial explosion.

When do solutions scale up?

Suppose a computer is to process some data. Normally the amount of work involved will depend both upon the particular approach that is taken to solve the problem and upon how many data are present. Just as in our fable regarding payment in corn, different types of computer solutions to problems react quite differently as the amount of data to be processed expands. Some algorithms and computer programs may continue to function nicely with larger and larger data sets. Other algorithms may work well for small sets of data, but may become impractical as the amount of data becomes large. New technology regularly boasts of its ability to efficiently process larger and larger amounts of data, but as you will see, as a problem scales up, or involves more data, the algorithms and processes needed may require considerably more processing. Let's take a general look at the effect that increasing data has on computer solutions and illustrate the issues with a few examples.

Linear Search: A museum maintains a guest log. People are asked to sign in when they visit, recording their comments. Out of curiosity, we want to count the number of visitors named "Sally" listed.

A natural approach would be to start at the beginning of the guest log, with a count of 0. Then we could look at each entry in turn, and add one to our counter each time the name Sally appeared. Technically, such a search of successive names, from beginning to end, is called a **linear search**.

How might this processing scale? Suppose n people have signed the book; we would have to look at all n names exactly once—either the name matched "Sally" or not—and we would adjust the count accordingly. If it took us ½ second to look at a name, then the total amount of time for our search would be $\frac{1}{2} \times n$ seconds. We could scan 10 names in 5 seconds or 1000 names in 500 seconds (about 8 minutes).

If we asked a computer to scan the names, and if the computer could process each name in one millionth of a second, then the amount of time required for various size guest logs is given by the first two columns of Table 6.2.

Table 6.2 Times Required for Various Computer Operations

Value of N	Number of Operations Required: n	n^2	n^3	n^4	2^n	3^n	$n!$	n^n
1	0.0000001 seconds	0.000001 seconds	0.000001 seconds	0.000001 seconds	0.000002 seconds	0.000003 seconds	0.000001 seconds	0.000001 seconds
5	0.000005 seconds	0.000025 seconds	0.000125 seconds	0.000625 seconds	0.000032 seconds	0.000243 seconds	0.00012 seconds	0.003125 seconds
10	0.00001 seconds	0.0001 seconds	0.001 seconds	0.01 seconds	0.001024 seconds	0.059049 seconds	3.6288 seconds	2.778 hours
20	0.00002 seconds	0.0004 seconds	0.008 seconds	0.16 seconds	1.04858 seconds	58.1131 seconds	7.8218×10^4 years	3.37×10^{12} years
50	0.00005 seconds	0.0025 seconds	0.0125 seconds	0.625 seconds	26.1979 years	2.3×108 years	9.77×10^{60} years	2.87×10^{70} years
75	0.000075 seconds	0.005625 seconds	0.421875 seconds	31.6406 seconds	1.2146×10^9 years	1.95×10^{22} years	1.95×10^{97} years	1.35×10^{127} years
100	0.000100 seconds	0.01 seconds	1.00 seconds	1.667 minutes	4.0×10^{17} years	1.63×10^{34} years	3.0×10^{146} years	3.2×10^{186} years

Notes:

1. This table assumes that the computer is capable of performing one million steps of the algorithm per second.
2. To gain additional insight on the length of some of these times, it is worthwhile to realize that scientists estimate the age of the universe to be between 10 and 20 billion years (($\text{between } 1 \times 10^{10}$ and 2×10^{10} years).

As this part of the table shows, the time for our counting increases as more people sign the guest log; in the last line of the table, it takes 0.0001 seconds to examine 100 names—assuming the computer can examine 1 million names in a second. Clearly, this amount of work seems manageable, and we could handle a very large number of names in only a modest amount of time. We might reasonably conclude that this solution scales up to large data sets nicely.

Class P

A general question in computing is whether a solution can be performed in a reasonable amount of time. "When is a solution feasible?"

While the answer to this question depends upon such matters as the amount of data present and the speed of the machines available, Table 6.2 can give us some guidance. The linear search is an example of a problem that scales up nicely and takes only a modest amount of time for various-sized data sets. Looking at Table 6.2 more closely, it would seem overly optimistic to consider a solution to be feasible if it required 2^n, 3^n, $n!$, or n^n units of work to process n data items. On the other hand, solutions requiring n, n^2, or n^3 units of work to process n items might reasonably be called feasible.

With this in mind, it is common to define a problem to be in Class P if the problem has some solution, where the number of steps to process n data items is (no more than) some polynomial involving n. For example, the problem of searching a collection of data to find a specified item is in Class P, since some solution (e.g., the linear search) requires only n units of work, and n is a polynomial.

With this definition, one can be reasonably optimistic and decree that a problem has a feasible solution if it is in Class P. Searching data is feasible by this definition, for example. Similarly, many common computing applications, including the storage and retrieval of data, fall within the scope of this notion of feasibility. All of these common examples support the idea that problems within Class P may be considered to have practical solutions. Conversely, considering Table 6.2, it seems reasonably safe to conclude that problems outside Class P could not be solved in any acceptable amount of time. That is, if all solutions to a problem with n data items require more steps than can be described by any polynomial, then the work for all solutions must be exponentials (e.g., 2^n) or factorials (e.g., $n!$) or worse.

Exhaustive Search: As a second example of how problems might scale, consider the following:

The Traveling Salesperson Problem

A salesperson is responsible for visiting a number of cities. In order to complete this task efficiently, the salesperson wants to find a route of minimal cost that goes through each city exactly once before returning to the starting point.

As an example, the map in Figure 6.1 shows several cities in the Midwest, together with the cost involved for flying from one city to another. Thus, the figureshows that it costs $134 to fly from Des Moines to Chicago. On the other hand, there are no direct flights between Des Moines and Grand Rapids.

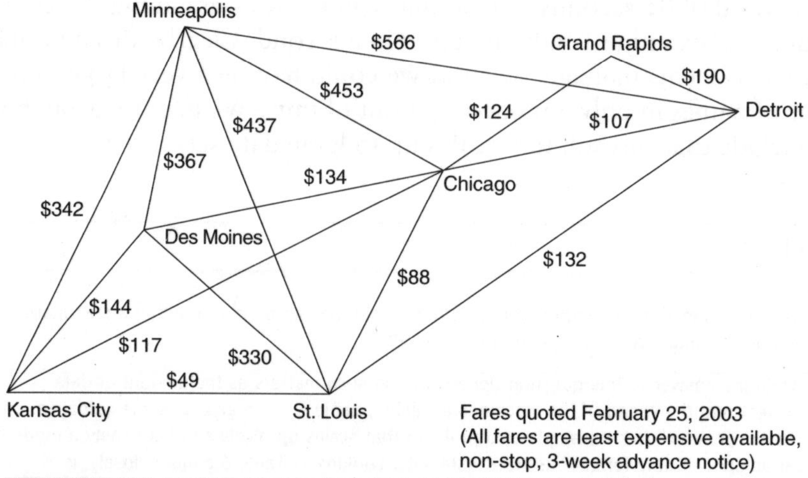

Figure 6.1
Airfares between selected cities in the Midwest.

Now suppose that a salesperson starts from Des Moines. Can she or he go to each of these cities exactly once and then return back to Des Moines? In reviewing the figure, this can be done in several ways. For example, two routes are:

1. Des Moines ⇒ Chicago ⇒ Grand Rapids ⇒ Detroit ⇒ St. Louis ⇒ Kansas City ⇒ Minneapolis ⇒ Des Moines
2. Des Moines ⇒ Minneapolis ⇒ Detroit ⇒ Grand Rapids ⇒ Chicago ⇒ St. Louis ⇒ Kansas City ⇒ Des Moines

Now that we know that a specific route is possible, which route incurs the least cost?

One way to find the solution to this problem is to search through all possible routes, compute the price of each, and then search the list of routes and prices to find the smallest price. Such an enumeration of all possibilities is called an **exhaustive listing**, and a search of all options is called an **exhaustive search**.

In this approach, each possible route (or permutation of cities) might be considered. In some cases, there may not be direct flights between some cities, so some routes might not be possible (one cannot go directly from Minneapolis to Grand Rapids, for example, so any potential route requiring this trip must be ruled out). If airlines had flights from each city to each other city, however, then this approach would require computing the cost for every possible route.

How many routes are there if the salesperson must go through n cities? The salesperson could start at home (she or he must start somewhere, so home is as good a place as any). After that, the salesperson might go to any of the other $n - 1$ cities (number of total cities minus the number of cities already visited). After that trip, the salesperson could go to any of the $n - 2$ remaining cities, and so forth. With this analysis, the total number of possible routes is

$$(n - 1) \times (n - 2) \times (n - 3) \times \ldots 3 \times 2 \times 1$$

In mathematics, this number is called $n - 1$ factorial, and written $(n - 1)!$.

Now suppose a computer could check 1 million routes in a second and evaluate 1) their cost and 2) the time they require. (This speed is probably unrealistically fast, but let's be optimistic.) To find the amount of time required for a computer to process the routes with various numbers of cities, look at the next to last column in Table 6.2.

Computing the best (most time efficient and least expensive) route when only a few cities are involved is fast. For example, if the salesperson had to visit 11 cities, then n would be 11, and our analysis indicates there would be $(11 - 1)!$ or 10! factorial routes. Looking at Table 6.2 with 10 routes to check, the computer's review of all routes would take about 3.6 seconds—a rather short time for checking. However, increasing the number of cities to 21 would mean 20! routes to check, and Table 6.2 indicates this would take 78,218 years to examine. We just about doubled the number of cities, but the processing time went from 3.6 seconds to 78 millennia.

Clearly, creating an exhaustive list would yield a solution, but the time involved could be substantial. It seems reasonably safe to conclude that exhaustive searches do not scale up very well.

Perhaps surprisingly, there are no known solutions to the Traveling Salesperson Problem that are fundamentally more efficient. Some improvements can be made to the basic approach of trying all possible routes through the various cities, but no solutions are known that require only one computer with reasonable or even feasible times. (Mathematical aside: If one thinks of the amount of time as a function that depends on the amount of data, then no algorithms are known for which the time is bounded by a polynomial! Such time functions grow much too fast to allow realistic computation of results for anything but the smallest data sets.)

Class NP

Class P identifies problems that have feasible solutions when one computer is available. With as many computers available as desired, could we find feasible solutions to other problems as well?

As an example, consider the exhaustive listing and search solution to the Traveling Salesperson Problem. In this approach, all possible paths are considered, and the shortest route selected. If this approach were tried with many different computers—one for each route, each computer could compute the cost for a different path. Next, each computer could compare the cost for its route with costs of routes computed by neighboring computers. When a computer discovers its route is more costly that another, it could drop out of the conversation, leaving processing to computers with relatively low-cost routes. This approach requires coordination and communication, and details are a bit tricky. However, it turns out that identification of the shortest route can be done in somewhat under n^2 units of time.

In this approach, the overall amount of work exceeds what is needed with only one machine, due to the overhead of communication among machines. Communication overhead is unnecessary when only one computer is working. However, when the overall work is spread over many computers, the resulting processing may experience a speed up in time.

This analysis motivates the definition that a problem is in Class NP if it has some solution that requires no more than a polynomial number of steps, given enough computers. For example, the Traveling Salesperson Problem is in Class NP. In addition, Class NP contains all problems in Class P; if the problem can be done efficiently with one processor, it certainly can be done efficiently with many processors. Just let one computer do all the work, and let any other computers remain idle.

Chess Playing: The game of chess offers another example of how scaling up can change a computer's rate of success. A variety of approaches are used to instruct a computer how to play chess, but the most common and successful methods all use the same basic approach:

- At each point in the game, the computer generates all possible moves, determines which approach is best, and selects the best-looking move.
- To determine which of these moves is best, the computer looks at all responses that could be made to each move, assuming the opponent makes the best possible response.

As a practical matter, it can be difficult to determine which moves are best without looking at all possible future moves for both sides. In the jargon of game-playing programs, a **ply** is the term used to describe a move made by either player. Thus, two plies occur if you move and then your opponent makes a move. With three plies, you move, then your opponent moves, and then you move again. With this terminology, the basic idea of most chess programs is to look ahead in the game through as many plies as possible to determine the possible consequences of each move. Once these consequences are known, the best current move can be selected.

Unfortunately, however, the game of chess is complex, and it has been estimated that, on the average for any given ply, a player will have to choose among about 20 possible moves. This number gives rise to the following rough analysis:

- In one ply, you will have about 20 possible moves.
- For a second ply, an opponent will have about 20 possible responses for each move you might make. Thus, there are about 20 × 20 or 400 possibilities at the end of two plies.
- For each of these 400 possibilities, you will have a choice of roughly 20 responses. This gives 20 × 20 × 20 or 20^3 = 8,000 possibilities at the end of three plies.
- At the end of *i* plies, there are roughly 20^i possible move sequences.

Thus, the number of possible move sequences is an exponential function of the number of plies considered. This number increases very quickly, so chess-playing programs can never hope to consider all possible consequences of every particular move; if a typical game involves about 50 moves, this analysis suggests that a computer would have to consider roughly 20^{50} different move sequences before it could choose the best response to the first move by an opponent. The combinatorial explosion is at work.

Consider for a moment that scientists estimate that the age of the universe is between 10 and 20 billion years. Assuming we began a chess game 20 billion years ago, a computer evaluating 20^{50} possible move sequences would have had to analyze about 1.3×10^{47} chess moves per second to respond by now to an initial move made at the birth of the universe. In contrast, the fastest modern computers can perform only about 10^7 to 10^8 instructions per second, and there is no prospect that increases in computer speed will have much real impact on this problem. Even major revolutions in computer processing speed would likely have little effect on problems dealing with huge numbers like this one.

Because the numbers related to chess playing and analysis are so large, modern chess playing programs must restrict what moves are considered in order to be somewhat effective. A particularly common approach is to look ahead only a specified number of plies. For example, several of the best programs currently available may look ahead eight or nine plies. Other programs may consider only some possible moves instead of all of them. Libraries of common board positions may also allow the machine to restrict the number of moves it must consider. Regardless of how the range of chess moves is restricted, computer chess programs are a particularly good example of the limitations that arise due to the combinatorial explosion. Each additional ply increases the number of moves to be considered by a factor of about 20. The consequences are parallel to what the king encountered in the fable. Any completely successful approach to playing chess will not be able to look at all possible moves, but rather will have to proceed differently (e.g., the king may abdicate). In Chapter 16, we will talk more about chess and the way it is played by both people and computers.

Overall, we might use Table 6.2 as a guide to determine what solutions scale up in a reasonable way. According to the table, if the amount of work or number of steps involved in processing a data set with n items is a polynomial (e.g., n or n^2 or n^3 or n^4), then the time involved for relatively large amounts of data may be manageable, and the solutions may scale adequately. However, if the amount of processing requires a factorial function (as in the Traveling Salesperson Problem) or an exponential (e.g., 20^n, as in chess playing, or even 2^n), then the solution probably does not scale up well.

We should, therefore, evaluate research boasting of dramatic advances in computer technology critically, keeping in mind the effects of the combinatorial explosion. Note, as a practical matter, that prototype systems often work on very small data sets. Thus, when we hear claims about how finished applications will work, it is important that we examine their approach very carefully. As we have seen, some types of solutions scale nicely, whereas others do not. One cannot always tell from advertising which is which, so if you are asked to invest in a company, be sure to check first!

How does complexity affect problem solving?

We have just observed that the time required to complete a task often depends on how much data are involved. How processing time relates to the size of a data set is called **computational complexity**; Table 6.2 shows that the time demands for some types of algorithms are much more difficult than for other types.

The next example illustrates that size also can affect the logic used to solve a problem. This effect is called **logical complexity**. Computers process data by running programs, and humans write those programs. As problems and programs gain complexity, the human authors must handle increasing logical complexity, and this can have an important impact on the effectiveness of new technology.

Preparing a Dinner

Consider the process of preparing a dinner. If the meal is only for yourself, then you might decide on a relatively simple menu: salad, stir-fry, lemonade, and cookies for dessert. Preparation of the salad might involve cutting up some lettuce, tomatoes, cucumber, and carrots, and then adding a small amount of dressing. Preparation could be done in one bowl—perhaps using a cutting board and knife in the process. Similarly, preparation of the stir-fry might involve cutting vegetables (and perhaps meat or another protein source) and adding spices during cooking. Because the stir-fry would take a little time to cook, you might start it first, because you would have time to cut the salad ingredients while cooking took place. Lemons might be squeezed into a glass, sugar and water added, and stirring done quickly with a spoon. Although this preparation of dinner involves several steps, each is fairly straightforward. Further, each step takes a short amount of time, so coordination of the various steps is relatively easy. In the case of the salad, preparation could use the bowl for serving, making cleanup relatively short as well.

Next, consider preparing the same menu for yourself and three guests. Preparation of the stir-fry might be about the same, although you would have to initially chop up about four times the amount of ingredients than before. Cooking might take somewhat longer, requiring you to stir frequently to maintain even cooking. Although this might require your full attention, you could still use a single frying pan or wok. If you wanted to be fancy, you might place the finished stir-fry into a serving bowl, and the guests could serve themselves from the bowl at the dinner table. With the need to supervise the cooking of the stir-fry, you probably would have to prepare the salad beforehand. As with the stir-fry, a serving bowl might be needed (although you might just prepare four separate salads). Turning to the lemonade, uniformity would require that you prepare the beverage in a pitcher. Again, this would need to be done beforehand.

Although I could add detail, even this outline of the dinner preparation for four people indicates that the process for four people is somewhat more complex than the preparation for one person. Serving bowls and pitchers are needed. Coordination is more difficult, because cooking requires mixing and the cooking time for four people is not adequate for the preparation of the salad or lemonade. On the other hand, the basic tasks are similar—and you still could take the cookies directly from the package.

As a third scenario, consider preparing the same menu for 200 guests. With this number, nothing may seem straightforward. First, you probably no longer have room to seat the guests in your apartment or home, so you would have to rent a hall. Then you would need to arrange for tables, chairs, and so on. (These might be arranged as part of the hall rental, but you still would have to work with the folks at the hall to set up tables, and the like.) Fixing just the salads might take one person several hours, and you might hire a person to do only this task. After the salad was prepared (perhaps using multiple serving bowls), space constraints might require that salads be served to guests as the food was put on the salad plates. Preparation of the stir-fry would be relatively complex, because cooking would require multiple burners—perhaps multiple stoves. To get all of this done in a timely way, you might employ several chefs. Similar troubles arise with the preparation of lemonade and the distribution of cookies. Serving of the food might involve several waiters or waitresses. Altogether, the preparation of this menu requires considerable negotiation for a hall; coordination of multiple people, numerous bowls, and serving stations; and orchestration of the serving and cleanup of dishes.

As we review the requirements for serving dinner to 1, 4, and 200 guests, we note that each stage added noticeable complexity. The simple process used for one hadto be adjusted somewhat for four, and coordination of activities required more attention. Similarly, the approach that worked for 4 did not extend well to 200. More people were involved; the workers had the potential to get in each others' way, making coordination particularly important; and new approaches were required for preparation and serving. In short, the logical complexity of dinner preparation may increase considerably with the size of the problem (i.e., the number of dinner guests).

Although this example focused on food preparation, complexity issues arise in the processing of data as well. As problems become more complex, simple solutions may no longer apply; special algorithms and programs may be needed to accomplish various required tasks, and coordination of activities takes on added significance. Also, as with food preparation, when problems and their solutions become more complex, there are more opportunities for mistakes, oversights, and other problems to arise.

What are some difficulties logical complexity causes in computers?

The following list suggests some of the difficulties of logical complexity for computing on an individual computer:

- If only one person will be using the computer, then there may be no need for a password or security system; the operating system need not be cluttered with mechanisms to verify that a particular user has authority to access specific files.

- If the computer will be doing only one task at a time—that is, if the computer supports single tasking, but not multitasking—then the operating system need not worry about how to allocate memory among users or how to decide how CPU time should be shared.

- If a computer allows only one window to be open at a time, then the operating system does not have to keep track of which window is active at any moment; any typing must be directed to the single window present.

Historically, early computers took these simple approaches and could function with only one user, one task, and one window at a time. This allowed early operating systems to be small, simple, and relatively easy to understand. Also, programmers could (mostly) understand an entire operating system and check it for errors. As capabilities have been added, operating systems have expanded with new algorithms and programs—just as our dinner-preparation crew expanded as the number of guests increased. Larger and more complex operating systems created new demands for coordination and cooperation—and new opportunities for mistakes, oversights, and other problems. Also, the coordination of multiple users, multitasking, and multiple windows places considerable demands on the CPU, and these chips now require more power just to do the same tasks done earlier in a simpler context. The new capabilities make the computers easier to use, but they also have added complexity to the problems.

Altogether, computers may be more helpful in solving problems if they can process more data and provide expanded capabilities. However, the greater computational complexity and logical complexity come with costs:

- Processing may require additional coordination and administrative oversight.

- New or expanded capabilities may place additional demands on computer hardware, requiring faster CPUs and larger memories.

- Greater complexity provides new opportunities for errors.

When does the cost of "more" outweigh the benefits?

Because "more" can refer to many qualities, we need to clarify just what we mean by the question. The following list suggests some meanings for "more" in the context of computers and computing:

- More features: Software can have more and more capabilities.
- Greater speed: Hardware components can move or process data more quickly.
- More graphics: Applications could make greater use of graphics, and users could utilize more images in their work.
- Greater accuracy: Answers, particularly numerical results, could be computed with more significant digits.

We now consider each of these areas in some detail. Although capabilities to support more users might also be on this list, I encourage you to think about such possibilities in the discussion questions.

More Features: In order to be helpful, software must provide the capabilities needed to perform the task. However, beyond a point, additional features may not be needed for the job at hand—and more features almost always mean larger programs and more complexity.

For example, some modern word-processing packages automatically underline text that the software identifies as a location on the World Wide Web. For example, if a user types www.cs.grinnell.edu/~walker/, some word-processing packages underline the address—independent of context. Of course, sometimes a user may want such underlining; however, other times such underlining is a nuisance at best. If software does not have this feature, then the user could still accomplish the same task by using any "underline" option that the word processor offers. But if the software does have this capability (even if the capability has been turned off), then the program must have special code that analyzes each word or phrase that the user types, that code must interact with various other program elements that affect font and style, and program elements must coordinate these various elements. Such features therefore contribute to program complexity; different people will debate whether all such features are actually helpful.

Lest you think that a concern regarding complexity is only theoretical in nature, let's consider a few illustrations related to the space shuttle. We have observed that computational and logical complexity can require considerable coordination and oversight, raise extensive hardware demands, and provide many opportunities for error. The following notes apply these observations to actual circumstances:

- In 1989, the on-board software for the space shuttle achieved what was called an "exemplary" error rate of only 0.1 errors per thousand lines. To achieve this "exemplary" level of correctness, NASA spent about $500 million to develop the overall software—about $1000 per line. Even with the 0.1 error rate, however, a program of 500,000 lines still contains about 50 errors. In 1981, one of these errors caused the first shuttle orbital flight to be delayed. Part of the reason for the cost of the shuttle software was that between 1981 and 1985, reports indicated that some 4000 changes were made to the software. This would translate to roughly 1000 per year, or perhaps 3 per day, including holidays and weekends. Each change cost NASA money.

  (From p. 112 of *The Limits of Computing*. From Edward J. Joyce, "Is Error-Free Software Achievable?" *Datamation*, February 15, 1989, pp. 53, 56.)

- "The Space Shuttle Ground Processing System, with over 500,000 lines of code, is one of the largest real-time systems ever developed. The stable release version underwent 2177 hours of simulation testing and . . . . 280 hours of actual use during the third shuttle mission." Errors detected during both testing and the actual mission were classified as "critical," "major," or "minor," and the occurrences of these errors is shown here:

	Critical	Major	Minor
Testing	3	76	128
Mission	1	3	20

  Thus, although many errors were caught during extensive testing and simulation, a fair number of problems were not encountered until the mission itself.

  (From p. 108 of *The Limits of Computing*. From Mira, "Software Reliability Analysis," *IBM System Journal*, Volume 22, Number 3, 1983. Quoted in *Software Engineering Notes*, Volume 11, Volume 5, October 1989, p. 16.)

- The problem of complexity in large programs is reinforced in an article by John Garman, former deputy chief of NASA's Spacecraft Software Division, reporting on the delayed first launch of the shuttle orbiter:

> The development of avionics software for the Space Shuttle is one of the largest, if not the largest, flight software implementation efforts ever undertaken in the nation. It has been very expensive, and yet it has saved money, saved schedule, and increased design margins time and time again during the evolution of the Orbiter and its ground test, flight tests, and finally the STS-1 mission. Since computers are programmed by humans, and since "the bug" [that delayed the first launch] was in a program, it must surely follow that the fault lies with some human programmer or designer somewhere—maybe! But I think that's a naive and shortsighted view, certainly held by very few within the project. It is complexity of design and process that got us (and Murphy's Law!). Complexity in the sense that we, the "software industry"[,] are still naive and forge into large systems such as this with too little computer, budget, schedule, and definition of the software role. We do it because systems won't work, can't work, without computers and software.
>
> (From *The Limits of Computing,* p. 113. This quotes John Garman in Edward J. Joyce, "Is Error-Free Software Achievable?" *Datamation,* February 15, 1989, p. 9.)

Of course, space shuttle software represents an extreme of very high complexity. Issues related to size and complexity arise in smaller projects as well. Here are some common examples:

- The addition of features to software requires both code for the individual features and code to coordinate those features with previous features. Thus, new features can compound complexity.
- Changes or adjustments to existing capabilities similarly affect both the algorithm for that material and coordination/administration. Because of interdependencies of features, work on one capability can affect others.

- In particular, the correction of an error in one part of a program sometimes creates a new error in another part of a large program. Thus, it is sometimes better not to correct a known error in a program, because the fix of that problem might have a reasonable chance of creating a new and unanticipated error elsewhere—and we have no way of knowing ahead of time if that new error will be critical, major, or minor.

From another perspective, major new releases of operating systems or application software often contain a large number of new features and capabilities. Also, factors such as those described earlier often result in a relatively high number of errors in these major new releases. The features may be nice, but at the cost of reliability (errors). For example, the software may malfunction or crash often.

After encountering such problems for some time, experienced users often wait to obtain major new releases for awhile—until a few rounds of corrections and adjustments come out. The later, corrected versions still may have some errors, but such problems typically are less significant than those found in the major new releases. When a new version of a program debuts, therefore, take a critical look at whether its new features are worth your investment in both time and money. What advertisers claim as a significant advance may or may not actually have the effect you want, and new software may contain some errors you would prefer to avoid.

Greater Speed: As with our discussion of features, we need to consider context while evaluating the significance of speed. Of course, computers can be helpful only if they process data in a timely manner. As individuals, we are annoyed if we must wait awhile at a computer screen while processing occurs—particularly if we cannot do anything else during that period. On the other hand, we are unlikely to notice if processing takes milliseconds rather than microseconds, or if one operation takes some time while we are doing something else. For example, we may not think about how long printing takes to finish if we have gone on to other tasks, so lowering printing time from 15 seconds to 10 seconds may not matter. Certainly, we would like to get answers quickly, but often our thinking and typing times are really the slow steps. In such cases, faster processing may arise more from our having a good breakfast than from getting faster computing equipment!

Another consideration regarding speed follows from the discussion in Chapter 1. In that discussion, we noted that computers process data though the interaction of many components. In such a context, increasing the speed of one component may not make much difference unless other components can take advantage of that faster speed.

We need, therefore, to consider what elements are limiting our work when we are trying to achieve significant speed-up. A faster bus or CPU may not help, for example, if the system is waiting for us or if the machine spends most of its time accessing data on CDs or disks. On the other hand, if much of our processing involves waiting for a disk for the storage and retrieval of data, then getting a faster disk might speed up our entire processing in a significant way.

More Graphics: One of the main areas for computing expansion in recent years has involved usage and processing of images (e.g., pictures). These enhancements require both faster processors and considerably more storage space. As we discussed in Chapter 2, graphical images require the computer to determine colors and intensities for each pixel. Because pixel-by-pixel storage requires much space, pictures may be stored in a condensed format, and the computer then determines the expanded pixel information. Image processing, therefore, requires either the storage and retrieval of extensive graphical information or computation (or both).

In many cases, the use of graphics enhances the usefulness of computers, and expanded use of images is most welcome. Recently, however, the increase in general use of digital images has demonstrated that images' demands on both storage and processing capability have their costs as well. Considering storage first, a high-resolution picture may require between 0.1 and 0.5 million bytes (megabytes) of storage; some pictures may require even more. Even low-resolution graphics may consume 0.05 megabytes.

In the mid- and late-1990s, before the extensive use of graphics, personal computers often had just 30 or 40 megabytes of storage overall. As computer users began to save pictures, and as the World Wide Web provided an easy way to obtain pictures, older computers ran out of space—often quickly. Computers that had seemed remarkably powerful and large no longer were adequate, and expanded machines were needed. Further, processing of graphical images could require extensive computation, taxing the CPUs that may have seemed speedy just a few years before. Although this may have pleased computer manufacturers, users (individuals, schools, and businesses) were faced with significant upgrade costs.

Today, modern machines have much greater storage capacity than before, and graphical applications are common. Picture sizes, however, still can be an issue in at least two ways. First, when pictures are sent from one machine to another (e.g., over the Internet), a great deal of data must be transferred. If machines are connected to high-speed Internet services, then such transmission may proceed quickly. However, if users have a slow connection—perhaps over a regular telephone line—then a single large picture may take minutes to transmit. (More details of the World Wide Web and Internet communications are discussed in Chapter 8 and later chapters.) With such time delays, slow transmission speeds may limit access to graphical content, because people are unable or unwilling to devote extensive amounts of time waiting for pictures to arrive.

A second impact of picture size may arise when users have e-mail accounts with limited space. Because pictures are large, e-mail with a few pictures may consume much of a user's account, and an e-mail service may block receipt of further e-mail until space has been freed.

As with other features, graphical capabilities can add considerably to the usefulness of computer applications, but lavish use of graphics can slow processing down and place strains on storage. When you are looking to buy a new computer, consider how you will use the computer and what demands you will place on the memory in terms of graphics. If you take hundreds of pictures on your digital camera, the expense of purchasing more memory may be more worth your while than if you tend to use your computer only for word processing. Weighing the costs against the benefits will help you make an informed purchasing decision. Being knowledgeable about your memory needs will also help you analyze new research that's purported to make serious advancements in memory capacity.

Greater Accuracy: As you have seen in Chapter 2, computers typically store integers only up to a certain size and real numbers only to a specified number of significant digits. Alternative storage formats could allow greater size or accuracy, but processing of those numbers takes a significantly longer amount of time. As computers expand in power, computations could be expanded to increase accuracy. However, before jumping at the chance to be more accurate, we need to consider what accuracy we expect or need.

For example, if you are working on a space mission involving a trip from the earth to Mars, then you may need to know the desired direction of travel to a considerable degree of accuracy. If the direction were off by even one degree, that one degree over thousands of miles could result in flying much too far from Mars to obtain orbit, or too close, which would end in crashing. Similarly, if you are timing runners during a track meet, then an error of 0.1 seconds could make a difference in who wins a race.

On the other hand, if you are determining how much paint you need to paint your house, and if house paint comes only in gallon containers, then computations need be accurate only to the whole gallon. Further, with variations of paint thickness, limitations on how accurately you can measure the height of your house, and fluctuations in your painting technique, your initial data for computations will be quite rough, and you cannot expect answers to many decimal places of accuracy if the beginning measurements are not very accurate.

Accuracy is vital in some contexts, but not in others. Further, accuracy in answers is limited by accuracy in initial measurements. We may not want computers to add considerable error to computations, but we should not take time and resources for unneeded accuracy, and we should not expect processing power to make up for errors in initial data.

As with considerations of features, speed, and graphics, we need our results to be sufficiently accurate to meet our needs; additional accuracy, however, may provide little benefit. Further, to obtain greater accuracy, a computer may require additional storage space or processing time. Thus, when you read about new computer systems with new capabilities, your analysis might first consider the extent to which reported advances will actually help in solving the problems you care about. You also should consider associated costs for equipment or processing, and whether new systems might create new frustrations as new errors are encountered. New or expanded systems can be most helpful in some situations, but of marginal value in others. Your decisions on new systems should depend on careful analysis, not just on appealing stories or advertising.

Summary

The amount of processing required to help solve a problem often depends on the amount of data involved. Computational complexity describes this relationship. Although some solutions scale up nicely, the work required for others quickly becomes very large as the size of the data set increases. For this reason, some solutions become impractical for data sets of even moderate size.

The size of programs and various interrelationships among parts of programs combine to yield logical complexity. When logical complexity is modest, programs can be built correctly and efficiently; however, as complexity increases, programs become large, and coordination plays a greater part.

Complexity can contribute to the introduction of errors into large software packages. Such errors may be extremely difficult to locate and correct. Further, in large, complex programs, the correction of some errors can lead to the introduction of others.

The introduction of new capabilities can be of great help in some applications but is not needed in others. Also, the expansion of features can add computational and logical complexity to programs, increasing the likelihood that programs contain errors. In addition, processing requirements and storage demands for new features may require the purchase of new computer equipment or the extensive upgrading of current machines. This can make new features expensive—particularly for applications in which these new features have only marginal usefulness.

Terminology from This Chapter

Class NP
Class P
combinatorial explosion
computational complexity
exhaustive listing
exhaustive search
linear search
logical complexity
Moore's Law
ply

Discussion Questions

1. This chapter's discussion of the combinatorial explosion describes five different formulae that might have been used by

the king in paying Paul. In these formulae, the number of kernels of corn paid for with one square of a chessboard were 2^i, $2i - 1$, i^2, $i!$ (i factorial), and i^i. Compute each of these values for a variety of values of i, and then plot the results with i on one axis and the number of kernels on the other axis. (Be sure all results are plotted on the same axes.) Describe in words how the graphs for the various formulae compare.

2. Consider how the themes of this chapter might apply to the number of users that a computer system can support. Are there advantages as a computer system expands from supporting one user to a few to many? Are there disadvantages or risks? Explain.

3. This question asks you to consider what accuracy is needed in results for several applications.

a. Consider the software that controls traffic lights at a four-way intersection. In each direction, lights shift from red to green to amber and back to red. After a light turns red in one direction, there is a small delay before the light(s) in another direction turn green—allowing traffic to clear the intersection one way before cross-traffic starts. How tightly should the timing of lights be controlled? That is, would it be satisfactory for times for lights to be controlled within 10 seconds? Within 1 second? Within 0.1 seconds? Explain.

b. Suppose I want to compute the amount of fabric needed to cover a sofa. How accurate might I be able to be in my measurements of the sofa? What implications does this have for my conclusions about fabric needs? (Possible research question: When buying fabric, how much accuracy is required?)

4. a. Identify an application in which final results are needed to two decimal places of accuracy.

b. Identify an application in which final results are needed to the nearest integer.

(Note: You may *not* use applications described either by the material in this chapter or by other discussion questions or exercises.)

5. A spreadsheet is a program that automates various computations in tables. Thus, spreadsheets are widely used in accounting, budgeting, and planning applications. A recent version of a popular spreadsheet program introduced the following feature: With a certain obscure sequence of keystrokes, a lunar landing game appeared. The user could explore a moonscape using various keys. Eventually, a careful explorer could uncover a tablet that contained the names of the members of the development team for the spreadsheet.

   a. Do you think the inclusion of this game was appropriate?

   b. What implications might the inclusion of this game have on the correctness of the spreadsheet?

   c. Could the inclusion of this game have any impact on users who did not know about this feature?

   d. If you were the manager of the programming team that included this game, what (if any) actions would you take in interacting with the individual programmers?

In each case, explain your answers.

Exercises

1. One theme for this chapter is the "combinatorial explosion."

   a. Give a definition for this term.

   b. For each of the other words or phrases in the "Terminology from this Chapter," provide a careful definition.

   c. For each term in part b, indicate how that term relates to the concept of the combinatorial explosion.

2. The first part of this chapter presents several different formulae for payments based upon the size of a chessboard. Determine how many kernels of corn would be required for boards with 20 or 50 or 100 squares for each of the payment algorithms given.

3. In a modern computer, the CPU might execute a million or so instructions per second. On the average, such a computer would finish one instruction every one millionth of a second, or a microsecond.

In the fable that opened this chapter, suppose Paul would serve a microsecond as ruler of the kingdom rather than take a kernel of corn. Thus, Paul's payment would be as follows:

- Paul would rule one microsecond for the first square of a chess board.
- Paul would rule two microseconds for the second square.
- Paul would rule four microseconds for the third square.
- Paul would rule eight microseconds for the fourth square.
- This pattern would continue, with successive doubling for each square, until payment was made for each square of a chess board.

Estimate how long Paul's reign would last using this payment system.

4. Figure 6.1 gives the costs charged for flying between several midwestern cities.

   a. Find the least expensive routing that allows someone to go to all of these cities exactly once before returning home.

   b. Suppose some additional air links were added to Figure 6.1 so that direct flights were possible between any two cities listed. (Make up some fares that seem reasonable for these new flights.) Now find the least-expensive routing covering each city once, and prove that your answer is the cheapest solution.

   c. Compare your approaches to finding the solution in parts a and b. Did you use some special properties of the graph in part a that you could not use in part b?

   d. Discuss how your solution to part b might be simplified if you could organize a team of people to help find the least expensive route.

Chapter 7

What can computers do for me?

Computers can help solve a very wide range of problems. In recent history, we have come to rely heavily on computers in everyday life, from e-mail to ATMs to weather forecasts to car manufacturing. On the other hand, computers have been unable to give significant assistance in certain other areas, such as reliably and consistently predicting the stock market. What makes a computer helpful in some areas and not in others? To fully understand when and how computers can help us, we need to consider what types of activities computers are good at and then look at our own needs. When our needs match computers' strengths, then computers often can help us considerably in our work. When we want to accomplish tasks that are beyond the abilities of computers, however, they may not be of much help. In this chapter, we'll look at what types of activities computers can help us with and what types of tasks are outside today's computers' capacities.

Additionally, in this chapter we'll explore whether some computers might be more helpful than others for what you want to do. The answer to this question involves a theoretical notion of "universality" of computing power. As we will discuss, at a conceptual level, it is likely that if one computer could help us, then virtually any computer also could be of assistance. In practice, however, the performance of one machine may be dramatically better than that of another; we'll look at how speed and capacity play an important role in determining how well a computer will perform a task.

What types of problems are computers good at?

At a very basic hardware level, computers perform three primary types of operations on data: the storage and retrieval of data, the comparison of different data items, and the arithmetic or logical manipulation of data. All of this work is done following specified instructions. Computers can be particularly effective when applications require a significant use of one or more of these operations. Further, computers are particularly useful to us when the work we have done corresponds well with their skills. Let's focus on what work you might have that could take advantage of a computer.

When would a computer's storage and retrieval skills help me?

Many uses of the computer involve variations on the theme of storing and retrieving data. Here we'll take a look at four common types of storage and retrieval activities that you may encounter: word processing, databases, multimedia filing, and networking and communication.

Word Processing

Word processing and desktop publishing provide good illustrations of how our needs mesh nicely with the characteristics available in computers. Word processing involves at least two types of work. Think of the last time you needed to write a paper for your English class: When you opened your word-processing application, what did you need it to accomplish? First, any English paper involves text—the words that form the raw data for the composition. This text must be stored and retrieved, and much of the value of using a computer for word processing arises from this data storage. When drafts of your paper are stored, they can be opened for editing, and you thereby can take advantage of information already present (you don't have to retype the whole document, thank goodness!); you only need to note modifications, and the computer incorporates your changes with the rest of the paper that has remained the same. Without the computer's ability to store and retrieve data, computers would be of little value in word-processing applications.

Databases

Sometimes in the storage and retrieval of information, we would like to identify only certain items. For example, suppose you maintain an address book, and in it you store names, addresses, telephone numbers, and birthdays. At any time, you may want to retrieve the names of those people who have birthdays in a given month or those that live in a specific state. To do so, you need to set up your information in an organized way and have the computer search through the information for specific items, based on your criteria. It is not surprising that various companies have written software packages to perform such storage and selective retrieval. These computer programs are called **databases**, and many computers arrive from the manufacturer with a database program as part of their general software. Some common applications for databases include the following:

- Keeping addresses of friends, colleagues, or business contacts
- Storing recipes—perhaps with information about the type of cuisine or the ingredients used
- Maintaining an inventory of your CDs and/or tapes—perhaps with information about the songs on each CD and about artists
- Keeping an appointment book, with your schedule for each day
- Storing lists of your insurance policies, credit cards, shopping needs, favorite Web sites, or other personal items

Multimedia Applications

Whereas databases typically focus on text, another type of application involving storage and retrieval keeps track of shapes, geometrical objects, colors, patterns, or sounds. For example, we may use a computer to plan the layout of cabinets in a new kitchen, help design a new piece of furniture, maintain the pictures from our recent trip, or organize the karaoke tapes we made at a nightclub. Although this list clearly could be extended at length, the point here is that the storage and retrieval of information need not be limited to text; both visual and aural data may be saved as well.

For the most part, storage and retrieval applications involve rather limited computation or communication. Rather, they use the computer as an extensive multimedia filing system.

Networking and Communication

Communication via computer involves the same storage and retrieval of information used in the previous examples, as well as computation of data (which we'll discuss soon), but in the context of our local computer interacting with computers elsewhere. For example, Internet banking may be considered as, fundamentally, an advanced financial program, with data stored and retrieved at a bank, and with communication lines available to allow you access to that data. Similarly, much activity browsing on the World Wide Web involves folks storing materials on machines throughout the world and you retrieving that material from your computer. The same general statement could be made regarding the use of e-mail—one person stores a message and another retrieves it with an electronic delivery system in the middle. Although a computer network expands the realm of what information you can obtain, many of the most popular Internet applications exploit the same capabilities that individual computers are good at—but on a larger scale.

How does a computer's computational capabilities help me?

Computers are capable of performing large mathematical and symbolic computations accurately and efficiently. This processing ability plays a major role in our everyday life. Let's look first at weather forecasting and then at some of our personal activities that are positively influenced by a computer's computational skills.

Weather Forecasting: Weather forecasting is a good illustration of making particularly good use of computers' ability to compute data. First, monitoring instruments record current conditions, determining such factors as temperature, wind speed and direction, visibility, and precipitation. These readings are taken at many observation sites, both on land and in the air (through the use of aircraft, balloons, satellites, and so on), and give a good description of the current weather. This phase of work requires the accumulation and storage of massive amounts of data, so computers are very well suited for this data-acquisition phase of meteorology. Computers can continually monitor sensors and store readings. Further, data can be scanned for reasonableness and consistency with nearby readings, and this can help identify malfunctioning hardware.

As a next step, meteorologists apply well-understood principles of physics (e.g., fluid dynamics) to their data in order to project where various weather systems will move and how those systems will affect future weather conditions. Computers play an important role in this process because:

1. Forecasting depends heavily upon applying detailed mathematical formulae to massive amounts of data.

2. The accuracy of the forecasts generally increases as the number of observation sites increases.

Meteorologists aim to analyze the weather with as much precision as possible, so the more data they can utilize, the better. More data, however, mean more computation is needed in applying the formulae. Without computers helping, computation on this scale would take years or more, and your daily forecast would be years out of date! This second phase of forecasting meshes nicely with the capabilities of computers to perform computations efficiently and in a timely manner. Computers are effective at number crunching, and forecasting is worthwhile only if the millions of computations can be performed quickly.

To be somewhat more precise, forecasting normally proceeds by dividing a geographical region into relatively small blocks in a three-dimensional grid, and data are collected for at least one point in each block. As an analogy, think of a house as being divided into rooms; you could record the temperature and humidity in each room to get a general picture of the comfort level of each location in the house. A more precise picture might include variations of temperature within a room. To be this specific, you might divide each room logically into four or more sections and take readings in each area. These additional readings would offer you new information; for example, they might show the locations of drafts of cold or hot air.

In weather forecasting, to determine weather patterns, computations are made for each geographical block (or room or section of a room) following well-known formulae. General trends can be established when these formulae are applied repeatedly to determine changes every six hours or every day. More accurate and detailed computations can be made if changes are noted every hour or every fraction of an hour. Throughout the work, the same formulae are used, but accuracy depends upon dividing the area in question into reasonably small graphical regions and computing projected weather conditions at each piece at frequent intervals (every hour or less). As you can see, the computational abilities are used throughout the weather forecasting process.

Organizing Finances and Personal Information: Another application that takes advantage of the computer's ability to quickly perform computations and that may apply to our everyday lives involves the organization of our personal data and information. For example, we might wish to utilize the computer to help us with our finances—perhaps with an eye to assisting with our need to file income tax returns each year. Part of such applications involve the storage and retrieval of financial information; we need to keep track of what money we have had as income (rarely enough), and we must record whom we have paid for what. To clarify our financial picture, we may want to place both income and expenses into categories. Income might include categories for wages, bank interest, tips, gifts, babysitting, walking a neighbor's dog, and the like. Expenses might include lodging (rent or mortgage), clothing, food, entertainment, transportation, medical expenses, and so on. Each month, we may want to know our overall financial picture—our total income and total expenses, but also our totals in each category. In keeping a budget, we may want to know how much we really spent on that party or for medicine. Further, if we have been careful in setting up our categories, then we also will have the information we need for the various parts of our income tax form. As with simple storage and retrieval of information, this use of a computer to store financial data has become quite common, and various financial and tax-return software packages are available to help.

The planning of budgets, personnel schedules, and multi-step tasks can also take advantage of a computer's abilities. For example, a civic organization may have income based on dues and gifts, and it may want to plan its program for the coming year. At first, leaders may list the various activities they want to do. Each activity might include such expenses as materials, refreshments, travel, and publicity. If an outside speaker is to be invited for a meeting, then there may be a need to pay travel and speaking fees. To prepare a budget, all costs can be estimated and totals compared with income. If there is significantly more income, then each event could be expanded, perhaps with fancier decorations or refreshments. If the expenses are too high, then some events might be canceled, or cheaper alternatives may be found (e.g., inviting local speakers instead of those requiring substantial travel costs), or dues might be raised. Altogether, budgeting requires numbers (costs) to be arranged in various categories, along with various computations (subtotals, totals, tax payments, tips, service fees) based on the items entered. Such computation-based software is called a **spreadsheet**, and these applications are sufficiently popular that many companies produce spreadsheet software targeted at a wide range of users and applications. As with databases, many computers are shipped initially with some type of general spreadsheet package.

What else can a computer help me with?

A computer also allows us to manipulate data and arrange it as we'd like. In word processing, for example, computers allow you to format text by changing margins, justifying lines, changing fonts, and aligning equations. Each of these tasks involves the logical manipulation of data. Spelling checkers also can review your text, making use of a computer's ability to compare words with dictionary entries. Indeed, each word processing task can be described carefully, completely, and precisely in logical terms. For example, justifying a line involves adding spaces between words to make both the left and right margins align properly. To perform this task, a computer determines both how much space to add and where to add it. Although this process requires some sophistication and subtlety to ensure that every page will look balanced and attractive, the key point is that in order for the computer to complete the tasks, all details are reduced to a basic list of rules. This helps the application make good use of a computer's capabilities, and the computer can thereby allow us to manipulate the data as we'd like.

What do good applications have in common?

A good application, like word processing or weather forecasting, solves a problem that requires the skills of a computer. Further, the task that needs to be accomplished can be described fully; complete, unambiguous specifications can be written for the application. Also, given the specifications, detailed algorithms are available to perform the desired tasks efficiently. There is little question about what to do or how to do it. The tasks of publishing, for example, have been performed for centuries; people have considerable expertise in solving the wide variety of problems that can arise in typesetting and composing a manuscript. The primary advantages of using a computer are that machinery can store, retrieve, and modify information as the manuscript evolves, and the computer then can perform the long, tedious, repetitive tasks for formatting and typesetting quickly and accurately.

To summarize, many good applications of computers have the following characteristics:

- The application has well-defined, precise specifications.
- The application draws upon strengths of computers, namely the storage and retrieval of data and the manipulation of data.
- The work environment provides an excellent opportunity for extended testing. The same capabilities are used very frequently, and this constant use of the same features makes it likely that any errors in hardware and software will be noticed promptly. In word-processing programs, for example, users normally proofread their work, and they can help identify situations when a word processor malfunctions. Further, with frequent use, typists or editors may learn ways to get around or resolve known errors or peculiarities in a word-processing package.
- The interaction between machine and users allows constant monitoring of results. In word-processing programs, users can correct errors naturally, as part of their work. In weather forecasting, input data can be monitored for problems with sensors, output data can be compared with known models, and predictions can be compared with the actual conditions that occur later. In such cases, people will notice and be able to take corrective measures, if hardware or software produce incorrect results.
- The application is such that constant review and revision of results are practical.
- Algorithms (formulae) are well established.

Why can a computer guide astronauts into space but not predict the stock market?

From the first chapter of this book, I have emphasized that a computer functions by following instructions, based on a relatively few built-in operations. For example, it can move data from one place to another—as needed for the storage and retrieval of data; it can perform basic arithmetical and logical operations—such as addition, subtraction, multiplication, and the comparison of numbers or letters to see which is bigger; and it can follow instructions quickly.

These capabilities are the foundation for all computer applications, including word processing, databases, spreadsheets, Internet banking, and Web browsing. When we buy or utilize existing software written by someone else, we may not think about the internal details. However, behind the scenes, someone (or a team of someones) has carefully thought through just what steps are needed to perform a task, and those steps have been specified in a program in remarkable detail. For example, even if we do not know just how to tally a budget or compute our taxes, we can still accomplish these tasks because someone, a program developer, has done the work for us in writing a program.

In general, to perform any task with a computer, a program developer must specify the individual steps required to accomplish that task. This list of steps is called an **algorithm,** and the thought process of identifying and presenting those steps is called **algorithmic thinking**. Since the algorithm is the basis for all computer activity, identification of an algorithm might be considered the most basic part of using a computer to help solve a problem.

Let's examine algorithms by taking a look at the launching of astronauts into space. In this endeavor, one must consider a remarkable number of factors: burning of rocket fuel, magnitude of burn, directions of the rocket and rocket thrusters, forces of gravity, masses and velocities of gases and the rocket itself, interactions with the atmosphere (e.g., friction with air, wind forces), and more. The full list of variables could fill volumes, but all ingredients follow basic laws of physics, and all activity can be charted through appropriate mathematical equations. The fact that each variable can be broken down and specified makes it possible to have an algorithm for space launch.

Let's look at this in more depth. When considering a space launch, scientists first identify all variables that might be relevant to the mission. They also identify output variables for all of the desired results, such as how much fuel should be pumped to the rocket engines at any moment or when a signal should be sent to separate one stage of the rocket from the others. All these variables are then related through equations or other relationships. When this basic framework is complete, attention turns to determining the steps, or the algorithm, needed to perform the various computations. This process is called **modeling**, or mathematical modeling, and such work provides the background needed to write computer programs to support the application—in this case, the launching of astronauts into space.

Also, well before the launch ever takes place, these same variables and equations can be used to determine what results might occur under various circumstances. For example, using assumptions about weight, rocket thrust, air pressures, and the like, computations could indicate whether a rocket would achieve earth orbit, and where that orbit might be. This type of hypothesizing, based on models, is called **simulation**, and simulations can provide a great deal of information on what might be—based on possible values for variables and assumed variable relationships and equations.

In the case of the launching of astronauts into space, the models and simulations are extensive and complex. However, physical laws provide a scientific background that guides the development of detailed algorithms and computer programs. The work is difficult, but the field is known for producing adequate instructions that enable computers to handle the computations involved in the design, monitoring, and control of the rocket systems required for rocket travel. As a result, it has been possible to launch astronauts into space.

On the other hand, no one has produced an adequate algorithm for predicting the stock market. This lack of success to date, however, has not been for lack of trying. Magazine articles and television programs regularly highlight interviews with various economists, investment consultants, and analysts who have developed a particular model for charting stocks and making predictions. These folks track a remarkable number of quantitative and qualitative data, plugging current information into equations and following charts and graphs. Their predictions may seem reasonably accurate for a period of time, but so far each system has eventually failed—at least from time to time.

In this regard, the basic problem is not a downfall of computers, for computers are designed only to follow the instructions they are given. Computers can produce many answers quickly, but the results are always based on instructions. In the case of the stock market, people do not know what models to follow or what instructions to specify. Think for a moment of all the factors that could influence the stock market: politics, economics, environment, and the list goes on. Some factors may even depend on human psychology—how people feel about their lives and their surroundings—but no one knows exactly how such factors will affect people's choices of individual stocks or investments. To date, we have only vague ideas about investment behavior, and stock-market predictions have some qualities of looking into a crystal ball. Unfortunately, this lacks the clarity required to produce an adequate algorithm. Thus, looking at the results of computer computations only reinforces this conclusion that people have not yet found an appropriate algorithm.

If computer programs that predict the stock market are unreliable, how I can tell when other computer programs might be giving unreliable results?

Unfortunately, this is a very difficult question to answer. In previous chapters, we have identified the stages of software development as specifications, design and algorithm development, coding, testing, and maintenance. In this chapter, we have commented on modeling and simulations. In practice, errors can arise in any stage of a computer program's development. Here are some examples:

- *Specifications*: One can never truly know if the specifications for a problem are complete and consistent. Various people can review specifications in an attempt to find omissions or inconsistencies, but this can only help refine the specifications—not ensure they are correct. After all, an omission in specifications could arise because no one thought of a particular scenario that might happen; if no one thought of it ahead of time, then no one will realize it was omitted until the situation actually occurs later. Overall, with complex problems, we can never be completely confident that our specifications cover all possible problematic occurrences, so in our subsequent problem solving we cannot be certain we are trying to solve exactly the right problem.

- *Design*: People design algorithms, and all people make mistakes—at least sometimes. Formulae may be wrong, either through errors in logic, difficulties in analysis, or typographical errors.
- *Coding*: Instructions to a computer must be extremely detailed and precise. In writing large and complex programs, the likelihood for error is very high—just as the chances are good that a book will contain at least one error somewhere. In writing programs, various tools can help identify common problems, just as spelling checkers can help us determine if any words we write in a paper are misspelled. However, tools cannot check our intent or our logical thinking; symbols or words may be valid according to a dictionary, but that does not imply that they are what we meant to say.
- *Testing*: Complex programs may encounter millions of different situations. Even in the context of word processing, just think of all of the possible combinations of fonts, styles, type sizes, and formatting. Because various parts of a program may interact in subtle ways, complete testing would require the checking of all possible interactions, for all possible combinations of input. Such exhaustive testing is not feasible for any but the simplest programs.
- *Maintenance*: When system components interact in complex ways, a change in one component may affect processing somewhere else. Thus, the addition of a new feature or the correction of an error in one place may generate an error somewhere else.
- *Modeling*: Models of processes and situations require the identification of relevant variables and the formulation of relationships and equations, based on reasonable assumptions. Errors may be made in the selection of what variables are relevant in identifying needed equations or in stating assumptions.
- *Simulations*: All simulations are based upon models, and all models in turn depend upon assumptions (either stated or un-

stated). Results of simulations can only be as good or valid as the assumptions that underlie them.

- *Hardware*: Although hardware tends to be more reliable than software, unanticipated hardware malfunctions can occur, with possibly serious consequences.

Altogether, we need to be particularly cautious in relying on computers for answers to questions. Every large-scale software package has errors. Some may be known, but we should expect to find new errors, even in programs that have undergone extensive testing. All of this suggests that we should not fully rely on computers in our work.

As a practical matter, the best defense against possible errors may be healthy skepticism and constant checking. If we do not automatically assume that a computer has produced the correct results, then we will compare its results with those from other sources. We also can ask ourselves if computer-produced results are reasonable. In reviewing models and simulations, we can ask what variables are used, how relationships were determined, and what assumptions were made. Of course, modern computers have a reasonable track record in producing helpful results—but they also malfunction (e.g., crash) from time to time.

With this record, it may be best to begin by assuming that computers are producing unreliable results until you have evidence that the data in front of you are correct. When using word processors, databases, and spreadsheets, such checking often is easy—you just look at what is displayed on your screen and compare it with what you intended. When using unfamiliar software or when working on more complex problems, you may need to take more extensive action to check. And if you will be investing your life savings—where the risks are high—you might want considerable evidence of testing and accuracy before proceeding.

For problems that a computer can solve, what process should I use to get an answer?

Sometimes a problem at hand is relatively easy; for example, we may want to add the cost of three items to double-check a bill we received from our telephone company. To do so, we likely can identify a software package on our computer (perhaps a calculator or spreadsheet) that allows us to do the job directly. Similarly, if we owe money on our credit card, we may want to compute our new balance after making this month's payment and then adding the interest that the credit-card company will charge us. Again, a simple calculator or spreadsheet may resolve our problem.

Unfortunately, relatively few problems are that simple. When we're working with complex problems, a helpful general approach is to break down our initial large problem and identify appropriate smaller ones. If we can solve the small ones, then we can put the pieces together to get our answer to the initial problem.

As an example, suppose we want to know our credit-card balance and the interest paid for each month until our debt is paid off—assuming we make the same monthly payments. We already have noted that we could use a calculator or spreadsheet to handle this task for a single month. Our next step might be to incorporate those calculations into a program that repeats this process until our debt is cleared. Such a process is called **repetition**, and computers are particularly good at this type of task. In repetition, we typically need to organize our data in a methodical way, and then we apply the computations systematically to the information we have stored. For example, in computing credit balances, we may organize our work in a table, with one row in the table giving the starting balance, payment, interest rate, interest, and final balance for a month. Successive rows would provide the information for successive months. In computing, data organized together in a logical manner is called a **data structure**, and much algorithm development focuses on identifying appropriate data structures and organizing their methodical processing to obtain the desired results. Our example actually involves two data structures: one containing the data for a row, and the second involving the entire table that has the rows as components.

In developing algorithms, we frequently begin by dividing a complex problem into subproblems in such a way that we would have the answer to the initial, large problem if we could answer each of the subproblems. We then try to solve the subproblems following the same strategy. Sometimes we may be able to solve a subproblem directly, but often that too may need further subdivision. As an analogy, you may note that this approach to problem solving matches reasonably well with the notion of outline form. In an outline, the main points are identified as points I, II, III, and so on. Often one of these main points is expanded with subpoints A, B, C and so on. If these topics still seem extensive, then points 1, 2, 3 may expand them further, and items a, b, c provide further clarification. Overall this yields an outline that might looks something like the following:

I.
  A.
    1.
    2.
  B.
    1.
      a.
      b.
      c.
    2.
  C.
II.
  A.
    1.
      a.
      b.
    2.
  B.

This same structure serves as the framework for the discussion questions and exercises at the end of each chapter in this book. The question numbers provide the main context and guidance for a problem, and sometimes this information is adequate to designate an entire problem; however, some questions involve several related subquestions, and these are designated a, b, c.

In the terminology of computing, this general approach to problem solving is called a **top-down methodology**. Think of the entire problem as being at a top level, and subproblems make up lower-level details. (Because an outline form uses indenting to show the level of each element, one might coin the term "left-to-right methodology" for the outline process, but such terminology is not in common usage.) The identification of subtopics within one problem or subproblem is called a **decomposition** of the problem or solution, and the process of developing the elements that belong under a heading is called **refinement**.

In practice, people have considerable trouble dealing with complexity; at some point there can be more items to think about than people can handle. A top-down approach is a very effective mechanism for dealing with this human trait. Once a problem is subdivided, we can focus on smaller and more manageable parts without thinking constantly about all of the pieces at once. In the development of software, dividing large projects into smaller subprojects allows the assignment of different people to separate tasks. Each person can work on one part of the software. If the pieces have been appropriately specified within a larger framework, then they will fit together to yield an overall software package that addresses the total need of the client or customer.

Can some computers solve problems that other computers can't solve?

Salespeople sometimes tout the advantages of one machine over another, citing special capabilities or outstanding features. (Return to Chapter 5 for more on computers and advertising.) And, from a superficial viewpoint, some of these claims are obviously true. A new computer likely comes with a built-in plug for connection to a network or the Internet, whereas a previous version may have required a separate add-on to make such a connection. One computer may have both a CD player and a separate disk drive, whereas another computer has only the CD player and thus cannot read disks directly. Old computers usually had black-and-white monitors, whereas most new machines have color screens. Such examples indicate that some computers have more or better "stuff" attached than other computers. Depending on your needs, some of this peripheral equipment may be important or particularly convenient.

However, in reviewing these examples, it is important to note that the differences involve peripheral devices—not the central CPU or the main structure of a computer. Most personal computers produced today have a common structure, although they may vary in some details. To be more precise, let's consider computers with the following elements:

- A CPU that can perform simple arithmetic and logical operations
- Some type of input and output device(s), such as a keyboard and monitor
- Some main memory—to hold a simple program
- A storage device that can be used to insert and remove disks, tapes, or CDs. (With a floppy drive or the equivalent, computers effectively have infinite storage capabilities; we can keep purchasing new disks when we fill the old. Even without a built-in drive, a computer likely contains a plug for an external drive or storage device, and we could use that capability to store any desired amount of information.)

Virtually all home computers satisfy these constraints. Some computers are more restricted or are specialized for a particular task. (For example, the electronics that control your microwave oven are basically a computer designed to cook your food; your car's engine is a computer created to move your car.) Although such restricted computers have limited capabilities, fundamentally all of today's computers for home, office, or a lab usually meet the listed criteria. What are the capabilities of our typical personal computers with the standard elements listed here? Remarkably, the answer relates to a theoretical model of a computer, called a Turing Machine.

What Are Turing Machines?

In 1936, Alan Turing first proposed a model for a computer, now called a **Turing Machine**. Although the details of Turing Machines require considerable discussion and a careful formalism, the basic idea is that a Turing Machine consists of an infinite tape, a read-write head for the tape, a table of potential actions, a mechanism to keep track of where it is within a computation, and a simple processor that reads the tape and responds according to the table. The mechanism for keeping track of what has been accomplished by the machine during processing is called a *state*.

To illustrate the idea of a Turing Machine, here are two (relatively) simple examples. In each case we use binary numbers to keep the number of states small in our Turing machine. Similar examples using decimal numbers are possible; although the format of such numbers might be more familiar, the corresponding Turing machines would be more complicated. (For example, the number of rows in each table would increase by a factor of 5 if we considered decimal numbers rather than binary numbers.) Please don't be intimidated by the binary numbers! Remember, most real computers work by processing binary numbers, 0s and 1s, as we discussed in Chapter 2.

Example 1

Assume that this Turing Machine has its read-write head at the left end of a binary number. The machine processes the number from left to right and then adds a 0 or 1 at the location following the number, so that the total number of 1's is even; that is, if the number has an even number of 1's already, then the Turing machine adds a 0 to the right of that number, but if the number has an odd number of 1's, then a 1 is added. (In case you care, this extra digit is called a **parity bit** and is important in checking the storage, retrieval, and transmission of data. We will have a chance to discuss this further in a later chapter.) Here is the description of what this Turing Machine does to place a 0 or 1 as the appropriate parity bit at the end of the binary number:

Possible symbols on each location of the tape: 0, 1, space where "space" means that the tape is blank at that location

Starting state: A

Ending state: C

(The Turing Machine also has a state B, corresponding to an intermediate point in computation, but state B neither begins the computation nor ends it.)

Processing Table

Current State	Input	Symbol Written to Tape	Tape Head Movement	Next State
A	0	0	Move right 1 character	A
A	1	1	Move right 1 character	B
A	space	0	Move right 1 character	C
B	0	0	Move right 1 character	B
B	1	1	Move right 1 character	A
B	space	1	Move right 1 character	C
C	0	stop		
C	1	stop		
C	space	stop		

Although processing is not very complex, on the surface the states of a Turing Machine may seem far from intuitive. Although formal processing by Turing Machines depend solely upon the table to guide what happens next, the developer of the Turing Machine usually motivates the states through an underlying idea.

To learn the idea of the states for this Turing Machine, let's look carefully at the table: The machine begins in state A and moves back to state A if an even number of 1's have been processed so far. Similarly, the machine proceeds to state B if cumulatively it has encountered an odd number of 1's. By keeping track of whether it is in state A or B, the Turing Machine has recorded whether the numbers read so far on the tape include an even or an odd number of 1's. With this information, the table of the Turing Machine identifies the appropriate activity when the machine encounters the space at the end of the number; according to the table, the Turing Machine writes the required parity bit on the tape and then moves to state C.

Because Turing Machines can seem abstract, understanding their processing often is aided by walking through an example. To better understand how this Turing Machine works, suppose that the number 10101 appears on a tape, as shown at the start of Figure 7.1.

As specified, this Turing Machine begins in state A, and the read-write head is positioned at the left digit of our input 10101. For the first step, the machine reads the input symbol (the digit 1) and then consults the table. In state A with input 1, the machine is to write a 1 to the tape (not changing what is already there), move its read-write head to the right one character, and go to state B for the next processing. The resulting configuration is shown as the second entry in Figure 7.1.

For step 2, the machine reads the next input symbol (the digit 0), and again consults the table. This time, the machine is in state B with input symbol 0, so the machine puts a 0 back on the tape, moves the read-write head one character to the right, and stays in state B. The resulting configuration is the third entry in the figure.

For step 3, the machine reads the 1, consults the table, prints the 1, moves right, and goes back to state A.

In step 4, the machine reads a 0, prints the 0, moves right, and stays in state A.

In step 5, the machine reads a 1, prints 1, moves right, and moves again to state B.

In step 6, the machine encounters a space or blank. Consulting the table for state B, the machine adds a 1 to the tape, moves right, and enters state C.

In step 7, the machine stops, and processing is complete.

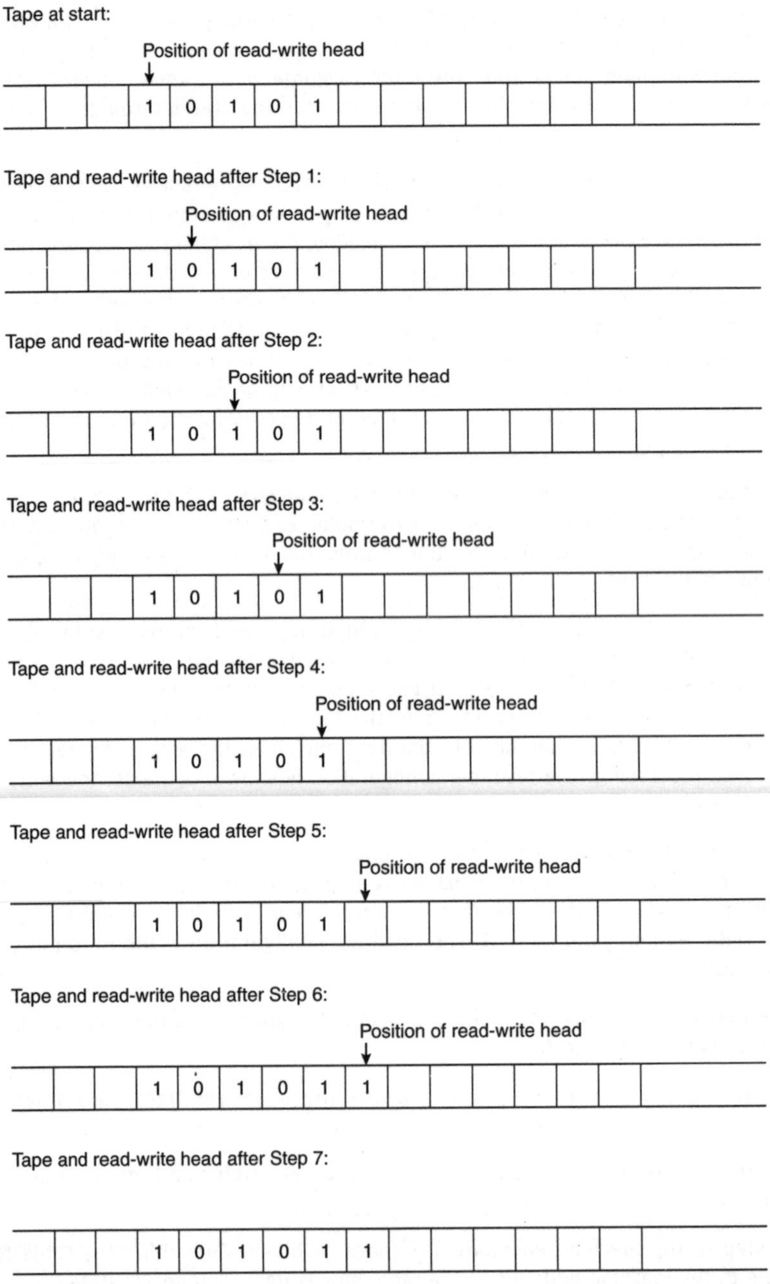

Tape at start:

Position of read-write head ↓ (at first 1)

			1	0	1	0	1							

Tape and read-write head after Step 1:

Position of read-write head ↓ (at first 0)

			1	0	1	0	1							

Tape and read-write head after Step 2:

Position of read-write head ↓ (at second 1)

			1	0	1	0	1							

Tape and read-write head after Step 3:

Position of read-write head ↓ (at second 0)

			1	0	1	0	1							

Tape and read-write head after Step 4:

Position of read-write head ↓ (at third 1)

			1	0	1	0	1							

Tape and read-write head after Step 5:

Position of read-write head ↓ (at first blank after 1 0 1 0 1)

			1	0	1	0	1							

Tape and read-write head after Step 6:

Position of read-write head ↓ (at new 1)

			1	0	1	0	1	1						

Tape and read-write head after Step 7:

			1	0	1	0	1	1						

Figure 7.1
Processing steps for a simple Turing Machine.

Example 2

The following Turing Machine also adds a parity bit, but this time the bit is placed at the beginning of the number. As with example 1, the machine starts in state A, moves to state A if an even number of 1's have been processed and moves to state B if an odd number of 1's have been processed.

Possible symbols on each location of the tape: 0, 1, space

Starting state: A

Ending state: E

Processing Table

Current State	Input	Symbol Written to Tape	Tape Head Movement	Next State
A	0	0	Move right 1 character	A
A	1	1	Move right 1 character	B
A	space	space	Move left 1 character	C
B	0	0	Move right 1 character	B
B	1	1	Move right 1 character	A
B	space	space	Move left 1 character	D
C	0	0	Move left 1 character	C
C	1	1	Move left 1 character	C
C	space	0	Move left 1 character	E
D	0	0	Move left 1 character	D
D	1	1	Move left 1 character	D
D	space	1	Move left 1 character	E
E	0	stop		
E	1	stop		
E	space	stop		

Processing for this Turing Machine begins just as it did for the previous machine. However, when the number is completely read from left to right, this machine has to move its read-write head to the left edge where it finds a space. Then the parity bit can be added. To accomplish this task, states C and D allow the machine to work digit-by-digit to the left. State C designates that a 0 should be added when the left edge is found, while state D designates that a 1 should be added.

Before going on, you should check your understanding of these Turing Machines by tracing their execution using another input string of your choice.

So, what do Turing Machines have to do with computers today?

Although Turing Machines may seem particularly mundane, they are important in the theory of computation for several reasons. First, because they can be defined precisely and their processing can be described rigorously, it is possible to prove various results about them. In particular, several variations of Turing Machines have been proven to have the same power. That is, whatever can be solved with one of these machines can also be solved on the others. Through theory, we can show that Turing Machines with the following capabilities can solve exactly the same problems:

- A Turing Machine with a tape extending infinitely far in both directions (an infinite two-way tape)
- A Turing Machine with a tape extending infinitely far in only one direction (an infinite one-way tape)
- A Turing Machine with several one-way tapes
- A Turing Machine with an infinite one-way tape and just the symbols 0, 1, and space
- A Turing Machine with several two-way tapes and an extended alphabet of tape symbols

These results indicate that adding tape capabilities or extending alphabets does not change what computers can solve. For example, although we may be more comfortable with numbers in decimal notation, Turing Machines that process decimal numbers cannot solve problems beyond those solvable by Turing Machines based on binary numbers.

Further, additional theory allows us to prove that Turing Machines have exactly the same power as the basic computer we discussed at the start of this chapter (with a CPU, main memory, and storage device). It may seem that today's computers are much more sophisticated than the historical Turing Machines; however, research shows that any problem that can be solved with one of today's computers also could be solved with a Turing Machine. And, conversely, any problem that can be solved with a Turing Machine can be solved with one of the basic computers we described earlier.

The Lambda Calculus

Also in 1936, Alonzo Church formally described algorithms using a theory of functions called the *lambda calculus*. This study motivated the development of the LISP programming language, now used extensively in the field of artificial intelligence. Remarkably, the lambda calculus also has the same power as Turing Machines.

All of these comments lead to the same basic conclusion that although computers may have various forms and descriptions, they all have the same basic computational power. This circumstance is sometimes described as the **universality of computers.** Each type of machine is universal, in that any computer can perform any computational task. The Computer Science and Telecommunications Board of the National Research Council notes that this notion of universality has several important implications:

- No computational task is so complex that it cannot be decomposed into instructions suitable for the most basic computer.
- The instruction repertoire of a computer is largely unimportant in terms of giving it power since any missing instruction types can be programmed using the instructions the machine does have.
- Computers differ by how quickly they solve a problem, not whether they can solve the problem.
- Programs, which direct the instruction-following components of a computer to realize a computation, are the key.

(From *Being Fluent with Information Technology*, National Academy Press, 1999, pp. 31–32.)

If all computers are universal, how do they differ?

As we have discussed, the principle of universality means that all basic modern computers can solve the same problems and run the same algorithms. We cannot distinguish among machines on the basis of their fundamental capabilities. Does this mean you might as well return your new Macintosh PowerBook computer and bring your parents' old Windows machine down from the attic to use in your dorm room? You could, but you might not want to. The principle of universality only says that computers can accomplish the same tasks; it does not indicate how fast the machines will be able to determine the results of an algorithm, how convenient they might be to use, or what nice input and output devices they might have.

For example, any computer with the basic capabilities will have a storage device. However, one computer may have large storage capabilities, so it can hold a great deal of data before having to utilize another CD or disk. Another computer may have very limited storage capabilities, so we may need to utilize several disks and swap them back and forth frequently to store a moderate amount of information. Both computers can do the same work, but one is more convenient for the user.

Similarly, some machines may process information faster than others. Also, some may have special processors and software to handle sound or pictures or multimedia materials. Such components may allow audio or video to be edited and merged with a simple interface for the user and with great speed. These particular computers would be more suited to your needs if you were handling multimedia components than slower computers that might require considerable time and effort (and generate much frustration) to perform similar tasks.

Internally, different computers utilize different CPUs and different operating systems, and thus they can run different programs. Although the principle of universality indicates that a program written for one CPU and one operating system can be translated to run on other CPUs and other operating systems, it does not follow that the actual translation has been done. Your new digital camera software, for example, may run on Windows XP but not on Windows 95, and you would need to have the software translated to work on your computer's Windows 95 operating system. The theory indicates the translation is possible, but that does not mean the product is actually on the market.

Altogether, different computers may work at varying speeds, provide different types of connections to various input and output devices, and have different types of interfaces for the user. Underlying these external trappings, the computers may be able to solve the same problems and run the same algorithms, but they may look and feel different for their users, and the actual programs on the market may work on some machines but not on others.

How can I decide what machine I should buy?

Today's market features a very wide range of brands of computers, operating systems, software packages, and special input and output devices (such as printers and scanners). The equipment also comes with a remarkable range of prices and sizes.

Given this diversity, do not begin your decision of what to buy by considering brands or operating systems or specific packages or specialized equipment. There simply are too many alternatives and combinations to think through. Rather, utilize algorithmic thinking to approach this question methodically. The first step in thinking about purchases should be to develop a realistic inventory of what you want to do with the computer. For many people, this might be limited to several common applications:

- Word processing
- E-mail
- Web browsing
- Databases for address books, recipes, and the like
- A finance package or spreadsheet
- Perhaps playing CDs or DVDs

Other people may have more specialized needs involving multimedia, work-related records or computations, games, or educational/learning packages.

Once this list of needs is established, the second step is to identify software packages that perform the tasks you want covered. You may want to review several packages that do the same work so that you can determine which one(s) seem best for your needs. In some cases, you may find that different software packages are available for different operating systems (e.g., Linux, Macintosh OS X, or Microsoft Windows). To stay organized, try maintaining separate lists—one for the software that fits your needs for each of those systems.

An optional third step arises if you will be using your computer within a broader context of school, work, or friends. In such a circumstance, you will need to determine what special requirements arise in that context. For example, if you will be using a spreadsheet at school, you should check what spreadsheet is used there and how it stores and retrieves information. Although you may not need to use the same software package on your own machine, you will want to be sure that your software can read files in the specified format and can store your information in that same format. As a specific example, this book has been written with word-processing software on three different systems. The publisher uses Microsoft Word on Windows-based equipment, I use ThinkFree Office on a Macintosh at home, and I use Open Office on a Linux system in the office. Although each of these word-processing packages has its own special advantages and disadvantages, the details do not matter greatly. The important point is that each can store and retrieve data in a format that is understandable by the other packages. Thus, I can work at home or in the office and can share files with the publisher easily. Such compatibility is important if your work will be moved from place to place or shared with others.

Once you have established your background needs and desired software, your fourth step is to review the software requirements to learn what hardware they need to run. What CPU is expected? How much memory is recommended? How large a storage device is needed? What input and output devices are expected? What plugs and connections (e.g., to the Internet) are advised? As you figure this out, it usually is best to identify the recommendations of the software packages that you might want to run and then to add a bit for expansion in the future, as we discussed in Chapters 3 and 4.

As a final step, you can select a specific system. You know what applications you will run, what software supports your needs, how your system might interact with others, and what hardware is required to make all of this work. At this point, you can look at price, convenience, warranty, and repair alternatives to see what fits your budget and personal preferences. If your needs are modest, then there is no need to spend a great deal of money for an extensive system that does a lot more than you will use. On the other hand, if you have extensive demands, then purchasing a basic system may not allow you to run the software you need.

Although much of this may seem like common sense, a careful analysis of what you want and what is available to you, as described here, can provide you with a completely adequate system for your needs—without requiring you to spend much more money than necessary. With all of the claims by hardware and software vendors, it is particularly easy to be swept up in a swirl of advertising and hype. A realistic and careful approach can help you cut through the distractions to obtain something that works for you.

Summary

Computers excel in storing and retrieving data, executing detailed logical or arithmetic operations at great speed, and presenting results in textual or graphical form. For this to be helpful to us in solving problems, however, several properties are needed:

- The problem must be translated into careful and precise specifications.
- A detailed algorithm must be developed to meet the specifications.
- A software package must be tested thoroughly to be sure it works as desired.
- Relevant data must be obtainable and entered into the program.

When problems do not have these properties, computers may be of limited use in finding solutions. Further, because complex programs normally contain some errors, reliance on results can be troublesome. Users should always be thoughtful in monitoring a computer's functioning, even when a computer is good at the task, such as in word processing, databases, spreadsheets, e-mail, and other Internet communications. Reliance on unverified results may add a risk—sometimes a high risk—to a task.

In using a computer to help you solve a problem, you can subdivide complex problems into relatively simple and manageable problems. This top-down approach provides a convenient mechanism to manage complexity. Your problem solving focuses on the development of solutions to pieces of the problem that together help you solve the original complex problem.

Although computers work at different speeds, have different CPUs and operating systems, and are connected to different input and output devices, basic computers share the ability to solve the same collection of problems. All basic computers are equivalent to Turing Machines in what they can do at a theoretical level. This universality of computers means that the choice of hardware should depend on such factors as ease of use, speed, and cost.

In selecting a computer system for purchase, a careful and methodical approach can be most helpful. This process involves an identification of your specific needs, review of software to satisfy those needs, consideration of what other systems you will want to work with, identification of the hardware recommendations given by the software packages you select, and consideration of such practical issues as price and ease of use.

Terminology from This Chapter

algorithm
algorithmic thinking
data structure
database
decomposition
modeling
parity bit
refinement
repetition
simulation
spreadsheet
top-down methodology
Turing Machine
universality of computers

Discussion Questions

1. Consider the following anecdote involving the use of computers to generate mail and to automatically process applications.

   A Dead Fish

   Fred Finn Mazanek, a one-year-old guppy, died recently, leaving an estate of $5000. A student at the University of Arizona received one of the computer-mailed "occupant" life insurance offers. The student diligently filled out the insurance form for this fish, listing the fish's age as six months, his weight as thirty centigrams, and his height as three centimeters. Another computer (or maybe the same computer who mailed the original offer) duly issued Policy No. 3261057 in Fred Finn's name from the Global Life and Accident Insurance Company and began billing and collecting premiums.

A few months later, the fish died, and the owner filed a claim. Although the insurance company was quite upset, they found it best to settle out of court for $650.

(From Dennie and Cynthia L. Van Tassel, *The Compleat Computer*, Second Edition, Science Research Associates, Inc., 1983, p. 22. Reprinted by permission of author.)

a. Does this story have any broader implications?

b. What does this story suggest concerning the role of computers?

In answering each part, explain your conclusions.

2. Answer the same two questions (from Discussion Question 1) for the following anecdote, involving a sales pitch commonly heard on radio and television.

Piano Sale

The Allen Piano and Organ Company of Phoenix advertised by radio that its computer had made a mistake in ordering inventory; the company was overstocked and was therefore holding a sale. A member of the Association for Computing Machinery called the company and offered to fix the faulty program for free. He found out that the Allen Piano and Organ Company did not have a computer and had not been using any computer facilities. The "computer error" was just a sales trick.

(From Dennie and Cynthia L. Van Tassel, *The Compleat Computer*, Second Edition, Science Research Associates, Inc., 1983, p. 233. Reprinted by permission of the author.)

3. Each of the following paragraphs describes a computer application. In each case, determine some characteristics of this computer application, and compare these properties with the list of things computers can do well. Then consider what elements of the application may not mesh well with a computer's strengths, raising the potential for errors or other problems. What are the risks inherent in using computers in this context? Are there steps that can be taken to minimize those risks?

a. A fighter aircraft may fly at speeds that are so fast that people cannot respond in time to avoid or correct various conditions. (By the time a pilot decides to turn to avoid another aircraft or a missile, for example, a collision may already have occurred.) Thus, much of the control of such an airplane is often turned over to a computer, where the response times can be quicker.

b. In a hospital, sensors attached to a computer may be used to monitor patients in a critical care ward. This allows constant review of a patient's vital signs, and it provides a mechanism to alert medical personnel if a patient's condition changes abruptly.

c. Extending the application in b, the computer may be attached to devices that can administer drugs and that can take other preventive or corrective measures. For example, a drop in a patient's blood pressure might signal the need to administer a drug intravenously.

4. Because each of the applications in question 3 involves hardware and software built by humans, each has the possibility of the computer system malfunctioning. In each case, describe what might go wrong. Then consider who might be responsible for the problem. (For example, who might be legally or morally liable?)

5. One policy that has been discussed for defending the United States against a surprise attack involves the concept of launch-on-warning. Under this policy, sensors (radar, satellites, reconnaissance planes, and so on) constantly monitor the skies for evidence of an enemy attack (presumably using missiles and/or aircraft). When sensors determine that such an attack has started, planes and missiles are launched immediately to retaliate.

   Proponents of a launch-on-warning policy point out that missiles can travel across the world in a very few minutes (perhaps 15 or 20 minutes). Thus, the United States has only a short time to retaliate before an enemy attack could eliminate much of the capability of the United States to respond. Effective retaliation may be possible only if the response begins before the enemy missiles and/or planes reach their targets. Times simply are too short to allow a lengthy review of possible attack data, and the consequences of an attack may be too devastating to ensure a reasonable response after the attack is completed.

Opponents of a launch-on-warning policy point to the potential for error in a response and the consequences of responding incorrectly.

a. Review this launch-on-warning approach in light of the known capabilities and limitations of computer systems. (You may need to do some additional reading to research both the launch-on-warning strategy and its possible defects. One Web site to check out is maintained by CPSR—Computer Professionals for Social Responsibility—at http://www.cpsr.org.)

b. Take a stand on this policy, either for or against, and write a strong argument supporting your conclusion.

6. Suppose your task were to catalog and organize all the books in a library. Consider the extent to which either the Dewey Decimal system or the Library of Congress classification system reflects a top-down methodology, with stepwise refinement. (If you are not familiar with either of these systems, this might be a good time to consult a librarian!)

7. For many schools, the goal is to provide a solid overall education. To accomplish this, schools often have various general-education requirements as well as requirements for various majors. Discuss how this framework of requirements fits within a top-down methodology to satisfy the overall goal(s) of the school.

Exercises

1. Consider the words and phrases from the "Terminology from This Chapter."

a. Some words and phrases identify types of software, some relate to elements or techniques within the problem-solving process, and some involve separate ideas. Organize each of these terms under the headings "software types," "problem solving," and others. In each case, explain your categorization.

b. Provide careful definitions for each word or phrase.

2. The chapter lists several applications of databases and spreadsheets. Think of three additional applications that might be appropriate for each of the following:

a. The personnel office of a company

b. The admission office of a college or university

c. A small, local grocery store

3. This chapter has not discussed computer games as a common application. In considering what you know about computer games, why do you think computers are good at running such games? For example, what capabilities do you think games require, and how do these requirements fit with what computers can do?

4. The discussion for the second example of a Turing Machine claims that the Turing Machine presented computes a parity bit and writes this at the beginning of a number. Using Figure 7.1 as a guide, trace the execution of this Turing Machine for the input 101, showing what happens at each step in processing.

5. Consider the following Turing Machine.

Possible symbols on each location of the tape: 0, 1, space where "space" means that the tape is blank at that location.

Starting state: A

Ending state: D

Processing Table

Current State	Input	Symbol Written to Tape	Tape Head Movement	Next State
A	0	1	Move right 1 character	B
A	1	1	Move right 1 character	C
A	space	space	Move right 1 character	D
B	0	0	Move right 1 character	B
B	1	0	Move right 1 character	C
B	space	0	Move right 1 character	D
C	0	1	Move right 1 character	B
C	1	1	Move right 1 character	C
C	space	1	Move right 1 character	D
D	0	stop		
D	1	stop		
D	space	stop		

a. Run this Turing Machine for each of the following inputs, and determine what is on the tape when processing stops.

i. 0000

ii. 1111

iii. 10011

b. Describe in words what this Turing Machine does.

c. Describe in words the motivation for states B and C. What do each of these states tell you about processing of the input?

6. The first example of Turing Machines in this chapter described an algorithm for computing a parity bit, based an even number of 1's in a number. This is called even parity. How would you change the Turing Machine so that the parity bit was set so the number of 1's was odd (e.g., odd parity)?

Part III Networking/ Distributed System Questions

Chapter 8

How are computers connected?

Have you ever taken a new computer out of its shipping carton and tried to hook it up? If so, you likely found that the computer manufacturer had organized and connected the various components inside the computer's cabinetry. Your responsibility was to connect wires and cables to electric power, printers and other devices, and perhaps the Internet. At that moment, you likely learned that a modern computer typically contains many types of built-in plug sockets, and that plugs and cables come in an assortment of sizes and shapes. A quick walk around your favorite computer store would further demonstrate that today's market contains hundreds of devices that could connect to computers. The wide variety can seem quite confusing—so why are there so many choices, and what are the differences between one type of plug or cable and another? This chapter addresses many of those questions, including the basics of how computers are connected, what the most common types of cables look like, and how wireless communications work. In addition to some practical mechanics, we'll explore the ideas behind how computers are connected.

How do you physically connect computers?

As you might expect, the simplest way to connect two computers involves running wires between them, much as land-based telephones are connected by wires. To understand the use of various cables for computers, we first need to review some basic concepts of wiring. Our discussion of computer cables follows from those concepts.

At a minimum, two wires are needed for a complete circuit, just as with most electrical circuitry. Think of one wire as fulfilling the role of an electrical faucet, if you will, bringing electricity into the device while the other wire has the role of the drain pipe and carries the electricity away from the device. In making connections for computers, wires usually come packaged as two (or more) metal wires, each of which is surrounded by insulation. Often, the individually insulated wires are, in turn, surrounded by a wrapper to keep them together in a convenient package. Usually, the wires that you plug into a power outlet are reasonably heavy to handle considerable voltage and electrical current. Such wires, often called a **power cord**, are usually bulky with a power plug at the end. For other connections, signals along the wires can work at low voltages and currents, so the wires need not be heavy or bulky. Even at these low voltages, however, the wires must channel electricity to the desired destination without interfering with wires going elsewhere, which is why all wires are securely covered in protective plastic insulation.

For reference later in this chapter, a few basic types of wiring are shown in Figure 8.1. The cable on the left in this figure could be used as a power cord. There are two individually wrapped wires of moderate diameter, and these provide the basic electrical connections that supply power and return it to a wall plug. The third wire is a **ground** that provides an additional path for electricity from your computer to the wall plug. In the cable in Figure 8.1, this third wire also is wrapped with insulation. In other cables, the ground may not be individually wrapped with insulation, but may appear as a bare wire within the overall cable. The motivation for this ground wire is safety; if something within the computer malfunctions, electricity coming in from the wall outlet might not be able to return along the second wire as planned. The ground provides an alternate route, acting something like an overflow drain in your bathtub or sink. Without this ground, if you inadvertently touched the computer, the electricity might try to use your fingers and you to complete the circuit, giving you a dangerous electrical shock. The ground wire makes this much less likely.

Returning to Figure 8.1, the second cable from the left contains four wires, arranged largely as a strip. In this flat cable, wires lie

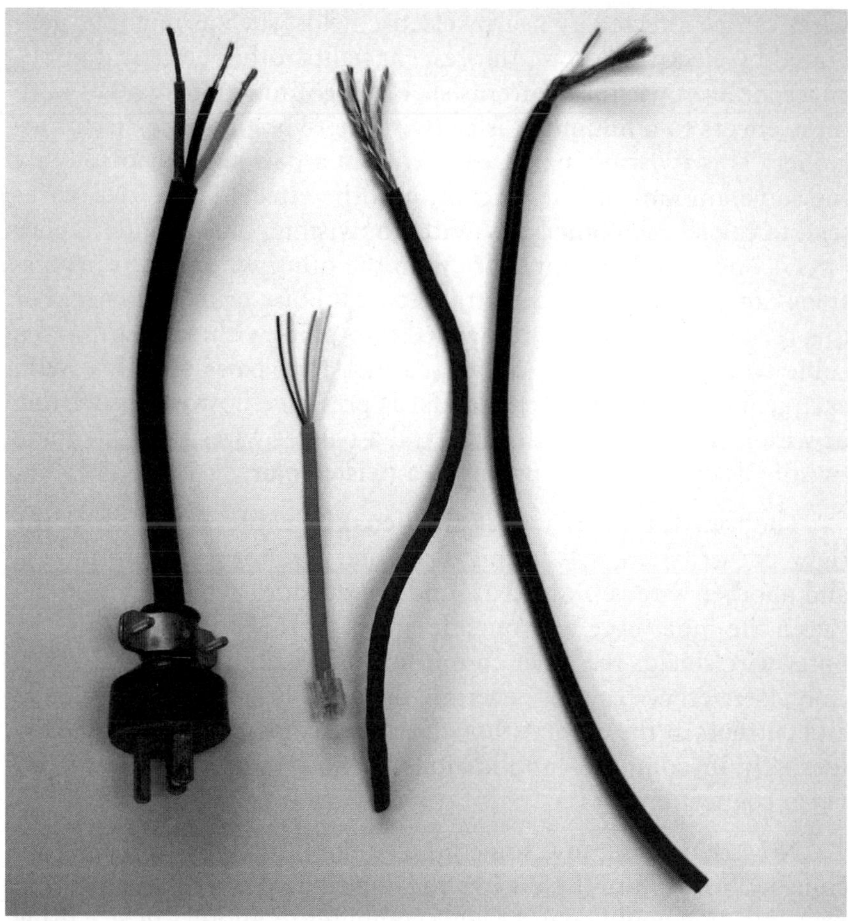

Figure 8.1
Four basic types of wires.

next to each other in the same configuration throughout the length of the cable. For convenience in identifying each metallic wire, the insulation for each wire has a different color. In using this wire, circuits often utilize pairs of wires, typically red and green for one circuit and black and yellow (sometimes blue and white) for the second circuit. Because these wires run next to each other, these circuits are said to utilize **untwisted pairs** of wires.

The right middle cable in Figure 8.1 contains four pairs of wires, and the metallic wires in each pair are twisted together. This aspect of their design has a specific purpose. Transmission of signals along wires can be affected by nearby electric fields, such as might be generated by electric motors, fluorescent lights, other electrical appliances, or even weather patterns such as lightning. One way to keep these effects to a minimum is to twist the two wires of a circuit together. This twisting makes each wire in a pair subject to roughly the same amount of interference, and the effects in the two wires tend to cancel each other out. With no twisting, outside interference affects one wire in a pair more than the other wire, and transmissions can experience much extra electrical noise or interference. For this reason, wires often are twisted into pairs within cables, and a cable with eight wires is organized into four pairs of wires (with each pair twisted together). Standards prescribe how much twisting of wire is needed to be effective, and a pair of wires with adequate twisting is called, not surprisingly, a **twisted pair**.

The fourth type of wire, called **coaxial cable**, is shown at the right side of Figure 8.1. In this form, one wire forms a central core, and another wire is braided around the outside, with insulation between the inner core and outside braid. In this configuration, the outer wire shields the inner core from electrical interference; electrically, interference cannot penetrate the outer braid to affect voltages and currents at the core. Although coaxial cable used to be used extensively in computer applications, it now is used primarily for video connections.

Now that you know something of the basic types of cable, we consider how to use these wires to connect computer equipment. In principle, you could connect your computer to another device using any wires and any plugs at their ends. However, there is great practical advantage in utilizing a standard plug, sometimes called a **connector**. A standard plug, for example, could be used for many different computers, telephones, and other devices, simplifying the need for extensive inventories of different plugs. Also, when a standard plug is used widely, manufacturers can take advantage of economies of mass production to produce the plugs reasonably cheaply. Cheap plugs that work well for a variety of our needs make us, the consumers, happy . . . and also safe; if a connector must meet specific standards before it's sold, then we can feel reasonably confident that the wiring is done correctly and that the insulation will work properly.

With the need for standardization, the Federal Communications Commission of the United States maintains a registry of standard jacks and how they are to be wired. Connectors and wires specified in this registry are called **registered jacks**. If you use headphones for your radio or CD player, those headphones likely come with a jack that you can plug into your audio equipment. A standard jack for telephones and computers serves a similar role for those devices.

For telephones and computers, the simplest of these jacks is the **Registered Jack 11 (RJ-11)**. A view of the front and back of several versions of this jack is shown in Figures 8.2a and 8.2b.

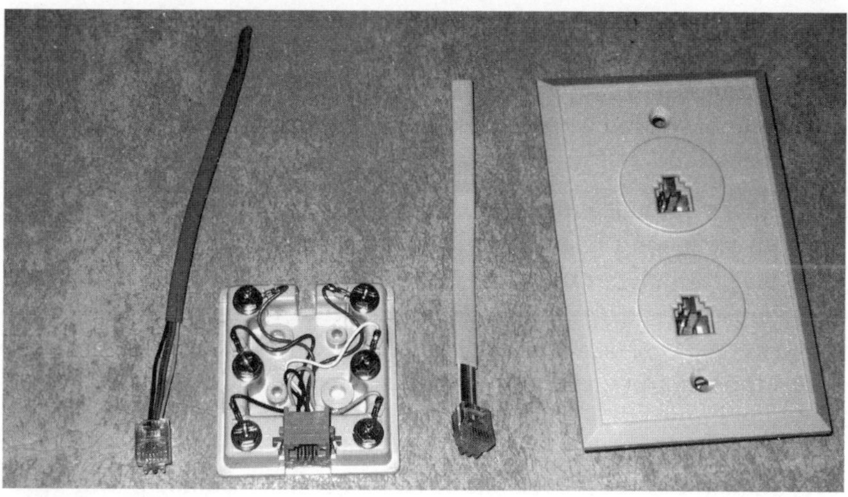

Figure 8.2a
RJ-11 jacks and sockets: front view.

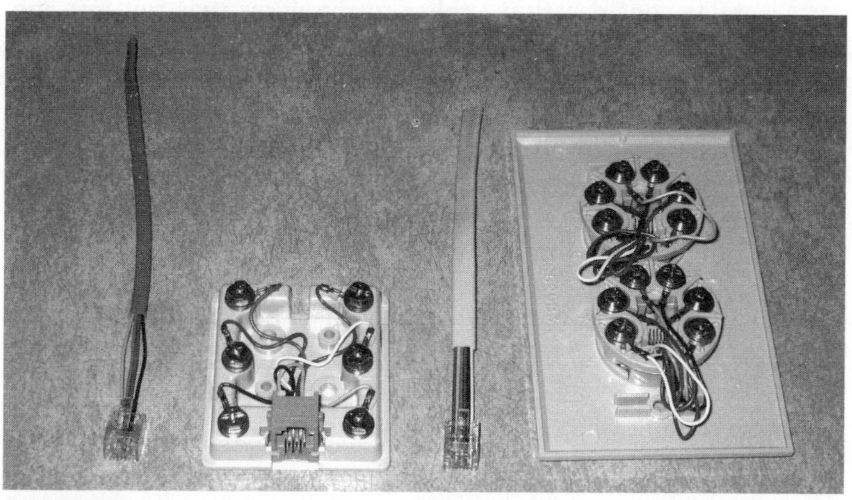

Figure 8.2b
RJ-11 jacks and sockets: rear view.

As shown in Figures 8.2a and 8.2b, a standard RJ-11 jack or socket may have six different wires, although many telephone cables contain only four wires. Historically, these wires were straight or untwisted, although modern cables may be either untwisted or twisted.

Although telephone wiring usually has four or six wires, only the middle two (the red and green wires) are usually used for basic telephone or computer connections. A four-wire version includes white and blue wires (or sometimes black and yellow wires), often used in telephone operations for multiple telephones, for signaling, or as spare wires. The six-wire version contains red, green, white, blue, black, and yellow wires.

So, why include extra wires if they don't do anything? The answer involves long-term flexibility and maintenance. Consider, for example, the telephone wires for my house. (You could check if your house or apartment is similar.) Because I am a residential customer who pays for a single telephone line, I need only one pair of wires (the red and green pair). However, in the future, the telephone company knows that I might want a second line or other special services. Because installing new wires is time consuming, labor intensive, and expensive, the telephone company has installed a four-wire cable to my house, and it maintains a connection box on the side of my house with connections for all four wires. Only two wires are used now, but the telephone company can provide additional services whenever I request them.

A similar consideration applies to the wires that run into my house from the telephone company's connection box. The wires themselves are small and inexpensive, but installing wires through the walls takes considerable time and effort. Because labor, not wire, is the primary cost of installation, most telephone wiring within a home involves four-wire cable. I may use only two wires for my basic service, but the others are available if I want more service. Also, as a backup, if I want just two wires but either the red or green wire breaks somewhere in a wall, having another wire in place allows an easy substitution. Altogether, the additional cost in going from two small telephone wires to four or six wires is low, but the cost of installing new lines is high. The use of the larger-than-needed cable allows long-term flexibility and aids maintenance at a low cost.

Returning to the RJ-11 jacks and sockets, note that the RJ-11 standard specifies which color wires are connected to which parts of a jack or socket, so that all wiring of such connectors is the same everywhere. Figures 8.2a and 8.2b show this ordering of wires for both the four- and six-wire variations. Notice, in particular, that the six-wire version includes the same connections as the four-wire version, with two more wires added.

As already noted, computer-to-computer connections using RJ-11 jacks and sockets normally utilize only the middle two (red and green) wires. The other wires are unnecessary—although reliance on the RJ-11 jack allows commonly available wire to be used in computer connections. When used, these wires can form a direct connection from one computer to another, which is called **point-to-point communication**. RJ-11 wiring, jacks, and sockets constitute one common mechanism for establishing this connection.

These wires make connecting computers an easy enough task, but the resulting communication is relatively slow; only one signal at a time can be sent along the wires. Transmission of a byte of data, for example, would require eight signals, and these would have to be sent one after the other on RJ-11 wiring. Such sequential transmission of data is called **serial communication**. In serial communication, one wire of the twisted pair is used to send a signal, and the other wire (sometimes called a ground) functions to complete the circuit. In order to send multiple signals at the same time, more than two wires would be used. In order to keep electrical interference to a minimum, a cable with eight wires (four twisted pairs) might be used to send four signals concurrently. By organizing the wires into twisted pairs, electrical interference for each pair is kept low. Such sending of several signals at once is called **parallel communication**.

This ability to send multiple signals simultaneously can greatly facilitate communication by increasing speed. Although different configurations of wire could be used to accomplish parallel communication, a particularly common choice uses eight wires, and is called **RJ-45** by the Federal Communications Commission. RJ-45 wiring, jacks, and sockets are shown in Figure 8.3; this type of connector also is commonly called an **Ethernet jack** and socket.

In comparing Figures 8.2 and 8.3, observe that the two jacks and sockets look similar; however, the RJ-45 jack has two more wires and is somewhat wider than the RJ-11. For comparison, Figure 8.4 shows the back of an Apple Macintosh PowerBook G4 laptop computer that contains both RJ-11 and RJ-45 sockets; the RJ-45 socket near the left is wider than the RJ-11 socket on the right.

Figure 8.3
An RJ-45 jack and socket.

Because the sockets have a similar appearance, it is not uncommon for computer users to confuse these two types of plugs and sockets when trying to connect their machines. Although the RJ-45 jack is too wide to fit into a typical RJ-11 socket, the RJ-11 jack often will fit into an RJ-45 socket. However, because the wiring standards are quite different for the two standard jacks, plugging the RJ-11 jack into the wrong socket could cause electrical damage to sensitive components.

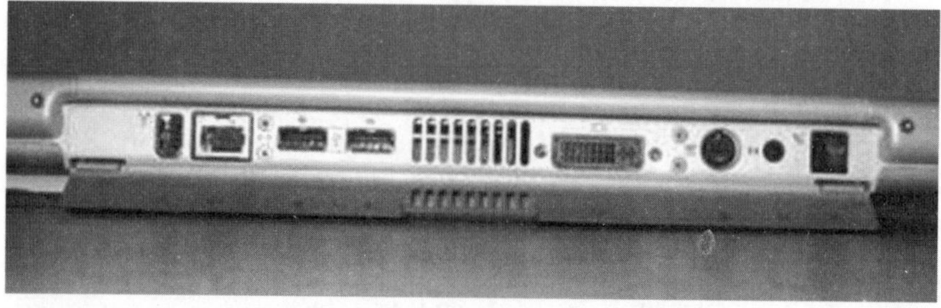

Figure 8.4
Sockets on the back of an Apple Macintosh PowerBook G4 laptop computer.

Check the jacks and sockets (for example, count the wires) before plugging cables into your machines!

Could you expand on the use of the eight RJ-45 wires?

The amount of data that can be sent reliably over a cable in a given amount of time (such as a second) depends upon what wires are used, how connections are made, what controls might be present to minimize interference, and what standards are involved in transmitting and receiving signals. Over the years, technology has evolved regarding the capabilities that are possible for cables with RJ-45 jacks and sockets.

As already noted, the wire for use with RJ-45 jacks and sockets contains four pairs of wires. Standards for connecting this wire to jacks and sockets were first defined in 1991, but then expanded and refined in 1995. Standard wiring using the RJ-45 jacks and sockets is said to be of type **Category 5**, or **Cat 5**. For reference, *Category 1* refers to the standard for simple telephones prior to 1983 that involved two pairs of wires, or four wires total.

How the eight wires connected to an RJ-45 jack are used has evolved considerably over the years, and three signaling standards now apply to the same Category 5 wires and cables: 10BaseT, 100BaseT, and 1000BaseT. The earliest and slowest of these standards was adopted in 1990 and is called **10BaseT**. Unraveling this name somewhat,

- *10* designates that 10,000 bits of information can be communicated per second.
- *Base* refers to a type of signaling called baseband signaling.
- *T* refers to the use of twisted pairs.

Although 10BaseT involves RJ-45 jacks and the eight wires of Category 5 cable, in fact only four of the wires (two pairs) are used for communication. One pair is used to transmit data, and the second pair to receive data. (With only two of the four pairs of wires needed for computer communication, some applications use the third pair for voice communications and the fourth pair for supplying electrical power.)

The next major step in communication speeds over these cables came in 1995 with the standard for **100BaseT**. This approach still uses just two of the four pairs of wires, but provides a mechanism for transmitting 100,000 bits of information per second. The next standard using RJ-45 cable for high-speed communication was ratified in 1999. This standard is called **1000BaseT** or **802.3ab** (following the standards' group at the Institute of Electrical and Electronics Engineers [IEEE]) and utilizes all four pairs of wires to communicate at the rate of 1 million bits per second. The newest standard, called **10GBaseT** or **802.3ae**, was adopted on June 17, 2002, and runs at 10 million bits per second, although it can transmit only over short distances using an enhanced RJ-45 cable; this most recent standard assumes that most communication at such high speeds will utilize more sophisticated cables and communication processes than are possible with RJ-45.

Although RJ-45 cable, jacks, and sockets describe essential elements of the wires and connectors, the wires can be connected to the jacks in several ways; this gives rise to a few different versions of RJ-45 cables. In many modern applications, RJ-45 cables connect a computer to a special device, such as a modem or hub, and wires at both ends of the cable connect in identical ways to the jacks; that is, pin 1 of the jack at one end of the cable is connected to pin 1 of the jack at the other end, pin 2 of each jack is connected, and so on. This is called a **straight-through cable**, and such a cable is used most often in connecting computers to networks.

When connecting two computers directly with a cable (point-to-point connection), however, a slightly different approach is needed. In particular, we noted that 10BaseT and 100BaseT standards involve one pair of wires for sending data and another for receiving data. Of course, when two computers communicate, the sending wires for one machine must correspond to the receiving wires for the other, and this requires connections for some jack pins to be reversed. When RJ-45 cables are connected to their jacks by reversing the wire connections at one end, the resulting cable-jack combination is called a **crossed cable**.

For the most part, if your connections involve RJ-45 jacks, you should use a crossed cable when connecting two computers directly, but you need a straight-through cable for most other connections between your computer and a network.

Are point-to-point connections used for networks or only for connecting two computers?

Although point-to-point connections are efficient for tying two computers together, this approach does not scale up well. For example, using this approach to tie 1 computer with 9 others would require 9 cables, but connecting all 10 computers to each other would require 45 wires. (*Computational aside:* To connect each of 10 computers to another, a cable could start at any of the 10 machines and end at any of the 9 remaining machines. This initially suggests 90 cables. Each jack, however, serves as both a start and an end, so only 45 cables would be required. Though smaller than 90, 45 cables are still far too many to make this an efficient way to connect computers.) Using point-to-point communication to join many computers to each other would require a very large number of cables. The size of cable jacks is also a practical issue that makes this technique less appealing. Further, as the number of computers increases, the bulk of the cables could become a problem. Clearly, point-to-point connections are not the best-suited connections for linking a large number of machines, and, therefore, they are not the most common form of network connections.

How are computer networks usually connected?

Rather than using point-to-point connections, computer and communication networks typically employ one of three approaches: star networks, Ethernet networks, or token-ring networks. Basic configurations for these networks are shown in Figure 8.5.

Star Networks: In a **star network**, each computer is connected to a central machine, and all therefore communications go through the center. With 10 computers plus the central machine, 10 cables would be needed. Also, regardless of how many computers were

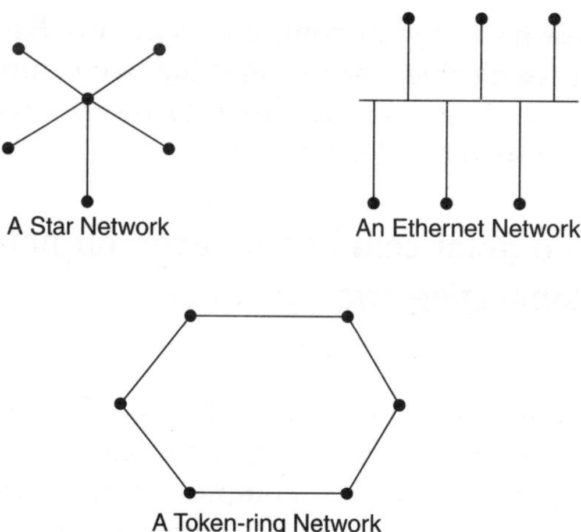

Figure 8.5
Star, Ethernet, and token-ring networks.

currently in a network, the addition of a new machine would always require just one more cable—from the new machine to the central one. Of course, this approach might involve some congestion of wires near the central computer, but wiring near the other computers could be reasonably simple.

The star network is often the approach used for telephone systems in small businesses or schools. The central machine in the telephone system is an electronic switch, and all telephones in the business or school have connections to that switch. In using this network, some communications go directly from the central switch to a local telephone. For example, were you to pick up the headset of your classroom's telephone, you would establish communication with the central machine, and you would hear a dial tone. The dial tone is the signal from the central machine, letting you know that your telephone is connected to the network and the system is prepared for you to dial. When you dial a number from your telephone, however, you're usually trying to establish communication with another telephone—not the central switch. Back in the early days of telephones, an operator would serve as the central machine: You would connect to the operator, the operator would ask you with whom you'd like to speak, and the operator would make the connection for you. Times have antiquated these personal connections, but the same basic principle applies as your information is transferred through the central machine to the person you're calling. Assuming for the moment that your desired number designates another telephone at your school, the central switch has the responsibility to pass information from your telephone to the one you have dialed and also to pass information back. In modern telephone systems, a central switch may make a temporary circuit between your telephone and the one called, and communications then utilize that circuit. Another approach would be for the central machine to receive a communication from one telephone, store that information centrally for a moment, and then forward it along to the desired receiver. Although this store-and-forward approach is not so common within local telephone switches, variations of this idea are used in various computer networks.

Star networks can work well (particularly for telephones) if the number of telephones or computers is reasonably small, as in a business, school, or small town. To serve more telephones or computers, a network could expand by allowing communication between central switches, as shown in Figure 8.6.

In a confederation of star networks, local communication still involves just a local switch or machine—talking on your dorm room phone with your neighbor down the hall would use only your school's small network. However, communication between tele-

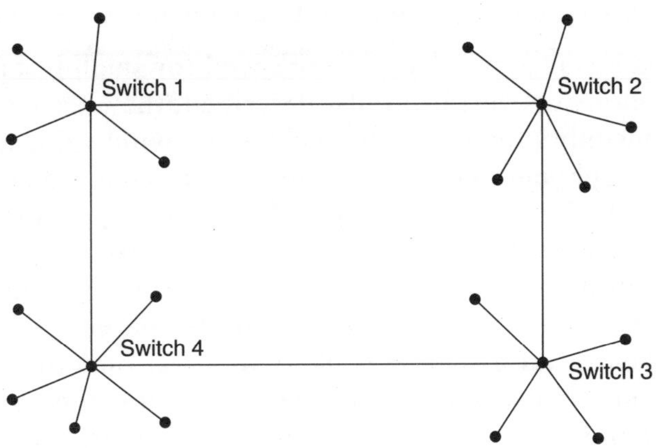

Figure 8.6
Four local star networks, connected in a network.

phones or computers attached to different centralized machines becomes a several-step process. In particular, when you make a long-distance call, you use your local telephone to send information to your local switch. That switch then uses its outside connections to send your information from switch to switch until it gets to the switch of the person you are contacting. That switch then uses the local connections to forward your information to the final party. So, when you call home from school on Mother's Day, your telephone wires carry your information through your school's central computer to the network in your hometown.

Suppose for the moment that your telephone is attached to switch 1 in Figure 8.6, and your best friend has a telephone attached to switch 3. When you dial your friend's telephone number, you send the number to switch 1. That switch realizes that the number does not correspond to a telephone attached to the same switch, but information must get to switch 3 instead to complete the connection. Modern telephone switching networks may use rather sophisticated techniques to handle your telephone call, but at a conceptual level, information will have to be sent through either switch 2 or switch 4. As you are talking, your voice information will go from your telephone to switch 1, be forwarded on to switch 2 or 4, and onward again to switch 3, where it can be sent to your friend's telephone. A similar process in reverse is followed as your friend speaks to you in response. Thus, even when you call someone who is not within your local network, your voice and the voice of your friend will travel through telephone wires from central machine to central machine, making it possible for you to communicate.

Although star networks can work well for small installations, as in the phone conversation just described, they place considerable responsibility on a central machine or switch. Star networks for either telephones or computers rely on the central machine for all activity. This allows relatively easy monitoring of communications and maintenance of equipment, because much work is centralized. This approach also has some advantages regarding reliability, in that the malfunctioning of any telephone or computer (outside the central machine) is likely to affect only that one machine. Further, if a wire is cut between a distant computer and the central machine, again, only the one local telephone or computer is affected. On the other hand, a malfunction by the central machine will likely affect communications for the entire network. The capabilities of that central machine also limit both communication speeds and the number of separate computers allowed. At a conceptual level, each machine requires its own wire to the central machine. In practice, some technology (called **multiplexers** and **concentrators**, in case you care) may allow several circuits to share the same physical wire, although such technology can help only to a point.

Ethernet Networks: Rather than rely on a central machine with a separate wire for each computer, an Ethernet network is based on the use of a single wire (or bus) running to all machines; that is, the same cabling system is used for all computers in a local network. This single-cable approach has several nice characteristics. Conceptually, the same wire or cable is shared by all machines, so separate wiring is not needed between each machine and a central point. Any computer can send information directly to any other computer without an intermediary, so communication is not limited by the capabilities of an intermediary.

Hubs Connect Local Computers to Form Small Networks

Although Ethernet systems generally rely on a cable rather than separate wires to connect computers, in practice, groups of machines may be individually attached to a single hub to maintain needed electrical properties. These hubs in turn would be connected to each other by cables, just like star networks are linked to make long distance phone calls possible. Ethernet networks normally use RJ-45, Cat 5 cables; and communication standards follow 10BaseT, 100BaseT, or 1000BaseT, depending on electrical interference and computer capabilities. In order to maintain appropriate electrical connectivity, computers on an Ethernet network plug into a local hub, making small sections of the network into a star network. Use of the hub, or central machine, also simplifies the difficulties of appropriately connecting the pairs of wires related to sending and receiving signals. Straight-through cables go from each local computer to a hub, and the internal circuitry of the hub does the actual connecting of machines. Hubs also can contain circuitry to check for transmission errors, allowing corrections to be made quickly when necessary. This enhances overall transmission speed and reliability.

Although hubs can form a star network in small areas, hubs also can be connected to yield large networks. Such connection of hubs is called **uplinking**. As with direct communication between computers, the connection of hubs requires that sending and receiving signals are sent on appropriate pairs of wires. Hubs may handle this administration internally and thus be connected by straight-through cables. Alternatively, hubs without this type of internal circuitry normally require crossed RJ-45 cables for connections to other hubs.

As with any venture that relies upon sharing, Ethernet networks require attention to several details in order to make communication reliable. First, because all computers in an Ethernet network are attached to the same cable, any communication from one computer will be received by all others. Information typically is supposed to go from one machine to a designated second machine, so the use of the common medium requires that all communications contain a header, indicating the intended recipient. With this header, all computers will receive a message, but then will look at the header. If the information is intended for them, they keep the full message; otherwise, they discard the information as they receive it. Thus, while all computers actually receive all communications, only the intended computer normally saves material intended for itself.

Second, Ethernet networks require special rules or protocols so that one computer does not interfere with communications by another. For example, when one computer wishes to send a message to another, it first listens to the cable to determine whether another machine is already sending a message. If so, the first machine waits some time before trying again. This rule suggests that once computers start sending a message along the common wire, others will not interrupt or interfere. Even with this rule of noninterference, however, it still could happen that two machines might want to send messages at the same time. They both could listen to the cable, determine the wire was free, and then start broadcasting their messages. Of course, this would mean that each transmission would be jumbled by the other. To handle this circumstance, Ethernet protocols require each computer to listen to the network as it transmits its messages—not just before the transmission starts. As it listens to transmissions on the network, a computer should receive the same message that it sends on the cable. If the message received is different, then another computer started sending at the same time. When two computers simultaneously send messages, each transmitting computer is required to stop transmitting, wait a random amount of time, and start the process again. The stopping clears the cable for later communications. Then, because the two computers wait random amounts of time before trying again, the time one chooses to try again will differ from the time the other tries to start. This should allow both to take their turns with minimal conflict.

Yet another concern regarding sharing could arise if one computer tried to dominate the cable—sending a steady stream of information without allowing others a turn for their work. To resolve this problem, Ethernet rules specify a maximum length for any message. If a computer wishes to communicate more information than is possible within this maximum, then the data are divided into multiple messages, and each is sent separately. With this rule in place, other computers will have the chance to send their materials during the gaps between the parts of any long message.

Altogether, an Ethernet network allows reliable communications at reasonably high speeds (now up to 1 and sometimes 10 gigabytes per second) at a reasonable cost. In order to function successfully, however, it does require that the communications of one computer do not interfere unduly with those of another. In practice, this means that individual messages must be relatively short, and that the network cannot become too busy. For example, if the network is busy more than 50% or 60% of the time, then interference among computers becomes problematic and communication can become bogged down. In addition, although it may support many machines, a simple Ethernet network maintains a single connection that runs from one computer or hub to the next. Thus, a single break in a cable or malfunction at one connection point will divide the network into two parts, isolating one piece from the other.

Token-Ring Network: Rather than connect all computers to a single cable or bus, a **token-ring network** organizes computers logically into a circle or ring; that is, each computer logically maintains two connections, one to the computer before and one to the computer after it in the circle. Communication also progresses in a single direction around the circle, so each computer receives messages from one side and sends messages to the other side.

For example, if we were to label computers consecutively along the circle as A, B, C, and so on, then computer A would send messages to B, B would send to C, C would send to D, and so on. However, B would never send directly to A, and C would never send to B.

Following this system, if A wanted to send a message to computer D, then A would send the data to B, B would forward it to C, and C would finally deliver it to D. To coordinate this transmission, and to know where messages were intended to go, each message has both a sender and an addressee designator. Thus, in sending a message from A to D, A would deliver the material to B—indicating it was to go to D and it was from A. B would read the header, realize the message was not intended for it, and thus forward the message on to C. Similarly, C would forward the information to D. D, however, would learn from the header that the message was intended for itself, and save the message for later processing. Also, to confirm that the information was received appropriately, D would then initiate an acknowledgement to A, forwarding this further around the circle (to E, F, and so on.) until the message got back to A. This circular process delivers messages systematically and provides confirmation of receipt. If the same message went fully around the circle and returned to A, then A would know that D somehow was no longer on the circle and the message had not been delivered.

To organize the sending and receiving of data, a token-ring network allows only one computer to send information at any given time. To do this, one computer is designated as the authorized computer. This designated computer is said to have a **token**, indicating this authority. When a computer has the token, it examines its pending work. If it has a message to send, then the computer sends this information on along the circle. If the authorized computer has nothing to send, then the computer passes the token to the next machine along the circle; this newly authorized computer checks its own pending work, sends messages, and then sends the token to the next computer, passing the authority forward.

In token-ring networks, the actual connection of computers to the network involves cables to a hub, and the hubs can be connected to expand the network. The use of cables and hubs can add error checking and increase speeds, just as with Ethernet. Also, a ring has the special property that it can be cut once and still work; the computers communicate by sending messages in the other direction. Thus, in sending a message from one computer to the next, record can be kept concerning whether the message was received. If not, then a computer might infer that the connection along the circle is broken. Instead of forwarding messages in the usual way, the computer could start passing messages back the other way along the circle. Messages then would move from machine to machine clockwise for awhile, then reach the cut, and be rerouted counterclockwise until all computers were appropriately contacted.

With only one computer having authorization at a time, concurrent transmission difficulties that can be found in an Ethernet do not arise; there is less potential for one computer to dominate the broadcasting of all messages. This allows token-ring messages to be somewhat longer than those in Ethernet, if additional length is needed.

Historically, both Ethernet and token-ring networks have had strong advocates, and both types of networks have been used extensively. When under development, both types of networks had strong positive characteristics, and both could achieve good speeds for the transmission of information. In recent years, however, advances in technology have increased communication speeds for Ethernet networks, so that they surpass the token-ring configuration, and Ethernet networks have come to dominate other wire-based forms. What type of network configuration does your school or business use? If it is indeed an Ethernet connection, you can see first hand how thousands of people can communicate via computer using one Ethernet network.

Can star networks or Ethernet networks connect an arbitrarily large number of computers?

Star networks rely on a single, central machine for communication, and Ethernet networks depend logically upon a single cable for communication. Limitations arise whenever technology depends on a single device or medium. Also, wires are subject to electrical noise and power loss, and such matters become more significant as the length of a wire increases. Expansion of networks must take these factors into account. Here are some ways this is done.

We have already noted that each computer in a star network places some demands on a central machine. Thus, as the number of computers in a network increases, the demand placed on the central machines increases. Eventually, the demands made on the central machine will slow overall processing down. The central machine can do only a certain amount of work, and performance suffers as that level of activity is approached and exceeded.

Furthermore, demands from separate computers rarely are evenly distributed. For example, in a business office, users likely place relatively heavy demands on computers during the day, but require little service from networks at night. Also, during the day, computer activity would likely be low during breaks or meetings, but much higher when employees are working at their desks. Moreover, some computing activity requires rather little message communication, whereas other work generates considerable traffic. For example, word processing largely depends on people typing and reading, so computers perform little extensive processing, and communication is limited to the sending and receiving of small text files. On the other hand, if people are reading graphical images from the World Wide Web, much data may need to be communicated over a network.

All networks typically experience regular variations in the degree to which they are used, so the people developing network systems can plan for these changes in demand. They create networks that are targeted to work their best when responding to only a fraction of the demands they are capable of handling. If a network has sufficient capacity, then it can handle short periods of high traffic. Otherwise, communication may be slow or even break down during spikes of high demand.

The difficulties regarding demand are compounded in Ethernet networks in which all machines use the same cable. For example, as traffic increases, two machines are more likely to try transmitting at the same time. When this occurs, they each stop, wait some time, and try again. The cable is in use for each unsuccessful attempt as well as for the time used for successful transmission, so when a computer has to send a message repeatedly, some potential capacity is wasted. Experience suggests that if an Ethernet cable is used to more than 50% to 60% of capacity, noticeable delays may arise, and the network may become bogged down.

To keep demand relatively low on networks, many organizations maintain separate, small networks, and then provide connections among those networks. This approach forms the basis for Figure 8.7, and the discussion of that figure illustrates how the approach might apply to star networks.

For Ethernet networks, electrical properties of cables restrict cabling between a computer and a hub to 100 meters (about 328 feet). For greater distances, hubs can be connected together, or devices called **repeaters** can be used to amplify the electrical signals. Within a small physical area, computers can connect to a hub, and then hubs may in turn connect to a more centralized hub, as shown in Figure 8.7.

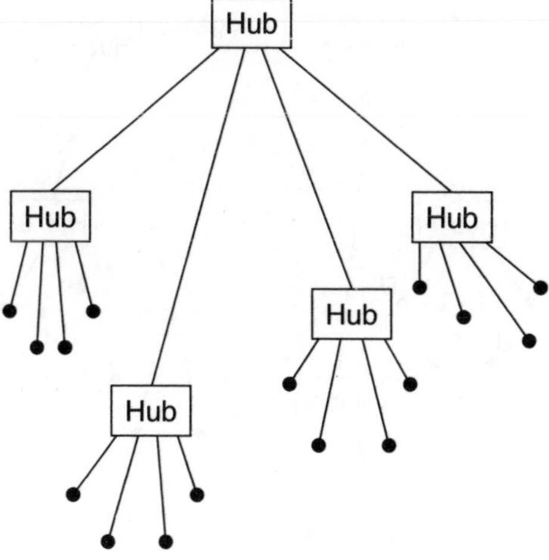

Figure 8.7
A hierarchy of hubs.

The overall structure shown in Figure 8.7 provides a hierarchy of hubs. Each of the computers and hubs is connected by Ethernet cables running 10BaseT, 100BaseT, 1000BaseT, or similar technology.

Although this hierarchical approach provides reasonable connectivity, each computer in the hierarchy receives the same signals, so each must share the same logical connections and cabling. The configuration that they form is called a **segment**, and each segment faces the constraints regarding capacities.

To address difficulties regarding capacities, a different approach may be employed, as illustrated in Figure 8.8, which shows two separate segments, one on the left and one on the right. Each segment has two hubs connected to local computers, and each of these hubs is connected to a more centralized hub. Within a segment, all hubs and workstations share the same logical cabling, and all hear the same communications. Thus, the mechanism is the same for computer A to send a message to computer B or to computer H. Computer A listens to its cable, and when the cable is free from other activity it broadcasts its message. That material is relayed by hubs 1, 2, and 3 to computers A, B, C, D, E, F, G, and H. Of course, if the bridge were a hub instead, then the same message would be sent to all other hubs and computers in the figure as well.

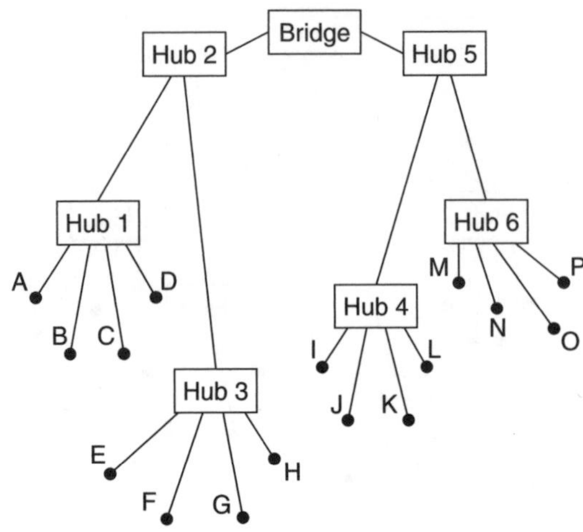

Figure 8.8
Two segments connected with a bridge.

The role of a **bridge**, however, is to keep track of the machines on one (or both) sides. When it receives the material from A intended for B or H, the bridge notes that all machines are on one side of the configuration. There is no need for material to be sent outside that left segment, so the bridge does not forward A's material to hub 5 for relay onward. In contrast, if A initiated a message to K, then the bridge would receive the message, realize that A was on one side but K was on the other, and the bridge would forward the message for delivery on the other side of the configuration. A bridge forwards messages when information must go from a sender on one side to a receiver on the other. A bridge does not forward messages when both sender and receiver are on the same side.

In effect, bridges allow local traffic on a segment or collection of segments to stay localized and not interfere with communications elsewhere. With such technology, communications for a department may stay within a department, or messages within a college or university may be contained within that school. A bridge also can serve as a protection from a malfunctioning machine that fills an Ethernet cable or network with messages. Although heavy traffic could cause local trouble on a segment, the bridge would prevent the messages from interfering with communications over other parts of a network.

In summary, large star networks and large Ethernet networks are made from connecting small networks. In star networks, connections run between central machines to form larger networks. In Ethernet networks, individual machines may be connected to hubs in a hierarchical structure to form segments, and segments are joined by bridges. Bridges allow segments to function separately and independently when only local communications are needed, but bridges provide connections among segments when broader communications are needed.

How does wireless technology work?

When you hear the term **wireless technology**, your first thoughts might involve your experiences with telephones. Not many years ago, wires connected all telephones to a central hub or switch. With the development of cordless telephones, a base station maintained the same wired connection to the central hub, but the base station communicated with your portable cordless handset using radio waves. When using cordless phones, you can move around the house, but your conversations are channeled through the same base station attached to your telephone connection in your home. More recently, you can use a cell phone that broadcasts your conversation to a radio tower in your area, but you are no longer required to be in range of that specific radio tower. Rather, when you move to a new area, your cell phone communicates with one nearby tower for awhile, but then may switch its broadcasts to another tower that may be closer.

This evolution of telephone communications has parallels with the development of wireless technology for computers. Because wireless communications extend Ethernet networks, just as cordless phones and cell phones extend wired telephones, the starting point is a wire-based Ethernet network. In Ethernet networks:

- Messages are divided into relatively short pieces or packets.
- Each packet contains a header that includes such information as the identification of which machine sent the message and which computer the message is intended for.
- Computers are attached logically to a single Ethernet cable.

- Only one computer at a time can transmit its message along the cable.
- All machines on the network receive every message.
- Each machine reads a packet header to determine the intended recipient, and the message is saved by only the designated computer(s).
- In order to enforce the sending of only one message at a time, machines check that the cable is not already in use before starting a transmission. Also, if two computers start transmitting at the same time, they both listen while transmitting to detect this condition, and then they cease their work for a random amount of time before trying again.

These ideas carry over to wireless communications, as well as with infrared signals or radio waves replacing the Ethernet cable. In a wireless setting, communication involves breaking messages into packets and utilizing headers to identify which machine is to receive the data. Further, because communication involves infrared signals or radio waves, all wireless computers in an area share the airwaves, receive the same messages, and determine if they are the intended recipient of each message. Also, two computers could start transmitting messages at the same time, thereby interfering with each other.

However, for wireless communications, the lack of a designated cable adds several complications:

- Frequencies used for computer radio transmission must be controlled so that computers can communicate with each other without interfering with other electrical devices, such as television sets, radios, or garage-door openers.
- Several wireless systems may be active in one location, just as one room might contain cables for several Ethernet cables for different networks.
- Electrical interference in an area may limit the speed at which data can be transmitted reliably.
- The transmission of radio waves can overwhelm a local receiver, so it may be difficult for a machine to determine whether another computer starts broadcasting a message concurrently with the first.

- Wireless computers, such as laptops, can move from place to place, and changes in location can affect whether they can receive transmissions.
- Because radio signals can be received by any listening device in an area, some care may be appropriate to prevent sensitive data from being received and used by unauthorized computers.
- If a portable computer uses wireless technology to establish a connection to the Internet through a stationary machine, then the Internet connection may need to be transferred to another stationary machine as the portable computer moves.

Let's consider some typical scenarios in a common wireless environment, consisting of two stationary computers (S1 and S2) connected to the Internet, and two portable laptop computers (L1 and L2). This configuration is shown in Figure 8.9.

In this configuration, both S1 and S2, the stationary computers, have wireless transmitters, and the range of transmission is given by the striped regions. Both can transmit to the region in the middle where the stripes overlap. Thus, laptop L1 can receive transmissions from S1, but not S2; laptop L2 can receive transmissions from both S1 and S2.

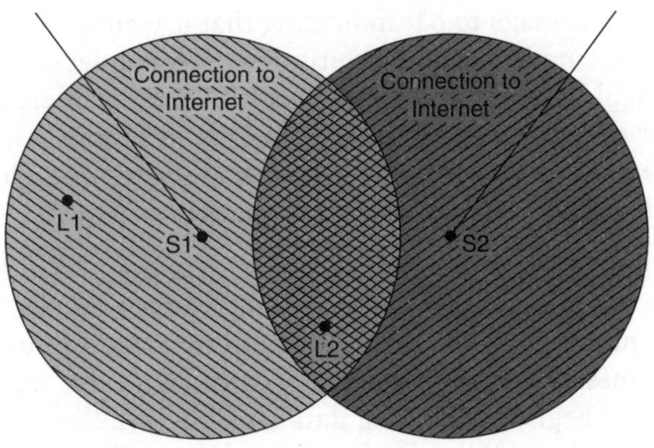

Figure 8.9
A wireless network with two portable and two stationary computers.

Because both S1 and S2 are connected to the Internet, these machines are called **access points.** (We will consider wireless networks without access points later in the chapter.)

Let's suppose that we have just switched on both S1 and S2; L1 and L2 remain off. During initialization, both S1 and S2 announce their presence to the nearby world by generating signals on the 2.4 GHz radio frequency band. Each signal is short, giving the identification number and other characteristics of these access points. These signals are repeated at frequent, but random, intervals, and this repeating of identifying information is called a *beacon.* By repeating the signals frequently, other computers in the neighborhood can learn of these access points in a timely manner. Although beacons are allowed on several different frequencies, each access point must choose a frequency, and it might happen that two access points could choose the same frequency. (As in Figure 8.9, these machines may be out of radio range of each other, so they may not know whether they choose the same frequency.) However, because beacon signals are short and repeated at random intervals, other computers in the area will be able to hear separate beacons even if their access-point machines happen to choose common frequencies. To summarize so far, when access points are turned on, they start up beacons, so others can know the access points are available for communication.

Now, let's turn on laptop L1. L1 will scan the relevant radio frequencies for beacons and determine that S1 is nearby. L1 then sends an *association* message to S1, indicating that it wants to make a connection and giving its station identity code. A connection also may involve special encryption instructions for security. If encryption is required for the connection, then L1 also would supply that information. (We will consider questions regarding security in Chapter 10, so we'll ignore encryption and security matters for now.)

Following L1's association message, access point S1 responds by authorizing communication and providing various details for subsequent transmissions, such as information regarding frequencies to be used for messages and transmission rates. With this information, L1 and S1 can begin exchanging data over this wireless connection. At this stage, radio waves take the place of the cables in an Ethernet, and material can flow smoothly between these two computers. For example, if the laptop user wants to access a Web page on the Internet, the user types in an appropriate address, L1 sends a request to S1, and S1 forwards the request along onto the Internet. When the Internet responds with data, S1 forwards this along the wireless connection to L1, and that information then can be displayed in the browser. S1 is essentially an intermediary, allowing the laptop to have access to the Internet.

The standards established for wireless communication involve considerable detail—most is beyond the scope of this book. However, a few general ideas may be of interest. First, separate standards are in place for both infrared and radio transmissions, so a specific machine may make use of a few media. Second, within the radio-transmission options, two main methods are used for communication. One (called *Frequency Hopping Spread Spectrum* [FHSS]) sends bursts of data over a narrow range of frequencies. Frequencies are changed in a predetermined pattern to reduce interference and to enhance security. A second option (called *Direct Sequence Spread Spectrum* [DSSS]) sends several bits of data concurrently on different frequencies, using a larger range of radio frequencies than in FHSS. Various standards for DSSS allow for different transmission rates. For example, one technique allows the transmission of 54 megabits per second, whereas another allows only 11 megabits per second to be sent, but provides a mechanism for rates to be slowed from 11 to 5.5, 2, or 1 megabits per second, to adjust for radio interference and to accommodate old equipment.

From a user's perspective, these details may not be of great concern, but you should note that response times may change as you move your computer from one place to another or as conditions around you change. When you are loading a Web page into your browser on one day, conditions might allow relatively fast data transmission, and your page may load quickly. On another day, there may be more radio interference or you may be connecting to a slow access point, in which case a page may take some time to load. This is all covered within the specifications for wireless communication.

Now let's get back to our scenarios from Figure 8.9. Suppose that laptop L2 now is turned on. Just like our L1 laptop did, L2 would listen for beacon transmissions. If it first hears the beacon from S1, it might make a connection. Alternatively, it might listen for all beacons, detect both S1 and S2, and ask the user which connection to make. After selecting an access point, L2 would send an association request and receive a response with authorization and communication information. For now, let's assume that L2 also has connected with S1. In the jargon of wireless communication, we say L1, L2, and S2 have formed an *infrastructure basic service set* (IBSS).

In principle, L1, L2, and S1 might all communicate directly with each other over the wireless network. However, as shown in the figure, L1 and L2 can be out of range of each other even if they are connected to the same stationary computer. Further, if L1 and L2 were just barely out of range and L1 were to move around, its signals might be received by L2 at some times and not at other times. To resolve such potential troubles, the access point in any IBSS relays any data sent by any portable machines in its IBSS. This guarantees that all computers with wireless connections to an access point hear the same information.

The transmission of data follows much the same approach used with an Ethernet connection—with one addition. Because several computers will be sending data over the same media (e.g., radio waves), messages are broken into pieces, and computers wait until they hear no messages from other machines. However, for wireless communications, listening for the lack of another transmission may not be sufficient. For example, in our scenario, L1 and L2 might each have data to transmit, but they may be out of range of each other. If they both started transmitting at the same time, then transmission to S1 could be muddled, but neither would know about the transmission of the other. (Even if they could hear each other in principle, their own transmission could overpower whatever they might try to hear, and they still might not realize that concurrent transmission had occurred.)

To resolve these concurrent-transmission problems, before sending a message, a computer first sends a request to transmit to another machine. The data are not sent until the initiating machine receives a message back to proceed. If no permission is forthcoming, a computer must wait for awhile and then ask again for permission. In this setting, if two requests are sent at the same time but the requests interfere with each other, then each party must wait until new requests are reissued and are transmitted clearly. If one request is received clearly, then it can be acknowledged and that machine can proceed. If L1 and L2 make simultaneous requests that are received, then S1 can respond to just one at a time.

Let's assume now that L1, L2, and S1 have connections to each other. They can all continue operating smoothly in their own IBSS, and S2 will continue on its own—until L1 or L2 moves. In particular, suppose L1 moves toward S2. For awhile it will continue to hear just S1's beacon, but after some time it will hear S2's beacon as well. If the connection with S1 seems effective—that is, if the signal from S1 is strong—L1 may ignore S2 and continue to communicate with S1. However, at some point, S1's signal may become rather weak, and reliability may prompt L1 to interact with S2. In order to switch its stationary computer from S1 to S2, L1 could drop its connection with S1 (with a *dissociation* message), but this would cause a loss of continuity for the user. For example, suppose you were shopping on the Web for books, and you had placed some titles into your shopping cart. You would want that session to continue no matter where you moved with your laptop L1, but switching to S2 with a new association request would break that continuity.

Instead, L1 can send a *re-association* message to S2. This provides the same authentication function as an association request, but it also specifies that current work is being done through access point S1. After S2 replies with appropriate information for a new connection, then S2 can contact S1 about any information pending for L1. For example, information on a new book title might have arrived from the online bookstore while L1 was conversing with S1 and S2. This information can then be relayed to S2. Also, because your initial contact with the bookstore was made through S1, that connection can remain for continuity, and information can be forwarded to S2 as needed.

As you move around with L1, perhaps to a new access point S3, your re-association message to S3 will allow it to retrieve pending information from S2 and then to inform S1 that further data need not go to S2 but rather to S3. Altogether, association requests allow a mobile computer to establish a link to the Internet, while re-association requests allow access points to forward current information to whatever access point might be involved with the current communications.

From a user's perspective, you can move your laptop L1 from one place to another to another without worrying just what access point is nearby. As long as your computer can connect with some access point in the network, then the sequence of re-association requests can allow machines in a network to perform the administration necessary to maintain Internet links you may have established throughout your travels.

If all of the wireless computers in an area are mobile and do not have Internet access, can they still connect?

If you find wireless communication available at a coffee shop or library, there must be an access point in the area; thank the shop owner or librarian for providing that computer and connection! But if no computer in a given area has a cable connection to the Internet, then wireless computers cannot access that technology. An Internet connection requires some point of access.

However, several laptop computers still could communicate with each other—at least if they all have wireless capabilities. A network between wireless computers is called an *ad-hoc network*. In an ad-hoc network, one of the laptops plays the role of an access point (but without the Internet access); that is, a laptop could be set up to establish a beacon for a new and independent network. Other computers then could issue association requests, and communication could proceed. In ad-hoc networks, the initiating machine (with the beacon) does not relay communications from other computers, so all computers must be within transmission range of each other. This simplifies communications, because all messages go directly to all parties, but the range of such transmissions may be limited.

Summary

The simplest way to connect two computers utilizes wires going from one to the other. A simple circuit requires only two wires. Multiple pieces of information can be transmitted by sending one piece at a time, but this serial communication can be slow. To transmit data more quickly, parallel communication sends several pieces of data over parallel wires at the same time.

Although, in principle, many types of wire, plugs, and sockets might be used for cables, standards provide efficient and reliable communication at reasonable cost. The simplest standard wiring cable is called RJ-11, and it uses four or six wires. Often only two of these wires are used for telephone and computer communication, but additional wires within the cable provide flexibility and aid maintenance. Within an RJ-11 cable, the wires may be untwisted, or they may be organized into pairs and the wires in each pair twisted together. Outside electrical interference has relatively little effect on twisted pairs used for circuits.

Cables that connect computers to networks often contain eight wires, organized as four twisted pairs; plugs for these cables are called Ethernet jacks. Wires within these cables may be connected to Ethernet jacks in the same way at both ends (straight-through cable); alternatively, connections of pairs at one end may be reversed (a crossed cable). These cables are called Category 5 or RJ-45 cables, and several protocols prescribe how communications work over these cables and at what speed. From slowest to fastest, these protocols are designated 10BaseT, 100BaseT, 1000BaseT (or 802.3ab), and 10GBaseT (or 802.3ae).

Cables running directly from one computer to another provide simple point-to-point communications, but this use of separate wires for each connection does not scale up well. Instead, a star network uses point-to-point communication to connect each computer in a network to a central hub. An Ethernet network allows several computers to connect to the same cable. A token-ring network arranges the computers into a circle with each computer connected to the ones just before and after it. Several computers in an area may constitute a natural group or segment; and star, Ethernet, or token-ring networks work well for segments. Bridges allow connections among multiple network segments.

Wireless technology utilizes many ideas of Ethernet networks. If some computers are connected directly to the Internet, these form access points. Portable computers use radio waves or infrared signals to communicate with a nearby access point. As portable computers move, they must interact with new access points as signals from previous ones become weak. Standards prescribe how a portable computer becomes associated with one access point or how it re-associates with another access point during travel. If no computers have direct connections to the Internet, portable computers still can interact with each other (but not with the Internet) through an ad-hoc network.

Terminology from This Chapter

access point
category 5 wire (cat 5)
connector
coaxial cable
10BaseT, 100BaseT, 1000BaseT, 10GbaseT
Ethernet jack
Ethernet network
parallel communication
point-to-point communication
registered jack
RJ-11 jacks and sockets
RJ-45 jacks and sockets
serial communication
star network
token-ring network
twisted pair
untwisted pair
wireless technology

Discussion Questions

1. Simulate the workings of an Ethernet network through the following group exercise.

   At the start, each person in the class is assigned two classmates, each of whom is to receive a separate communication. Each overall communication is to be three to five medium-length sentences. To communicate with classmates, each person must speak aloud, giving first the intended recipient's name and then saying up to six words of text. Because communications are several sentences of multiple words, the full text of the communication will have to be divided into several distinct messages. To speak, each person follows these rules:

   - The person waits until no one else is already speaking.
   - When the room is otherwise silent, a person can start a name/text message.
   - If two or more people start speaking at the same time, then the speakers must stop and wait a random amount of time before trying again. (To maintain some level of randomness, each person might be given a list of random numbers initially, with the idea that the person uses the list to determine how long to wait. If a person has to wait a second time, the length of the wait is the second number on the list.)
   - Although everyone hears all messages, a person writes down the text spoken only if the message included her or his name.

The process continues until all communications have been completed, at which point each person is asked to report each message that person received.

Additional Suggestion: If people can see each other during this exercise, there may be a tendency to use motions or other nonverbal hints for folks to determine when they can talk without interfering with others. To counter this tendency, participants might sit in a circle facing outward, so they cannot easily see each other.

2. Consider the popular children's game of tag. In this game, one person is designated at being "it." When that person tags someone else, the tagged person becomes it, so this designation is passed along from one person to another. However, in the game, the quality of being it passes from one person to anyone else; there are no constraints on whom the designated person can tag.

a. How would the game of tag have to be changed in order to simulate a token-ring network, in which the tagged person would correspond to the computer with the token?

b. In the usual game of tag, one person could be "it" very often, but another might avoid this designation by always running quickly away from "it." In a token-ring game of tag, could any person or computer avoid becoming it? Explain briefly why or why not.

c. How might your answer to part b affect how much fun participants have in a token-ring game of tag?

d. To what extent does your answer to part b affect the effectiveness of a token ring for communication among computers?

e. Suppose a computer in a token ring could send the message-passing authority to any computer rather than to its neighbor, using the model of a game of tag rather than the circle model in the usual token-ring network. To what extent might the resulting network work effectively in promoting communication among computers? That is, to what extent could the game of tag be used as a model for message passing in a computer network? Briefly justify your answer.

3. Discussion Question 1 outlined a process in which members of a class could simulate an Ethernet network.

   a. Outline a process in which members of a class could simulate a token-ring network.

   b. Follow your simulation in part a so class members have the experience of applying the relevant rules of token-ring networks.

   c. Assuming you have participated in simulations for both Discussion Questions 1 and 3, compare the effectiveness of the two approaches. Does your experience suggest any advantages or disadvantages to either approach?

4. Ask a manager or director at the computer center at your school or business to describe the various segments, hubs, and bridges in use for computers near you. Some points to consider might be:

   a. How many machines are placed on a single segment?

   b. How are computers organized (e.g., by department, lab, application)?

   c. How many bridges are in use, and how are they organized?

   d. How does your school or business connect to the rest of the Internet?

Exercises

1. Consider the words and phrases in the "Terminology from This Chapter" section.

   a. Organize this terminology under the headings "Network Types," "Hardware to Connect Computers," and "Other Terms."

   b. Provide careful definitions for each word or phrase. In each case, be sure it is clear why the term is in the category that you selected in part a.

   c. While the "Terminology from This Chapter" section identifies the major terms, this chapter also contains definitions of various supporting elements. Find six additional terms introduced in this chapter, and provide careful definitions of each.

2. The chapter outlines a computation indicating that 45 cables would be needed to connect each of 10 computers to each other using point-to-point communications.

   a. Follow a similar approach to determine how many cables would be needed for connecting 100 machines to each other using point-to-point communications.

   b. Use a similar approach to determine the number of cables needed in general for connecting n computers following point-to-point communications.

3. Another difficulty with multiple point-to-point communications for a single computer arises from the number and size of the jacks needed for the task. A single RJ-11 jack measures about 3/8" by 5/16", and each jack must plug into an appropriate socket. Although the socket must have some insulating materials around its outside, let's ignore that for now to keep computations simple.

   a. Focusing just on the size of the RJ-11 jack, how much space would be required for 100 jacks?

   b. The Internet contains millions of computers. Suppose these were connected by point-to-point communications, each with its own jack. How much plug-in space would 1 million jacks require?

   c. How does the space computed in part b compare with the size of a typical modern laptop computer? (You will need to measure a laptop—use your own machine, the laptop of a friend, or a computer available in the school, an office, or a store.)

4. The discussion of star networks indicates that some central machines form temporary connections from one computer to another, so computers can send messages directly through an established circuit. As an alternative, a central machine could receive data from one computer, store that data temporarily, and then forward the data onward to the intended recipient. Consider each of these approaches for communications in the context of bridges from one Ethernet segment to another.

   a. Could a bridge make a direct electrical connection from one segment to another so that messages could go simultaneously over both segments?

b. Could a bridge use a store-and-forward approach to communications between segments?

In each case, explain your answer.

5. The discussion of wireless communications identified seven complications that wireless technology had to address beyond the general approach used for the Ethernet. Discuss how each of these complications is addressed by the details of the wireless standards.

6. In Figure 8.8, the bridge connects two small segments, and it might be reasonable for the bridge to keep record that computers A through H are on the left and computers I through P are on the right. In another context, however, computers A through H might be on one side with the entire Internet on the right. Explain how a bridge could record only the identities of computers A through H on one side and still perform its function.

7. Standards and technologies for wireless communication are designed to support effective communication between access points and mobile stations over a range of electrical conditions.

a. Suppose wireless computers were not allowed to be mobile; that is, they used radio technology for communication, but they were not allowed to move from one place to another. Which, if any, elements of wireless communication might be simplified?

b. Could any elements of wireless communication be simplified if wireless computers were not allowed to access the World Wide Web or other hardwired network?

In each case, briefly justify your answer.

Chapter 9

How do users share computer files?

When was the last time you collaborated with a group to write a paper or lab report? Did one member of your group write the whole thing? Did a few of you sit together in a public computer cluster and write the paper together? Or, did you each take turns working on the same file by sharing it electronically? Sharing files via a network has taken group projects to an entirely new level of efficiency. No longer do you need to run out in the rain, disk in hand, to a friend's dorm so that she can edit your draft of your group paper. Instead, you and she can separately log on to a computer network, you can exchange files, and you're one step closer to a finished paper. But how is this great convenience possible?

In the past, when machines worked in isolation rather than in computer networks, each individual machine kept track of its own files. When a user typed a document on her or his machine, the machine stored an appropriate file on its own local hard drive. Today, most of our computers are connected in networks, and files can be distributed widely. You could, for example, easily write a group paper with a fellow student who's studying abroad in Australia, and it would be almost as simple as if she were in the room next door. Networks allow individuals to access files stored on many machines, and in some cases several people can access the same files concurrently. This type of file sharing is certainly convenient, but the underlying technology is highly complex. In this chapter, we will address basic questions on how files might be accessed and how several users might share data in the same file.

What are file servers and how do they work?

One of the more convenient advances in computer technology over the years has involved the ability to store files on centralized servers. In the early days of workstations, all machines worked individually with their own files, and the computers were not connected in networks. In this environment, users stored their work on their computer's hard drives, disks attached to the computers where the users were working. For portability, they would save their files onto a removable disk, which is sometimes called a floppy disk, because the original products were indeed quite flexible. Thus, if a user moved from one machine to another, she would first save her files from the first machine onto a removable floppy disk, and then she would hand-carry the disk to the second machine. With the walking from computer to computer, this approach to file sharing has come to be called *sneaker net* by some modern pundits.

With the development of computer networks, information now can be transferred quickly and easily from one computer to another, and no one has to leave their desks. These days, files can be stored in a general area that can be accessed by machines throughout a network. In computing terminology, that local computer used for storing many files is often called a **file server**. With this centralized storage of information, users do not have to worry about which machine to use when they want to work on a specific file. In a large lab, all computers may have access to the same file server, so a user who saves her work on the file server can work with the same files she did yesterday—regardless of where she sits or what machine she used yesterday. She may not even be aware of just where the file is stored; she simply identifies the logical name of a file, and the local computer interacts with the network to locate the material. In some cases, the physical location of the file can be changed from one server to another without the user even knowing it has moved.

Let's explore these ideas of file sharing by taking a look at several ways that Karen, Ella, and Steve might work on their group science paper. The three students live in separate dorms but want to make equal contributions to the project, so they decide to enlist the help of their school's network. Note that Karen's computer uses a Microsoft Windows operating system, whereas Steve's uses Linux, and Ella's uses the Macintosh OS X.

As a very simple model for file sharing, Karen, Ella, and Steve could maintain their own separate files for their group paper, and each could e-mail copies periodically to the others. This approach utilizes three separate and independent file servers, one for each system, as illustrated in Figure 9.1. Using this model, Karen begins their group paper and saves it on her computer system as

H:\compsci105\groupwork\finalpaper.doc

When Steve works on his portion of this paper, the full name for his file on his Linux system is

/home/steve/comp-sci/papers/finalpaper.sxw

and Ella's file for her portion of this work on her Macintosh OS X calls this file

/home/ella/cs105/homework/finalpaper.wrf

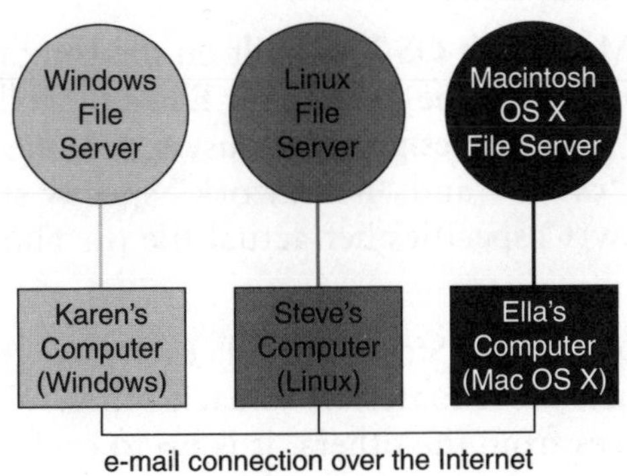

Figure 9.1
Three separate computer and file systems, connected by e-mail.

On Karen's Windows-based system, "H:\" designates a disk that happens to be located across campus and is accessed through a network. A main directory for Karen is maintained on that disk. Within her main directory, Karen maintains a subdirectory called "compsci105" (for the course number); "groupwork" is a subdirectory of "compsci105," and a draft of her part of the final paper in Microsoft Word format is found within "groupwork." In this context, the designation "H:\" indicates a logical location, but not the physical location of the file. By logical, we mean that if the current file server were to be replaced by one or more other machines, the designation "H:\" could still apply. This ability to identify a file location logically and change the actual physical location without changing the name is called **location independence**. The designation "H:\" does indeed suggest a specific location somewhere, but that somewhere can be changed if necessary so that the "H:\" designation always locates the correct files.

On the Linux-based system, "/home" designates the collection of all users, and "/home/steve" is Steve's main directory. Within that framework, "comp-sci" and "papers" represent subdirectories, and "finalpaper.sxw" designates the actual file (in OpenOffice format). Notice that the full Linux name contains no indication of a file's location whatsoever (i.e., it has no parallel to "H:\"). It turns out that materials for "/home/steve" are stored on one of several centralized file servers, but just which one changes from time to time to balance storage demands. In this case, the name does not even hint at the physical location of the file; this level of abstraction is sometimes called **location transparency**.

Because the Macintosh OS X is built on the Unix operating system, a variation of Linux, the naming for Ella's file follows a similar form as Steve's: "/home" designates all users, "/home/ella" is Ella's main directory, "cs105" and "homework" specify subdirectories, and "finalpaper.wrf" specifies her actual file (in ThinkFree Office format).

In this example, Karen, Steve, and Ella each have their own files, but they can e-mail those materials to each other. When each student receives pieces from the others, it is up to each student to incorporate the new pieces into her or his copy of the overall document. Although this simple model involves sharing only through e-mail, we will learn shortly that other, more sophisticated models allow greater levels of sharing.

How do people access and use files on the network?

Technically, access to files on other machines can follow any of three basic approaches:

1. The user may make a copy of the centralized file and make edits on that copy only, so that work on the local copy does not affect the centralized version.
2. A single copy of the file may be maintained on the network, but that copy may move from one place to another, according to where the user is working at the moment.
3. The user may work directly with the centralized copy of the file, so changes made by the user will modify that centralized copy.

In practice, approaches 1 and 3 are in common use, whereas the migration of files from location to location described in approach 2 is not used as frequently. Let's focus on the more popular approaches here.

File Transfer Protocol: A particularly common approach for the sharing of files involves a user requesting a copy of a file from a centralized server. In this form of file sharing, each copy of a file is maintained independently, and no effort is made to coordinate versions. Stripped to its basic elements, the approach requires a user to send a specific request for a file to a relevant server, and the file server responds by sending back a copy of the desired file.

If Karen, Steve, and Ella used this model to share their group project, they would decide on a common format for their paper—perhaps Rich Text Format or (RTF), and they would maintain a single, common file as their standardized copy. Depending upon their school's networking capabilities, this file could be located in one of the students' directories mentioned earlier, or the file might be located on a commonly accessible file server, as shown in Figure 9.2.

Using this model for file sharing, the file server contains the most recent draft of the full paper for the group. Karen, Steve, and Ella can each access this file through the school network. If Ella, for example, wanted to work on the document, she would download a copy of the current full draft from the common file server to her own computer account. She then could add materials and edit other sections, saving the result back within her own account. When she was done, she would upload the revised copy from her account back to the common server.

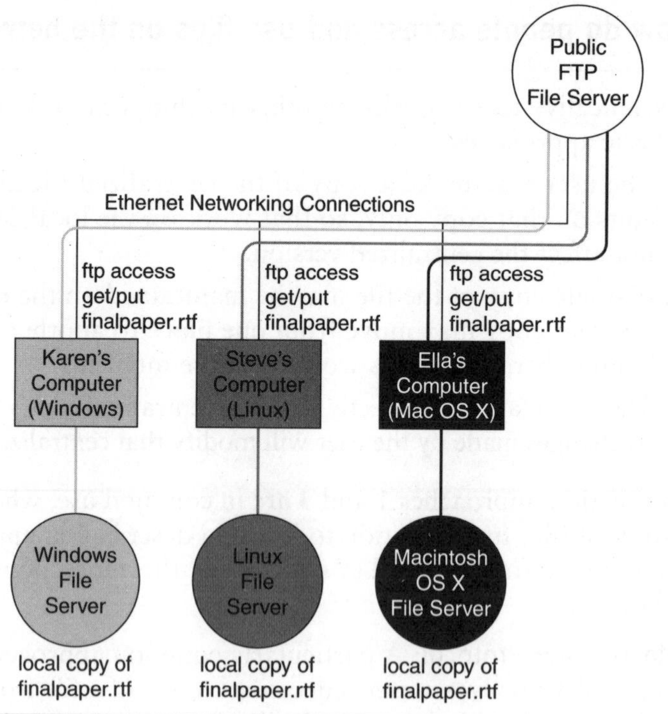

Figure 9.2
Three file systems, together with a common file server.

On Ethernet and wireless networks, a particularly common mechanism for this interaction follows standards developed in 1971, called **File Transfer Protocol (FTP)**. A typical FTP interaction involves the following steps:

1. A user initiates a session, indicating to the machine where the remote file is stored.
2. The remote file server asks the user for authorization information, such as a user name and password.
3. The user responds with the requested information.
4. Assuming the supplied information matches what was expected, the interaction continues.
5. Communication proceeds, following a command/response format.

a. The user issues a command (for example, "get finalpaper.rtf" asks the file server to send the file "finalpaper.rtf" to the user; the statement "put finalpaper.rtf" asks the local machine to send the file to the file server).

b. The client machine and file server respond with the information requested.

6. When the user has moved the desired files, the user issues the command "quit" to end the interaction.

Altogether, FTP transfers one or more complete files between a local computer and a file server. By accessing an FTP site, for example, Steve could successfully retrieve the version of the paper made available by Karen or Ella, as illustrated in Figure 9.2. After he has edited it, he would want to upload his latest version of their work. When the goal is to update a file stored on a server, the process entails three basic steps:

1. Use FTP to copy the file from the server to the user's local computer.
2. Use the local computer to revise the copy of the file stored locally.
3. Use FTP to copy the new version of the file back to the file server—often overwriting the old copy stored there previously.

In technical terms, FTP is a simple example of a **client/server** model of computing. The **server** provides a service or resource in response to requests by a **client**. In our group-project example, Steve's computer would be the client, requesting the common file server to allow him to download the latest version of the file. The FTP framework provides a careful specification for a limited range of client requests, and the server responses are similarly limited and precisely defined.

Remote File Access: The other common approach for accessing files involves a **remote-service mechanism** that allows an ongoing interaction between a client (the user) and the file server. In the case of editing a file, the user may want to view various parts of a file, delete sections, make additions at any point in the file, or revise portions. Ella, for example, may want to add more to one of Karen's introductory paragraphs or edit their paper's conclusions. From Ella's perspective, editing the remote file would have the same appearance in a window as editing a local file. Behind the scenes, however, Ella's machine must make a constant series of requests to the server so that the file can be viewed and updated. Some requests will leave the file unchanged, and others will modify the file. It is important to keep track of what work is done by the client computer and what is done by the server. One way to accomplish this is to make edits and additions directly onto the file server's copy of the file itself.

If you use a word processor (such as Microsoft Word, Open Office, or ThinkFree Office) on the file server itself, the application would tell the server about every keystroke the user makes, and send updates to the user's machine whenever something visible changes. Consequently, using a word processor on the file server generates a great deal of traffic. Thus, although this approach occurs in some applications, most applications provide for some processing on the user's machine. For example, part of the computer science paper may be sent from the file server to Ella's computer, the client Ella may edit that section, and updates would be sent periodically back to the file server. With this piece-by-piece communication, one can think of the local machine as providing another level of cache for the file server, just as cache memory holds frequently used data items or program parts, and just as main memory holds recently used segments of virtual memory. During editing, the word-processing software (such as Word or Open Office) runs on the *client* machine, and asks the file server for at least enough of the file to fill the editing window on the screen.

With remove file access, reading and displaying a file is reasonably straightforward. The client computer requests a part of a file, and that material is displayed on the screen. When the user moves to another part of the file, the client computer requests the information in the next section of the file. If the user has only read or displayed the old material—not changed it—there is no need to copy material back to the file server, because the server already has the original version of that material. Thus, when requesting new material, the client computer can simply throw away any previous part of the file that might still be stored in the client computer.

The process of modifying a file, however, is somewhat more complicated, because any changes in one portion of the file must be reported back to the file server. After all, the file server maintains the authoritative copy of the file, so the server's copy of the file must reflect any changes or additions. At a tactical level, however, a question arises concerning when the updates should be reported. Unfortunately, although updates may be done in several ways, each approach has difficulties. Here are some of the choices:

- *Immediate update (sometimes called write-through)*: The file server could be notified immediately every time a user makes any change in any part of a file. At an extreme, a message would be sent from the client to the server for each character added or changed in the file. Although this keeps the server's copy up to date at all times, extensive editing generates considerable network traffic. Such traffic can interfere with other work being done over the network and can slow processing speeds of the word processing itself.
- *Update at the very end (sometimes called write-on-close)*: The client could keep track of all changes made in a file, and notify the server only when the user completes the work, exiting the word processor. This approach generates little network traffic—just at the end of a session. On the other hand, this requires the local machine to store a considerable amount of data. Further, because no revisions are changed on the server as they are made by the user, all updating work may be lost if the hardware or software malfunctions. Of course, if a user opens a file, makes a simple change, and quits, then write-on-close and write-through may turn out to be quite similar.
- *Batched updates (sometimes called write-delayed)*: The client could delay notifying the server about updates or additions rather than reporting updates as they occur. Effectively, this allows the client to keep track of changes as they occur and report several changes at once to the server. This is a compromise approach between the two extremes and has elements of many compromises. Batched updates generate network traffic periodically—not with every change, but also not just once at the end. Similarly, this approach saves changes that the client has made to the file in batches. After a malfunction, work from the last regular server report would be lost, but that might be only a few minutes of work.

Remote file access often involves running an application on the client's machine with delayed reports to the server regarding modifications. This provides a reasonable balance between generating network traffic and providing a convenient and reliable environment. The analysis becomes more complicated, however, if other users want access to the same file at the same time, and we consider this issue next.

 How are files shared?

Some uses of file sharing already have been implied through our example involving Karen, Steve, Ella and their group project. Let's look at those examples again and expand them with details and variations.

Sharing with FTP: One way to share files is to make them available on a common server, telling the file server that others are allowed to read the specified file. Users then utilize FTP to make their own copies. When you post a file to the file server using FTP, it can be accessed only by those who have permission. Thus, the first part of any FTP session requires use of a user name and password. As with many computer systems, files involving FTP are organized by account, and anyone who has an account on the file server automatically can access the information related to that account. This is because some FTP commands allow moving through a file system from directory to directory, as long as owners have given permission for such browsing. Thus, once someone has logged in to the server using FTP, they could find your file (assuming the permission and directory structure were appropriately configured) and copy the file to their account.

Alternatively, Karen, Steven, and Ella could agree to place their common file within an account with user name "anonymous"; this approach involves the notion of "**anonymous FTP.**" In this approach, a file server may have a special account, called "anonymous," and this account has a special directory for publicly available files. Within this framework, users can run FTP and log in with the user name "anonymous." Often they provide their e-mail addresses or their user names on their client machine as their password. Once logged in, access to files is limited to this special directory and its subdirectories. If you have placed a copy of a file in this area, then others will be able to use anonymous FTP to make copies of your file. Karen, for example, could place a copy of her draft into the anonymous FTP folder and anyone could access it, even people who were not privy to general access to her school's network. Steve (or even Karen's mother) could download the draft of the group paper from this FTP site either from on-campus or from off-campus, supplying only an e-mail address as a password. Note that anonymous FTP does not allow general access to a file server, and you may have to make a conscious effort to move files to the special FTP directories. Other files you might have, or even updates to your files, will not be available to others unless you copy them to the special FTP area as well.

Sharing with Remote File Access: Turning to remote file access, if you have authorized others to be able to read your original file, they may be able to view it directly with an editor, such as Word or OpenOffice, directly on the network. There are, however, a few logistical problems with having many authorized people able to read a file. A remote file service can send many copies of a file to various folks, and all can view the same material without interference.

Complications arise, however, if the file changes. For example, suppose many people can read the file, and you are the only one who makes a change. Each viewer of the file has a separate cache copy on their local machine. When you make a change, their copy is no longer up to date, creating what is called a **cache coherence** problem; all copies of the file are no longer identical. Resolution of this problem may take one of two basic approaches. The first approach, called a **client-initiated update**, is reasonably passive. The file server simply waits until a user asks for an updated version of the file, supplying new copies only on demand. Thus, when you altered the file, all cache copies for the various people around the network became out of date, and they stay out of date until those folks ask for revised versions. Of course, if those people know you are editing, they may ask for updated versions frequently so they can refer to the newest information. On the other hand, if they do not know you are updating, or if they simply do not want to be bothered, then the materials in front of them could be outdated for an extended length of time.

A second approach to resolving a cache-coherence problem, called a **server-initiated update**, requires a file server to keep track of all clients currently viewing a file. Whenever you change a file, the server notifies all clients of the update, so that the cache at all client computers can be revised. As you might expect, this approach requires some administrative overhead for the server to keep track of current clients and can generate network traffic—particularly if you update the file often. Server-initiated updates require effort, processing time, and network communications, but they can keep multiple copies of a file synchronized. Of course, the importance of keeping copies up to date may depend greatly on the specific file and circumstances. Server-initiated updates are not implemented in many applications, because the gain does not seem worth the effort for just a few users on occasional files. However, some applications may require that everyone have completely current information, and server-initiated update might be explored in these cases.

The most complex environment for the cache-coherence problem arises when several users might want to access and change all or part of a remote file. The problem, called the **concurrent update problem**, is that one user might try to make a change in one way, while a second user tries to do something contradictory. For example, suppose that both Steve and Ella are using remote access to view and edit Karen's draft of their paper. If Steve and Ella both have plans to edit the introduction, how will the network know what changes to make to the original file? One way the network could handle this situation is to take the *ostrich approach* and just ignore the problem (just as ostriches are reported to stick their heads in the sand). Is this irresponsible? Maybe, but it can work fairly well if multiple users agree to take turns editing the file, or if their work schedules dictate that only one will be changing the file at a time. In this scenario, several people have the potential to modify the same file, but only one actually tries to change the file during any interval of time. To work, all parties would need to be in good communication; for example, Steve would tell Ella when he's working on the file and vice versa, so that two people are not working on the paper at the same time. Effectively, there is no need for a complicated solution in software to a potential problem that has been resolved in another way.

Alternatively, the network could enforce a policy that only one person can change the file at a time. In this mode, any person asking for access to a file must indicate whether the access will involve reading only or possibly editing. Those interested in reading the file are allowed access at any time. However, if someone asks to edit the file, then the software checks whether someone else already has editing privileges. If not, then the request can be granted, but if so, the second person is denied access. We say the first person activates a **lock** on the file, and this lock prevents others from changing the file's contents. Thus, if Ella were making changes on the paper,

Steve would know as soon as he opened the document off of the remote server, and would not be allowed to edit it on the network.

In practice, the lock often corresponds to the existence of a special file, one that identifies a document or file as "locked." When a new user runs an editing program, the program checks for the existence of this particular type of file. If the file is present, then some other user must be editing the file, and the new user is blocked. If the file is not present, then the editing program creates a special file as a way to communicate to future users. When editing is completed, the editing program removes the locking file, and others will be able to proceed. As an alternative, a special bit can be set within the editable file itself, indicating that someone is editing the file. If the bit is set, then others are denied permission to start editing.

Although the concept of locks works well, some applications require many people to work on different parts of a single file, making it difficult to limit editing access for the entire file to just one person at a time. In such cases, locks may be put in place for small pieces of the overall file. For example, in a college or university, several people in the registrar's office may be involved with updating student records and class records. When grades are being recorded, different workers may need to type grades corresponding to different courses. If only one lock were allowed for the entire file, then only one worker could enter course grades, and the process could take a very long time. However, if locks were associated with each course, then the locking mechanism would guarantee that two people did not interfere with each other by updating the same course—but many workers could enter grades for distinct courses.

Why can some machines (e.g., Windows, Macintosh, Linux) access some files, but not others?

In order to use a file, a machine requires several capabilities:

- The machine must be able to physically access the file; that is, the machine must be able to establish a physical connection or link to the device holding the file.
- The user must have appropriate permission to view or edit the file.
- The user's machine must be able to interpret appropriately the file data it receives.

So how do different operating systems influence access to files? As we consider this question, let's review the previous points more closely. This chapter has examined the use of computers attached to a network to communicate. Such communication involves several logical layers—often involving the standards called TCP and IP that we will discuss shortly. Although these standards provide many capabilities, they require that machines be physically connected to networks, and those networks in turn must be connected to each other for communication to take place.

Sometimes within a lab or an office, computers may be connected to each other, but not to the outside world (the Internet). For example, computers in a law office or medical facility may not be connected to the Internet as a mechanism to prevent unauthorized access to sensitive information. As another example, computers for a college course on networking may be connected to each other, but not to machines outside the lab. This configuration would allow students to learn about details of networks and to run experiments without interfering with computers and users outside the lab when something goes wrong.

Even when machines can communicate with each other, operating systems maintain records of who is allowed to access what data, as noted in Chapter 3. Typically, the person who creates a file has complete authority to view and change the data; however, others also may be allowed to read or to modify the information. When such permission is granted, others might use FTP or remote file access to view or edit the material. Note, however, that permission to view or modify one file does not necessarily carry over to the same permission for another file. Thus, it is quite possible that you could read or even change one file on a remote machine but not have the same privileges for another file.

Further, the ability to view a file's contents does not immediately imply that the file is intelligible. For security reasons, some information may be stored in an encrypted form, so the material makes sense only if you or your software knows how to decode the stored material. (More about this in the next chapter.)

In addition, various programs may place data in one format or another to enhance processing. For example, word processors often insert information on fonts and spacing within files. The format, for that information, however, may vary remarkably from one word processor to another—or even from one version of a word processor to the next version by the same vendor.

As a very simple example, consider what happens when you hit the "enter" or "return" key on your keyboard. Typically, in striking this key, you intend two actions to take place: The next material should move to the next line, and it should start at the left margin. On some machines (for example, those using the Windows operating system), such an action is recorded as two separate characters ("line feed" and "return"). On machines running Unix or Linux, the action is recorded as a single character ("return"), and the second action is inferred. Although such details may seem remarkably picky, they can have an effect when a file is viewed on different systems. When a Windows-based file or Windows-based e-mail is viewed by a Unix or Linux machine, the viewer may treat each character as designating a new line. Taken together, the result is to make two new lines that yield double spacing. Alternatively, additional characters may seem to appear in files—the one ("return") is treated normally, but the other ("line feed") may generate an unwanted mess (often "^M" or "=20"). In contrast, when a Windows-based machine views a file created by Unix or Linux, the text may seem run together without the desired spacing between lines. Thus, a table may seem nicely formatted to a Windows-based editor, but a Unix viewer would not find an expected pattern of characters for starting a new line. Instead, the file may be viewed under Unix as a continuous stream of text without the expected line breaks or new paragraphs, and formatted tables may appear with data from successive lines run together.

Although appearance issues can be resolved fairly easily, more complicated problems can arise when files are opened using different operating systems. For example, files generated by one word-processing package may be unintelligible to other packages if the file formats do not agree. The second word processor is expecting data in one format, does not find that format, and then experiences trouble. Fortunately, many contemporary word-processing packages recognize this difficulty and scan files to determine which of several formats might have been tried. However, if the file does not follow any of the known formats for that word processor, the material displayed may appear as a random jumble—or the word processor may simply generate an error message indicating it does not know how to proceed.

Similar issues arise for many applications, not just word processors, and care must be taken in saving files to anticipate how they might be used and who might use them on what machine(s).

When someone wants a file from a server, how does the server know whether to use FTP, remote access, or other programs?

Most computers send messages over an Ethernet network following a standard approach called **Transmission Control Protocol/Internet Protocol (TCP/IP)**. As part of the Internet Protocol, computers are required to include information about which application should be used for each message. This information is stored in the message's title, or IP header. To be somewhat more precise, an IP header includes a *port address* (actually a 16-bit number) that indicates the program that should receive the included data. For example, port 21 is the identifier used to indicate that a message contains FTP commands. Thus, when a computer receives a message specifying port 21, the machine knows to pass the information along to the program handling FTP. Therefore, when Karen posts her draft of the group paper on the common file server, her computer sends the "upload" command in a message specifying port 21. The server then knows that the message will contain an FTP command and presents that message to its FTP program. Similarly, port 20 indicates that the message contains file data related to an FTP command. Thus, after an FTP user types the command "get finalpaper.rtf", the user's computer packs the command into a message that includes an identifier indicating "port 21." When the file server receives the message from the network, it reads the "port 21" field, realizes the message has to do with FTP, and sends the "get finalpaper.rtf" command to its FTP program. When FTP on the server processes the command, it locates the relevant file, divides the data into messages (called packets), adds the designator "port 20," and sends the data back to the client. When the client receives a message indicating "port 20," the client computer knows the information received has to do with FTP file data, and the data then are forwarded to the relevant FTP file-handling program.

The use of port numbers can work smoothly, provided all computers agree on which numbers to use for which applications. For example, 21 indicates an FTP command, and 80 indicates access to the World Wide Web. In fact, the nonprofit Internet Corporation for Assigned Names and Numbers (ICANN) maintains a list of well-known port numbers, under contract with the United States government, the Internet Society, and other groups. Such assigned ports are numbered between 0 and 1023. Because applications change over time, the list of these port numbers also changes. A current list of assigned numbers is now maintained in an online database; although responsibility for such matters continues to evolve, if you're interested, you might search the Web at http://www.icann.org for various details. You could also search under the name of ICANN's predecessor, the Internet Assigned Numbers Authority (IANA). Table 9.1 shows assigned port numbers for some common applications.

Although numbers above 1023 are not formally assigned, the ICANN does maintain a registry of numbers above 1023 that are used for various applications. When new applications are created, the writers can officially register their port numbers so that the computer community will know which port numbers they use. (If you want to claim a port number for your application, you should contact ICANN about their procedures.) Nonregistered applications may use registered port numbers for communication, as long as the client and server applications agree on which port to use. To avoid interfering with other applications, however, those who are writing new applications are encouraged to review the current registry before deciding what numbers their applications might use and choose unique numbers for their applications. For whichever ports the writers use, in order to conform to TCP/IP, the port numbers will be contained in the IP header.

What makes TCP/IP work?

As you might expect, transmitting materials from one computer to another requires many details to fit together smoothly. To successfully coordinate all the activity that must take place for communication,

Table 9.1 Some Common Port Numbers

Port Number (Decimal)	Application Description
20	FTP data
21	FTP control
23	Telnet (a simple approach for logging into computers at a distance)
25	E-mail (Simple Mail Transfer Protocol)
80	HTTP, used for the World Wide Web

computers divide the work into distinct logical levels, meaning that a hierarchy of "who's doing what" is established. Each level addresses specific details and functions, and activities to be accomplished at higher levels can make use of lower-level functions. The idea here is much the same as discussed in Chapters 1 and 4 on applications and operating systems, where various details (such as how to manage specific printers or disks) were resolved in libraries of functions, and these materials then could be used in higher-level problem solving.

For standard computer-to-computer communication, the International Organization for Standardization (ISO) has specified an Open Systems Interconnection Reference Model (OSI) with seven distinct levels. The seven levels identified in the OSI cover the range of needs for communications, and are outlined in Table 9.2.

Rather than focusing on the details of the OSI model, let's look at the basic plan outlined by OSI. First, the title OSI highlights the term "Open Systems." The open systems premise emphasizes that communication is possible only if all computers involved agree on how they will function. With the open systems approach, the workings of the communication system are distributed publicly for reference by all manufacturers of computer hardware and software. The OSI model is not a trade secret; rather, all machines can follow the same standards, so we can expect that equipment from one manufacturer will work with that purchased from another source.

Let's consider the communication layers of the OSI model from the bottom layer upwards. Layer 1, the Physical Layer, handles the tangible details of transmission from one machine to another. For

Table 9.2 Layers of Computer-to-Computer Communication

Layer	Name	Description
7	Application Layer	Layers 5–7 involve various high-level capabilities for applications
6	Presentation Layer	
5	Session Layer	
4	Transport Layer	Organizes application data into packets; provides delivery mechanism
3	Network Layer	Routes packets (groups of bits) from source to destination
2	Data Link Layer	Moves frames (groups of bits) from one machine to the next
1	Physical Layer	Moves bits from machine to machine

Ethernet, this involves listening to a cable to determine when the cable is not being used by others and sending materials bit by bit. Matters of transmission media and speeds are handled at this layer.

Layer 2, the Data Link Layer, handles groups of bits, called **frames**. When a message is sent, the material is broken down into frames and is monitored by the Data Link Layer. In this layer, materials go from one machine to the next, and some checking is done to be sure that the data sent match the data received. When frames (groups of bits) are received in jumbled form, the receiving machine asks the sender to retransmit the material. Because of this work, we can have some confidence regarding individual transmissions of data from one machine to the next.

Layer 3, the Network Layer, involves routing a message from a source (such as a client) to a destination (such as a server). Although the Data Link Layer handles data transmission from machine to machine within a single segment, broader communications may require messages to move along several segments to reach their desired destination. For example, in the case of the World Wide Web, a message may have to move from machine to machine repeatedly between countries and across continents. The Network Layer handles how the message is routed to get to its destination. Messages within this layer are sometimes called **packets**. Computers can move the packets through the network and towards their destinations with the help of Internet Protocol, or IP. Thus, the IP part of TCP/IP specifies a way of sending packets of information from a source to a destination along a network. (Another common mechanism for the Network Layer is called a *connection-oriented protocol*, and is used by telephone companies and other public networks.) As has already been suggested several times and as may be inferred by its name, IP is the communication mechanism of choice for much of the Internet.

In considering IP, know that each packet is routed separately, according to a variety of factors, including the congestion of various Ethernet segments. This means that if you have requested a large amount of data through your browser and if that data were split into several packets, then the various packets or parts of the data might have each followed different routes from the Web server to your browser!

Layer 4, the Transport Layer, divides large messages into smaller packets that can be sent over the IP layer, and then recombines those packets in the receiver. This layer also can monitor what packets are actually received during a transmission and detect packets that appear lost; lost packets can be re-sent. Although several approaches may be followed at Layer 4, TCP is widely used and provides reliable communications for applications.

Layers 5, 6, and 7 provide additional services for the programs that send and receive messages. Layers 5 and 6 offer specialized services, such as the ability to monitor large messages and to review specific fields of messages. Many applications do not need such capabilities, and some networking books do not mention them. Services, such as FTP, e-mail, and remote file access, run as applications in Layer 7. As you explore this topic, focus first on understanding Layers 1 through 4, as these provide the basis for the higher-level layers.

Thus, the abbreviation TCP/IP identifies a basic approach to machine communications, highlighting two specific layers. TCP indicates a protocol at Layer 4, in which large messages are divided into packets, and IP specifies a mechanism at Layer 3 by which those packets are sent from a source to an intended destination. When the packets get to their destination, TCP also indicates how the material should be reassembled to get the original message. Further, as part of this process, TCP checks that no data are lost, asking for the retransmission of data as required.

Summary

When several people collaborate on a project, they may wish to share files and programs. This sharing could occur in three basic ways. Each person in the group could maintain her or his own copy of the material, and they could e-mail versions among group members. Alternatively, the group could agree upon a common file format and place the current version of their work on a common file server. Group members then could use File Transfer Protocol (FTP) to download a copy of the current version from the common server to their machines, edit their copy of the file, and upload a revised copy back to the server when they are done. FTP may involve accounts and passwords for individual users or "anonymous FTP" for general use. As a third alternative, group members could work directly with the file on the common server, using remote file access.

When an individual uses remote file access to edit a file, the user's changes may be communicated as they are made (write-through), when the user has finished editing (write-on-close), or in batches (write-delayed). When several people wish to make changes in the same file, different copies of the file may contain different versions of the material, and care is needed to determine which copy is correct. Solutions to this concurrent-update problem may follow an ostrich approach or a file-locking mechanism.

When several people use different operating systems to share common files, complications can arise if the computers follow different file formats. When a file following one convention is viewed by a system using another convention, the file may seem garbled or unintelligible.

Underlying file sharing, computer networks often use Transmission Control Protocol/Internet Protocol (TCP/IP) to organize information into packets and send those pieces of information through the network. As part of the transmission process, each message contains a port number so the receiving computer can identify what application to give the information to. Common applications have port numbers specified by the Internet Corporation for Assigned Names and Numbers (ICANN).

Terminology from This Chapter

- Anonymous FTP
- Cache coherence
- Client
- Client-initiated update
- Concurrent update problem
- File server
- File Transfer Protocol (FTP)
- Frame
- Location independence
- Location transparency
- Lock
- Port address
- Packet
- Remote file access
- Server
- Server-initiated update
- Transmission Control Protocol/ Internet Protocol (TCP/IP)

Discussion Questions

1. Suppose caching is used for remote file access.
   a. Why would it be important for a client computer to have either a large main memory or a disk?

b. To what extent would it be helpful to have both?

c. What might happen if the client machine did not have a disk and its memory was small?

d. Do you think it matters if a file server had only a small amount of memory? Briefly explain your answer. (Of course, the server must have a reasonable-sized disk to serve as a file server!)

2. Consider the following list of applications. In each case, consider whether locking is likely to be needed in maintaining a file. If a lock seems advisable, consider whether the lock should be associated with an entire file or with specified parts of the file (and specify which parts).

a. A word-processing file for a student's term paper

b. A word-processing file for a group's term paper, in which the group has divided the paper into sections with each person responsible for one section

c. A word-processing file for a group's term paper, in which the group has divided the paper into sections, one person is responsible for writing each section, and another person is responsible for editing the section once it is written

d. A database file to keep track of prices of items in a grocery store

e. A database file to keep track of patient records in a hospital

f. A database file to keep track of tickets and seats for a theater

3. In the party game of telephone, participants are arranged in a line. A message is given to the person at one end of the line. Then each participant, in turn, whispers the message to the next person. Messages are repeated only once from one person to the next, so each person must try to make sense of whatever he or she has heard without benefit of clarification. Eventually, the person at the far end of the line proclaims the message as received, and that message is compared to the original.

a. Determine some possible similarities and differences between the message passing used in this party game and in TCP/IP.

b. Identify various pitfalls that might go wrong with communication during this party game.

c. How might the various layers of the ISO OSI model help avoid or overcome the pitfalls mentioned in b?

4. Suppose a user is editing a file using remote file access and the file server crashes, but the client computer continues to run. To what extent could the user continue to edit the file—perhaps saving the result when the file server is rebooted?

5. Much of the success of the Internet relies upon standards and agreements so that all interested parties follow the same conventions. The Internet Society is a key part of this process. The Internet Society is composed of professional members, both individuals and organizations.

   a. Look up information about the Internet Society on the World Wide Web to identify its various roles.

   b. Identify at least six groups that the Internet Society works with to help set standards. In each case, indicate the specific role of the group and how that group helps coordinate activities on the Internet.

Exercises

1. **a.** In reviewing the words and phrases from "Terminology from This Chapter," some terms relate to high-level concepts or applications, some relate to low-level communication issues, and some involve ideas at an intermediate level between concepts and details. Organize the terms into 3 or more levels from high-level concepts down to low-level technical matters.

   b. Explain your categorization of terms in part a.

   c. Provide careful definitions for each word or phrase.

2. Chapter 3 discusses the principle of locality and describes how it is applied to the effectiveness of cache memory and virtual memory. Discuss how the principle of locality might impact the generation of network traffic in remote file access:

   a. When the file is being read only

   b. When the file is read and then modified

   For example, would the principle of locality tend to increase network traffic, decrease network traffic, or have no effect?

3. When editing a remote file, this chapter discusses three approaches to address the cache-coherence problem: write-through, write-on-close, and write-delayed. Suppose a user is

in the middle of editing a file when the local computer crashes—perhaps due to a power failure. Discuss the likely state of the remote file when power is restored. For example, consider which, if any, of the user's changes might be found within the centralized copy of the file.

4. Most word processors allow a user to save the current file, at which time a client computer sends updates to the central computer. To what extent is this capability compatible with write-through, write-on-close, and write-delayed approaches to the cache-coherence problem? For example, what effect would a "save current file" command have if the word processor used a write-through strategy for the cache-coherence problem?

Chapter 10

When can I consider my personal data secure?

With today's widespread use of computers, the safety of your personal information should be of great concern to you. When was the last time you ordered something online and provided your credit card information? How many times a week do you enter your password and log in to your e-mail account? Each time you access the Internet, you put your computer at risk for viruses, and each time you exchange information via the Internet, you are potentially compromising your privacy. In some cases, just keeping your computer turned on while it is connected to the Internet can threaten your privacy and security. In this chapter, we'll discuss ways to safeguard your computer and your information.

When we store information on a computer, we want that data to be available later, whenever we need it. We expect that our files will be saved, that we can access the files freely in the future, and that computer malfunctions will not cause information to be destroyed or damaged. Further, although we want unimpeded access to our material, we also may want access denied to unauthorized folks. In essence, we want to control who can read or change our material, and we want to trust that it is stored safely.

Back in the misty eons of time (perhaps even as recently as 50 or 100 years ago), ensuring reliability and security for vital or sensitive information was a relatively straightforward matter. Computers were not yet used, and photocopiers were devices of the future, making it relatively easy to protect important documents. Within a company, for example, data might be collected and tabulated on paper, organized into folders and file drawers, protected by fireproof vaults, and monitored by police patrols and guards. These measures ensured that authorized personnel could work with the data, but that personal or sensitive information could not circulate. A limited availability of specific pieces of information made it easy to monitor their safety, but it also led to some difficulties. The primary difficulties can be divided into three categories:

1. *Physical threats*: Files might be damaged or destroyed by physical means, such as fire or water.
2. *Insiders*: People within the company—employees with authorization to work with the data—might copy or memorize information and bring it with them for outside circulation.
3. *Outsiders*: People outside the company might physically break into buildings and disturb the files.

To protect against these problems, a company could make sure that their vaults were built fireproof, waterproof, and so on; that the backgrounds of workers were checked and monitored; and that security guards patrolled the buildings. They could also enforce special procedures that would limit both access to data and the movement of documents in order to supply further protection.

Today we might have many of the same goals for reliability and security of data in computers as generations before us did for their information, but data access and manipulation in computers involve programs, operating systems, operating personnel, and interconnected hardware components. Each computer may store a vast amount of information, and these data may be shared potentially by all machines within a network. The range of security issues, therefore, must extend to each of these areas as well as to the data themselves.

Let's begin this chapter by discussing data reliability. Today's problems are generally similar to those in earlier times, although the nature of electronic media adds subtleties and sophistication. The availability and control of data become complicated, however, when we consider that computers might crash or malfunction or that computers may be interconnected in networks. Many old problems still arise, but opportunities for data loss and for security violations are much harder to control. Ultimately, security in any age depends upon the actions of people and how they handle the responsibilities and trust they are given.

How can I be sure my files will be available when I need them?

In Chapter 3, we identified several layers of memory: registers with a CPU, cache, main memory, and disk or other physical storage devices. Of all of these regions of memory, only disks or other physical devices can provide **persistent storage**; that is, data in registers, cache, and main memory are lost during a power failure or when an application program finishes. Only data stored on a disk or other medium are expected to remain after a user session.

With this in mind, we can be sure our data will be available to us over the long term only if the data are saved to one of these permanent media. Thus, when editing information, users are well advised to save their work frequently during their session. For example, when working with a computer, I normally try to save work every 10 minutes or so throughout a session. If the computer crashes in this context, the most recent work may be lost, but the saved version includes any changes made 10 minutes ago, and only the most recent changes might have to be re-created.

Following this same philosophy, some software packages are programmed to save changes automatically on a periodic basis—perhaps every 10 or 15 minutes. Although these changes may be placed in a special file—separate from the actual file you are editing—software packages often provide a mechanism to recover both the file and those changes should your work be interrupted by a machine malfunction.

Note, however, that subsequent access to any of your files always depends on the disk or other device functioning properly. If a disk or disk drive malfunctions, the computer may not be able to retrieve files, even if they were stored properly previously. A similar problem might arise if files were stored on a removable device, such as a floppy disk or tape, and that medium was subjected to magnetic fields or other interference. The original files may have been fine, but subsequent events may make those files unreadable. For such reasons, prudence suggests making one or more backup copies of a file and storing that material separately from the original files. The backup copy provides some security in case the computer cannot retrieve the original material properly; one can try the backup if the original files are not usable.

Even when backup files have been made, however, some care is needed—and the more sensitive or important the data, the more care that may be required. For example, suppose you save a file on one floppy disk, make a copy on another floppy disk, and then pack both together in a briefcase. Having two copies provides some protection in case one disk malfunctions. However, trouble arises if the briefcase is stolen or is subjected to the same magnetic field. Separating the two copies could reduce risk, so if one disk were subjected to a problem, the other disk would be relatively unlikely to experience the same problem. In the business world, a common guideline suggests storing a backup copy of vital company files in a separate building from the main office or computer center. That way, if fire or water damage were to affect one site, the backup copy would be safe. The key is maintaining independent backups so that the conditions of one do not have an impact on the other.

To pursue the concept of backups somewhat further, an initial tendency may be to make a full backup of all files on a regular basis. Although this approach may work well, it may require the storage of massive amounts of data. If files change frequently, backups may be needed every day—or even every few minutes!

To resolve this, backups are generally handled in one of three ways. Each approach makes full backups of all files on a periodic basis; differences arise in what happens between those full backups. First, you could have your files regularly scanned to identify what has changed since the last backup or scan, and copy only files that have changed. Alternatively, you could have the changes themselves tracked rather than entire files, and add those to your backup at certain intervals. With either of these approaches, the changed files or changes are called **incremental backups**. With either approach, if a failure destroys files, you can restore them by going to the full backup and then copying the changes.

Finally, you could use a variation of incremental backup and have only the inputs that generated the changes recorded. For example, a word processor may record each keystroke you make when editing. To use such data to restore a lost file, the word processor begins with the last full backup, replays each command or keystroke you took, and applies the same processing to the document, thereby updating it. Effectively, your previous work is repeated, but presumably at a much faster pace than when you were typing earlier.

Although incremental backups can be relatively fast and take up relatively little space, file recovery involves updating based on the last full backup, an interaction that involves processing. Many reliability guidelines therefore suggest that you check this process regularly; that is, on a periodic basis it is important to take an old full backup, apply changes, and check that the system really can be restored correctly. Backups can provide a valuable measure of reliability, but only if they work properly.

As an additional precaution, if something does go wrong, you should be careful in how you use your backups. For example, if a disk drive malfunctions, ruining the copy of a file on one disk, then inserting the backup copy into the same disk drive might well ruin the backup copy as well. At the very least, care is needed to determine the cause of the problem first, to be sure the same problem does not occur again.

Your computer files and information, therefore, can be relatively secure when they are under your care and you back them up as necessary. You have a good chance that they'll be there when you want them. It becomes more of an issue when you trust your files to someone else or to a resource beyond your control. Take, for instance, your money; you likely use ATMs all the time, entrusting a computer networking system with your hard-earned cash. How can you be sure that the machines running your transactions are completing them as instructed? What would happen if the ATM crashed? Let's take a look at ATMs and explore this further.

How reliable and secure are ATMs?

As you might expect, maintaining bank records requires considerable care, and special procedures are established to anticipate the various circumstances that might arise related to computer crashes and malfunctions. Let's consider three situations that might arise when you try to transfer money from your savings account to your checking account:

1. A crash or malfunction occurs before you try to make your transfer.
2. A crash or malfunction occurs after you have made your transfer.

3. A crash or malfunction occurs as you are in the process of making your transfer.

Crashes or Malfunctions Before You Try to Make Your ATM Transfer: The process of making an account transfer using an ATM typically involves several steps:

1. You insert your bank ATM card and enter your personal identification number (PIN).

2. You select menu options to indicate the desire to make a transfer, you indicate the relevant accounts, and you specify the amount.

3. The ATM sends relevant account, PIN, and transfer information to the bank.

4. The bank indicates the transfer is legitimate (that is, the accounts and PIN are appropriate, and there is adequate money to cover the transfer), makes the transfer, and reports that the work has been completed to the ATM.

5. The ATM reports that the transfer is complete and returns your bank card (if it has not been returned earlier).

In this outline, observe that the process involves a dialogue between the ATM and your bank; the ATM sends a message, and it expects a response. The ATM banking system, however, has established time limits for all such messages and responses. If the ATM sends a message but does not receive a response in the specified time (perhaps 50 seconds), then the ATM cancels the transaction, displays a "time-out" message for you, and returns your card.

Fortunately, this time limit handles the situation when the bank's computer crashes or malfunctions before you enter your bank card at an ATM. Following the prior sequence of events, suppose you insert your card, type your PIN, and enter the transfer information. When the ATM packages this material into its message, the computer crash will prevent a timely response, so the ATM will cancel the transaction, and you receive your card back. At that point, your transfer deposit did not take place, you have been notified of this failure, and you can try again later.

Crashes or Malfunctions After You Make Your ATM Transfer: If your ATM or the bank's computers crash after you made a transfer, processing has involved the entire outline through step 5. You have requested a transfer of money, the bank has performed the relevant processing, and the ATM has notified you that the work is done. At this stage, you want assurance that the balances in each of your accounts are correct; the risk of a computer crash or malfunction would be that the record of your transfer was lost. To resolve these types of problems, financial activities are considered as a sequence of events, called **transactions**. Accounting standards require banks to maintain logs, called **audit trails**, of each transaction. An audit trail is simply a record of each event: an ongoing record of activity for your accounts and all other accounts as well. In maintaining these audit trails, editing is never allowed. Once a transaction occurs, it can never be erased. If a mistake is made, then a new transaction is performed to correct the error, so both the error and its correction appear in the audit trail.

Because of this system, the bank will have a record of your transfer on its audit trail—even if the machine subsequently crashes or malfunctions. After the ATM or bank's computer system is repaired, these audit trails can be used with backup files to restore all files, regardless of what information may have been damaged in the malfunction itself.

Crashes or Malfunctions While You Are in the Process of Making Your ATM Transfer: So what happens when a transaction is interrupted in the middle? In this case, processing starts, but does not finish properly. To handle these circumstances, many modern systems process transactions in multiple phases. At the start of a transaction, the computer records the current state of data. Then, as the transaction proceeds, the information is updated tentatively, and final updating of records is deferred until all parts of the transaction are completed. With this approach, any errors cause the transaction to be canceled, with the original state of data restored. In the terminology of databases, the computer *rolls back* transactions, discarding updates.

In the case of your ATM transfer, the bank may have withdrawn money from one account, but not made the corresponding deposit to your account at the time of a computer crash. No account's records, however, are finalized until all relevant processing has been done correctly; there is no chance that one account record will be updated without the other having the corresponding revision. Altogether, the roll back assures us that our records will stay consistent for any banking transaction.

Timeouts, audit trails, and roll backs are common in many transaction-based applications—not just ATM deposits. Similar techniques are common whenever updates involve steps that must be done together. A transaction may require the updating of several pieces of data, but a roll-back mechanism ensures that either all pieces are revised or the entire transaction is canceled. Altogether, these types of capabilities can provide considerable security that files are maintained in a timely and consistent manner; in the case of financial transactions as might be found in banks, variations of these security measures are mandated by both accounting standards and legal regulations.

Security for your ATM account, however, goes beyond ensuring that the system is functioning correctly. The **Personal Identification Number (PIN)** that you are required to enter serves to identify you in a way similar to password protection systems in your computer.

How well do password systems work?

Limiting access to data requires that a computer distinguish one person from another. For example, if multiple people will be using one computer, each person can be given a separate computer account and password. The system then operates under the assumption that each individual knows her or his password but others do not. Data are restricted when a potential intruder cannot supply the required access code.

Unfortunately, password systems often work better in theory than in practice for several reasons.

- Users often choose codes that are easily guessed, because they do not want to forget their own passwords. Common favorites include their own names or nicknames (sometimes repeated twice), names of relatives or friends, well-known dates (e.g., birthdays, anniversaries), and popular words or phrases. For example, some studies have found that as many as 40% or 50% of the passwords on a system can be guessed following a few simple rules and guidelines.
- Users often tell their friends their passwords, so that their friends can use a particular program or data set.

- If non-mnemonic names are chosen, users often post passwords next to their workstations, so they won't forget what to type. Of course, others will find this posted information equally helpful.
- Passwords are often so short that they may be determined by simple trial-and-error. (Until recently, for example, one business used a system where passwords for all users consisted of exactly two capital letters.)
- System flaws, operator errors, or procedural mistakes may allow users to access the file that contains all passwords. Numerous stories tell of lists of current passwords appearing on terminals or printers, for example.
- Most computers allow system managers special privileges, so that the machines may be run smoothly and so that updates and operations may be performed effectively. Managers normally have the power to peruse all files on a system, regardless of password protections that might inhibit other users.
- If outsiders or regular users are able to break into a manager's account, then these people also can examine and modify all files. (In one system known to this author, an administrator was worried about forgetting the manager's password, so he left it blank. Individual accounts were well protected, but anyone who tried to log in as manager had no trouble whatsoever obtaining special powers with a privileged status.)

Overall, then, passwords have the potential to limit access to information, but any system depending on password protection must be used carefully, following well-established protections and procedures. Carelessness may open such systems to a wide range of abuses.

Besides password systems, what else can I do to protect my files?

A different approach for the protection of data involves the encoding of information, so only authorized users can make any sense of the information present. With the processing power of modern machines, programs sometimes encode data automatically before storing any data and decode all information before it is displayed to an authorized user.

The Caesar Cipher: With encoding and decoding, of course, the level of security depends upon the ciphering system actually used. During the Gallic Wars, Julius Caesar encoded messages to his troops by replacing each letter by the third letter after it in the alphabet. Applying this idea to the modern English alphabet, "a" would be encoded as "d", "b" as "e", and so forth. At the end of the alphabet, "w" would be coded as "z", "x" as "a", "y" as "b", and "z" as "c". Although this system, now called a **Caesar Cipher**, seems very simple, the code was never broken by Caesar's enemies, and it served as a secure form of communication.

Today, the art and science of cryptanalysis has become very sophisticated, and simple codes such as a Caesar Cipher can be broken very quickly and easily.[1] Secure codes must be much more sophisticated.

The Caesar Cipher, for example, has at least two major weaknesses. Every letter is coded by the third (or fourth or *n*th) letter after it, so once the code for one letter is determined, the codes for every other letter also are known. To illustrate, consider the coded message

```
Igkygx iovnkxy gxk kgye zu ixgiq
```

and suppose you know (or guess) that this has been sent using a type of Caesar cipher, but you do not know if the shift is one letter, two letters, three, or more.

To decipher the message, you could simply try each of the 26 possible shifts of the alphabet and see which line makes sense. In the case of the previous message, the choices are shown in Table 10.1.

With this approach, a simple trial-and-error process produces the actual message with little difficulty. (In this case, A was coded G.)

A second weakness inherent in the Caesar Cipher is that every letter in the actual message is encoded each time by the same letter in the cipher alphabet. (In this example, A always appears as G, etc.) This allows people trying to break a code to take advantage of statistical properties of English. Although there can be variations among different texts, E, for example, is usually the most frequently used

1 For an interesting account of a variety of simple techniques for breaking codes, see Abraham Sinkov, *Elementary Cryptanalysis, A Mathematical Approach*, The New Mathematical Library, New York: Random House and the L. W. Singer Company, 1968.

Table 10.1 Message Decodings with a Caesar Cipher

Shift by	Alphabet Coded By	Possible Decoding of Message
0	ABCDEFGHIJKLMNOPQRSTUVWXYZ	Igkygx iovnkxy gxk kgye zu ixgiq
1	BCDEFGHIJKLMNOPQRSTUVWXYZA	Hfjxfw hnvmjwx fwj jfxd yt hwfhp
2	CDEFGHIJKLMNOPQRSTUVWXYZAB	Geiwev gmtlivw evi iewc xs gvego
3	DEFGHIJKLMNOPQRSTUVWXYZABC	Fdhvdu flskhuv duh hdvb wr fudfn
4	EFGHIJKLMNOPQRSTUVWXYZABCD	Ecguct ekrjgtu ctg gcua vq etcem
5	FGHIJKLMNOPQRSTUVWXYZABCDE	Dbftbs djqifst bsf fbtz up dsbdl
6	GHIJKLMNOPQRSTUVWXYZABCDEF	Caesar ciphers are easy to crack
7	HIJKLMNOPQRSTUVWXYZABCDEFG	Bzdrzq bhogdqr zqd dzrx sn bqzbj
8	IJKLMNOPQRSTUVWXYZABCDEFGH	Aycqyp agnfcpq ypc cyqw rm apyai
9	JKLMNOPQRSTUVWXYZABCDEFGHI	Zxbpxo zfmebop xob bxpv ql zoxzh
10	KLMNOPQRSTUVWXYZABCDEFGHIJ	Ywaown yeldano wna awou pk ynwyg
11	LMNOPQRSTUVWXYZABCDEFGHIJK	Xvznvm xdkczmn vmz zvnt oj xmvxf
12	MNOPQRSTUVWXYZABCDEFGHIJKL	Wuymul wcjbylm uly yums ni wluwe
13	NOPQRSTUVWXYZABCDEFGHIJKLM	Vtxltk vbiaxkl tkx xtlr mh vktvd
14	OPQRSTUVWXYZABCDEFGHIJKLMN	Uswksj uahzwjk sjw wskq lg ujsuc
15	PQRSTUVWXYZABCDEFGHIJKLMNO	Trvjri tzgyvij riv vrjp kf tirtb
16	QRSTUVWXYZABCDEFGHIJKLMNOP	Squiqh syfxuhi qhu uqio je shqsa
17	RSTUVWXYZABCDEFGHIJKLMNOPQ	Rpthpg rxewtgh pgt tphn id rgprz
18	STUVWXYZABCDEFGHIJKLMNOPQR	Qosgof qwdvsfg ofs sogm hc qfoqy
19	TUVWXYZABCDEFGHIJKLMNOPQRS	Pnrfne pvcuref ner rnfl gb penpx
20	UVWXYZABCDEFGHIJKLMNOPQRST	Omqemd oubtqde mdq qmek fa odmow
21	VWXYZABCDEFGHIJKLMNOPQRSTU	Nlpdlc ntaspcd lcp pldj ez nclnv
22	WXYZABCDEFGHIJKLMNOPQRSTUV	Mkockb mszrobc kbo okci dy mbkmu
23	XYZABCDEFGHIJKLMNOPQRSTUVW	Ljnbja lryqnab jan njbh cx lajlt
24	YZABCDEFGHIJKLMNOPQRSTUVWX	Kimaiz kqxpmza izm miag bw kziks
25	ZABCDEFGHIJKLMNOPQRSTUVWXY	Jhlzhy jpwolyz hyl lhzf av jyhjr

letter, with T second, and so forth.[2] Thus, another approach to breaking a code (given enough text to study) is to count the number of times each coded letter occurs. The chances are quite good that the letter appearing most frequently will be an E or T, for example.

Approaches to Improve the Caesar Cipher: With these basic weaknesses in the Caesar Cipher, improvements could be made in several ways. First, during encoding, instead of simply replacing a letter by the third (or *n*th) letter after it, each letter could be matched with a random letter of a new made-up alphabet. This

2 Sinkov, op. cit. presents more frequency count information on p. 16.

new cipher alphabet would be the key needed to decode the message, as in the following example:

Plain Alphabet: A B C D E F G H I J K L M N O P Q R S T U V W X Y Z

Cipher Alphabet: R V I N T O Q F Z P A X H B K D C J W U M E Y G L S

Here, each letter in a message can be replaced by the corresponding letter in the cipher alphabet, so that "FUN" is encoded by "OMB." This approach resolves the first major deficiency in the Caesar Cipher, because a knowledge of part of the code (O stands for Y) does not appreciably help decipher other parts of the code.

The second deficiency is often addressed by following one of two approaches. In the first approach, a different code is used for each subsequent letter in the message. Thus, to encipher "FUN," the letter "F" is enciphered using one cipher alphabet, "U" using a second, and "N" using a third. Certainly, if this approach is used, with a different coding scheme for each letter, and if the pattern of coding schemes is changed for each message, then the messages may be unbreakable. However, as a practical matter, using different cipher alphabets for each letter in a message is unwieldy. Both the sender and the receiver must agree on the sequence of codes to be used, and management of many different codes can be difficult.

Thus, in practice, it is not uncommon to use one basic cipher alphabet, but then to use different shifts for subsequent letters. For example, the sender and receiver might agree that the first letter of the message would be coded by the cipher alphabet, shifted by 3 letters (as in the original Caesar Cipher), the next letter shifted by 1 letter, the next by 4, then by 1, 5, 9, 2, 6, 5, 3, 5, and so on (where this sequence of shifts may be remembered as the digits of the mathematical number pi). To simplify the logistics further, the pattern of shifts might be repeated after a certain number of letters. For example, once the first eight letters are coded by shifts of 3, 1, 4, 1, 5, 9, 2, 6, then the next eight letters also are coded by the same pattern of shifts.

Codes produced in these ways are much better than the simple Caesar Ciphers. The simplifications needed to manage their logistics (like shifting to the numbers in pi), however, also can open potential weaknesses that may be exploited by those trying to break the code to obtain the underlying data. Statistical methods used for single alphabet codes often may be extended to these multiple cipher approaches, at least when patterns repeat or when they can be predicted.

To help prevent decoding by statistical analysis, encoders can code several letters at once, rather than coding letter by letter. For example, a code could be constructed so that pairs of letters were coded together (coding "ED" by "RM," for instance.) With this approach, counts of individual letters would not give much information to potential cryptanalysts, because the code was not based on individual letters. Even here, however, when reasonably large amounts of text are collected, patterns could be observed and statistical analysis of groups of letters may provide insights. Coding pairs of letters may create some difficulties for cryptanalysts, but these are rarely insurmountable.

Increasing the size of the groups, however, can greatly complicate the work required to break a code. When 50 or 100 letters are encoded as a group, for example, the task of cryptanalysis may be sufficiently time-consuming such that codes can be cracked only after many years (at which time, the data may no longer be sensitive or even relevant).

Encoding reasonably large groups of letters together is the basis for one of today's most popular encryption schemes, called **public key systems**, which are often used with modern computer systems. Public key systems typically involve three main elements.[3]

First, each group of letters is interpreted as a number n. (If a group had only one letter, we might consider A as 01, B as 02, C as 03, and so on. If a group had two letters, then the combination CA might be 0301—putting the numbers for C and A next to each other. The number n in what follows would be 01 or 0301 or whatever letters formed a group within our message.)

Second, the number n is put into an arithmetic formula to get a coded form. For example, the formula might specify numbers e and m, so that the coded number c is $c = n^e \bmod m$; that is, the group's number n is raised to the power e, and the remainder is computed after dividing by m. With this approach, c is easily computed (assuming you have a good calculator that raises numbers to powers and also takes remainders).

Third, when e and m have been chosen carefully, it turns out that a similar formula may be used to decipher the message. In particular, there may be a number d where $n = c^d \bmod m$. The security of the code then depends upon the difficulty of computing d. For a public key system, a person wishing to receive coded messages will publish m and e, so anyone can send him or her information. The

3 For more information, see Donald W. Davies, *Tutorial: The Security of Data in Networks*, IEEE Computer Society, Los Angeles, CA, 1981. The discussion here follows the general treatment given in Part II of Davies' tutorial, pp. 115–134.

coding scheme is straightforward, fast (at least when machines do the computation), and public. On the other hand, under certain circumstances, the computation of d may be expected to require so much time that data will remain secure for a long time.[4]

With these formula encryption systems, there is always the possibility that a new discovery or insight will suddenly allow d to be computed easily and quickly from m and e, but this is beyond the capabilities of current knowledge. Thus, this approach currently is viewed as reasonably secure, at least if m and e are chosen carefully. When you use public-key encryption to store data or to send messages, therefore, you can have some confidence that your material will be secure for that storage or transmission. However, before the encryption (before storage or transmission) or after decoding (when you retrieve your data from the file or when the message is received), the data still will be vulnerable, and this can threaten the security of your information.

What internal security threats do computers encounter?

Unfortunately, even limiting access to accounts and files by passwords or encryption does not guarantee that data on multi-user machines will be safe. At least three other types of risks should be considered:

- Programs accessing data may make unintended copies of the material. An offending program could copy data to another user's account as it was doing its work for an authorized user. An intruder then could obtain information by just waiting for an authorized user to access it. Alternatively, the offending program could use an Internet connection to transmit your data to another location. Often, you might expect such of-

4 In one popular version of a public key system, developed by Rivest, Shamir, and Adleman, m, e, and d are obtained as follows: One starts with two large prime numbers, p and q. Then let $m = pq$ and let $L = lcm(p - 1, q - 1)$, the least common multiple of $p - 1$ and $q - 1$. Then d and e may be computed by taking any solutions to the equation $de = 1 \mod L$. Although such computations are easy once p and q are known, the discovery of p and q is difficult given only n, because the factoring of very large integers can require a large amount of time and energy. Although further motivation for such work and the reasons this works are beyond the scope of this book, details may be found in Davies' *Tutorial*, already cited, or in the original paper, R. L. Rivest, A. Shamir, and L. Adleman, "A Method for Obtaining Digital Signatures and Public-Key Cryptosystems," *Communications of the ACM*, Volume 21, Number 2, February 1978, pp. 120–126.

fending programs to come about because they were altered by someone who hacked into your computer; however, it is also possible that you obtained the program in that form originally! The program might e-mail periodic updates to its owners to indicate how it is functioning and to document any errors. Such notifications might be considered legitimate to help the development of future versions of the software. However, the same e-mail could transmit your secret data as well. When you use your word processor, for example, do you know what it really does behind the scenes?

- Unauthorized people could access old versions of sensitive files that remain after the originals are no longer in use. To be complete, erasing should involve two steps: First, disk or file space should be overwritten, so no sensitive data remain. Second, the space previously occupied by the data should be deallocated, so it may be used again. (Translating these steps to paper files, paper should be shredded before it is recycled.) Unfortunately, on many systems, only the second step is performed. Overwriting disk files is time consuming, and this step is often omitted. Without overwriting, information can be obtained by looking through space recently deallocated. (Again, in a paper world, this is not unlike looking for information by searching through someone's trash barrels.)
- Two programs running on the same processor can communicate, either directly or indirectly, thereby making confidential information vulnerable to prying eyes. For example, a process using sensitive data might send messages to another person's program if it's running at the same time. Material can also be compromised when messages are sent indirectly between programs; processes may take advantage of an operating system's scheduling of work in order to transmit data.

Although this communication between accounts or programs is reasonably complex and certainly requires some collusion, possibilities such as these arise whenever users share a single machine. Overall there are many ways that unauthorized people may obtain sensitive data through clandestine or defective software, as well as by sloppy file handling. Multi-user machines, therefore, have considerable potential for allowing the unauthorized distribution of data and programs.

What external (networking) threats do computers encounter?

When individual processors or computers are linked to a network, the potential for security leaks expands significantly. The problems already identified for single processors remain, but small difficulties on a single processor may be used as wedges to open wider leaks in a distributed system. In addition, some new types of problems may arise.

Keyboard Sniffers: When you work at a computer, you typically provide information to programs by typing at the keyboard or using a mouse. In normal usage, you expect your data to go directly to that application. Also, you may expect that data will be encrypted before it is stored or sent to another machine. Unfortunately, all of this potential security can be undermined if a special type of program, called a **keyboard sniffer**, is constantly monitoring and recording everything you do at your keyboard. And, once a keyboard sniffer has recorded your information, it can do whatever it wants with what it finds. For example, if you entered a credit card number as part of shopping online, a keyboard sniffer might have the capability of identifying that number as being an account. If your computer is connected to the Internet, the keyboard sniffer then could send that information to any designated location in the world. Although these types of spying programs are still relatively uncommon, the technology currently exists for such programs to be installed behind the scenes where you may not notice them, but where they could record and transmit everything you have done on the machine!

Wire Tapping: At a physical level, any network of machines must use some medium to transmit data from one place to another. When all electrical components are physically close to each other, communication between machines can be monitored carefully by security personnel to prevent unauthorized individuals from connecting to the transmission medium and copying information as it is sent. As distances between machines become longer, however, physical observation becomes much more difficult, and the information is more vulnerable. For example, exposed wires and junction boxes can be tapped, radio waves can be intercepted, and electromagnetic fields from electrical cables can be monitored. In the latter two cases, someone could capture data without any physical connection to a wire. When opportunities for eavesdropping and wire tapping like these exist, data can no longer be considered invulnerable during transmission. Outsiders may have an opportunity to receive data as they move from one place to another in a network.

Coordinating Processor Security Levels: When physical channels are secure, interprocessor security is still complicated because people generally have different capabilities and requirements on their machines. As a simple example, someone with a personal computer at her or his home or office may have complete freedom to access and modify anything on that system. The owner may work with all data and programs at will, with virtually no constraints. When that machine is connected to a network, however, the office machine may limit the information available through the personal computer. The individual may need the same material both at home and in the office, but data flow over the network may be restricted.

As the needs of users expand through a network, each machine must monitor who is allowed to access what data, and different levels of users enjoy different privileges. In many cases, each machine has to trust what it is told by other machines in the network. For example, a request for data may include the identity of the user, and a machine receiving the message may trust that the user's identity is correct.

Frequently, on large systems on national networks, a person with special system privileges on one machine may be given expanded privileges on another connecting machine. If the person is responsible enough for one system, the assumption may be made that she or he will be equally trustworthy on the next system. Such an assumption may be shaky, but to limit this person's privileges could greatly restrict the usefulness of the network and the ability of a responsible worker to do her or his work. On the other hand, granting these privileges also aids an intruder on one system in gaining access to other systems in a network. If a person breaks into one machine (perhaps by guessing a password), that person may be able to then break into accounts on connecting machines.

In a related problem, guessing passwords can be easier on distributed systems. As a simple illustration, if one machine can interact with a second, then the first simply might try to log into an account on the second by trial and error. If an account name is known, for example, the first machine could simply try all possible passwords, one after another. Such a brute force approach could take a very long time if an account's password was a random collection of characters, but the process might go quickly if a user had chosen a simple word or name. (To reduce the possibility of a computer guessing an account on another computer, many systems will stop accepting attempts to log in if passwords are consistently wrong, or alarms may be triggered to warn of attempted break-ins.)

In general, gaining access to one machine or to an account on one machine often opens up many ways to break into other accounts.

Trojan Horses: Another way people can interfere with your work involves the exploitation of generally accessible file areas. These file areas would include commonly used programs that may be grouped in a directory that many people can access. Routine administrative tasks using materials in these file areas may be done automatically by running programs stored in special locations. Under normal circumstances, these activities would not pose any problems. If security measures within a system are somewhat lax, however, a clever user might be able to introduce a new program into a system area, and this program then may be run automatically as part of administration or accidentally by another user. If the foreign program were to copy sensitive data or grant special privileges, then the original user might gain access to restricted information. These programs are called **Trojan horses**; unfortunately stories of security violations that are due to Trojan horses are quite common.

Viruses and Worms: Two other types of subversive programs that can undermine system security and reliability are viruses and worms. The mechanics of these programs differ in their operation and in the ways they spread through a system, but the ideas behind both viruses and worms are reasonably similar. Each case affects the functioning of an operating system by entering a machine from a source that is trusted to be secure. Once within the machine, the program is run and it affects the further operations of the machine. Sometimes the effects may be harmless, but in other cases data may be lost or modified, or a system may be unable to continue functioning. In each case, system security has been breached, and system users may no longer know what operations and data are reliable. (As a preventative method several years ago, one major company shut down its computer operations on a Friday the 13th, because of rumors of difficulties that might occur when that date was reached.)

Viruses typically are transmitted in e-mail or on diskettes that are used on one machine and then another. When a user receives a virus via e-mail, the text itself may be reasonably safe; however, if the e-mail contains an attachment, then opening the attachment may run a program (such as a word processor or spreadsheet) that activates the virus within that attachment. To expand on this somewhat, modern word processing systems and spreadsheets often allow users to write small programs (sometimes called *macros*) for use within a document. One simple part of a spreadsheet, for example, could compute the sum of the numbers in a row. More complex instructions could tell the word-processing package or spreadsheet to access files, change data, send e-mail, or erase materials. A virus is a set of such instructions within a document that instructs a word processor, spreadsheet, or other program to carry out unwanted activities when a document is opened.

Because you are running the program (word processor or spreadsheet) on your computer, the program has the capability to access your files. With that access, the virus embedded in an attachment could cause your word processor or spreadsheet to change your files, access your lists of e-mail addresses, or send e-mail. Like any program, once a virus is launched, it is difficult to monitor. Because you have little control over what an unknown attachment program might do, it is strongly suggested that you *not* open e-mail attachments unless you know who they are from and what will happen.

On another front, when a diskette is inserted into a machine, the computer reads some initial data to learn about the type of material present. If this initial information is altered, the computer could be instructed to change its programs, data, or mode of operations. In this way, disk viruses can cause just as much damage as attachments, and you should be equally careful in working with e-mail attachments and potentially infected disks.

Worms typically enter machines over network communication channels that we trust to be reliable. A worm takes advantage of weaknesses in one system to transmit itself to other machines, where the program may be duplicated and retransmitted. The scope and seriousness of its effects depend upon its design, as well as particular networks and machines.

In many cases, both worms and viruses are designed to perform some unusual or clandestine operation, and then they tell the computer to make additional copies of themselves. These additional copies may then be transmitted and run on either your computer or other machines to cause further deterioration of a system or network. Sometimes this duplication process has the potential to destroy a great deal of data or to bring normal operations to a halt. As in medicine, a single virus program (or cell) may be relatively harmless by itself, but as it reproduces (producing more copies of itself), the result can overwhelm the health of a system.

Stalking the Wily Hacker

Let's take a look at several types of security leaks through one celebrated case described by Clifford Stoll.[5]

In his commentary, Stoll reports that an intruder gained access to the Livermore Berkeley Laboratory (LBL) computers in August 1986. While trying to track down the identity of this person over the following 10 months, Stoll (with the support of LBL and the help of personnel at other sites) followed this individual's attempts to break into about 450 other computers. More than 30 of these attempts were successful. Stoll reported that half of the 450 attempts were unsuccessful because the computers were unavailable. Of the remaining 220 attempted log-ins,

- 5% were refused by a distant computer (set to reject LBL connects [no one at LBL was allowed access to these machines]).
- 82% failed on incorrect user name/passwords.
- 8% gave information about the system status.
- 1% achieved limited access to databases or electronic-mail shells.
- 2% yielded normal user privileges and a programming environment.
- 2% reached system-manager privileges.[6]

Thus, about 5% of the attacks against Internet computers were reasonably successful. In this case, the intruder was particularly interested in military or classified information, and one might expect computers involved in such applications to be more secure than machines used for general computing. It is not unreasonable, therefore, to expect that the percentage might have been higher for machines with more general uses. In the same article, Stoll compares his results with other, independent studies of attempted break-ins to systems and concludes, "break-in rates of 3–20 percent may be expected in typical network environments."[7]

Such rates suggest that although many computers may be somewhat resistant to intruders, persistence can pay off. Different attacks on the same machine, trying different user names and accounts, or taking advantage of different characteristics of a system can allow an outsider to find holes and to take advantage of potential weaknesses. For example, in reviewing this work of the intruder, Stoll writes

> The intruder conjured up no new methods for breaking operating systems: rather he repeatedly applied techniques documented elsewhere. Whenever possible, he used known security holes and subtle bugs in different operating systems, including UNIX(R), VMS(R), VM-TSO(R), EMBOS(R), and SAIL-WAITS. Yet it is a mistake to assume that one operating system is more secure than another: Most of these break-ins were possible because the intruder exploited common blunders by vendors, users, and system managers.[8]

The intruder also guessed account names and passwords to gain access to other accounts and machines. Overall then, the intruder gained access to a wide range of computers around the world by taking advantage of many of the potential security problems mentioned in this book, including software errors, easily guessed passwords, and procedural errors. Throughout this work, potential weaknesses were present in each system, and the person methodically took advantage of these circumstances. As Stoll reports, "the person we followed was patient and plodding, but hardly showed creative brilliance in discovering new security flaws."[9]

Given that he used relatively well-known techniques, the scope of the intruder's activity is impressive. The intruder lived in Germany and used the local telephone exchange to obtain access to a nearby machine. This computer then allowed him to enter various national and worldwide networks. (Long distance charges were borne by some of the installations under attack.) After several stages, the intruder was able to connect to the LBL computers (where monitoring of his activities started), and this gave the intruder access to the Internet for access to many machines and networks throughout this country. Altogether, he made use of a remarkable diversity of machines and involved an impressive range of locations through interconnected networks.

As a postscript to this story, the identity of this intruder finally was determined only through a long-term, concentrated effort by Clifford Stoll and others. Various monitoring and tracing capabilities were utilized in the work, but tracking the individual still required great effort and resourcefulness. The presence of an intruder was first determined during an investigation of an accounting error, because the intruder had created a new account with no corresponding billing number. He obtained access to this accounting information through a subtle error in a standard text editor and was then able to gain system manager privileges. To trace his progress, investigators attached printers to users' lines, so they could read everything the intruder typed. They constantly monitored all of his account's activities, and they traced his telephone calls. The complete story of the monitoring and eventual identification of the intruder makes fascinating reading. If interested, read the full account in one of the sources listed in the notes.

Since the LBL example occurred, both security measures and hacking techniques have progressed significantly. One way that organizations and companies now increase their defense against unwanted visitors is by installing protective measures such as firewalls.

---

5 Stoll writes a fascinating account of his efforts to track down an intruder to the Livermore Berkeley Laboratory computers in his article "Stalking the Wily Hacker," *Communications of the ACM*, Volume 31, Number 5, May 1988, pp. 484–497. His story has also been described in a program produced for Public Television. Various other accounts of this material have also appeared in several publications.

6 Ibid., p. 494.

7 Ibid.

8 Ibid., p. 484.

9 Ibid., p. 485.

What do firewalls do, and how do they work?

Many security threats arise from unauthorized access to computers by people at a distance, so an important component of any defense against these threats involves the prevention of such access. Remember how Chapter 9 described that communication from one computer to another proceeds by sending packets of information, and these packets contain an identifier number, called a port, to specify how they should be handled? (For example, port 21 indicates a message has to do with commands for the transfer of files via FTP, and port 80 has to do with the transmission of data for browsers of the World Wide Web.)

Ports provide application-routing information for every message, so one way to limit access over a network to known applications is to limit which ports can be used for communication. For example, if you know and trust the applications for ports 21 and 80, you may decide messages for these ports should proceed. However, if you know nothing about applications for port 12345, then you may wonder about the purpose of any messages received on such ports. Screening of ports is a primary function of a *firewall*. More generally, a **firewall** is a filtering program that monitors all network traffic to a computer.

Overall, message filtering can be quite sophisticated, and firewalls typically allow you to accept messages to only certain ports. In addition, messages from specific other sites or computers can be explicitly accepted or rejected, so sources of known trouble can be prevented from communicating directly with your computer. By setting parameters to correspond to your intended uses and experiences, a firewall can block messages to unknown application programs, thus preventing information from getting to programs you may not trust or even know about.

Summary

When you use a computer, you expect your information will be stored reliably and processing will proceed correctly. You also expect that your data will be secure.

Some measures that can enhance reliability and correctness include the use of full backups, incremental backups, timed transactions (to defend against crashes), transaction processing, audit trails, and roll backs.

Computer security involves granting authorized people access to your confidential or sensitive data, while preventing others from using this information. For some simple, isolated computer systems, this problem may be solved reasonably well, because the machine can be placed behind locked or guarded doors, where only appropriate people can get near it. Once several users have access to a machine, however, problems multiply. When several machines are interconnected on a network, difficulties are only compounded further. Some common threats include keyboard sniffers, wire tapping, poor coordination of processor security levels, Trojan horses, viruses, and worms.

Some technical methods to address these problems include password systems, encryption, full erasure of old files, anti-virus packages, and firewalls. In addition, users must utilize care in monitoring behavior of the software they use, in handling attachments in e-mail, and in reviewing files obtained either over the Web or on disks.

Terminology from This Chapter

Audit trails
Caesar Cipher
Firewall
Incremental backup
Keyboard sniffer
Persistent storage
Personal Identification Number (PIN)
Public key encryption
Transactions
Trojan horses
Virus
Worm

Discussion Questions

1. Discuss whether or not it is ethical for a student or employee to write a password-guessing program.
   a. How would you respond to the argument that a password-cracking program provides an intellectual challenge?
   b. If a student is successful in learning the password of another student or an instructor, should the student be punished for reporting to the other student or instructor that his or her password is not secure?
2. On many machines connected to national networks, "guest" or "anonymous" accounts are established to allow people

from around the country to log on to the machines. With such accounts, anyone can log on to a machine without having to know a password. Typically, the capabilities available from such accounts are somewhat restricted, but they do allow interested users to locate, copy, and edit publicly available data and to run programs. Such sharing of data can support a wide range of research and development efforts, and much educational software and materials are exchanged at low cost through such opportunities.

Although anonymous accounts can aid legitimate access to publicly accessible data, they also can provide a convenient starting place for people wishing to obtain sensitive data. Review various ways of obtaining unauthorized access to data on distributed networks, and describe at least two major ways that such anonymous accounts could be used in breaking into restricted data or accounts.

3. One way the problem of trust is complicated for computers is that a very large number of people may have a legitimate responsibility for part of a system. Determine what capabilities each of the following people should be given in order to do their jobs, and consider how each of them might use those powers to obtain or transmit unauthorized information if they wished.

   a. Computer operators

   b. Software developers

   c. System managers

   d. Repair/maintenance personnel

   e. Users on a multi-user computer

4. Suppose a programmer teamed up with a member of a testing or system administration group. Describe a few ways (at least two) where the two people could work in collusion to obtain sensitive data in a way that would be difficult to detect. For example, how could one person cover for the other?

5. The following questions raise issues about the trust that a person might have when using a computer. In each case, clarify the issue(s) and determine the extent you think this should be a concern for computer users.

   a. When you use a word-processing package, how do you know that the program is not making another copy of what you type, so that copy could be accessed by someone else? (Any program you run will have access to your files, of course, because you are the one running it, and you certainly can access your own files.)

b. In a related matter for a program with several users and printers, when you ask the machine to print some information, how do you know that the operating system or the print procedure does not make a copy at the same time, perhaps printing the copy on another printer?

c. If you buy new software for your personal computer (perhaps you purchased a new word processor, spreadsheet, or video game), how do you know that the diskette containing the software does not contain a virus? (Some commercially available packages have been contaminated in the past.)

d. If you use a virus checker on your own personal computer, how do you know that it works as claimed? More generally, how do you know any software package does what it claims? How can you be sure that something odd will not happen when the package is run a certain number of times?

e. When you log on to a large computer system, how do you know that the operating system is not displaying your password to someone else? How do you even know that the log-in process is genuine (i.e., not being simulated by some other program that is designed to capture your password or to copy your files)?

f. When you call a service or repair company, how do you know that the person who comes to your business has not attached a wiretap to your data communication lines?

g. In a bank environment, how would you detect if a programmer in the computing department had added a piece of code that would allow his or her account to be overdrawn? Similarly, in computing interest to the nearest cent, how would you know that any extra fractions of a cent were not credited to the programmer's account? (This latter event has happened, where the total amount of interest accumulated checked out correctly, but the programmer became rich by getting thousandths of fractions of a cent daily whenever interest for any account was computed.)

h. If your computer has a modem that can connect it to telephone lines, how do you know that some piece of software does not automatically call a toll-free number (or a local number) periodically when no other processing is occurring to transmit updates on data files?

6. The End-User License Agreement for version 6.4 of the Windows Media Player by Microsoft stated:

> Digital Rights Management (Security). You agree that in order to protect the integrity of content and software protected by digital rights management ("Secure Content"), Microsoft may provide security related updates to the OS Components that will be automatically downloaded onto your computer. These security-related updates may disable your ability to copy and/or play Secure Content and use of other software on your computer. If we provide such a security update, we will use reasonable efforts to post notices on a web site explaining the update.

With this agreement, Microsoft is authorized to download anything it feels is appropriate to handle any circumstance it deems a threat, and it can disable programs you have purchased from other sources. Discuss the implications of such a policy from the standpoint of data reliability and computer security.

Exercises

1. a. The "Terminology from This Chapter" section identifies several mechanisms that unscrupulous people may use in an attempt to gain access to unauthorized data or to cause mischief on a computer. Most other terms relate to the protection of data or the prevention of mischief, although a few terms may be more general. Organize the terms into the categories "threat," "prevention," and "other." In each case, explain why the term belongs in the category that you chose.

b. Provide careful definitions for each word or phrase.

2. One commentator stated "it is virtually impossible to ever be completely sure that any computing system of any size is completely secure" (*The Limits of Computing*, Chapter 9, question 9.5). In view of the possibilities for unauthorized access to data described in this chapter, evaluate whether you think this sentence is overly guarded, overly pessimistic, or about right. For example, consider the following questions:

   a. Is the statement overly guarded? Could the word "virtually" be omitted? In other words, can you describe any reasonably sized computing system that could be guaranteed to be secure? How would you know it did not have security leaks?

   b. Is the statement overly pessimistic or alarmist? Would it be more accurate to state, "Although it may be somewhat difficult, it is quite feasible to create and operate a secure computing system."

   Justify your answer.

3. The March 20, 1989, issue of *Time* magazine (pp. 25–26) discusses the potential for security violations within networks of computers within the military. For example, *Time* reported that "the U. S. arrested and expelled a military attache for allegedly trying to steal details of computer-security programs." The article then considers the following hypothetical scenario:

   - An enemy agent in the Pentagon sends a computer virus through the World-Wide Military Command and Control System, which the U.S. commanders would rely on in wartime for information and coordination. The virus sits undetected. When hostilities begin, the agent sends a message that triggers the virus, erasing everything in the system.

   - A different virus is introduced into NATO's logistics computers. Triggered just as the Soviet army marches into West Germany, the virus alters messages so that all allied supplies are sent to the wrong places. By the time the mistake is corrected a day or two later, key parts of NATO's defense line have collapsed.

   a. Discuss some ways that such a virus might be injected into such a computer network. Who might be able to plant the virus? How?

b. How could the possibilities for this type of threat be reduced or prevented?

c. *Time's* article states that "officials differ about the likelihood that such sabotage could be carried off." What do you think? Justify your answer.

d. To what extent do you think circumstances have changed in the years since this article appeared?

4. Firewalls can prevent programs on other computers from establishing communication connections with your computer. Explain why such firewalls may not be effective in preventing troublesome effects that might arise from opening attachments to e-mail.

Part IV
Web/Internet Questions

Chapter 11

How does the Internet work?

It's a Wednesday evening, and you've just sat down at your computer. In a matter of minutes, you're scanning an e-commerce site for you aunt's birthday present, you're composing an e-mail message to your professor via your school e-mail account, you're listening to your brother's radio show broadcast live from a college hundreds of miles away, and you're using your computer for an online chat with a friend from home. Without the Internet, none of these actions would be possible. Think about how much you depend on communicating via your computer—it may be much more than you realize. When was the last time you actually mailed a letter in paper form? But what exactly happens to make e-mail and work with the Web possible? Where does the information reside, and how do monitors know what to display. To begin, let's recall what we already know about hardware and network organization.

On a small scale, the organization of computers into coherent networks can follow simple principles discussed in Chapters 8 and 9. For example, a small number of computers may connect to a single Ethernet cable, forming a network segment. Segments, in turn, may be connected in a hierarchical manner using routers. Organization of a small group of computers within a school or company typically follows a basic, coherent, and understandable structure. The Internet, on the other hand, involves millions of computers, connected in complex ways to a maze of local and regional networks. With so many computers and connections, and with additions and changes happening continuously, how can anyone know just how all of the pieces fit together, and how can it possibly work?

Despite the complexity, however, millions of people receive e-mail, use Web browsers to find information, move files via FTP, and generally utilize the Internet for a wide range of communications each and every day. This chapter addresses how such communication is possible—even with the Internet's inherent intricacies. First, we'll consider matters of organization. How do various pieces fit together in a way that allows machines to get information from one place to another? We'll then discuss questions of Internet ownership and access: who owns what parts of the Internet and how funding is generated to pay for this infrastructure. Once we've covered these basics, the chapter addresses common questions about experiences you may have in using the Internet, such as how a browser works and the role of standards. Let's begin with the organization of the Internet.

How is the Internet organized?

Although you may think of the Internet as a single logical entity, a more accurate image would involve a confederation of cooperating local, regional, and national networks. To understand this structure, some history may be helpful.

In the 1960s, most computing was done on large computers, called **mainframes**. Mainframes were not quite the portable and user-friendly personal computers that we know today; rather, they were large, heavy machines that were usually operated by experienced technicians. In many cases, these machines worked by themselves or in clusters that were physically close to each other. When connections between distant machines were needed, companies used telephone lines to dial up from one location to another. After establishing a connection between locations, the computers used these dial-up lines for communication. When greater capacity, or **bandwidth,** was needed for communications, companies sometimes leased telephone lines from one location to another. By leasing a telephone line, a company made an exclusive physical wire connection with a different location, and no longer needed to dial up their telephone box. Leased lines also could be somewhat more reliable than depending upon a dial-up telephone. Both dial-up and leased lines worked reasonably well, as long as volume was relatively low and one machine always communicated with just a few others.

Then, in 1969, for various practical and strategic reasons, the U.S. Department of Defense (DoD) established an experimental network connecting four research computers—at the University of California at Los Angeles and at Santa Barbara, at SRI International, and at the University of Utah. Funding for this network came through the Advanced Research Projects Agency (ARPA) within the DoD, and this network was therefore called ARPAnet. Through the 1970s, the number of locations attached to this DoD network expanded gradually, and people connected to these computers also found other types of uses for the network, beyond those initially envisioned by the DoD. For example, file transfer with FTP was developed in 1971.

In the 1980s, the initial network established by the DoD combined with other networks funded through the U.S. National Science Foundation (NSF). In particular, the main network, or **backbone,** involved a few main computer centers, or **nodes**, and other institutions obtained access by connecting to these centers (or to institutions that in turn had connections to the backbone centers). Overall, these inaugural connections might be envisioned as a web or expanded star network, with a backbone computer in the center, a few connections to that center for "first-tier" institutions, connections to the first-tier computers to form a "second-tier," and so forth. Thus, when a new institution wanted to establish a connection to this network, it would first identify what other organizations in the area already had a connection. Then, the new institution would negotiate to run (or lease) one or more cables from its own computers to the already-connected organization. Typically, institutions in an area might be connected to the same backbone node—either directly or through its neighbors. Connectivity to other regions typically involved going through backbone nodes.

Computer connectivity was becoming increasingly useful, but funding came largely from the NSF, which is chartered to conduct scientific research and development. With this focus, the NSF limited connections to the network to research organizations, scientific laboratories, and academic institutions. Commercial traffic was not allowed. For example, e-mail was first developed in 1972, when Ray Tomlinson at BBN wrote the first basic software to send and receive e-mail messages. In the mid 1970s, e-mail emerged as a very popular application, and folks at universities could communicate over the NSF network via e-mail. This network, however, was not connected to commercial networks that had emerged separately. Thus, a scientist at a research university might be able to e-mail a research assistant at another university, but not a colleague who worked at a private company in the next town. In 1989, the NSF lifted its e-mail restriction and allowed e-mail connectivity for two commercial network vendors, CompuServe and MCI Mail. By the start of the 1990s, the NSF network connected many research, scientific, and academic institutions; and several private and commercial networks had emerged for other purposes. E-mail and file transfer applications were used widely.

Then, in 1991, two major changes occurred. Commercial restrictions began to be phased out, and the NSF developed plans to turn its Internet over to the private sector. Originally, privatization involved identifying several companies to run national operations, called **National Access Points (NAPs)**. Each NAP was run by a separate company, called a **National Access Provider**, and based in a different location. Regional and local organizations, called **Internet Service Providers (ISPs)**, could attach to a NAP to provide Internet access for companies, schools, individuals, and other interested parties. By 1995, the move toward privatization was largely complete with four NAPs: Ameritech ran the NAP in Chicago, MFS Corporation ran the NAP in Washington, D.C., Sprint ran the NAP in New York, and Pacific Bell ran the NAP in San Francisco.

Today, the various NAPs and ISPs operate as separate companies, but standards organizations specify how communications will take place. Further, standards allow for expansion, and new companies can join the Internet without requiring any changes to existing NAPs and ISPs. This has allowed connections to the Internet to grow at a remarkable rate. For example, www.thedirectory.org maintains a listing of ISPs based on regions of the country and organized by telephone area code. In their January 7, 2002, materials, the directory stated that "As of November, 1998 . . . we had almost 200 companies that were nationwide providers. . . . We now have over 1,300 nationwide providers in our database and the number is still increasing." They go on to state that some areas of the United States had as many as 1500 ISPs.

With all of these independent companies and networks, protocols describe formats for messages in considerable detail, so communications can proceed from one provider to another without difficulty. Overall, you can consider the United States's NAPs and ISPs as representing a confederation of companies, with guidance and standards coming from various specified national or international committees and agencies.

You can find more information on the early history of the Internet through the Internet Society, including "A Brief History of the Internet" by Leiner et al., www.isoc.org/internet/history/brief.shtml.

How is the Internet organized at the global level?

Because the DoD and NSF operate within the United States, their decisions formally apply to networks only within that context. However, because the Internet began in the United States, the NSF and DoD's policies and approaches have had a major impact on networking in other countries as well. To expand somewhat, each country has the power to determine companies and service providers for national, regional, and local networking within that country. However, to enable networking communications to take place among countries, any country involved with the Internet must follow consistent standards. Thus, various international committees oversee standards, and interactions from one country's network(s) to networks in other countries may be based on negotiated contracts and agreements.

Overall, one might consider the model of NAPs and ISPs as now applying worldwide, where NAPs from various countries provide top-level service and connectivity for a type of network backbone. Then within countries or regions, ISPs connect individuals, groups, and companies to the NAPs.

Who owns the Internet?

As the discussion of the Internet's history suggests, ownership of the Internet has evolved over the years. At the start, one might argue that the U.S. Department of Defense or the National Science Foundation owned the Internet, because those agencies provided primary funding. Ownership was even more clear with private networks, such as MCI Mail or CompuServe, because one company controlled and ran each network.

With privatization and internationalization, however, the term *ownership* today is misleading. The United States and other countries who host NAPs could be viewed as owning parts of the backbone or main interconnection points of the Internet. Also, one could consider regional or local ISPs as owning segments of regional networks. National and regional networks, however, have overlapping capabilities in the United States and other countries. Thus, all networks must cooperate with regard to standards, and no single network or provider has the ultimate control. Further, if one provider curtailed its services, then others are in place to take over. Thus, no one company or country can be considered as the owner of the Internet; rather, ownership is shared among many entities, and responsibilities are divided among participants.

Now that the Internet is an international entity, coordination of the Internet is largely accomplished through the Internet Society (ISOC). In particular, its Internet Engineering Task Force (IETF) focuses on various hardware matters, while its Internet Architecture Board (IAB) defines the network's architecture—its backbones and the networks attached to them. Information about each of these organizations exists online—see, for example, www.isoc.org for the home page of the Internet Society. This page, in turn, has links to both the IETF and IAB.

Within a country, a government may designate certain agencies or groups to control various standards, protocols, and agreements. For example, in the United States, the U.S. government has designated the Internet Corporation for Assigned Names and Numbers (ICANN) as having primary responsibility for specifying what Internet name is assigned to whom and what port numbers are reserved for which use. (More about Web addresses shortly.) In other countries, different groups may have similar responsibilities for those areas. In some sense, one might argue that these committees and agencies own or control their components of the Internet, but those groups can function only within the constraints of international agreements and specified standards.

Does it cost anything to connect to the Internet?

Despite the fact that no one specific company or organization owns the Internet, connecting to it is not free. Both national and regional providers must maintain their networks, including cables, computers (servers), routers, and all the other pieces that make up the Internet. Connections between providers require cables, transmission lines, satellite links, and the like. Such infrastructure obviously incurs considerable costs—for setting up initial equipment and connections, for maintaining that equipment, and for upgrading components to keep up with new demands of users. Although the Internet is more of a confederation than a single entity, the various components all incur costs that must be offset by income.

Who pays for the Internet?

When the DoD or NSF maintained much of the Internet backbone, many of the basic costs for national connectivity were met by the United States government. Any academic, scientific, and research organizations that participated in the Internet needed to cover their own costs of connecting with the backbone, plus some of the operation of the backbone itself. The Internet, however, was not expected to earn a profit, and many basic costs were subsidized by the government.

With the privatization of the Internet, economies changed in substantial ways. The government still maintains a role in the Internet, but the national and regional providers now operate as businesses and must earn a profit on their investments. The national ISP America Online, for example, works continuously to maintain up-to-date service and charges its subscribers a monthly fee to offset its expenses and make a profit. Today, the role of government continues to diminish as commercial interests become increasingly important. Serious revenue is required to offset all of the expenses that the Internet incurs, and these days such costs must be covered by users—companies, organizations, and individuals.

Where does the money go?

In considering the costs of the Internet, many expenses have to do with basic infrastructure: servers, routers, communication lines, and the like. When this equipment is running smoothly, electrical signals move from place to place, and processing continues in a way that is largely independent of usage. Of course, demands for handling a large volume of message traffic may require more equipment than what is needed for a small volume. Generally, however, once the infrastructure is in place to accommodate a basic level of activity, the costs of running this equipment do not vary much whether the traffic on a particular day is heavy or light. Expenses largely have to do with setting up and maintaining the network rather than communicating individual messages.

For this reason, what you're charged for Internet usage typically depends on the materials you need to buy to establish connections (cables, computers, junction boxes, and so on) and the general level of capacity you anticipate. Fast lines may be more expensive to install and maintain than slow lines, for example, but your needs may make them more useful to you than the other. Once equipment is in place, you can send many messages or just a few with virtually no change in cost. For this reason, charges for the Internet to you, your school, or your company usually are not associated with individual messages. You pay a flat fee (perhaps monthly) for a level of service to support the infrastructure, but you do not pay per message. Part of your payment to an ISP then goes toward the NAP for the national infrastructure.

Once you have connectivity to the Internet, you have access to an incredible wealth of information and the ability to communicate with people around the world. For many people, these advantages make up for the expense of a monthly subscription to an ISP. In addition to e-mail, the Internet allows you to navigate, or surf, through Web sites that cover virtually any topic. You probably have some favorite Web sites, and their names all conform to a standard format. Let's turn now and take a look at what's behind an Internet address.

What is an Internet address?*

When you type in a Web address, you provide the computer with the information it needs to find the location you are trying to access. All locations on the Internet may be described at three levels: the **domain name**, the **Internet Protocol number (IP number)**, and the **Ethernet address**. Let's now examine each level.

Domain Name: The domain name is the logical name for a computing system attached to the Internet. If your school hosts a Web site, then its domain name is likely included in the Internet addresses for its Web pages. For example, cs.utexas.edu is the logical name as-

*(From Dale and Walker, *Abstract Data Types*, pp. 144–146.)

sociated with a central machine for the computer sciences department at the University of Texas at Austin, while grinnell.edu refers to a central academic computing machine at Grinnell College. In fact, the names form a hierarchical structure: .edu indicates that these are educational institutions—grinnell.edu and utexas.edu are main subjects within the .edu category. cs.grinnell.edu and math.grinnell.edu are two subcategories under the Grinnell College heading, used for the computer science and mathematics areas.

More generally, the suffix of a domain name (such as .edu) is called a **top-level domain** (TLD), and these are coordinated through the Internet Corporation for Assigned Names and Numbers (ICANN). Currently, 13 names are used within the United States for different types of organizations. A full list of these TLDs is shown in Table 11.1.

Beyond these suffixes used in the United States, other countries typically are assigned a suffix for their own use, and each country determines how domain names are assigned within its jurisdiction. For example, the suffix .uk is used for domain names within the United Kingdom, while .gr is used for Greece, .tv for the country of Tuvalu, and .cn for the People's Republic of China.

Table 11.1 Top-Level Domain Names for the United States

Abbreviation	Use or Purpose
.aero	air transport industry
.biz	businesses
.com	commercial
.coop	cooperatives
.edu	four-year educational institutions
.gov	U.S. government
.info	general use
.mil	U.S. military
.museum	museums
.name	individual people
.net	general use
.org	not-for-profit organizations
.pro	professionals (accountants, lawyers, physicians)

IP Number: An Internet Protocol (IP) number is a 32-bit address that often is written as a four-part decimal number. You usually do not type this part of the Internet address when searching for a site, although you could. Rather, the domain name you do type in corresponds to a central computer that has a specific IP number, and this number is communicated to your computer by a server. For example, cs.utexas.edu corresponds to 128.83.139.9, so when you type in "http://www.cs.utexas.edu," your computer consults a server that identifies this address as corresponding to the IP number 128.83.139.9. This allows your computer to contact the central computer named cs.utexas.edu.

IP numbers also are arranged hierarchically. For example, consider the IP numbers corresponding to Grinnell College, as shown in Figure 11.1. All of Grinnell's addresses begin with 132.161. . . , and the machines related to academic computing begin 132.161.10 . . . . The machines related to the Grinnell's mathematics and computer science departments are divided into three subnetworks with IP numbers 132.161.31 . . . , 132.161.32 . . . , and 132.161.33 . . . . As with domain numbers, IP numbers are defined so that no two correspond to the same location or machine.

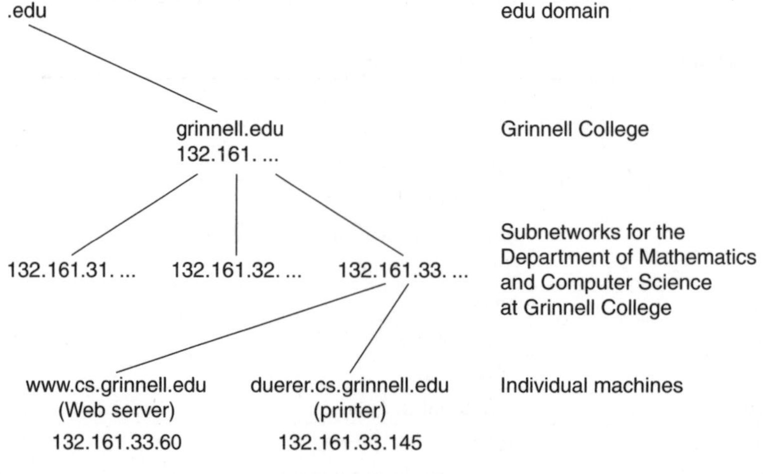

Figure 11.1
The IP number hierarchy for computers at Grinnell College.

Internationally, three nonprofit organizations assign and distribute IP numbers:

- The American Registration for Internet Numbers (ARIN) assigns and manages IP addresses for North America, South America, the Caribbean, and sub-Saharan Africa.
- The Réseaux IP Europééns (RIPE) assigns and manages IP addresses for Europe, the Middle East, and the rest of Africa.
- The Asia-Pacific Network Information Center (APNIC) assigns and manages IP addresses for Asia and the Pacific basin.

Ethernet Address: The third level of an Internet address is the Ethernet address, a 48-bit address that is built into each actual machine or Ethernet board. Manufacturers register these numbers with the IEEE Registration Authority, a body within the Institute of Electrical and Electronics Engineers. When machines are repaired or when Ethernet cards are replaced, new circuitry has a new Ethernet address, even though the rest of the computer may be the same. This underlies the distinction between IP numbers and Ethernet addresses: IP numbers are associated with specific computers and do not change, whereas Ethernet addresses correspond to Ethernet circuitry and can be attached to any computer. New Ethernet hardware warrants new Ethernet addresses, because you are using a physically different chip or board. However, when you replace the Ethernet hardwired in your computer, your IP number likely remains the same as the designation for your machine within the communication network.

How are domain names, IP numbers, and Ethernet addresses related?

When a user wants to send a message, she or he normally designates a domain name, such as cs.utexas.edu. The machine then must translate this to the Internet IP number and communicate it to the network. IP numbers in turn must be translated to Ethernet addresses when machines send actual packets of information over specific cables.

The translation between domain and IP numbers, or between IP numbers and Ethernet addresses, requires your computer to consult an Internet authority, as I will describe shortly; various Internet authorities maintain tables of domain names and IP numbers, and other authorities store tables of IP numbers and Ethernet addresses. In considering these tables, the Internet is now so large that it is not practical for any one machine to record all possible addresses. Instead, central machines are designated as authorities for various parts of the network, and a local machine may or may not record the few domain names, IP numbers, and Ethernet addresses it actually uses. Any machine attempting to contact another machine must first contact a central computer in charge of keeping track of the necessary IP addresses so that it has access to that information.

To see how this type of lookup is done, suppose the local machine (steenrod.cs.grinnell.edu) needs to determine the IP number for cs.utexas.edu. When the machine is first turned on, it has no information concerning other IP numbers, but its initial configuration includes information that a local **domain name server (DNS)** can be reached at grinnell.edu—IP number 132.161.10.11. If this server is unavailable, it has the IP number for a secondary **network information server (NIS)**. The DNS and NIS machines maintain databases with domain names and IP numbers in a binary format that facilitates quick lookup. In fact, for efficiency, this information is often stored in two tables—one based on domain name and the other on IP number—so that searches by either domain name or IP number can be performed particularly fast.

In searching for the IP number for cs.utexas.edu, the local machine first asks its local DNS, which is the authority for the local network, but which may or may not know about the rest of the world. In handling this request for information, this local DNS consults its tables to attempt to locate the needed IP number. If this information is not in the table, the search fails, and the local machine then asks its secondary NIS source, which is the authority for a wider area of the network. If this fails as well, eventually a request is generated for the DNS for all .edu addresses. This DNS then either returns the information requested or indicates that it is available from a more specialized DNS, which handles information down one branch of the domain name hierarchy. (For example, the .edu DNS may indicate that information regarding cs.utexas.edu can be obtained from a DNS specializing in utexas.edu, and give the IP number for that corresponding specialized DNS.) In short, to determine the IP number that corresponds to a given domain name, a local machine may consult several specialized DNS machines that look up the desired information name in appropriate tables before finding one that returns the appropriate IP number.

Of course, it might be that all designated DNS machines are unavailable when your local computer attempts to find the IP number that corresponds to a particular domain name. Because of this possibility, some systems also maintain a table for some local machines that are commonly accessed. Although this table is often in text format rather than binary format, it can serve as a backup resource. Local machines can refer to this system's table for IP numbers and also can store IP numbers in this local table for future reference.

Once the local machine learns the IP number for the destination of a message, it then must send the message itself. However, as noted earlier, the IP number designates a logical machine, not the physical connection of an Ethernet controller to a cable. Thus, another translation process is needed, and another table is used: The machine needs to determine the Ethernet address associated with an IP number. To identify the correct Ethernet address, the computer consults another table—this one often stored in main memory.

At the start, this table is empty. Thus, the machine broadcasts a message to all machines on its local network, asking "Which of you has the following IP number: . . . ?" If the message is being sent to another machine in the local network, then the desired machine replies, and the machine can send the message. If the machine is outside the local network, no response is returned. Instead, the machine packages the message in a packet to a default router, which in turn can follow a similar process until the packet is delivered to the correct location.

In summary, Internet communication requires at least two types of lookups: one to receive IP numbers from domain names, and one to obtain Ethernet addresses from IP numbers. Because the Internet involves a vast number of machines, it is impractical to keep all of this information in a small local computer. Instead, a local machine may keep a table of recently obtained information, because it typically needs only a few Ethernet addresses at a time. These addresses are often kept in a small table in main memory, where a simple search can find the needed information. The computer will then consult other machines when data are unknown. These central authorities for domain names are (as we discussed) domain name servers, which use specialized tables for fast retrieval of information.

All of this discussion, of course, fits within a context in which desktop computers are connected directly by wires to an ISP or other Internet outlet. Because desktop computers are reasonably heavy, they usually stay where they are first connected. In contrast, laptop computers often move from one place to another, and this adds challenges.

How do laptops connect to the Internet?

As we have learned, when connecting to the Internet, each computer must have an IP address. The question then arises as to what IP address laptop computers should use, because they are portable machines and can join a variety of networks at any time. Typically, laptops obtain IP numbers in one of two ways. This address can be specified manually; that is, a lab administrator or an ISP may assign an explicit IP address for your machine. This number then is entered into various network tables, and you may need to enter the number into your laptop. Thereafter, all network communications utilize this address. Such an approach is called a **static IP address**, reflecting that it is static rather than dynamic or changeable.

An alternative approach involves your computer asking the network for an IP address when you plug it in and turn it on. In this approach, called **Dynamic Host Configuration Protocol (DHCP)**, the IP address changes each time you use your computer, as new IP addresses are obtained each time they are needed. With each connection to a network, your computer makes a new request for an IP address, and the IP address it receives will likely be different than what it had previously—even if it connects to the same network.

A computer can function on a network only if it uses the network's preferred method of determining an IP address. Thus, if the network expects a static IP address but you haven't entered yours, then your computer and the network cannot communicate properly. Similarly, if your laptop operates on the basis of a manually specified IP address but the network expects the DHCP approach, communication again fails. If, however, both expect DHCP, you likely can just connect your computer to the network and let the equipment handle the details. When that occurs, your manual work is done. If, however, you move from one network with static IP addresses to another that expects a different static IP number, you likely will need to enter the IP address each time. Today, many laptop computers are designed to simplify the process of connecting to networks, and they can handle many details. However, they cannot guess static IP addresses, so you always will have to intervene when networks follow that approach.

Now that we've discussed how computers connect, are identified within a system, and communicate, let's take a change of pace and look at what you see on your monitor when you access the Internet, and how that material comes to be displayed.

How do Web browsers display text and images?

As with other processing within computers, a browser displays text and images according to specific instructions. Recall that a Web browser is an application that runs on your computer. You type in the name of a document, including a domain name as I just described. The browser then interacts with the Internet to locate the document, retrieve it, and display the material on your computer's screen. Three browsers in common use today include Microsoft's Internet Explorer, Mozilla, and Netscape Navigator. Because computers use different browsers to view the same Web pages, Web text and image information need to be communicated so that every system will understand how material should be displayed. The system of specifying and communicating Web documents often uses rules and conventions called the **Hypertext Transfer Protocol (HTTP)**. This may clarify the prefix *http://* that is often typed at the start of many Web domain addresses. HTTP denotes the standard or protocol that your browser will utilize when it communicates with the Web server that stores the document you request.

As part of the delivery of material from a Web server to your browser, the server indicates the nature of its instructions in one of two ways. For example, if the server is sending you information to display an image on a Web page, it will tell your computer that the information it is providing is for an image. One way it accomplishes this is to informally allow the browser to infer the format based on the suffix of a Web document name. Table 11.2 shows a few frequently used examples.

Table 11.2 Some Common File Name Endings and the File Types They Often Denote

File Name Ending In	Format Used in Document
.hmtl or .htm	Hypertext Markup Language
.pdf	Portable Document Format
.ps	PostScript
.gif or .jpeg	graphical GIF or JPEG format, as discussed in Chapter 2

As this suggests, a document with the full name

http://www.cs.grinnell.edu/~walker/index.html

would be located on the Web server www.cs.grinnell.edu in the account of user walker. The file itself is called index.html. The computer uses the suffix html or htm to know the format used in the document. As with much material found on the World Wide Web, this file contains formatting instructions based on a system called the **Hypertext Markup Language (HTML)** to specify how the document should look. (We will talk more about HTML shortly.)

As a second, more formal, approach for communication of types of documents, a Web server may precede its sending of a file with a specific message, notifying the browser about the nature of the document. In this case, a server may indicate the forthcoming document will be in PDF, PostScript, or another format, regardless of the suffix used in the document name. In such situations, a browser is supposed to interpret what follows in the designated way (although occasionally a browser may not function properly).

Once a browser knows or infers the format of material it is receiving, it interprets the document using one of two mechanisms. If the format of the document is common (like HTML), the browser may know how to process it and can display the document directly. Alternatively, the browser may consult a table of formats and run a designated, special program to carry out the actual display. Such a designated program is sometimes called a **plugin**. Through the use of plugins, a browser can respond to a wide range of materials, and new formats can be added without changing the browser. (Only the table of plugins need be updated.)

How does HTML work?

HTML is P reasonably streamlined approach for specifying formats and display information for Web documents. To be somewhat more precise, HTML indicates a family of formats, with each version clarifying capabilities and providing new features. Each version is specified by the World Wide Web Consortium (W3C) and represents a standard for use by all browsers. Two versions in particularly widespread use are HTML 3.2 (version 3, release 2), developed in 1996, and HTML 4.01, developed in 1999.

As the name "markup language" may suggest, HTML provides instructions, called *tags*, within a document to specify various details of format. The first tag, at the very beginning of a document, is

<html>

The corresponding tag, at the very end of a document, is

</html>

These HTML tags tell the browser that the document uses Hypertext Markup Language to communicate how its text and images should be displayed. As this example indicates, HTML tags are placed within angle brackets < >, and the starting tag (html) has a companion closing tag (/html) with the same name plus an initial slash character. A similar convention is followed for a variety of formatting specifications. To denote italics, for example, the tag <i> tells a browser that what follows should use an italics font, while </i> indicates the italics section is over.

Some other common tags include:

<b> </b>	Use a bold font.
<p> </p>	Consider the intervening text as a paragraph (the </p> tag may be omitted, however).
<title> </title>	Placed directly after the initial html tag; use the identified material as the title at the top of a browser window.
<table> </table>	Place what follows in tabular form.
<ol> </ol>	Consider what follows as a list of numbered items (items within the list are designated by an initial tag <li> for "list item").

Beyond these paired tags, HTML contains a variety of tags for special purposes. For example, <br> specifies a break in the current line, moving to a new line.

Another type of tag indicates where to insert pictures or other material. For example,

<img src="my-picture.gif">

indicates that the .gif file called my-picture should be inserted at the designated location on the page.

In basic formatting with HTML, the text and images are given with simple instructions, and a document's author allows the browser to interpret various details according to local circumstances. For example, a computer's display may have high resolution or low resolution depending on how tightly dots or pixels are packed together. Low-density screens typically have relatively large pixels, so text may appear relatively large. On the other hand, if the same material is shown on a high-resolution screen, then that material may appear quite small in size. Computer monitors also may display colors in different ways, and a browser may be set to accommodate particular equipment. Beyond these equipment-related variations, some computer users have better eyesight than others, and they may set their browsers to show letters in a smaller type font than users with worse eyesight. Because of such practical considerations, many Web documents provide only basic formatting instructions, allowing a local browser to refine details according to specific equipment and user preferences.

Such considerations notwithstanding, HTML allows a document's author to specify spacing, font, and color information in considerable detail, if desired. Such elements typically fall under the heading of "style" and provide remarkable control regarding the appearance of materials. Author-supplied formatting instructions normally overrule preferences set in a browser. However, because equipment varies (resolution, color settings, size of screen), even tightly controlled documents may look quite different on different machines.

Between formatting instructions and style information, HTML provides a wide range of instructions for formatting Web documents. For information beyond the basics given here, I encourage you to consult one of the many books on HTML. Also, standards for HTML are maintained online by the World Wide Web Consortium at http://www.w3c.org.

Why do browsers sometimes fail to display Web pages properly?

Have you ever opened a Web page and had parts of it fail to open or seen the page framed awkwardly as though it were not being displayed correctly? One reason this happens is that from time to time, browsers may contain software errors or bugs. Much software malfunctions in one circumstance or another, and browsers are no different than other software packages in this regard.

Your browser, however, may be displaying the site incorrectly because of more substantial reasons, those based on the code in the instructions. For the most part, browsers correctly handle standard HTML—at least for versions that were known when the particular browser was written. For example, HTML version 2.0 was published in November 1995, HTML version 3.2 was developed in 1996 and published in January 1997, HTML version 4.0 was published in December 1997, and HTML version 4.01 was published in December 1999. A browser written in 2002 is likely to work appropriately for HTML 4.01, but it might not display pages written in a form of HTML that was released after that time. An old browser might work fine for HTML 3.2, but not for HTML 4.01.

Unfortunately, however, various developers of browsers sometimes decide to include features or alternatives that do not fit within standard HTML, and Web authors or some word-processing packages may utilize these nonstandard features. For example, a browser may allow additional tags for formatting, and the "save as HTML" option for a word processor may include those tags in the files it generates. Of course, when the resulting files are displayed on the expanded browser, they look fine—perhaps even elegant. However, such files may be interpreted in peculiar ways or not at all on other browsers.

As with most Web applications, standards make a difference. When Web pages follow the standards, authors can be reasonably confident that their pages will appear as they want them to on most any browser and on most any computer system around the world. When standards are violated, however, an author is throwing herself or himself on the mercy of the computer to do the right thing, and the results may not be predictable.

In case you are interested in reviewing standards more closely, you should note that the World Wide Web Consortium maintains a general Web site at http://www.w3.org. As a further resource, the consortium provides a service that allows you to check whether any Web page conforms to the international standards. For details, you can consult http://validator.w3.org.

Although HTML allows authors to write simple Web pages according to standards, Web authors also can utilize more elaborate languages when writing their Web pages. These languages provide more capabilities (such as animation), and standards exist for these languages as well. Let's take a look at JavaScript, a common Web page development language often used in association with HTML.

What is JavaScript, and what can it do?

HTML allows browsers to interpret and format Web pages, but the format and capabilities that it facilitates are static; that is, a Web server sends information to a browser, and the browser displays this information in a predefined format. Except for following instructions for display, the browser does not process information, and activities (such as mouse movement) by a user do not affect the display. Although this model works well for the basic communication of information, it relies on the server for most processing, and therefore represents **server-side processing.**

With server-side processing, changes in the Web page's display require a three-step process: the browser sends information to the server (perhaps after a user enters data), the server analyzes the new information, and the server's response is sent back to the browser. As this outline suggests, such activity has two potential problems: the server must handle all processing, and the network must carry traffic for even the simplest processing tasks. Thus server-side processing can place significant burdens on both servers and networks.

An alternative approach would be to allow a user's browser to handle some processing requests. For example, after filling out a form, the browser might check that all boxes were completed before transmitting the information along the network to the server. In this case, the browser handles some error checking, and potential problems can be corrected before the browser transmits any user requests to the server.

This alternative can cut down significantly on server demands and network traffic, but it requires that processing instructions be conveyed to a browser so that it knows how to process some of the data before transmitting anything to the server. JavaScript is one common tool for writing such instructions within an HTML Web page. JavaScript provides a mechanism for writing various types of computer programs within a Web page to allow the browser to handle some processing chores. When a Web page instructs the browser on how to do some processing, it has initiated **client-side processing**. As with many parts of computing, client-side processing capabilities have both advantages and disadvantages. The major advantage? JavaScript processing allows local processing. The major disadvantage? JavaScript processing allows local processing.

To explain, local processing with JavaScript allows fast response to user interactions, keeps network traffic to a minimum, and places little burden on servers. All of these capabilities offer significant benefits. Local processing with JavaScript also means, however, that a user may run unknown programs with little or no supervision. This may or may not cause problems with your computer. In principle, JavaScript is designed to have only a limited collection of capabilities, and the processing possibilities are not supposed to harm your local computer. For example, JavaScript cannot open files on your local computer, erase your files, send e-mail under your name, or otherwise interact with your local computer without your explicit permission. On the other hand, because JavaScript allows users to run unknown programs and because computer software sometimes contains errors, some people worry that JavaScript programs might exploit weaknesses in a browser with detrimental results. When a user downloads a Web page, the user may or may not even know if the page contains a JavaScript program, and the user rarely will have reviewed the program ahead of time to determine that it functions in a desirable manner. For this reason, some computer users set their browsers so that JavaScript programs cannot be run. Even though most JavaScript programs work nicely, people using Web pages cannot be certain who wrote the JavaScript programs, and thus cannot know what these programs actually do. Thus, although running JavaScript may have potential advantages, JavaScript programs also may open the user to possible risks, and skeptics are not willing to take chances.

Summary

The Internet began in the late 1960s and 1970s as a small network, initially funded by the Advanced Research Projects Agency (ARPA) of the United States Department of Defense (DoD), called ARPAnet. The network expanded with funding from both the DoD and the National Science Foundation (NSF), but remained as a research enterprise through the 1980s. In 1991, the NSF phased out various commercial restrictions and began a program to turn the Internet over to the private sector. National access points (NAPs) now run national operations within the United States, and Internet service providers (ISPs) work regionally and on the local level. The network is designed so that new networks can join without affecting current networks. This has allowed for explosive growth; in the United States alone, some 1300 companies now provide national service, and some regions have as many as 1500 companies that provide local service. In order to function, all of these groups must conform to standards that are set by international organizations. Outside the United States, governments organize Internet access in a similarly cooperative manner.

All locations on the Internet are described at three levels: a domain name, an Internet Protocol number (IP number), and an Ethernet address. The domain name provides an easily remembered identification (for example, cs.utexas.edu for the computer sciences department at the University of Texas at Austin), the IP number provides a technical identification (128.83.139.9 for cs.utexas.edu), and the Ethernet address identifies a specific electrical board plugged into the local computer. Desktop computers often are assigned IP addresses manually, but laptop computers may operate through DHCP (Dynamic Host Configuration Protocol), through which they request a new IP address whenever they are plugged into the network.

When your computer is connected to the Internet, you may use a Web browser to identify materials and have those materials displayed. Web pages are identified through a specific address; the suffix of that address often identifies the type of document being retrieved. Web pages often contain formatting information written in the Hypertext Markup Language (HTML), and Web browsers use these formatting instructions to display data on your screen.

JavaScript allows HTML to be extended so that some processing can occur within your browser in response to your work.

Terminology from This Chapter

Backbone
Bandwidth
Client-side processing
Domain address
Dynamic Host Configuration Protocol (DHCP)
Domain Name Server (DNS)
Ethernet Address
Hypertext Markup Language (HTML)
Hypertext Transfer Protocol (HTTP)
Internet Service Provider (ISP)
IP number
National Access Point (NAP)
Node
Server-side processing
Static IP address
Top-level domain

Discussion Questions

1. The first part of the chapter states, "Both dial-up and leased lines worked reasonably well, as long as volume was relatively low and one machine always communicated with just a few others." Identify some reasons why low volume or communication with few other machines might be a necessary condition for the success of computer communication using dial-up lines or leased telephone lines.

2. With your browser, call up the Web site http://www.cs.grinnell.edu. This is chosen as a fairly straightforward Web page that conforms to the W3C HTML standards, but other standard pages also might be consulted. After viewing the page in your browser, use the browser menu options to view the source material. This will allow you to see the HTML that generates the page you see in your browser.

   a. Compare the look of the page with various HTML tags. Make a list of tags and see how many you can decipher; that is, for as many HTML tags as possible, try to write a sentence or two describing what that tag does.

   b. The bottom of the page shows a yellow rectangle with the W3C symbol. Click on that symbol and describe what happens.

3. A survey of the members of one organization suggested that about one-quarter of Internet users have disabled JavaScript in their browsers as a safety precaution. Upon learning this, developers of various Web sites for the organization concluded that checking Web forms for errors should be done both client-side and server-side.

   a. (Easy) Why might client-side error checking be inadequate for this organization's Web applications?

   b. (Requires a bit more thought) Why might developers include client-side error checking at all in their Web materials if it will be disabled by many users of the site?

4. Owners of laptop computers sometimes complain that they can connect their laptop computers to the network in some labs or hotel rooms and the machines work fine, but their laptops do not work properly on other networks. Identify some possible causes of these difficulties.

Exercises

1. a. Identify words or phrases from the "Terminology from This Chapter" section that relate to the location of material on the Web. Write a definition or describe the meaning of each of these terms.

   b. The "Terminology from This Chapter" section includes several terms related to translating a Web location or address from one form to another. Identify these terms, and explain the role each might have when you are searching the Web for a document.

   c. The chapter's terminology includes several terms related to standards or agreements on how information will be communicated. Identify these terms, and provide explanations of each.

   d. Some terminology in the chapter relates to computers themselves and their connections to the World Wide Web. Identify and explain these terms.

   e. Review the "Terminology from This Chapter" list for any remaining terms (not covered in parts a through d). Provide careful definitions for each word or phrase.

2. Because the beginnings of the Internet were strongly influenced by the United States Department of Defense and the National Science Foundation, some elements of the Internet may seem to have an American bias. For example, domain names for groups in the United States often do not carry a .US designation, whereas domain names for groups in other countries do carry a national designation. Thus, utexas.edu is associated with The University of Texas at Austin—without explicitly stating the United States—whereas the University of Kent at Canterbury in England has the domain names ukc.ac.uk and kent.ac.uk.

   a. Can you find other examples where practices associated with the Internet might be interpreted as having a bias toward the United States?

   b. Can you find examples where current practices seem clearly international; that is, where the practices seem to treat the United States as equal with other countries?

3. This chapter discusses three groups (ARIN, RIPE, and APNIC) that assign IP addresses.

   a. Investigate why this task is handled by three nonprofit organizations rather than by just one.

   b. How do these three organizations coordinate their work so that IP numbers in one region will not be confused with IP addresses from another region?

4. Current IP addresses utilize 32 bits (according to Internet Protocol version 4). However, in 1997, the Internet Engineering Task Force (IETF) approved a new standard (Internet Protocol version 6) that will utilize 128 bits.

   a. Why do you think the new standard expands the number of bits in IP addresses? Be as specific and precise as you can.

   b. Do you think a similar expansion will be needed at some point for the size of domain names? Explain your answer.

5. Pick a country outside of North America.

   a. Investigate what group has authority for each of the following:

- Assign and register domain names
- Assign IP addresses
- Determine national access point(s) to the Internet for that country
- Make actual connections between national access points and the Internet outside the country

b. In each case, also determine who or what authorizes these groups to perform these tasks.

Chapter 12

How private (or public) are Web interactions?

Think about the last time you worked on the World Wide Web. What was the first thing you did after you opened your browser? You probably began by entering the location of a Web page that you wanted to view. Your computer then generated a request to a Web server, and by doing so, you sent information through the Internet. Have you ever stopped to consider what information exactly you've offered to the network in that brief exchange? Once the request reaches the Web server, the server identifies your desired page and sends the relevant information back. The low-level details of this exchange followed the protocols discussed in Chapters 8, 9, and 11, but what information was actually transmitted? How much of your personal information was released to the Internet so that you could view that Web page?

In some cases, Web pages ask us to enter information as part of a transaction. The part of a Web page where we enter this information is, naturally, called a **form**. A form typically contains blank areas where we can type, buttons we can select, menus from which we can make selections, and boxes we can check. For example, when we search the Web using such tools as yahoo.com, google.com, or askjeeves.com, we enter words or phrases into a blank text area to guide the search. When we order merchandise, we supply our shipping address and credit card information. But, in providing this information, we may wonder how secure the information is as it moves from our browser to the Web server.

Overall, our interactions with the World Wide Web involve the communication of much information. In this chapter, we'll explore what records are kept of our work, what materials are public or private, and how secure various pieces of information might be. Understanding these important topics can help shape how carefully you interact with the Web. Feel free to investigate them further by reading the latest publications on the Web. It's a controversial and popular subject that is bound to intrigue you.

How is information transmitted from a browser to a server and back?

To begin, let's look carefully at the information we supply in our browser when requesting a Web page; these exchanges can potentially compromise our privacy, as you'll soon see. A simple example of a request for a Web site might be:

http://www.cs.grinnell.edu/~walker/fluency-book/web-info.php

Such an expression is called a **Uniform Resource Locator (URL)**, and it provides a primary format for specifying Web pages on the World Wide Web. The URL acts as the directions to the Web site's address, and when you hit Return, the network forwards these directions to the server about the file that you're looking for. As we have discussed before in Chapters 9 and 11, we can decipher elements of this URL as follows:

http:// Tells your browser and the Web server to use the Hypertext Transfer Protocol for the transmission of this material from the Web server to the browser.

www.cs.grinnell.edu Specifies the domain name for the Web server for the computer science program at Grinnell College.

~walker/fluency-book Indicates that the document is located in the fluency-book subdirectory of Walker's Web directory.

web-info.php Identifies the name of the file itself (that happens to be written in a scripting language called PHP rather than in HTML).

In general, the URL begins with a protocol specification, followed by a domain name, a specification of directories and possibly subdirectories, and finally a file name. In some cases, if the file name is omitted, the Web server will look in the directory or subdirectory for files by a default name, such as index.html. If you have used the World Wide Web, then you have typed URLs in searching for various documents.

An extended form of a URL also is possible. The first part of this version has exactly the same information (protocol, domain name, directories, file name) as the URL with which you're familiar. This information is followed by a question mark and any desired text. Here is an extended version of the previous example:

http://www.cs.grinnell.edu/~walker/fluency-book/web-info.php?Computers are useful!!!

Here, the data "Computers are useful!!!" has been added after the question mark.

When this material is entered into the browser, the browser uses the first part of the URL to generate the request for the page, just as you would expect, and the Web server deciphers that material to locate the desired page. However, the browser also packages up the remaining material and passes that along to the server as well. When the server processes the material, it identifies the question mark and then makes the remaining material (after the question mark) available to the specified Web page. If that page involves running a program at the server, then that program can use the information as it tries to respond to your request.

For example, if you actually type the previous extended URL into your browser, the Web server reads the last portion of the URL and notes that web-info.php is a program, that program is run, and that program is given the data "Computers are useful!!!". In this case, the program uses that information in deciding what it will place on the page sent to your browser. With this particular program using this information, the page displayed in your browser includes the following section:

Query String

Your query string was: Computers are useful!!!

Your query string reversed is: !!!lufesu era sretupmoC

That is, this particular program prints out your query string forward and backward. In other cases, the information following the question mark might indicate a person's name, and the program might search a directory for that name.

Because URLs are so easy to use, this extended version of a URL is one common way of sending information from a browser to a Web server. In fact, this is one of two approaches frequently used when you enter information into a form. One approach, called the GET method, uses this extended version of a URL. When you complete a form and click "Submit," the browser packages your information, adds it to the URL, and passes the entire URL along the network to the Web server. The Web server "GETs" the information you provided from the extended URL. Although Web developers sometimes employ tricks to hide the information you send in a URL, you often can see the entire URL—with your information added—in your browser's URL field when the new page is loaded. Thus, although the GET method is convenient, a browser may display your information publicly where anyone looking over your shoulder can see it. Because of this display possibility, any data you enter should be considered public!

A second approach for data transmission packages the data in a form that is sent behind the scenes. This second approach, called the POST method, transmits data in packets over the Internet, but does not attach data to a URL. The basic idea of the POST method is similar to the GET: The browser gathers information you might enter in a Web form, packages the data, and transmits the material to a Web server. The Web server locates the desired page, runs any designated program, and forwards your form material to that program. However, because your information is not attached to the URL, that information will not be displayed directly in your browser. From this standpoint, forms using the POST method do not display information as publicly as those relying on the URL. Be warned, however, that there is still a question of how public your material might be when the POST method is used, and I will address that question shortly.

The POST method provides somewhat more privacy for your data than the GET method, but the actual approach used for any Web-based form is predetermined by that form. You cannot control how your information will be transmitted. At a technical level, each Web form contains one of the following elements:

```
<FORM . . . METHOD="GET" . . .
```

or

```
<FORM . . . METHOD="POST" . . .
```

and this specification determines the form used to transmit your data. (In many cases, if you display a page containing a form in your browser, you can request your browser to display the HTML source—the Web page with formatting instructions as well as the content. As you scan this source file, you likely can find one of the listed elements for each form on the page.)

Further, if the form is designed to utilize the GET method, then you also can expect that the script you activate when pressing "Submit" expects data communication through the GET method. If you were to edit the form to change "GET" to "POST," your data would be transmitted differently, but the program you called would likely not recognize the data. Your revised form used the "POST" method, but the program on the Web server still expected "GET."

Overall, you may find it interesting to observe which methods are used when you use various Web applications, but unfortunately you cannot adjust forms and programs written by others.

What information about me is routinely transmitted when I use the Web?

Although a browser does *not* send your user name or e-mail address to the server when you use the Web, your browser does transmit a moderate amount of information. Here are some elements that are conveyed as part of the HTTP protocol:

- The IP address of your machine
- The IP address of the machine responding to your request
- The operating system that your machine uses (such as Windows XP, Linux 7.0.2, or Macintosh OS X version 10.2.6)
- The browser you are using (such as Internet Explorer version 5.2 or Mozilla 4.6)

IP addresses and operating systems do not directly indicate your identity, but they do identify the machine you are using. Of course, the sending of packets along the Internet requires IP addresses for both the sender and the receiver, so this information can hardly be kept secret. Also, on the surface, it may seem peculiar that a Web server would be told details of your operating system and browser, but this practice has a rational and practical justification. In particular, different browsers on different operating systems may have different capabilities and idiosyncrasies. Relatively old browsers may not be able to interpret new versions of HTML, specific browser versions may not handle PDF files correctly, and so on. For this reason, some Web-page developers tailor their Web pages to specific environments. For example, you already read in Chapter 11 that various developers of browsers may extend HTML standards in differing ways. Tags specified for standard HTML may work in all browsers, but expanded tags for Internet Explorer may not work for Netscape. Thus, if Web developers can detect that you are running Internet Explorer version 6.0 on Windows 2000 Professional, they may generate only those formatting tags they know will work properly on your browser, and that might be different than if you were running Mozilla 1.2b on Macintosh OS X. Also, they may know that a particular browser does not properly handle PDF files based on a stated application type, and thus they may use an HTML document rather than the normal PDF document that is sent in response to requests from other browsers. Thus, the exchange of operating system and browser information with the server can actually work to your benefit and can help tailor Web pages to your browser's capabilities.

To experience directly some of the information routinely transmitted to a Web browser, you may wish to view

http://www.cs.grinnell.edu/~walker/fluency-book/web-info.php

which is the URL mentioned earlier in this chapter.

What information about me is routinely recorded when I use the Web?

As already noted, Internet communication requires the IP addresses of both sender and receiver. The Web server and the page you request therefore will know your machine's IP address during Internet communication, but not specifically your personal identity.

In addition to passing IP address information to a Web application, a Web server may log or record where every URL request comes from (domain name and/or IP address). This information can be useful, for example, to track the demand for various Web pages, to identify which pages are most popular, and to explore patterns of usage. For developers of Web sites, such information can be very valuable in determining how effective their pages are. Pages used often may be judged more useful or effective than those used rarely. Similarly, pages that people use repeatedly may have particular value.

Sometimes, to track particular details of a page, an e-commerce developer may include a transparent one-pixel by one-pixel image on the page, referring to a specific URL. Such a small image represents just one dot, and the image may be transparent. Thus, the user is unlikely to be able to see this image. (More about such images shortly.) Despite its invisibility, this small image can be used to track references to the URL, so the developer can determine specific usage details of individual sites or groups of sites. This can be particularly useful, for example, if a page contains advertising and the advertiser wants proof of how often its ad was viewed.

Although all of this information does not automatically identify specific users, records like these in conjunction with other information might be sufficient to identify exactly what you used the computer to do. For example, if the computer were in your dorm room or office, it might be safe to assume that you are the only person who uses that machine. If the computer requires that you log in, the computer may keep a record of all logins, so a comparison of times for Web requests and times for logins might provide good evidence about what you were doing while using the computer.

Although computer systems are not legally required to log Web usage or logins, the maintenance of some logs can be quite helpful. For example, if someone sends harassing e-mail or uses a hammer to attack a computer monitor, then a log might help identify whose account was being used on that machine at the time. Of course, once logs are kept to anticipate security questions, the same logs may be available for other purposes as well. To know for certain what is happening with the computers you use, you should check with the school, company, or ISP that supports your computer and its networking to determine what logs and records are kept. Unless you know otherwise, you probably should assume that some system or networking administrator could track down what you view on your Web browser. This assumption may not be true—but it also might be!

And even if your school, company, or ISP does not maintain or review logs, some of your activities might be inferred by an examination of cookies kept on your computer or in your account—a topic we discuss next.

What are cookies?

You may have had the experience of going to a Web site for some work and returning to that site later to discover it seemed to remember what you did previously. For example, you may have purchased a book on an e-commerce site. When you went back to the same e-commerce site a week later, the site may have greeted you by name or suggested new titles on the same subject as the book you purchased. If you bought an airline ticket at a travel site, then the next visit to the site may have resulted in a highlighting of special offers originating from the same airport you left the first time.

In each of these cases, the Web site seemed to remember who you were and what you did previously at that site. *Cookies* provide a common mechanism for enabling this type of interaction. More precisely, a **cookie** is a small piece of information that a Web site saves on your computer when you visit the site, and your browser maintains a list of these cookies. When going to a Web site, your browser checks this list to determine if a cookie has been placed there previously by that site. If so, the cookie is sent back to the site as part of your Web request. With this piece of history, the Web site may determine something about your past involvement at that site—either directly from the cookie or by using the cookie's information to search a database. Altogether, cookies are small pieces of information stored on your computer that help identify you to specific sites you have visited on the World Wide Web.

As with many records of past history, cookies have potential advantages, but also have an impact on your privacy. On the positive side, cookies have the potential to streamline and personalize your interactions with Web sites. By knowing who you are and what you have done at a site, a Web site can tailor what it displays on its pages to your preferences and interests. Further, by knowing your identity, a site may not require you to complete some forms, or it may be able to fill forms with information you have supplied previously—making your interactions easier the second time you visit the site.

Regarding privacy, Web browsers send cookies only to the sites that they came from initially; browsers do not distribute cookies that originated on one site to other sites. Thus, one Web site cannot directly determine what other sites you might have visited. We have, however, already noted that a Web site may contain small (one pixel), transparent images. Sometimes these images actually come from other Web sites, in which case they are called **Web beacons** or **Web bugs**. Because these special images are associated with specific Web sites, those sites also have the capability of storing cookies on your computer—even if your Web request only asked for a page that happened to contain Web beacons or bugs. Cookies obtained in this way are called **foreign cookies** or **third-party cookies**. In recent years, some Web companies, such as DoubleClick, have contracted with various commercial Web sites for general tracking of customers. In such cases, a Web beacon of the DoubleClick or other Web tracking company is placed on a commercial Web site. When you view the commercial site, you also load the Web beacon for the tracking company, and your browser will return any cookie related to that information to the Web tracking company. Because cookies identify your computer, and because the tracking company knows about the current page you are viewing, the tracking company can maintain a log of what commercial sites you have visited over time through its Web beacons. The tracking company may not know your personal identity, but it can keep track of what contacts your computer has had with the Web sites it is monitoring. Log information can provide commercial sites with valuable information about the interests and preferences of their users, so it is not uncommon for commercial Web pages to contain Web beacons.

What defenses do I have against cookies?

Up to this point, we have discussed three ways that sites or servers can record information about your Web browsing:

1. By logging your computer's IP address in interactions between your browser and a Web site
2. By placing cookies on your computer or in your account
3. By tabulating third-party cookies by Web-tracking companies

The first of these helps identify your computer to the Web site, while the second and third indicate something about the history of your computer usage. None of this information directly reveals your personal identity—only the IP address of your computer. Outsiders cannot determine who you are by using just these pieces of information. Comforting as that may be, understand that the addition of personal information to the records need not be a major step. For example, many commercial sites ask you to register. You cannot order a book or an airline ticket without giving your name, address, and credit-card information. Of course, once a company has this information, the technology is available to connect it with other information it already has—perhaps from cookies.

With this in mind, users of the Web are well advised to check the privacy policy of commercial sites before supplying personal information.

- How will a company use the information you supply?
- Will the company share this information with others?
- Can you limit access of others to this information?
- What protections are in place to keep this information secure?

As a separate matter, note that cookies typically are stored in files in your computer account. Thus, if you have a computer account at school or work, then the computer system there likely has a record of cookies from the sites you have visited. At many schools and companies, system administrators have the technical ability to view those files. Similarly, if you use an Internet service provider for Web access at home, it might be possible for managers of that ISP to read your cookies file. Should administrators or managers look at a file of cookies, they would know something about the Web sites you have visited recently.

Because viewing of cookies and Web logs is technically possible, you should review the privacy policy of any institution, company, or ISP whose computers you use. A privacy policy may explicitly forbid access to this information, or such access may be allowed only in certain circumstances. On the other hand, managers or your school's IT people may be allowed to view such information at will.

Before using a computer at work, you are strongly advised to review policies to know what access your boss might have to review your Web usage!

And, even if policies restrict access to such information by others, you should realize that technicians might inadvertently access such information when systems malfunction. For example, suppose you have been using a computer for some time when it crashes or when its connection to the Internet seems to malfunction. Despite your efforts, you cannot get your computer to work properly again. Naturally, you call a technician to help resolve the problem. Depending on the symptoms, the technician may use software to scan various files in your computer to identify potential problems, and during this work it might well happen that the technician views your file of recent cookies. The technician's goal was to solve one problem, and the investigation led to the viewing of your recent cookies. (Lest you think such situations are only hypothetical, I know of several instances where this specific scenario actually happened!)

If you are worried about others viewing your file of recent cookies, one approach is to regularly delete that file. Some computer users set up their accounts so that their file of cookies is deleted every time they log off their computers, so any list of cookies will include only the current session's activities.

Although this can reduce some risks, understand that specific details to delete files of cookies may vary from one system to another. Suppose, for example, you regularly use several computers and your files are stored on a common server; you might use several machines in a lab, but you access all your files from a departmental server. In such a situation, you might have to investigate whether files with cookies are stored on the local computer you use, on the central server, or both. Trying to erase the file in the wrong place might make you feel better but would not bolster your privacy. In addition, you should be aware that cookies are different from the "history" file that some browsers maintain. Cookies contain specific data that are defined by a Web server and are stored in one file. A history file, if present, contains a list of URLs that you have visited recently, but does not contain information sent by those sites. Erasing a history file will have no impact whatsoever on your file of cookies.

How secure is information transmitted through the Internet?

As I noted in Chapter 8, the transmission of information over the Internet begins with your computer broadcasting one or more packets of data on your local Ethernet cable en route to the Web server. Because you use public cables to transmit data, you cannot be confident that your data are entirely secure. Nearby computers listen to these Ethernet cables and could potentially read the data you send. If the destination of your communication is beyond your local network segment, then those packets are forwarded from one server, bridge, or router to another, as your data move from one segment to the next, eventually reaching the desired destination. Altogether, this segment-to-segment movement of information implies that each packet of data might be read by dozens or hundreds or even thousands of computers. In most processing, each computer on this path either ignores your data (as not being intended for it) or forwards your information to the next location; computers en route normally do not examine or analyze your data. From this standpoint, you might think information transmitted through the Internet seems reasonably secure.

However, because your information is sent on many segments, there always is the potential that some computer on some segment will copy, analyze, store, or otherwise process the information, even if all other computers ignore it. For example, a program on an intermediary computer might be programmed to look for sequences of characters that could be credit-card numbers, recording each such sequence of digits. The interconnection of computers provides an opening for message monitoring, and the capabilities of modern computers could easily provide a snooping program with the ability to review a massive amount of information. Although the likelihood may be reasonably low, the cost of such an information interception could be quite high, and it is best to assume that data in any packet are susceptible to being read by an unauthorized party.

Of course, some data you send may have little value to anyone else. Someone might intercept your request to view a Web page, but you are unlikely to care if someone discovers that you went to a Web page to purchase a book; find information about Grinnell, Iowa; or review a flight schedule. These Web sites are publicly known, and the information they contain is not secret.

On the other hand, you might well care that your personal information cannot be read by others. If you use the Internet to make purchases, for example, you would want complete confidence that by sending data through the Internet you were not compromising your bank account or credit-card information. Similarly, if you were making inquiries about medical symptoms you might be experiencing, you might not want that information made available to your employer or insurance company. Because the information in packets has the potential to be read as it moves along a cable, the best approach to secure your information is to encrypt your data before placing it in those packets. When the data are encrypted, others might intercept the encrypted information, but they would not know what it means. Of course, such data might still be susceptible to unauthorized access if others could decipher your information, so even encryption is not a guarantee of completely secure data transmission. However, if one of the better encryption systems is used, such as public-key encryption discussed in Chapter 10, then the time necessary to break the code may be sufficiently long (years, decades) that the data would be of little use if anyone actually goes to the effort of discovering how deciphering might work.

You should utilize **encryption** whenever you send sensitive information along the Internet, but understand that this works only if the recipient also can **decrypt** the information. Luckily, for many common uses, browsers and other transmission programs offer their own encryption protection. For example, although HTTP transmits information in plain text (without encryption), **Secure Hypertext Transfer Protocol (HTTPS)** encrypts the data before transmission and decrypts the information at the other end. Thus, if you regularly use a Web browser, you may have encountered a pop-up box that indicates that you are starting to use a secure page. Another pop-up box may appear later, indicating that you are leaving a secure site. When these messages appear, they often notify you that encryption is being used—both for the transmission of data to your site and for the sending of your information to a server. Such pages often use an HTTPS protocol with encryption.

Similarly, if you have occasion to log in to another computer remotely over the Internet, the telnet program handles communication without encryption, but the **secure shell (ssh)** encrypts information before putting it out on the Internet.

How safe is it to use credit cards online?

To address this question, let's first consider some issues related to actual plastic credit cards that you might carry in your wallet. Ignoring the Internet completely, at least four scenarios could result in the abuse of your credit card:

1. You might lose your credit card, and the finder might use it to charge items to your account or sell it to someone else who misuses it.
2. Someone might watch your transaction in a store, record the number, and use it (or sell it) to make unauthorized charges. Alternatively, someone might obtain your number by taking the carbon paper or other impression involved with a regular transaction.
3. You might use your credit card in a regular transaction with a business, but the business might not provide the services or goods you think you paid for, or the company may make additional charges or otherwise overcharge you.
4. You might use your credit card regularly, but the company involved with the transaction might sell or share the card information with others who then abuse it.

Of the above scenarios, the first two clearly involve the theft of your credit card number. In the first case, the card is physically stolen, while in the second case someone has learned the number while you retain the card itself. The other two scenarios describe situations where you have provided your credit-card information to a business, as in any regular transaction, but the business misuses it. Charging you for services not rendered is an example of credit-card fraud, and unauthorized distribution of your credit-card number is both a violation of confidentiality and can possibly be considered theft or fraud.

In each case, at some point you will discover that your credit card has been misused. If you've physically lost the card, you might notice your card is missing and contact your credit company directly. If a company is abusing their access to your credit card, there is the chance that you'll see an unaccounted-for extra charge on the bill before you sign the receipt, but otherwise it might take some time before you realize the anticipated services or goods are not going to materialize. At that time, you might first contact the company for clarification—although this might be impossible if the business disappeared. In many cases of fraud, you would not notice an irregularity until reviewing your monthly credit-card statement, and your only recourse may be to report the problem to your credit-card company.

Although this review of the risks of plastic credit cards may seem familiar, it is important to realize that of the scenarios described, only physical theft of your card is impossible using the Internet. Your plastic does not physically leave your presence during a credit-card transaction over the Internet, so it therefore cannot lead to the physical theft of your card. On the other hand, each of the other types of abuse is possible. Let's consider each of these alternatives in more detail.

How can someone obtain my credit-card number online?

As we have noted, your credit-card information is open to anyone watching the Ethernet cable if it were sent through the Internet without encryption. Even with encryption, however, theft of your credit-card information is still possible; the data could be obtained from your machine before encryption takes place. For example, someone might install a keyboard sniffer on your computer—an unauthorized program that records each key you type. The sniffer monitors your keyboard before computer processing performs the encryption, so your credit card numbers and other information are available directly as you type. When a sniffer program finds a pattern that looks like a credit card, it may record the number or send it over the Internet to an accomplice site. Because sniffer problems usually arise because someone had unauthorized access to your computer, your best defense against them is to carefully control who has access to your machine and to keep track of what programs are in place.

Another, less clandestine way that your credit-card information could be obtained is if you ask your browser to record data you type into forms. As a convenience, many browsers offer to monitor what you enter into forms so that you do not need to type the same information time after time whenever you use a site. This service can save time and effort, particularly if you use the same site(s) frequently. However, it also implies that others using your account have similar access to your information. If this saved information includes your credit-card number, than anyone gaining access to your computer and account could charge materials to your credit card.

How can online companies defraud me during a regular transaction?

When you enter your credit card into a Web form in anticipation of services or goods, you run the same risks you might encounter in using plastic directly—except that you have not had physical contact with a salesperson or other company representative. If the company does not really exist, if it goes out of business, or if it engages in unethical business practices, you may be charged and find it difficult to recover your money. Recovery of charges on transactions over the Internet can be particularly difficult, because you may have only a domain name as the address of the business involved. In practice, the business may involve only a Web page, and a charge on your credit-card statement might refer to anywhere in the world.

Recovery of online credit-card charges can be difficult, so your best defense against such abuses is to be quite certain of the sites where you do business. Some companies, such as amazon.com, have well-established records of providing appropriate goods and services. Conducting business with less-established companies, however, may carry a greater risk.

How can online companies abuse my credit-card information after a regular transaction is complete?

Once a company has your credit-card number, we expect the company to protect that information. For the most part, legal requirements and ethical expectations apply similarly to both Internet and plastic transactions, and demand that the information is kept confidential. Internet transactions, however, are subject to the same additional risks already outlined for obtaining goods and services. A company could theoretically make unauthorized purchases on your card once it has your information, or it could sell your number to someone else. If you do not know where the business is located, or if the business closes, you have nowhere to go to seek reparations. Remedying your situation may be particularly difficult if the business is located thousands of miles away in a different country where laws, law enforcement, and customs may differ substantially from what you know.

As an additional risk, the submission of your credit-card information over the Internet implies that the data are stored on a company's machine—at least for a short time—and that machine is connected to the Internet. If that machine is the target of an unauthorized intruder, then your number and many others might become available. Because this is an obvious vulnerability, many companies install specific protections, such as firewalls, to guard against such unauthorized access. Although these security measures may provide a reasonable level of protection, Internet-connected computers cannot help but carry some ongoing level of risk. You therefore make your credit-card numbers vulnerable when you shop online, even if it is only to a minimal extent. Credit cards, however, are not the only susceptible information you have when you work on the Internet. Other personal information can likewise be compromised.

What information of mine can others learn over the Internet?

Let's discuss what personal information can be accessed over the Internet by first distinguishing between two types of data: public files and private files. Public files include information you post on the World Wide Web for use by anyone who might want it. For example, if you maintain a Web home page, any information on that page is likely public—and you intend it to be. Similarly, you might place public information in documents and files accessed by links from your home page.

Other information may be available because people can happen upon it if it is stored in public places. For example, as a convenience to your family and friends, you may maintain a folder of pictures you have taken during recent activities or trips. The folder is not identified on your home page, and there are no other links to this folder of pictures. Your intent is to give the URL of this folder to selected friends and relatives for their enjoyment, and you make the folder public so that these designated folks have access to your pictures—regardless of where they might be. Because you have kept this URL reasonably secret, you hope that others will not know about it.

Although this may be convenient, it involves some risks. Suppose, for example, you named the folder "photos"—an easily guessed name. If someone typed your home page and added "photos"—just as a guess—then they might be able to click on any file in the directory. Because you made your folder public over the Web for your friends, others guessing the folder name also could access it. On some systems, you may be able to set permission codes to specify whether individual directories and files are publicly accessible. If so, you may be able to control just which files anyone can read.

These controls can work well, but be aware that accidents happen when directories and files are moved or changed and permissions are relaxed by mistake. For example, in late June 2003, Apple Computer was updating its Web pages in anticipation of an announcement of new products a few weeks later. In the process of adding new pages, however, permissions were relaxed for just a few minutes, and several people read about the new products. Apple corrected the permissions quickly, but the new product line still was discussed that evening on the national news.

Beyond materials you explicitly post on your Web pages, information about you may find its way onto the Web when you register at Web sites or even at public locations, such as museums. For example, a few years ago I was teaching a class for first-year students and noticed one registered student had a reasonably distinctive name. In searching for this name on the Web, I discovered the student had visited a museum in Florida on a particular date earlier that year. Although the student did not care that this record of a family trip was posted, the student was quite surprised that I knew about it at the first class meeting. (The example provided the class with a wonderful example of the availability of information on the Web.)

And, of course, once material does become available on the Web, search engines may find it and place it in indexes for fast and easy retrieval. (More about this in the next chapter.)

How can I secure my private computer files?

All of these comments reinforce a common theme from recent chapters: Ask about how information will be used or distributed before you provide personal information to anyone—either through an Internet form or when completing paperwork with an institution or company.

Although you expect information that you have posted as "available" to be public, you also expect information in private files to remain private. After designating files as private, their unauthorized release to others requires at least two steps:

1. Access to the machine where the data are stored
2. Access to the files on that machine.

Blocking such access can focus on either of these steps.

To block access to a machine, you might utilize several strategies:

- Install a firewall to restrict ports that can be used for Internet communications to your computer. This approach was discussed in some detail in Chapter 9.
- Require users of your computer to have an account and password. Although outsiders might be able to guess account names and passwords, this step at least has the potential to slow intruders down.
- Utilize anti-virus software to check all incoming materials for viruses, so subversive software (such as viruses) cannot come into your computer through Web pages, e-mail, FTP file transfers, or corrupted disks. When installed on your machine, such virus programs may gain access to files, so the best countermeasure is to prevent their introduction.
- Carefully monitor all new programs, games, and other files you bring into your system. Few commercial companies knowingly distribute viruses or other security links with their

software, but such troublesome programs may be found from time to time on commercial software. Of course, you have little control at all over software you download over the Web, so you need to be particularly cautious before installing any new programs onto your system. (The first virus file I ever received was in e-mail sent inadvertently by the director of a statewide organization related to the computing industry.)

Expanding on these last two points, programs obtained from others may have wonderful capabilities, but they also might have "features" that undermine the security on your computer. Further, if you download a program and then run it, the program likely has full access to all of your materials—after all, you have chosen to run the program from your account, and therefore have responsibility for any work done on your account.

Outside of monitoring what programs you download, having anti-virus software, using passwords, and creating firewalls, you should carefully monitor what permissions you grant to each of your files. For added security, you can separate public and private files into separate directories to help avoid inadvertent relaxing of permissions. If you place private files in your private directories, then permissions must be relaxed for both a directory and a file in that directory before outsiders can view the information. Although mistakes still can happen, protection via two permissions is generally more secure than protection based on only one permission.

Does leaving a computer (or laptop) connected to a network compromise its security?

In principle, firewalls, password protection, anti-virus software, and the like should provide reasonable security for your machine when it is connected to the Internet. And, of course, no processing whatsoever occurs if the machine is turned off, so we only need to discuss risks if the machine is turned on.

In practice, however, operating systems and other programs are quite complex, and thus prone to containing errors that in turn could create vulnerability and allow someone to access your computer through the network. Vendors of operating systems (such as

Microsoft, Apple, and Linux) constantly monitor their products and release periodic updates to resolve security risks and other errors. Careful attention to these updates, with prompt installation of security updates, can help considerably in reducing risks, However, because complex software almost always contains errors, and because these errors might involve security, you take some risk that an outsider could gain access to your computer whenever you attach it to the Internet, either directly or through a modem or DSL link.

For wireless networks, risks can be higher—at least in some common circumstances. In particular, Chapter 8 indicated that wireless networks can work in two modes: either with or without a password. Passwords, of course, control what other computers and users can access the network, and thus directly control access to your machine. However, direct-access connections without passwords are in common use, and any computer connected to such a wireless network may be open to snooping by outsiders. For example, recent folklore includes stories of people stopping on a street, turning on their laptops, and immediately having full access to a local wireless network. Rarely do these tales discuss invasions of privacy or malicious activities by the intruders, but the stories do suggest that wireless networks without password protection may constitute a greater security risk than other networks.

Summary

When you work with a browser for the World Wide Web, you typically begin by specifying an address or Uniform Resource Locator (URL), and your browser uses this information to communicate with a Web server that provides you with desired information. Beyond URL information, however, this exchange between your browser and the Web server also conveys data about your browser, your machine, cookies, and the contents of forms and query strings. Various methods are used to transmit this information, and many allow limited privacy for your data. E-commerce developers may utilize cookies, Web beacons, and Web bugs to help tabulate your behavior on the Web, allowing them to promote their products, refine their marketing, and adjust their interactions with you.

The use of a browser may not identify you individually, but developers may be able to combine browser information with data you provide to online companies, so your personal habits may become known. Materials stored on your computer by browsers or by yourself may provide further data regarding your transactions. You should examine the privacy policies of companies, schools, and Internet service providers to clarify how your personal data might be used and what protections you might have.

Data traveling on the Internet typically moves along many segments, so you should assume that any information you supply could be intercepted and read by others. Encryption can provide a measure of security for your data. This can help you if you use credit cards for online transactions, but the use of credit cards on the Web is subject to the same abuses as the use of these cards in stores. Risks for credit-card use rise when you cannot verify the identity of a company.

When your computer is connected to the World Wide Web, there is some potential for outsiders to gain access to your materials. Firewalls, password protection, anti-virus software, and the like should provide reasonable security, although errors in software can create opportunities for breaches in security. Wireless networks can have somewhat higher risks, particularly if connections are not password protected.

Terminology from This Chapter

Cookies
Decryption
Encryption
Foreign cookie
Form
Secure Hypertext Transport Protocol (HTTPS)
Secure Shell (ssh)
Third-party cookie
Uniform Resource Locator (URL)
Web beacon
Web bug

Discussion Questions

1. Why do you think Uniform Resource Locator (URL) is the name given to addresses we use in designating an item on the World Wide Web?
   a. What might be meant by "uniform" in this context?
   b. Why might the word "resource" be used rather than document or file?
   c. Why might one use the term "locator" rather than "location" or "address"?

2. When you send a letter or postcard in paper form through the post office, you first place the item in a mailbox. The letter or card then goes from mail carrier to mail carrier, until it reaches its recipient. Compare the security of this relaying of information from carrier to carrier to the transmission of data packets from machine to machine over the Internet.
   a. Ignoring the Internet for this part, are there potential differences in security between the sending of letters and the sending of postcards? Explain your answer.
   b. Is communication over the Internet more similar to the sending of letters or to the sending of postcards (or is the mechanism about the same)?
   c. In what ways are security issues similar for paper mail and Internet communication?
   d. In what ways are the issues different?

3. Many institutions and companies state on the Web their privacy policies regarding any data they collect.
   a. Find the privacy policy for your school or company.
   b. Find the privacy policies for at least three ISPs, such as America Online, MSN (the Microsoft Network), and a local ISP that serves your town.
   c. Compare the policies you have found in parts a and b.
      - To what extent might personal information be available to officials in the school, company, or ISP?
      - Might the school, company, or ISP share your information with others?
      - Do you have any control over what data might be distributed?
      - Are there other similarities or differences in policies?

4. FTP, the traditional File Transport Protocol, does not use encryption in moving a file from one place to another. Thus, files moved by FTP have some risk of being intercepted and read. Identify the extent to which you might protect yourself against unauthorized access to file information transported using FTP. To what extent do you think FTP can be considered safe and secure?

Exercises

1. a. Provide careful definitions for each word or phrase listed in "Terminology from This Chapter."

   b. From this list of terms, identify those that have to do with typical Web pages; that is, terms that involve the display or communication of information between a user's browser and a Web server.

   c. From the list of "Terminology from This Chapter," identify those terms that relate to behind-the-scenes accumulation of data about a user.

   d. From the same terminology list, identify those terms related to keeping information private and away from unauthorized parties.

2. This exercise assumes you have access to a computer connected to the Internet.

   a. Determine the current IP address for your computer. Details of determining the IP address will depend on your particular environment. Often, this will be identified as a Network option within a System or Preferences option. Alternatively, you might open a command or terminal window and issue an IP-lookup command. On some systems, this command might be called nslookup or host.

   b. If you are working in a lab with several computers, determine the IP address of several other computers in the same lab. What parts of the IP address are the same for all computers in the lab? What parts are different? Can you explain any similarities or differences?

3. Many computers on the Internet have a command to find the IP address of any site on the World Wide Web. Use the command on your computer to check the following addresses given in this chapter:

   a. grinnell.edu

   b. cs.grinnell.edu

   c. cs.utexas.edu

   d. ukc.ac.uk

4. a. To what extent do you think the use of plastic credit cards for a person-to-person transaction involves some trust between the customer and the business person? Explain your answer.

   b. The use of plastic credit cards is protected in some ways by various laws. Explore the laws in your country or area to determine what safeguards are provided by the legal system for your use of plastic credit cards.

   c. To what extent does the use of credit cards over the Internet involve the same level of trust between customer and business, and to what extent does this usage over the Internet require greater trust?

   d. To what extent do laws protect you in your use of credit cards over the Internet? Explain your answer.

Chapter 13

How do Web applications work?

Imagine that your friend Aimee is sitting at her computer, navigating through the Web and exploring a variety of sites. She goes to a search engine to locate possibilities for tonight's entertainment in Boston, and as she does so, an icon on her desktop indicates she has just received new e-mail. She clicks to her e-mail account, determines the new mail is spam, deletes it, and clicks back to her browser to continue her search for evening activities. The search engine provides her with several sites that seem related to what she's looking for, from newspaper Web sites, to entertainment guides, to travel brochures. As she scans these sites and learns what she wants to know, a few pop-up ads appear offering her subscriptions to entertainment magazines and discounts on tours of Boston. After a few minutes, Aimee has finished scoping out Boston's evening scene, so she logs off the network and calls her friends to plan for the night's activities.

This brief Internet work involved a number of Web applications (search engines, e-mail, spam, pop-up ads), but how did they work? How did the search engine know which sites to direct Aimee to so quickly? Why did she receive a piece of unsolicited e-mail? How were the pop-up ads chosen to cater to her query? To discover the answers to these questions, we need to understand some basics of these computer applications.

All computer applications depend upon computer programs to provide specific instructions that describe exactly what the computer is to do. The instructions, or sequence of steps for performing work, are called an *algorithm*, and Web applications (or other computer packages) all rely upon detailed algorithms. In many ways, algorithms are like recipes, offering the computer a list of specific instructions that result in an application. Each application utilizes a different algorithm. Similar Web programs by different vendors may utilize different algorithms, or the algorithms may follow a similar approach but differ in their details. In rare cases, algorithms may be identical. In many cases, details of algorithms depend upon trade secrets, and companies are reluctant to disclose those secrets publicly. Think about your local town or county fair and its pie-baking contest: Although anyone interested in apple pies knows the basic ingredients and steps, you'll never know your Aunt Linda's secret recipe that makes her pie win each year. In a similar way, at a very detailed level, we often cannot know just how various applications work.

On the other hand, just like the basic recipe for an apple pie, applications often follow common approaches for processing. We may not know some specific details, but we may have a good idea of the main elements of various algorithms. In this chapter, we consider some of these general algorithms for several common Web-based applications, such as search engines, Web advertising, and e-mail.

How do search engines work?

In a typical interaction with a Web search engine, you enter one or more words into a text box. When you click "submit", your browser sends your query to the search engine, the search engine idntifies Web pages which match all of your words, and you receive the results of the search as a listing in your browser.

To expand somewhat on this process, the work performed by most search engines has these general characteristics.

1. A search engine performs a search, based on a query given by the user.
2. The search engine maintains a database of Web pages.
3. Information about Web pages often involves at least four areas: category, description, title, and URL.
4. Your query string is used to search the information areas for the database of Web pages.

5. Relevant Web pages are ordered according to perceived relevance, according to some (proprietary) criteria.
6. The results are returned to your browser.

Let's explore each of these points in somewhat more detail. When you type terms or phrases into a search engine form and click "Submit," your request typically is added as a query string to the URL after a question mark (recall our discussion of extended URLs in Chapter 11). For technical reasons, blank spaces usually are replaced by plus signs (+); otherwise, you can read your query just by looking at the last part of the URL, which you can view in the address or location field of your browser when the new page loads. The search engine uses the query string as input to a program, and that program compiles the results of your search, which are sent to you when it finishes. This query-response format is common to virtually all Web applications; what makes search engines special has to do with the middle points listed earlier: the database, information areas, searching, and ordering of results.

How do search engines find out about materials on the Web?

Every search engine maintains a database containing information about Web pages; that is, when you initiate a search for specific pages, a search engine does not start scanning information out on the Web to locate material you might want. Rather, that material already has been collected by the search engine, so the process focuses on identifying material already found rather than looking for new material. For example, in April 2004, the search engine Google stated that it provided "access to more than 4 billion web pages" (http://www.google.com/help/features.html). The same press release states,

> Google takes a snapshot of each page examined as it crawls the Web and caches these as a back-up in case the original page is unavailable. If you click on the "Cached" link, you will see the page as it looked when we indexed it. The cached content is the content Google uses to judge whether this page is a relevant match for your query.

Other sources from Google and elsewhere indicate that the search engine's database of pages is stored on over 10,000 PC servers that are running the Linux operating system.

Why store so much information?

The quick answer as to why search engines store millions of Web pages is speed. If you have had experience loading Web pages into your browser, you probably have found that some pages take a long time to load. Sometimes the pages are very large, and it takes time to transmit all that material. Sometimes servers or communications are heavily loaded with traffic, and the material must wait its turn for transmission. Sometimes transmission lines to a server may operate only at slow speeds. Search engines would have similar troubles in scanning Web pages if all those pages had to be loaded from their sources for each search. And, if loading each page takes a long time, then a search engine would take at least that long to obtain the pages and scan them in response to your query. Storing pages within a search engine's database eliminates the need to consult the actual sites in trying to respond to your query. In addition, as you will see shortly, this advanced downloading of pages also allows the preparation of various indexes to help facilitate the search process.

How are the pages obtained for a search engine?

Historically, search engine companies have used two basic approaches for obtaining and **indexing** Web pages. The first involves reviews by humans, whereas the second uses automated programs. When people maintain the databases for a search engine, the company employs a team of folks to locate Web pages and organize those materials in its database. This basic approach was employed for the Yahoo! search engine, from its beginnings until October 2002. Ask Jeeves also used this technique when it started, at one time employing about 100 editors.

The second approach to organizing Web pages uses computer programs to methodically surf the Web. These programs, called **Web crawlers,** may start on one page and then systematically follow all its Web links to identify additional pages. Each new page gives rise to another collection of links and new pages. Repeating this process over time allows the computer program to cover a vast number of Web pages, and each can be stored in a search engine's database. Many search engines now use Web crawlers to locate pages, including Google, Ask Jeeves (which runs the Teoma search engine), All The Web (also used by Lycos), and Inktomi (purchased by Yahoo! in March 2003).

Although Web crawlers' process of finding links works well, one complication arises when pages reference each other. For example, suppose my page (A) has a link to your page (B), and your page also has a link back to mine. If a Web crawler were not careful, it might start at my page (A), then go to yours (B), then go back to mine (A), then back to yours (B), and so on. Such a pattern is an example of an **infinite loop** and could allow processing to continue forever. To prevent being caught in such fruitless loops, Web crawlers must keep track of what pages they have already visited. If links would cause them to revisit a page, then that link may be ignored as not providing any new information.

Although Web-crawler technology predominates in the development of databases for search engines, a combined approach is still used by a few companies, such as Yahoo! and MSN Search. These companies employ human editors to help guide common search queries, but the search engines utilize Web-crawler technology for relatively uncommon queries.

Whatever technology is used to locate and store Web pages, note that the pages in a search engine's database reflect only material from the time the pages were stored. If pages change, those changes are not immediately reflected in a search engine's database, and the results of your search may show out-of-date information. You cannot assume the references you get from a search apply to current pages; instead, the search results are based on past pages. For this reason, search engines not only have to frequently download Web pages for their databases, but also must regularly update those pages to reflect any revisions made to them.

How do searches locate information for my specific search requests?

Although a search engine's database resolves time delays of accessing Web pages, storage alone is not adequate to provide a quick response to your queries. Scanning billions of documents—

even by computers—requires considerable time and cannot be accomplished fast enough to give you a response in just a few seconds. Instead, search engines maintain various indexes to help guide their processing. Although the technical details for particular search engines are trade secrets, I can describe the basic idea with a familiar example.

Suppose you want to learn about "virtual memory" in this book. How might you proceed? If you have a particularly good memory, you might remember that this was a topic in Chapter 3, and turn directly to that material. Alternatively, you might start on page 1 of the book and scan each page until you found the relevant passage. As a third technique, you might consult a glossary to find a basic definition. None of these approaches, however, is very general. The first requires that you already know approximately where to look, the second assumes you have sufficient time and patience, and the third gives only a short definition.

Instead of any of these approaches, a more effective and general strategy would be to take advantage of the index. An index contains a listing of terms and the page numbers where they are discussed. In this case, you could look up "virtual memory" and (hopefully) find appropriate page references to read. As a variation, you might look up the word "virtual" to get one listing of passages, and you might look up "memory" to obtain a second listing. Comparing common references on both lists would provide you with information related to both topics. By looking up each word separately, you might not find the term "virtual memory" itself on a specific page, but you would expect both terms to be used in some way—perhaps in different paragraphs—on the page.

Search engines use this same idea of an index to speed up their searches. When a search engine company stores a Web page, it also updates its indexes that keep track of where to find various terms. Thus, if you conduct a Web search for the word "virtual," the search engine will consult an appropriate index for this word and identify Web pages that contain this word. Similarly, if you search for "memory," you will get a corresponding list of Web pages.

A search for "virtual memory" could proceed in either of two ways. Often, if you do not place these words in double quotes, the search engine will consult the indexes for the words "virtual" and "memory" separately and then find which pages contain both references. Presumably the pages you obtain would include references for "virtual memory," but other references might be included as well. For example, if one page indicated that "virtual reality applications require a significant amount of main memory," then that page would be retrieved as having references to both terms. On the other hand, if you conduct your search with double quotes around these two terms, then the search engine will look for only those pages where the word "memory" comes immediately after the word "virtual."

Just as with searching for material in a book, search engines prepare their own indexes for finding materials related to your queries. As with the storage of Web pages, search engine companies utilize two approaches for the actual preparation of these indexes: human and automated compilers. In their early years, both Yahoo! and Ask Jeeves employed people to scan pages, select the most helpful pages for their indexes, and identify themes for each page. Software tools developed by the vendor then would compile lists of themes and pages from the indexers and provide the search engine with the information necessary to respond to queries. An important advertising point of each of these sites was the human oversight to their search results; sites selected by people were thought to be generally more helpful than those selected by machines. Thus, even though queries to search engines with human-compiled indexes might result in relatively few responses, the sites that were identified often were of fairly good quality.

The second way to compile indexes is to turn the problem over to programs. In this approach, the challenge is to clarify relevant rules for assessing the content of a site so that an index contains only relevant references. Due to practical constraints, current search engines often maintain several indexes to address this issue. For example, one index might consider keywords specified by the author, another index might capture the title of the document, another might look at the body of the page, and another might scan for words in the URL itself.

However indexing is done, indexes must be updated whenever new pages are scanned, and index entries must be revised when new copies of pages take the place of earlier versions.

How are the results of searches ordered so that the most "relevant" sites appear first?

With billions of Web pages stored and indexed, search engines often identify thousands of pages that might be relevant to your search query. Finding the most "relevant" is indeed a challenge, but search engines want to return to you the most helpful sites so that you will continue using their service and they will continue to profit from advertisements. In producing their listings, search engines do not want their selections to be unduly manipulated by commercial sites. Commercial sites often want to be listed first, where they will have the greatest visibility and thus the greatest likelihood of being utilized. As a Web-based company, they may have a wonderful site, but few folks will visit that site if it appears on page 100 of a search engine's listing! Sometimes companies are given the opportunity to purchase space on a search engine, but often they must rely on the relevance of their site to the user's query. Thus, commercial companies may try to refine their Web sites so they appear most relevant or important. (We'll discuss how they work to achieve higher visibility later in this section.) This commercialism leads to a continual tension between orderings by search engines and manipulations by commercial Web sites. Were a commercial site to know exactly how a search engine orders its materials, it could try to alter its content to include everything that would make it listed first. Consequently, a search engine company rarely makes public many details about just how it determines the order of its search results. On the other hand, even with details buried within trade secrets, some common approaches such as the following five are well documented.

PageRank: PageRank, a registered trademark of Google, determines a page's importance by considering what pages link to it and the importance of those pages. At a basic level, if many pages refer to a given page, that page is considered relatively important; if few pages refer to a page, that page is relatively unimportant. At a more sophisticated level, a page is considered important if many important pages link to it; a page is less important if only a few important pages link to it or, alternatively, a page is less important if many unimportant pages link to it; and finally, a page is unimportant if few pages link to it—either important or unimportant. The interested reader will discover the computations involved in this process to be an elegant application of a mathematical subject called linear algebra (involving eigenvalues and eigenvectors).

Review of Title or Keyword Information: Every Web document can contain a title (often displayed at the top border of your browser window) and a list of keywords. Search engines can utilize this information to determine the relevance of a page to your query. For example, in your search for "virtual memory," the body of a page may contain both words, but the title or keywords may indicate the main topic involves Hollywood movies. Because your terms do not appear in important locations, this page may be considered less important than one giving your terms a higher profile.

Combinations of Words in Your Search: In your search for "virtual memory," the search engine might locate many pages that contain both "virtual" and "memory" somewhere in the page. Greater priority might be given to those pages where these two words are next to each other, just as you typed, rather than appearing separately in the document. (If this approach is used in ranking search results, a search for "virtual memory" may not produce the same results as a search for "memory virtual.")

Click Popularity: Click popularity measures how many people click on various links. When a search engine displays pages, it counts how many times users select which pages. Those pages that users select are given an increased ranking.

Stickiness: Stickiness measures how long users stay on a selected page. If a user selects a page referenced by a search engine, the user might scan the page and immediately return for another selection, or the user might spend some time reading that selected page. A search engine might work to record this amount of time, and pages are given high ratings if users stay on them for long periods of time.

Search engines probably use several of these techniques in some combination. Some materials from Yahoo! suggest that it gathers data on keyword and title information as part of its ordering process. Some third-party studies suggest that Google includes both PageRank and keyword/title information. Click popularity and stickiness are reported to be used by Lycos, Hotbot, and MSN Search. Undoubtedly, search engines use other factors as well, but these give a general idea of the types of strategies available to search engine companies.

Why do topic searches often yield porn sites?

The answer to this question includes a combination of social behaviors, economic forces, and technology. For better or worse, sites featuring pornography, violence, and sexual themes are remarkably popular. Although relatively few people (that I know, at least) admit that they frequent these Web sites, considerable evidence indicates these sites are quite popular. Although we could speculate on the nature of the audience, some statistics help clarify both the magnitude of this audience and something about its makeup.

- According to Jupiter Media Metrix, approximately 40.6 million people in the United States, 36% of all Internet users, visited an adult content site in February 2002. This is greater than the total visitors to online auction sites, such as eBay, in the same period, as reported in Yahoo! Finance.
- A report by the National Research Council estimates that there were between 2 million and 8 million official subscribers to pornography Web sites in 2002.
- Curiously, SexTracker reports that 70% of all Internet porn traffic occurs during the 9-to-5 workday. Also, various sources report results by eMarketer.com indicating that employees earning \$75,000 to \$100,000 annually are twice as likely to download pornography at work as those earning less than \$35,000.

Further, a significant number of these visitors are willing to pay for viewing, products, and the like. Altogether, adult Web sites generate millions of dollars in revenue annually, and this amount has been increasing steadily. Here are some further statistics:

- Jupiter Media Metrix estimates that online pornography revenues in the United States will grow from \$230 million in 2001 to \$400 million by 2006. (Source: eMarketer)
- The report by the National Research Council cited earlier estimates that subscribers to pornography Web sites paid between \$40 and \$100 a year, for a total of approximately \$200 million in 2002.

With so much money involved, companies and individuals who maintain these Web sites have a strong incentive to promote their sites and to entice the general public to visit their sites rather than those of others. After all, Web sites generate profits only if visitors utilize those sites so site owners want their sites to be visible. All of this generates considerable motivation for owners of pornographic and other adult Web sites to make their sites as visible as possible. To be listed in the "top 20" references of a search engine is an especially coveted position, because it implies the site would be listed on the first page of responses given to a user. A listing at rank 1 or 2 by a search engine would put the site at the very top of the page—in the most visible position.

 How do sites increase their visibility?

We have already discussed how companies often want to manipulate their sites so that they appear most relevant to a user's query, but this is not the only way that they can achieve Web site visibility. Two other common strategies include purchasing space on search engines and working within browsers. Many search engine companies generate revenue from ads or from highlighted references that they place at the beginning of their pages of results. These advertisements, paid for by companies promoting their Web sites, can be an important source of income for search engine companies, making them a viable business enterprise. Typically, the ads or highlighted references that appear on a search engine page are related to the queries you make—at least according to keywords on the reference pages. Adult sites, for example, have a strong incentive for publicity, so the keywords that call up their Web sites in a search engine may be more general or inclusive than some viewers might prefer.

Search engine companies using references that have been generated through automated searches typically take a different approach when it comes to ranking their search findings. These companies usually have a clear policy that they will not adjust ratings based on pressures or payoffs. Further, the search engine companies typically keep the details of their ratings' computations private in order to reduce the manipulation of these ratings by commercial sites. However, even without public disclosure of ratings formulae, commercial companies and consultants work to identify relevant criteria to improve ratings and visibility. For example, entrepreneurs may conduct experiments to learn what factors seem to have the most effect on ratings. A recent review of materials from several consultants and referenced on the Web highlighted several mechanisms for improving visibility:

- Include important phrases in titles and headers (for example, put "virtual memory" in both the header of your page and in the title of the browser window).
- Identify keywords—perhaps several times in a "title" or "meta" field within an HTML page.
- Arrange directory and file names to contain content phrases (for example, use "virtual-memory.html" as the file name, or place page "paging.html" in a "virtual_memory" subdirectory).

Also, when search engines track click popularity or stickiness, some commercial sites may utilize programs to "browse" the Web to increase tracking data. To counter such maneuvers, search engine companies may penalize sites that are caught trying any of these sly activities. With huge profits to be made, however, many commercial developers have great incentive to improve their Web site's ranking, and often are willing to devote considerable time and effort to refining their sites to make that happen, regularly trying new approaches to improve their ratings and visibility.

Another tactic a company could take to improve its Web site's visibility is to influence your browser's behavior. For example, some browsers provide a mechanism that allows an alternative page to be loaded when a desired page is not found. The idea is that if you enter the URL for a non-existent Web page, you may be presented with the web site for a search engine or a generic Web page rather than recieve an awkward "not found" message.

When a browser has this capability, however, it may be possible to change just which alternative Web page is presented. Sometimes you may specify this alternative explicitly, but sometimes it may be changed by a script located in a Web page or e-mail. That is, the alternative page for your browser may be reset when you view another page or when you recieve e-mail.

Of course, when others set this alternative page for you, you may find yourself viewing material you have no interest in seeing. According to some reports, some users have found themselves viewing gambling sites or hardcore pornography in their browsers after recieving e-mail.

This capability reported for some browsers suggests that your browser settings may be changed if you visit various Web sites. We will discuss this topic in greater details, shortly, but take note that interacting with a Web site or reading e-mail may have side effects that can influence your future Web experiences.

How are pop-up boxes created?

To explore pop-up boxes, let's first consider a basic Web page, written in simple HTML, and its interaction with a browser. As a hypertext markup language for Web pages, HTML provides formatting marks that tell a browser how textual material and images should be displayed. As shown in Figure 13.1, after a server sends an HTML page to your browser, the browser displays the material in the browser window by following the HTML formatting instructions. This process is reasonably simple and straightforward; HTML has no built-in capabilities for creating pop-up windows.

The process for displaying a page written in PostScript or PDF is similar. PostScript and PDF, as you will recall from Chapter 2, involve files of a particular form that contain both information to be displayed and extensive instructions regarding how that information should be formatted. In this case, the browser may not know all about these formats, but it calls on a plugin display program to handle those chores. Figure 13.2 shows this process for a file that contains PostScript formatting instructions. Although this process may require the extra step of calling a program to interpret the PostScript, it still is fairly simple, and no pop-up windows can appear.

We lose some of this simplicity, however, if the Web page utilizes JavaScript, VBScript, or another scripting language. These Web page capabilities are designed to supplement your basic text and

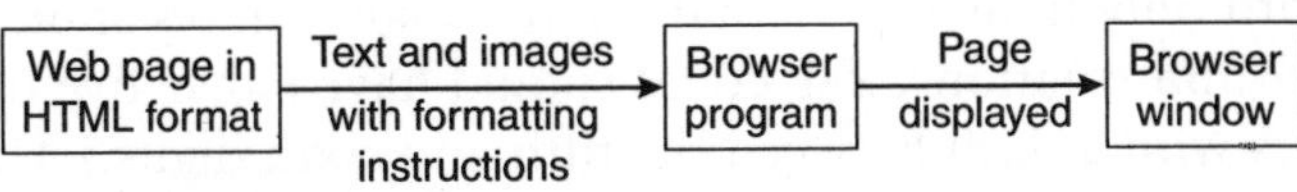

Figure 13.1
Processing an HTML page.

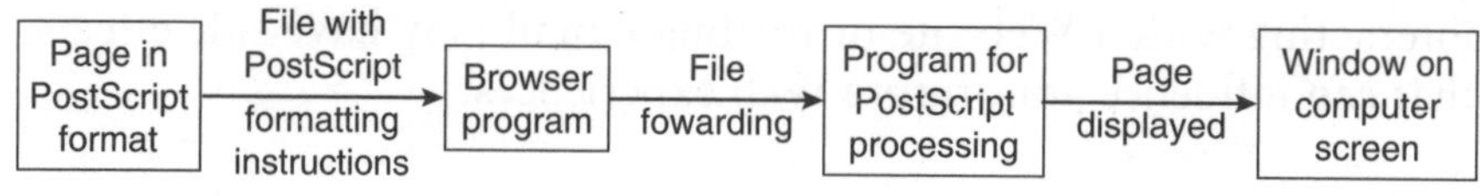

Figure 13.2
Processing a page utilizing PostScript formatting instructions.

formatting instructions with programs that respond specifically to something you do on a Web page or to other events related to your browser. For example, one program or script may be run when you type material into a text box, and another program may be run when you click "Submit." Such programs can be linked to most any activity, such as typing, pressing a mouse button, or releasing the mouse button. In addition, a program can be run when the page first loads into your browser, and a final program can be run when your browser completes its work on your page and goes onto another page. Technically, each such activity you perform on a Web page is called an **event**, and HTML allows a Web programmer to associate a script or program with a wide range of events. This type of programming is called **event-driven programming.**

As an example, consider a Web page that helps you prepare to ship a package. On the Web page's form, you will need to supply your own address, the address the package is going to, the type of shipping (postal mail, United Parcel Service, Federal Express), and the speed of delivery (overnight, second day, regular delivery, bulk rate). In return, the Web site will let you know how much your package will cost, and your shipping office will be able to print a special shipping label for you when you deliver your package. As an example, Figure 13.3 shows such a form, used by the Grinnell College mail service.

Now, let's consider possible supplements to this form. First, we might want a table of cities and ZIP codes to appear in a separate window. Second, as a user fills out the form, we might want to check that the address is reasonable. (Names should contain mostly letters with only limited punctuation and digits, states should have two-letter abbreviations, ZIP codes should have either five digits or nine digits with a dash between the fifth and sixth digits.) Thus, we might associate a script to each field in the form, which would check the field as it is completed. Third, when the user clicks "Submit,"

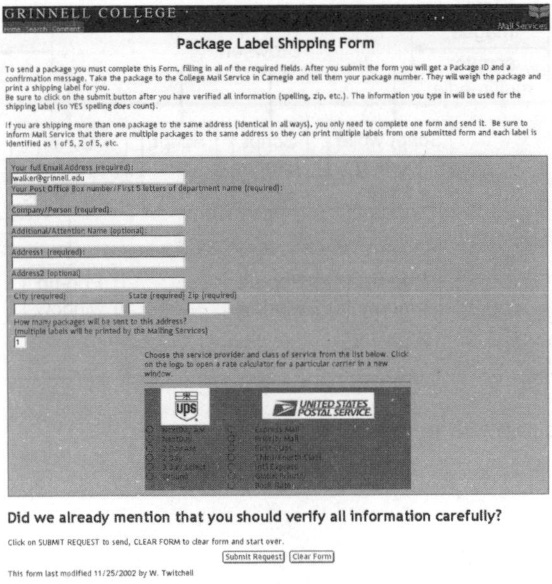

Figure 13.3
Form used by the Grinnell College mail service. Courtesy of Grinnell College.

we might want to confirm that all fields are appropriately filled out and that no required information has been omitted.

All of this special processing can be accomplished using a scripting language, as illustrated in Figure 13.4. Using either JavaScript or VBScript, the first part of the code for a Web page could instruct the browser to open a second window when the mailing form loads. Additional scripts could check each field of the form as the user fills them in, and the scripts could report an error message in a pop-up window if problems are found. A final script could check the information at the end—again using a new pop-up window to indicate any omitted fields.

This hypothetical example illustrates several helpful uses of scripting: pop-up windows can present a user with supplementary information; scripts can review text as a user types it; scripts can make final checks in a form; and new windows can display warning or error information. None of these capabilities are available directly with strict HTML, but adding them to a site can make a perceptible difference in how user-friendly and interactive the site is.

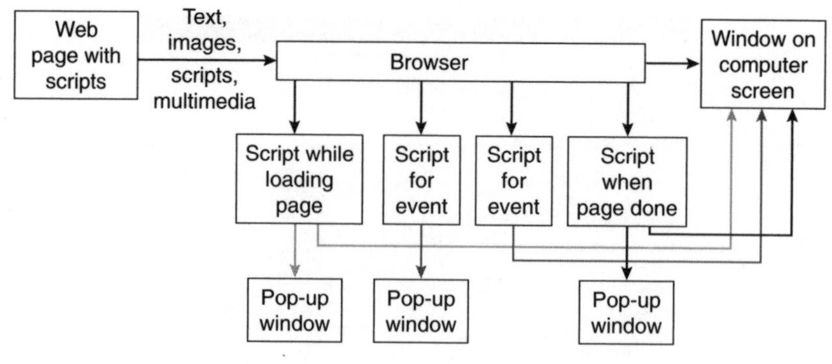

Figure 13.4
Processing a Web page with scripting.

The addition of scripting capabilities can help us with common tasks, and the automatic generation of new windows can provide us with worthwhile information.

How can pop-up windows be controlled?

As we've discussed, pop-up windows can be generated when Web pages take advantage of scripting languages. These windows may be programmed to appear when a page loads, when it finishes, or when the user performs various activities while viewing the page. In essence, because scripts control the appearance of these windows, and because Web developers can write the scripts as they wish, JavaScript, VBScript, and other scripting languages can trigger new windows to appear at any time during the viewing of a Web page.

For the most part, the appearance of these windows is outside the control of you as a viewer of the Web page. Often they materialize on your screen with useful information and enhance your Internet experience, but at other times they provide unwelcome solicitations or promotions that are more annoying than helpful. Unfortunately, when activated, a browser will follow the scripts it receives, and windows will appear following those instructions, regardless of the content of those windows.

Although most of this activity happens automatically, you usually can employ one countermeasure. In particular, browsers normally have a setting to turn off JavaScript or other scripting languages. If these languages are disabled, then your browser will format the HTML it receives, but it will ignore any requests to run scripts. In particular, turning scripting off will prevent the appearance of any pop-up windows (as well as eliminate ad animation and the creation of new windows for advertisement). On the other hand, turning off scripting also will turn off all error checking in forms and other aids that you might find helpful. It is technically possible for browsers to allow you to run a scripting language but block processing related to new windows. However, details of such an option, if available, would depend on your specific browser.

As a practical matter, some people have concerns that scripting also may allow Web developers to take advantage of security problems in a browser, and thus open up a user to destructive or annoying programs. I would estimate that approximately one-fourth of educational computing professionals routinely turn off scripting for security reasons. These people avoid potential annoyance, but they also miss helpful features of error checking and form processing.

How are topic-specific ads generated?

As we have already discussed, companies have strong incentives to publicize their products, so they often want to place ads where potential customers will find them. In Web applications, this includes paying vendors, such as search engines, to include links to the commercial sites and display ads within other Web pages. We also have noted that scripts within Web pages can generate pop-up windows at various times. Because Web developers can control the content of these windows, it is hardly surprising that pop-up windows sometimes contain advertising.

The display of these ads may be further refined by two additional factors. First, scripting allows the dynamic display of material. In particular, scripts can change the appearance of pages over time. This allows one ad to be replaced by another and also allows some animation of ads. Second, we have already discussed in

Chapter 12 that a Web server may seek to store a cookie on your computer or in your account. If your browser is set to allow this, then a Web server knows something about your past history and can apply that knowledge to the pop-up windows it displays. In particular, cookies could allow a Web server to know what you have purchased or what you have browsed on its site in the past, and this special information could be used to tailor ads to your apparent interests. For example, if you purchase fishing goods on an e-commerce site, then that site will have a record of your having purchased an aquatic animal guide, a fishing pole, and a fishing vest—perhaps in a customer database. Through the use of cookies, the company could identify that you are a customer, and if so, which one (the one who bought fishing gear). It could then initiate a pop-up window advertising a deep-sea fishing tour of the coast of Nantucket, which would please the tour company because the money they are paying to advertise on this site is going to good use: you, their target audience, are seeing their ad. Thus, by using a cookie, the company could review its customer database, identify your past purchases, select ads for related products, and send those ads to your browser for display either in its regular page or in pop-up windows.

When you're browsing the Web and pop-up advertisements or the like appear on your computer screen, they may not be welcome, but often you can recognize that they are appearing in response to an action on your part (e.g., submitting a search request for fishing, loading a previously viewed page, or purchasing fishing gear). Why, then, do people receive random, unsolicited e-mail if they have never expressed interest in anything remotely related to the spam mail's topic? This, in part, results from the way that e-mail works, which is our next topic for discussion.

How does e-mail work?

Electronic mail (or e-mail) was first developed in the mid-1970s to send simple textual messages. Early e-mail messages contained characters you could type on a keyboard, and there was no worry about fonts, colors, pictures, audio, and the like. Communication was relatively straightforward, using the Internet packets discussed in Chapters 8 and 9—an e-mail message was placed in one or more packets, each of which indicated the addressee to whom the message was being sent, a return address, a few administrative details, and the characters making up the text. In these beginning stages, as noted in Chapter 11, the NSF-sponsored Internet allowed e-mail exchanges only within its network; smaller commercial networks had emerged, but were restricted in their effectiveness by NSF's exclusive network. Through this early period of development, commercial activity was not part of Internet traffic, and e-mail was largely restricted to communication between friends or professional contacts. In 1989, the NSF-sponsored governmental network linked with commercial networks, and e-mail expanded to connect a much greater number of people, but the nature of the communications still involved only text. With the simple nature of this material, processing of e-mail was like simple HTML processing by browsers, as shown in Figure 13.5.

In the early 1990s, interest in e-mail grew dramatically, as did the desire to augment e-mail's basic text capabilities. It became clear that a new approach was needed to allow multimedia, such as pictures and sound, to be packed up and included within e-mail messages. This led to the development of **Multipurpose Internet Mail Extensions (MIME)**, an effort at Bellcore (Bell Communications Research) in New Jersey, led by researcher Nathaniel Borenstein. The first multimedia message was sent on March 11, 1992, and included the picture shown in the sidebar on the next page.

This work led to an international MIME standard—a formal agreement or protocol among nations for the transmission of multimedia information over the Internet. If you use e-mail, your e-mail program likely takes advantage of this standard every time you send or receive an attachment in your e-mail.

With the addition of multimedia components, e-mail messages naturally become more complicated, because different types of

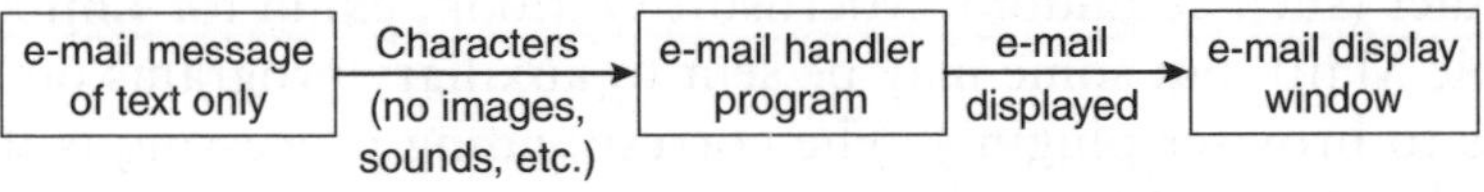

Figure 13.5
Processing simple e-mail.

The First Multimedia Message

This picture comes from the first multimedia e-mail message, sent on March 11, 1992. As you can see, this picture shows "the infamous Telephone Chords, the world's premier (= only) all-Bellcore barbershop quartet, singing about MIME." This group of scientists includes (from left to right): John Lamb, bass; David Braun, baritone; Michael Littman, lead; and Nathaniel Borenstein, tenor. Their song followed the tune of "Let Me Call You Sweetheart," and a recording of this song also was part of this first multimedia e-mail message. See http://www.guppylake.com/~nsb/mime.html for additional details.

Sidebar Figure 1 Bellcore's Telephone Chords in the first MIME e-mail message. Personal photo of Nathaniel Borenstein and appears with his permission.

material must be interpreted by your computer in different ways. Some of these media usually can be handled directly by an e-mail handler (such as Eudora, Microsoft Outlook, exmh for Linux, or Apple Mail), but some may be sent to auxiliary programs (analogous to browser plugins). The corresponding processing is illustrated in Figure 13.6.

From your experience with e-mail, you may know that textual information now commonly comes formatted in HTML or in a

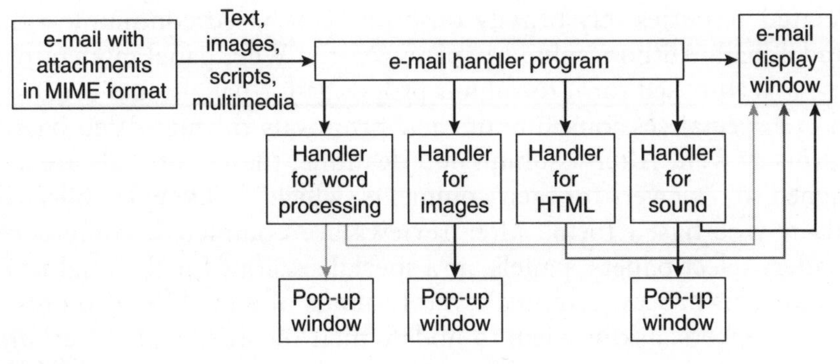

Figure 13.6
Processing multimedia in e-mail.

form designed for a word processor. Although such formatting sometimes has benefits, it also can raise the same issues that we've already discussed for browsers and scripting languages. E-mail attachments can contain scripts for scripting languages (such as JavaScript), references to Web pages, embedded images, and the like. Viewing any e-mailed material, therefore, can cause scripts to run as programs, which, as we know, may or may not be a desired effect. Although Figures 13.5 and 13.6 largely clarify how e-mail is processed, we will discuss some implications of this processing shortly.

Can I be certain who sent me an e-mail message?

As you would expect for any communication via the Internet, your e-mail handler can report only the information it receives within TCP/IP packets. Thus, your e-mail handler naturally determines the sender of an e-mail based on the information it finds in the e-mail. There is no requirement that this information indicate the actual sender of a message and no effective mechanism for checking.

This lack of a tie between actual sender and reported sender may seem peculiar, but it can be quite helpful when applied to certain situations. For example, for several years I have developed and administered software for an international conference. Conference-related activities rely heavily on both Web-based communication and e-mail. Authors submit papers over the Web; panel moderators use a Web-based form to submit proposals for panels; and organizers of special sessions submit their proposals through Web-based forms as well. After a submission deadline, these materials are assigned to reviewers for their comments, which are likewise collected via a Web-based form. After reviews are completed, conference leaders select papers, panels, and special sessions for the final program. This process requires several rounds of e-mail: first to previous reviewers, asking them to update their records; next to authors and session proposers, asking them to verify the correctness of their online submissions; then to reviewers, telling them their reviewing assignments; and finally to authors and proposers, indicating whether their materials were accepted for presentation. In the course of this communication, several conference leaders collaborate to prepare e-mail communications, but one person typically is designated as a conference contact. Thus, although several people may be involved in sending e-mail, the "From" line of an e-mail reports it comes from the contact person—a symposium chair, a program chair, a panels chair, or a chair for special sessions. Likewise, when a conference leader prepares the e-mail, she or he usually prepares a general note and instructs a script to use the central database to fill in details for each e-mail recipient.

In considering a specific e-mail, the person preparing the e-mail information and initiating the correspondence may or may not be the designated contact person. Also, regardless of who actually sends the message, the e-mail draws from a central database, and all e-mail actually comes from the same physical server that is connected to the database. To accomplish this processing, when a message is sent, scripts insert the appropriate "From" and "To" lines within each message, based on the conference leader designated as the contact. This feature allows conference leaders to share the work of organizing correspondence while maintaining a single contact person for various tasks.

As this example suggests, many scripting languages allow you to send anonymous e-mail or e-mail with an altered "From" line; you just specify both where the message goes and who the e-mail should say the message is from. The example also illustrates that this capability is completely appropriate in some circumstances.

This example, however, also illustrates that scripting languages make it remarkably easy for users to insert any e-mail address they wish in a "From" line or other part of an e-mail message. Although many e-mail users are responsible when using this capability, some have chosen to take advantage of the technology for their own goals. As a result, you indeed have no way to be sure just who really sent an e-mail message.

The use of scripts within e-mail attachments, which we discussed earlier, further compounds this issue. As I have already noted, these scripts can work as programs that run when you try to read the e-mail messages or attachments. When these programs are running on your computer, they may have access to some of your materials, including any address books or listing of e-mail addresses you might have. If these programs can gain access to your addresses, then they also can generate new e-mail to those people. As a result, scripts or programs in an attachment you receive could, in fact, send new e-mail to your friends under your name. Depending on the circumstances, you might not even know the e-mail was sent; you could be reading the e-mail note with little indication that a script was communicating with your friends behind the scenes!

Why is e-mail susceptible to viruses and worms?

We have already noted that e-mail may contain scripts for sending more e-mail to your friends and acquaintances, and these scripts can be activated when you open an e-mail or attachment for reading. Of course, such processing is not limited to sending e-mail. Exactly the same approach could be used to imbed programs in your e-mail containing viruses and worms. If a virus is contained in an e-mail attachment, then opening the attachment likely will run that virus program. You can see how e-mail is a convenient, efficient way for viruses to spread; many people open attachments without considering first whether they are expecting the file, if they know the sender (which, as we discussed, may not be worth anything), or if their e-mail handler automatically scans attachments for viruses.

The best way to protect your computer from e-mailed viruses is, as with browsers, not to give these embedded scripts a chance to run. Turning off scripting and other automated options in e-mail–related applications will provide some measure of defense.

Another approach is to employ software filters to scan messages as they arrive. This approach, however, has its own limitations, as we will discuss in the next chapter.

Why is e-mail susceptible to viruses and worms?

As you may know, **spam** (in the context of e-mail over the Internet) is sometimes defined as the sending of unsolicited e-mail to others—often on a massive scale. In recent years, the volume of spam messages has ballooned. Here are a few statistics:

- On June 16, 2003, the *Seattle Times* reported that America Online stated it was blocking 2.4 billion spam e-mails *every day*.
- MessageLabs, an Internet filtering firm, estimated that 55% of all e-mails sent in May 2003 were unsolicited messages—up from 40% just the previous month.
- In a court case filed by Earthlink against Buffalo Spammer, the spammer sent some 825 million messages to Earthlink ISP customers and cost Earthlink $1 million just in terms of bandwidth.

Altogether, the generation of unsolicited messages or spam has grown in huge proportions in just a few years. What is it about e-mail that makes spam the incredibly popular form of advertising that it is? Most notably, e-mail involves only a few pieces of information: a sender's address, a receiver's address, a subject, and a text body, and not all of these are actually required. Of these, the only essential item is the receiver's address, so mailers will know where to send the message. With access to lists of e-mail addresses, programs have little difficulty putting the pieces together to generate e-mail; thus, the only challenge facing mass e-mail programs is determining potential addresses. Once those lists are established, spam can be distributed in huge quantities quickly and at low cost.

To gain addresses, spammers utilize at least four approaches:

Scanning Web Sites: We have already noted that search engines often utilize programs to follow links on the Web to browse sites and collect pages for indexing. Much the same approach can be used to search the Web for e-mail addresses; programs can follow links throughout the Web, but store only e-mail addresses rather than full pages. This suggests that any e-mail address you post on a Web site has the potential to be identified and used as the target of spam.

Utilization of Information You Supply: When you supply your e-mail address to a commercial site, a chat room, or another organization, your address becomes part of a listing by that company or organization. In a chat room, your e-mail address also may be distributed to other users of the chat room. Depending on the group's privacy policy, that e-mail address might be used for only restricted communications, or it might be available for the sending of spam. If you do not know just how a company or organization will use an e-mail address you supply, you should assume that your information may be used to generate e-mail—perhaps on a massive scale.

Exchange of Lists: Once one company has obtained your e-mail address, the company may sell it to someone else, or several companies may exchange lists. Again, these activities should be covered by privacy policies, and you should check whether your information will be distributed before you supply information. Even if a policy indicates that your information will remain private, however, it does not follow that the same policy will remain in effect in the future. Although a company currently may intend to guard your privacy, circumstances may change. For example, if the company encounters difficult financial times, and an outside firm offers a large payment to purchase an e-mail list, then the company may feel some pressure to change the privacy policy and distribute the list of addresses.

Random Spamming: By scanning Web sites, a potential scammer can identify possible locations that host e-mail accounts. This does not give information about specific e-mail addresses, only where they might be based, but the spammer might just make up possible addresses and send e-mail. If e-mail bounces as being undeliverable, then the spammer knows the address is invalid. If the e-mail yields no response, then the spammer does not know whether the address is valid or not. However, if a user sends back a note—even to indicate that she or he wants to be removed from the list—then the spammer knows the address is valid and may add the address to the list for future reference. This strategy of spammers suggests that you should never respond to spam—you may be confirming that a potential address is valid, thus inviting a barrage of further messages!

These four strategies suggest that you should be extremely careful in giving out your e-mail address: Always check privacy policies first, and even then act cautiously. Remember that responding to spam is a certain way to verify you are reading your e-mail, and encourages further activity.

How is spam controlled?

If the volume of spam you receive seems relatively low, then you may decide simply to review each incoming message and delete the spam that you encounter. This strategy, however, can become difficult as the volume of the spam you receive increases. Thus, you may be drawn to follow a more active approach to handling spam. Here are some strategies, both short term and long term.

In the short term:

- You could change your e-mail address and be particularly conservative in giving the new address out—following the ideas presented in the previous section. You would have to tell your friends of your new address, but it might take spammers quite awhile to locate your new location and send you spam.
- You could install a filter to scan your e-mail and remove or redirect some of it. Many filter software products have appeared on the market in recent years, so you might utilize one of these commercial packages—or perhaps your ISP already utilizes a package for you. Basically, filtering software can follow two approaches:
  - If you want to receive e-mail only from a known list of friends, you could use the filtering software to look for e-mail from your list, and separate it from all other pieces of mail. Messages from your friends might go to a special e-mail area; other messages could be either deleted or sent to a "junk" area for you to review when you have nothing better to do.
  - If you expect to receive legitimate mail from a wide range of people, known and unknown, you could set a filtering program to scan messages for likely terms, phrases, or content. In effect, the filter might grade each e-mail to determine how likely it is to be spam, and the filter would take action on messages that seem most likely to be inappropriate.
- Some institutions and companies set a policy that any e-mail message with more than 6 (or 10, or another number) recipients is likely spam, and thus automatically discard all such messages.
- Some organizations may utilize firewalls to block e-mail from specified sites that have previously been identified as

sending spam. Although this does not protect you against new spam-generating sites, it may reduce spam from common sources; that is, until they move to new sites.

Over the long term, to reduce the amount of spam received, individuals can be careful in posting e-mail addresses, giving those addresses to others, and handling spam. Of course, a main motivation for sending spam in the first place is to make money through sales or other business practices. From this standpoint, the best long-term attack against spammers is to carefully avoid buying goods from folks that distribute spam. You may find spam annoying and complain to various Internet groups, but if you buy those products, then you are providing direct financial encouragement for continued spamming.

Can laws help?

Although we might hope that laws could help control spam, this approach has several practical difficulties:

- *Message headers*: Message headers can be faked, so it can be extremely difficult to determine exactly who sent spam in the first place. A message may indicate it came from one source, but it might actually have come from another—even a competitor. To enforce laws, one must know who to charge with a violation, and the identification of e-mail senders can be difficult.
- *Subcontractors*: When a company begins an advertising campaign, it may contract with a second party to run specific ads. That company may subcontract specific parts to third parties, and so forth. At some point, a subcontractor may begin an automated campaign using spam, but this may be quite different from the intentions of the original company. Further, because spam usually is generated through independent computer programs, spam can be tricky to stop once the programs begin. With such an array of companies engaged in advertising, it turns out that the original company often loses control of its advertising campaign. It may tell its immediate subcontractor(s) to avoid spam or to stop a current spam campaign, but it can be difficult to reach the actual subcontractor sending out the e-mail!

- *Laws apply within jurisdictions*: Laws of a country apply within that country, and laws of a state or province apply only within those areas. With the international dimensions of the Internet, laws passed in one geographical region often cannot be enforced if the offenders are located elsewhere. Thus, even if the United States passed a law with stiff penalties for unsolicited, mass e-mail campaigns, the law would not be enforceable for spammers located in other countries. Further, if spammers were living in the United States when the law was passed, there would be little preventing them from continuing their activities from another country. A full ban would require international agreements covering *all* countries, because any abstaining country could become a haven for commercial spammers. Realistically, such a wide-reaching international agreement would be most difficult to obtain.
- *Variations in laws and technology*: By their nature, laws must be specific in identifying what constitutes a problem or violation; therefore, courts would require a precise definition of spam that clarifies the boundaries between spam and legitimate mailings in order to consider a potential law. Courts often throw out vague laws that are not being sufficiently clear in guiding behaviors. Also, laws typically address specific technologies and approaches. Because spam is an invention of technology, and because technology continues to advance, laws often lag behind practices. When a law addresses one behavior, folks find new ways to operate, and laws that once would have been effective no longer resolve the problem they were designed to address. Thus, there is a constant tension between laws and behaviors. This is not to say that laws related to the Internet cannot be helpful in reducing some types of behaviors. However, with the international dimensions of the Internet and spam, it may not be reasonable to expect resolution of technical problems and behaviors through legal means.

Summary

All computer applications depend upon algorithms to specify the steps computers must follow to accomplish their work. Web search engines organize this work into several steps. Search engines constantly utilize programs or employ indexers to store and tabulate Web pages within a database. When you request information on a particular topic, the search engines identify relevant Web pages according to their indexing. Algorithms then order these pages according to their perceived relevance, based on a variety of criteria.

Commercial sites gain business according to the visibility of their Web pages, and this may lead companies to adjust their materials to manipulate ratings and perceived relevance. Pop-up boxes and browser scripts can be used to supplement information at your browser, for error checking, and to enhance product visibility.

E-mail started in the mid-1970s as a mechanism to send simple messages, but the MIME format now allows the transmission of multimedia materials. When you receive e-mail, your mail program can display what it receives, but data in messages, such as the sender, can be faked; you cannot have confidence about who sent an e-mail. Commercial companies may collect e-mail addresses from many sources and guess about other e-mail addresses. With lists of potential e-mail addresses, marketers may broadcast unsolicited e-mail or spam in great quantities as an inexpensive way to advertise products to large audiences.

Both Web pages and e-mail can contain programs, including viruses. Although laws can provide some help in controlling unwanted programs and spam, your best defense involves caution and vigilance.

Terminology from This Chapter

event
event-driven programming
indexing
infinite loop
Multipurpose Internet Mail Extensions (MIME)
spam
Web crawler

Discussion Questions

1. An assignment in one course asked students to write a paper describing an application of a particular type of algorithm. One student typed the name of the algorithm into a search engine, examined one of the references returned, and wrote a paper explaining that application. It turned out, however, that the referenced application had nothing to do with the

type of algorithm in question. That type of algorithm was not even mentioned in the Web site. Consider how it might have happened that the search engine's response to the student query contained such a reference.

2. Recent statistics suggest that gaming and gambling interests are becoming at least as popular on the Web as pornography. Here are a few statistics:

   - The research group Datamonitor forecasts that the online gaming market will grow from $670 million in 2002 to $2.9 billion in 2005. Although South Korea was the largest market for online gaming in 2003, NUA Internet Surveys indicates that the United States will bring in the most online gaming revenue by 2005.
   - A research report published by the Informa Media Group (and reported by eMarketer through various third parties) estimates that worldwide revenue from e-gambling will reach $14.5 billion by 2006.
   - With such projections, Jupiter Media Metrix predicts that revenues from online music, games, and audio-visual entertainment will far outweigh revenue from online porn by 2006.

   Such statistics and projections raise several questions.

   a. How might such business ventures influence what we see in our browsers or in e-mail in the coming years?

   b. To what extent can such ventures be monitored or regulated through governmental policies or laws?

   c. What impact will Internet traffic related to gaming or gambling have on the use of the Web for other purposes?

   Conduct some additional research on any of these areas, and discuss possible answers.

3. Suppose you were writing a filtering program to identify and divert e-mail that might be spam. One approach might be to scan messages for various keywords that might be considered objectionable. However, this simple approach does not always work. In the following examples, determine why looking for specific words might not catch some spam messages, or why it might label some appropriate messages as spam.

a. An e-mail message contains an attachment—perhaps in PDF format—and that attachment is encoded for transmission.

b. The text of an e-mail message is written in HTML and contains some comments (not displayed on your screen) along with regular text.

c. An e-mail message contains pictures or sounds, perhaps in GIF or JPEG format.

4. Consider the section of this chapter entitled, "Can I be certain who sent me an e-mail message?" While this section contains 6 full paragraphs to answer the question, some might argue that the short answer is simply "no." Do you believe this shortened answer would have been adequate? Why or why not?

Exercises

1. a. Give a careful definition for each of the words or phrases listed in the "Terminology from This Chapter" section.

b. Use each term in two or three sentences to explain its significance and clarify its relevance to this chapter.

2. When you obtain the results of a query from a search engine, it sometimes happens that a reference no longer works; that is, you click on a reference to find that page is no longer available.

a. Explain how it might happen that a search engine produces a reference to a nonexistent Web page.

b. The Google search engine anticipates the possibility that such broken links might arise and allows a user to view an old copy of the page. In Google's terms, this is a "cached" copy. Based on your reading in Chapter 3, why do you think this copy is called "cache"?

3. This chapter discusses possibilities for e-mail scripts to send e-mail from your account or to activate viruses and other programs. As another example, consider what might happen if an e-mail message was written in HTML format. Suppose further that your browser was configured to accept cookies, display images, and run scripts.

a. Suppose someone sends you e-mail. How might they be able to confirm that you have actually viewed their message?

b. How might a company be able to set a cookie on your account based on e-mail you have received?

4. Suppose someone wants to develop a list of valid e-mail addresses, perhaps for the purpose of sending spam selling the address list to others for spam. Toward this end, this person identifies valid Web site names and makes up possible user-names (e.g., henry01, henry02, . . .). Suppose further that this person sends out numerous e-mail messages to all of these potential users, and these messages are written in HTML.

Describe how you could set up your HTML page and handle subsequent processing to determine which of the possible user names and addresses were in use. You can assume that a user might read your e-mail, but you should not assume that the user will consciously reply to that e-mail.

5. Suppose you ran a Web-based company, so you would want your company's pages to be listed early on search engines. Suppose you knew or suspected that a particular search engine used click popularity or stickiness as a factor in determining which sites to list before others in giving its search results.

a. What technique(s) might you employ to manipulate the search engine's statistics regarding click popularity for your Web site(s)? That is, what might you do to give your site(s) a higher rating for click popularity?

b. What technique(s) might you employ to manipulate the search engine's statistics regarding stickiness for your Web site(s)?

Part V
Social/Ethical Questions

Chapter 14

How universal is access to computers and the Web?

The concept of access to computers and the World Wide Web is quite complex. Think about what defines "access" in this context. Does it depend on how the technology is used? How convenient must the technology be in order to be considered accessible? How much should it cost, if anything. Once you have a sense of what it means for computers to be accessible, you must consider a myriad of diverse factors that influence accessibility, including technological capabilities, political power and privilege, cultural norms, social circumstances and class, economic means, scheduling constraints, and personal interests and motivations. This chapter examines many of these topics, considering possible levels of access and identifying potential issues. Although the material in this chapter can only begin a discussion of accessibility, you are encouraged to build upon the base provided here and bring these issues to your local communities. Try to determine what needs to be done in order to provide more uniform access to all, and to work with community groups and individuals to make such expanded access happen.

Let's now consider what it means to have access to computers and the World Wide Web, and as we do so, we'll talk about a number of examples that show the reality of how much computer access varies.

What different levels of access are there for computers and the Internet?

Let's consider access on a continuous scale, from not available at all to being easily available to anyone for any application at any time.

- Computers and Internet access never available
- Some accessibility to a computer and the Internet, perhaps at specified times through a communal installation or a common account
- Limited ongoing access to individual accounts, perhaps with significant restrictions regarding convenience, cost structures, or social circumstances
- Ongoing access to individual accounts, perhaps through slow computers or limited communications channels
- Easy ongoing access for individuals using high-speed technology

Graphically, this scale is shown in Figure 14.1.

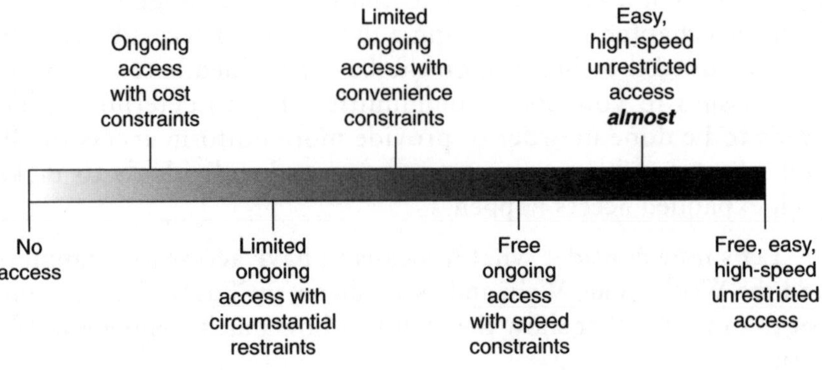

Figure 14.1
Levels of computer and Internet access.

Let's look at each of these in more detail by considering several case studies. Although Case Study 2 is eight years old, the others have occurred within the last three years or so. To protect privacy, selective details have sometimes been omitted.

Computer and Internet Access Never Available:

Case Study 1

In a rural and isolated area of a third-world country, people have virtually no computing equipment, and communities have no infrastructure for telephones or other communication lines. This lack of technology has kept farmers reliant upon outside brokers for sales of crops, and agricultural sales regularly are well below market prices elsewhere. In one such community, farmers are actively seeking a communal computer with a satellite-based connection to the World Wide Web so they can interact with outside brokers and participate in the world market. There is reasonable expectation that a single computer with Internet access could provide the information needed to double or triple the prices the farmers receive for their crops.

Case Study 1 identifies a setting in which computers are not easily available at present. Relative to the local economy, computer technology is very expensive and thus beyond the reach of most people. Even if a computer did become available, it would be difficult to use it regularly, given the lack of supporting technology. The community does not have dependable electrical power, so a desktop computer would continually crash and recharging batteries on a laptop would be difficult, because to restore battery power voltage fluctuations might destroy any equipment that is plugged in.

Furthermore, if computer technology were obtained and problems of power resolved, the community still has no telephone structure or other wired communication network. This particular community is also physically isolated by mountains, and establishing a traditional telephone network would require spanning hundreds of miles of rough terrain. Because of this location, a computer cannot be plugged in to any existing network to gain Internet access at any speed. Similarly, the community has no transmission towers or installed networks for cellular telephones, making standard wireless technology difficult.

With virtually no local infrastructure, this community is currently working on the installation of a generator for ongoing electrical power and the use of a satellite station to make contact with a base station over 1000 miles away. Their lack of access to a computer and the Internet, then, principally arises from their lack of technology and infrastructure. Conversely, for these farmers, the dream of access may mean a single machine for the community, perhaps with one account, one e-mail address, and so on. From this perspective, privacy, individual accounts, and transmission speeds are relatively minor issues—access means having something that works well enough to interact with markets and buyers.

Limited Ongoing Access with Cost Restraints:

Case Study 2

A university in an urban setting in a developing country was able to establish e-mail access for faculty, staff, and students. However, for political, economic, or social reasons, users were charged per kilobyte for e-mail they received. At the specified rate, a one megabyte file (such as a single picture) included as an e-mail attachment might cost the equivalent of a graduate student's monthly salary.

Case Study 2 portrays a different situation. For folks involved in this example, computers *were* available, and these machines *had* access to the Internet. Anyone associated with the university could, in principle, obtain a computer account; however, in practice, potential costs were prohibitive. The receipt of even a simple e-mail message could cause severe economic hardship. Thus, in reality, only the economically well-to-do could afford computers with Internet access. Limiting available Internet access to an exclusive group of people is not uncommon and is achieved in a variety of ways. In other settings, governments sometimes have restricted access to computer networks and the Internet according to political stature, economic class, or other cultural position. Alternatively, Internet administrators can arrange their networks so that only members of a ruling political party or influential business people might be allowed access. On the surface, their policies may specify that many or all citizens can access the World Wide Web, but a closer look may indicate difficult rules or extreme practices that greatly restrict the use of this technology by the general public.

To expand upon the university example, it turned out that all e-mail to the university went to a single administrator's account. Those in correspondence with people at this school were told to place the intended recipient's name in the "Subject" line, so people would know who should receive the e-mail. In this case, all individuals had access to all e-mail, but were supposed to read just those messages meant for themselves. (In different circumstances, an administrator instead could forward each e-mail to the intended recipient.) In practice, this approach to e-mail implied that no message could be considered private. Rather, both senders and recipients needed to assume that the administrator and any other users had full access to any message that might be sent or received by anyone.

Limited Ongoing Access with Circumstantial Restraints: When Internet access is available and not denied to anyone because of economic or political reasons, a number of situations can arise that limit how accessible computers really are to those who want to use them.

Case Study 3

A public library has a few computers attached to the Internet for general use. Potential users can reserve times to use these machines, although users are supposed to limit their use to 30 minutes if others are waiting. In practice, the 30-minute time limit is enforced only if a customer complains to a librarian, and then the librarian normally just reminds the current user to finish up. If the current user is slow in finishing, it can easily take 15–20 minutes of the next time slot before the next user can use the machine. Due to restricted budgets, no machines are available for a short search of the Web that might take two or three minutes.

In Case Study 3, computers are available for anyone to use in the public library. Moreover, any library user has access to the equipment on an equal basis. The library's limited resources, however, require some time rationing, and that could lead to interpersonal difficulties when time limits expire. In practice, folks who are relatively assertive are more likely to gain greater access than those who are relatively shy.

Time limits also may discourage users with either short or long tasks to accomplish from working on a computer. If you wanted to search for just one item on the Web—perhaps following up on a reference for an assignment—you might have to wait 30 minutes or an hour or even longer for your time slot only to use the computer and Internet for 5 minutes. With such a perceived hassle, you might well decide not to use the computer. Similarly, if you needed to type a 10-page paper for a class, you might find it difficult to work in 30-minute sessions. As soon as you started on one section, or began researching one topic, your time might be up, and you would then have to wait for another turn. Overall, limited resources may force institutions to create policies to allocate computer and Internet usage, but any such policy will likely encourage one type of usage and discourage others.

Case Study 4

A family purchased a personal computer with a high-speed Internet connection. Although the family had both a son and a daughter in high school, the computer was placed in the son's room so it would be more convenient for him.

Uneven access to computers regularly occurs even in situations that do not have time-limiting regulations and would otherwise offer excellent accessibility. Case Study 4 illustrates a common, but sometimes subtle, form of access discrimination. When a computer is in a public area, as our library example showed, some folks may feel less comfortable accessing the equipment than others. When the computer is placed in a less public area, such feelings can intensify. In this case, a family may tell the daughter that she may use the computer whenever she needs to. However, in practice, it may seem intrusive to her to go into her brother's room on a regular basis; or, if he's particularly messy, his room may be an unpleasant environment for her, and her overall experience with the computer would be compromised. Environmental factors play a role not only in someone's comfort level, but also in her or his productivity level. In the previous example, the son may have needed to request a better lamp or chair in order to use the computer without straining his eyes or back. These details influence the quality of his Internet accessibility.

Limited Ongoing Access with Convenience Restraints:

Case Study 5

Iowa has developed a state-wide communication network, the *Iowa Communications Network (ICN)*, with connectivity to the World Wide Web. State law mandates that every public school district be connected to this network. Some state funding has been made available to underwrite the costs of the connection, and some extremely innovative programming has been developed for this visionary network. Although some school districts have incorporated this infrastructure into their courses and curricula, others have little equipment for student use, few instructional areas (such as classrooms) where such equipment might be placed, and few teachers with appropriate training for using the equipment. Thus, in some school districts, the Internet connection goes to a few computers housed in a maintenance or heating building some distance from classrooms and regular instructional spaces.

The circumstances of school districts in Case Study 5 illustrate another vital factor in computer access: convenience. Even if you have access to computing equipment, you may not be willing to use it regularly if that access is inconvenient or requires some hassle. In the case of the school district that placed the computer in another building, any teacher was allowed to use the Internet-connected equipment whenever she or he wanted; the equipment was available, and the district would be delighted to have the equipment used. However, to use the equipment, a teacher had to take her or his class to another building, turn on computers and display equipment, and start up programs. At the end of a class, the teacher had to follow a reverse process. In practice, this process took both time and effort, and teachers preferred to spend their time on other activities that they found more interesting, productive, or convenient. Teachers in the district might show films or include parts of television programs in their courses, but they almost never used the state-supported computers. Experiences at other institutions indicate that teachers are much more likely to experiment with computer-based learning and exercises if the equipment is readily available in their classrooms. Even moving down a hall seems to present a barrier for consistent usage of equipment, whereas the same teachers may utilize these materials regularly when their classrooms are already computer equipped.

Ongoing Access with Speed Constraints: The speed with which folks can access the Internet also plays a role in the overall quality of their computer access. In some cases, a slow speed may reflect technical challenges, but in other cases the issues may be more related to politics or social circumstances.

> ***Case Study 6***
>
> A university in a modern, but geographically isolated, country provides free computer accounts and Internet access to all faculty, staff, and students. Due to transmission limitations, Internet connections with international sites are often quite slow, and it may take several minutes to download files that are several megabytes in size. Even typing simple text through an Internet connection may involve several seconds delay; that is, if you type something into a window, it sometimes takes 30 seconds for your text to appear in your window due to communication delays.

Sometimes slow speeds arise from geographical distances or limitations in network capacities. In Case Study 6, everyone at that school had Internet access, and that connectivity worked very well for many local applications. However, other Web applications required considerable interaction with servers at a distance (in another country), and sometimes this work took a long time, even for simple tasks. This time delay had several consequences. Sometimes a user would decide not to pursue an application in anticipation of long delays. At other times, a user would set her or his schedule to take advantage of anticipated periods when communications might work relatively well. In the case study situation, for example, connections outside the country generally were much faster during mornings, and the connections slowed down in the afternoons and evenings. Sometimes work in the morning might proceed three or more times faster than the same work in the afternoon. Overall, although users theoretically had access to computers and the Internet at all times, in practice, they had good quality access only at certain times throughout any day, and were often pressured by the slow connection to skip or delay work that came up during heavy Internet hours.

Easy Ongoing Access with High-Speed Technology—Almost: As we've moved through these case studies, you've seen that a variety of social forces can impact accessibility to the Web. Included in these influences are social problems unrelated to government-enforced rules or overt discrimination. Economic and political issues sometimes arise for the Internet Service Providers (ISPs), which in turn impact the end user.

Case Study 7

One telephone company in Iowa indicated it would provide only dial-up service to its customers until the state legislature changed the tax structure. The company claimed, for example, that a more efficient **DSL (Digital Subscriber Line)** connection was technologically possible, but too expensive for the demand. At the same time, many local telephone companies in the same state were providing DSL connections to their customers without complaint.

On the same subject, a resident of an urban community near Los Angeles complained that advances in technology were needed so he could get DSL connections at his house, at the same time that DSL was commonly available in rural Iowa.

Case Study 7 illustrates a nontechnical constraint on access related to politics and economics. Technology was available to supply fast DSL service throughout rural Iowa, and some customer-oriented companies made that technology available in their areas. The other company wanted to change public policy, and it held DSL access hostage to its interests in taxes and profits. Thus, access and its limits are not always based on technology; other factors may be at least as important. Consider the second part of Case Study 7, in which DSL connections were not readily available near the city of Los Angeles. If technology can allow access over hundreds of miles in rural Iowa, certainly the same technology could allow connections near urban Los Angeles. Sometimes access is more a matter of will than technology.

The DSL connection example also highlights issues of cost and capacity for consumers. In particular, although DSL service provides continuous access to the Internet—often at reasonably high speed—a non-DSL connection over telephone lines typically is slow and requires a telephone call to an ISP. Slow connections may limit access by requiring long periods of time to transmit files, and telephone calls required for access can incur long-distance charges. Thus, the simple means by which someone connects to the Web has influence over the quality of their Internet experience.

What factors affect the ability of people to access the Web?

The discussions thus far have focused on a number of factors related to Web access. Here is a reasonably concise list of the basic influences we have considered:

- *Technical considerations and infrastructure*: Internet access requires a computer, an ongoing source of reliable electrical power, and a mechanism to connect the computer to the Internet. Although many people living in developed countries may take computer technology and infrastructure for granted, the distribution of this technology is not universal. Some areas of developed countries lack proper computer infrastructure, and as of today it is certainly not available throughout all developing countries.
- *Economic considerations*: Individuals or groups can use technology only when it is available at an acceptable price. Barriers can include high costs of equipment (relative to standards of living of potential users), costly access charges, and expensive charges for specific applications.
- *Political considerations*: Governments or institutions may seek to control access to computers or to the Internet through restrictive laws; only people in certain groups may be allowed access.
- *Social, cultural, or religious considerations*: Some groups may feel discrimination regarding their use of computers. For example, subordinates may be unwilling to challenge those in authority, women or minorities may be made to feel uncomfortable or experience harassment when using equipment, positioning of equipment may give priority to some groups over others.
- *Individual considerations*: People with some personality traits may experience preferred access to computers. For example, those with assertive personalities may dominate those who are more shy.

Altogether, access relates both to what you want to do and what is available for you to use. If you are lucky, you have the resources to accomplish what you wish and feel your access is quite satisfactory. However, you may instead be subject to constraints that limit your computer access and inhibit the ease with which you can work with computers. With this general observation, we next consider in more detail what factors about who you are influence the degree to which you encounter Web access constraints.

How universal are Web constraints?

As you've come to see in our discussion, many people cannot access the Web or cannot access it easily, because of political, economic, or social considerations. Further, access can be difficult or impossible because of more blatant problems, such as a lack of technology, legal constraints, or high costs. In many of the circumstances that we have discussed, it takes little analysis to conclude that some groups have easy access, whereas other groups do not, and it takes little effort to have an idea of who can and cannot access the Web. In many other cases, however, the matter of who has Web access is considerably more subtle.

To illustrate this, consider our previous example involving time-limited computer access in a library. From one perspective, the library's policy provides equal access. Anyone can sign up for a time, and a librarian will enforce the policy when notified that an infraction is taking place. In practice, however, the system inadvertently rewards antisocial behavior. A user can stay overtime by being slow, ignoring a request by the next user, or waiting for a formal complaint. These behaviors create a hassle for the next user. If this happens a few times, that next user may want to avoid a confrontation and forego using the computer. Also, if a current user turns out to own a local business and the next user works in that business, then that next user may be reluctant to talk to a librarian about an expired limit. Folks in different social circumstances similarly may feel uncomfortable working to enforce time limits. In practice, such policies may give priority to some groups of users over others.

Beyond social situations that impact computer use, our cultures and genders also influence our levels of access and experiences with computers. For example, much of our behavior is shaped in part by cultural norms, and different groups may be encouraged or discouraged in different ways. For example, studies suggest that negative experiences with computers affect women and ethnic minorities significantly more than white males. Although experiences of women and men may be similar during elementary school in the United States, the American Association of University Women (AAUW) reports in their study *TechSavy* that girls are often discouraged from using technology during the middle-school years, and these experiences are compounded in the years that follow. Some issues involve access; others include matters of self-image, public images of computer professionals as "geeks," antisocial behaviors of middle-school boys, perceptions of computing as "hacking," and lack of encouragement.

At the college level, Allan Fisher and Jane Margolis reported on an in-depth analysis of computer science majors in their study, *Unlocking the Clubhouse: The Carnegie Mellon Experience*, published in book form by MIT Press in 2002 and summarized in the *SIGCSE Bulletin inroads* in June 2002. In considering why some students leave a computer science major, the researchers reported that, for women, a drop in self-confidence often *precedes* a drop in interest. The researchers continue, "This drop in confidence is usually driven not by low academic performance, but by students comparing themselves unfavorably with others . . . ." Interestingly, these researchers discovered "women's exit statements that they are "just not interested" to be a misleading endpoint to a complex process . . . ."

Although the complex social issues for women in computing extend well beyond access to computing equipment and the Web, access can be a factor. Recall our case example in which the family's computer was placed in their son's room. This type of subtle constraint is certainly not uncommon. Although the placement of a computer may reflect a long series of events and family dynamics going back years, the end result adds a level of difficulty to the daughter's computer access. She may feel that she has less access, even if in principle she is supposed to have equal access with her brother. Policies and practices like this one often may appear on the surface as providing all groups with equal access, but the effects ultimately give priority to one group over others.

One important consequence of such subtle circumstances regarding access and social pressures arises in the context of who participates in computing degree programs and the computer-oriented workforce. Computing has a strong history as a well-paying career area that can fit nicely with various individual professional and personal goals. Further, both men and women of many ethnic groups have shown outstanding abilities in the field and have made vital contributions. Moreover, periodic shortages in the workforce have created strong incentives for people to consider entering the field. Despite numerous efforts at recruitment, however, the statistics show clear underrepresentation of various groups. Tables 14.1 and 14.2 show some figures for 2002, reported in the Taulbee Survey of the Computing Research Association in March 2003, based on schools offering a Ph.D. degree in the United States and Canada. They illustrate what percentage of computer science majors receiving each of the listed degrees is male versus female.

Turning to the workforce in the somewhat more general field of information technology, statistics are similarly out of balance. The following comes from a May 5, 2003, press release from the **Information Technology Association of America (ITAA)**:

> Among the most striking findings of the report is that the percentage of women in the overall IT workforce fell

Table 14.1 Gender of Degree Recipients for Computer Science Majors

	Bachelor's Degree	Master's Degree	Doctoral Degree
Male	81.2%	74.1%	82.2%
Female	18.8%	25.9%	17.8%

Table 14.2 Ethnic statistics for Degree Recipients

	Bachelor's Degree	Master's Degree	Doctoral Degree
Nonresident Alien	8.5%	55.7%	44.8%
African-American, Non-Hispanic	3.4%	1.1%	1.3%
Native American/ Alaskan Native	0.4%	0.2%	0.3%
Asian/Pacific	21.7%	15.7%	11.5%
Hispanic	3.6%	1.2%	1.6%
White, Non-Hispanic	57.8%	24.5%	39.0%
Other/Not Listed	4.7%	1.6%	1.6%

> from 41% to 34.9% between 1996 and 2002, and the percentage of African Americans in the overall IT workforce fell from 9.1% to 8.2% during the same period. However, when administrative positions were removed from consideration, . . . percentages of both groups rose slightly over the six years. The percentage of women IT professionals rose from 25% to 25.3% of the workforce, and the percentage of African American IT professionals also rose slightly from 6% to 6.2% between 1996 and 2002.

The ITAA findings indicate that while these small gains have been made in the number of women and minorities in the workforce, the groups still are underrepresented in the IT workforce as compared to their representation in the whole U.S. workforce. Women comprised 46.6% of the U.S. workforce [in 2002, as compared with their 25% representation in computing] and African Americans represented 10.9% of the U.S. workforce in 2002 [with only 6% representation in computing].

Of course, access to computing represents only one component of the causes that lead to this type of imbalance. Of particular interest is the *cumulative* effect of less-than-preferable access to computers with respect to gender and ethnic minorities and their career choices; presumably limited access over time has a real impact on comfort with and interest in computers, although to what extent we do not know. Computer access is, however, a highly visible factor related to the computing industry, and thus may provide one focus for discussions and policies.

How do software filters influence Web access?

Software filters are, in general, programs that scan information (Web pages, e-mail messages, other files) as it comes into your machine and then block selected information according to predetermined criteria. Anti-virus software represents one type of software filter, comparing all incoming files to lists of known viruses; if the anti-virus software identifies a likely virus, the software may throw it away, place the file in a special area, delete or change the infected part of the file, or otherwise take action to try to protect your computer. In the context of this discussion, however, we consider software filters that go beyond scanning for viruses, looking instead for files containing material that someone has defined as having "objectionable" content. In this context, filters typically have the goal of limiting Web access; in particular, software filters commonly are used in today's society to prevent children from accessing objectionable materials on the Web. And thus, we encounter our first social difficulty related to filters: There is no universal consensus regarding what might be objectionable. As a simple example, people in Scandinavia generally are much more tolerant than people in the United States regarding sexual content, but generally less tolerant regarding violence and guns. Even within the United States, people disagree about the extent information regarding such matters as birth control or guns should be available to minors. Similarly, obscenity laws within the United States often refer to local standards of decency—a standard that is particularly difficult to interpret in the context of the international Internet. On a related matter, politicians, community leaders, and parents debate the extent to which medical information should be available over the World Wide Web. If children are not allowed to view health-related clinical information for parts of the body (such as genitalia), then the question arises as to whether children should be allowed to search online library catalogs.

Once developers of software filters determine what is and is not objectionable, the next challenge is to determine just what blocking of materials a filtering program should provide. Several issues arise:

- Should filters apply to images only, text only, sound only, or some combination of these?
- Does "effective" mean that 100% of all "objectionable" material is blocked? or 95%? or 80%?
- To what extent should "effective" filters allow free access to "nonobjectionable" materials? Should 100% of these materials be available? or 95%? or 80%?
- Should filters block materials that are encrypted? For example, if an image were sent as a text file (perhaps using ASCII characters), then the text might be meaningless but a simple reinterpretation of the file as an image might allow viewing. If an image were sent in binary format as a number, should filters block certain numbers as potentially representing objectionable pictures? (Is 10010110011 an objectionable number or not, and how would you justify your answer?)
- If filters are to decode encrypted materials, how will the filters know which encryption scheme is used and how to de-

code it? If a file could be interpreted in several ways, perhaps as text or as a number or as an image, which interpretation should the filter use?

Deciding What to Block: Any software filter is a computer program, and programs follow algorithms; therefore, any software filter must have a set of instructions or rules for determining which materials can pass and which must be blocked. To provide flexibility, the filters may offer a range of rules that the user or administrator can establish for her or his computer. Regardless of the specific technology, however, at some level the software must depend upon rules to decide its actions. These rules may follow several approaches, such as the following:

- A filter may contain a table of Web sites that are known to have appropriate material; the filter passes material from sites on the list, but sites not listed in the table are blocked.
- A filter may contain a table of sites known to have objectionable material; the sites listed are blocked, but others are assumed acceptable.
- A filter may search for certain "objectionable" words or phrases and block pages in which those are found.
- A filter may rely upon keywords or other information prepared by the authors of pages. Those pages with acceptable keys are allowed to pass, but others are blocked.
- A filter may rely upon keywords or other author-obtained information, and the keywords may be used to identify "objectionable" pages.

Unfortunately, none of these approaches are very effective in blocking inappropriate materials while allowing appropriate materials to pass. For example, relying on a table of acceptable Web sites certainly blocks much objectionable material. However, with the dramatic and ongoing growth of the Web, it takes time for new reasonable sites to be added to the filter's list, and such sites would be blocked—at least for some time. As a particular example, for awhile one well-known filtering package allowed material from the "National Republican Party" to pass, but blocked material from the "National Democratic Party." According to the vendor, someone had thought to add a URL for one of these to the list of acceptable sites, but no one had thought to add the other. Of course, relying on a table of objectionable sites has the opposite problem, as new objectionable sites likely appear with the same frequency as new appropriate ones.

Screening based on the occurrences of groups of letters, words, or phrases typically ignores context and almost certainly cannot determine literary merit, and thus often fails to provide appropriate screening. For example, on September 28, 2000, the Digital Freedom Network published the following as the two winners of their "Foil the Filters Contest."

> Grand Prize:
>
> > Joe J reports being prevented from accessing his own high school's Web site from his own high school's library. Carrol High School adopted filter software which blocked "all questionable material." This included the word "high."
>
> Runner-Up:
>
> > You wouldn't think someone named Hillary Anne would have censorware problems, but all attempts to register hillaryanne@hotmail.com. were rejected because censorware spotted the hidden word "aryan." Hillary says "I had to email and fight the system like crazy to actually be able to use my registered nickname again."

Filtering based on author-provided keywords or information has at least three problems. First, the filtering software depends on the accuracy of the information provided, but authors may not be forthright or they may follow different standards than those expected by the software. Second, only a small fraction of the total material available on the World Wide Web contains keyword information. Without this background material, filtering software either would have to block a vast amount of reasonable pages or let pass much clearly objectionable material. Third, without international standards with universal legal penalties, any laws enacted by one country to mandate keywords or the author-based classification of materials would be unenforceable for much of the World Wide Web.

How effective are filters?

With all of the interest in software filtering, reports of difficulties abound. Material that should be accessible, isn't; material that shouldn't be, is; and alternatively, material can appear in a somewhat different form than anticipated. To clarify this third option, a filter can allow a page to load, but replace questionable text so as to make the result more appropriate. With this in mind, the following "Inspiration Award" from the Digital Freedom Network may be illustrative:

Winner:

> Attributed to EPIC's Marc Rotenberg, and though we are not sure if it's a real case or not, it says it all and we couldn't pass it up. Thanks, Marc.
>
> "Congress shall make no law abridging the freedom of sXXXch, or the right of the people peaceably to XXXemble, and to peXXXion the government for a redress of grievances."

Turning from anecdotal statements to more systematic studies of the overall effectiveness of software filters, various reviews and analyses report different results. In its September 25, 2001, issue, for example, *PC Magazine* reports:

> For this roundup, we looked at six content-filtering products designed for home and another six for business. In testing, most products blocked more than 85 percent of objectionable content—good enough to make a serious dent in inappropriate Internet usage.*

The March 2001 issue of *Consumer Reports* provides results on both the filtering of objectionable materials and the blocking of "a list of 53 web sites that featured serious content on controversial subjects." In their tests of the ability of sites to block objectionable materials, *Consumer Reports* stated, "Most of the products we tested failed to block one objectionable site in five." In considering the sites with serious, but controversial, subjects, they noted, "Results varied widely. While most blocked a few sites, . . . [two filtering programs] blocked nearly one in five. . . .[A third program] blocked 63 percent of the sites." The editors of *Consumer Reports* concluded, "Our results cast doubt on the appropriateness of some companies' judgments."

*Karen J. Bannan. "Clean It Up" *PC Magazine*, September 25, 2001. 20(16): 103.

With the rapid development and increasing sophistication of Web sites and the corresponding evolution of filtering software, effectiveness measures and comments about specific filters are in constant flux. Although many reviewers report that filtering software can reduce the possibility of viewing objectionable material while allowing access to other sites, objective reviewers seem to consistently conclude that no filtering software does a perfect job at both tasks, and that, when it comes to children accessing the Web, such filters cannot replace parental supervision.

The interested reader is encouraged to find recent reviews and reports of filtering software to better understand the current state of the art. Of course, vendors of the software tend to promote their side of this matter, and you are advised to seek out objective reviewers who do not have a stake in their conclusions. You also may want to locate materials from the Digital Freedom Network or to search the Web for further examples of situations in which software filters have behaved badly. Although examples can be humorous, they also illustrate how difficult it can be to create an algorithm that identifies exactly the "objectionable" materials and leaves other materials alone.

Who uses filtering software?

Because parents have primary responsibility for their children, some groups argue that parents can legitimately choose filtering software as a tool in helping to screen what their children can view on the World Wide Web. Informed parents should understand that the software may still allow some objectionable material through, or the software may block some appropriate material. Altogether, however, parents may decide that imperfect filters are still preferable to not having filters at all. Of course, other groups argue in opposition, believing that filtering imperfections undermine any potential value of the filters, that filtering software inhibits free speech, and that the only effective approach to filtering involves active parental oversight.

Parents are not the only users of filtering systems. The September 25, 2001 issue of *PC Magazine* reports that "Today, 33 percent of businesses monitor employees electronically, which includes examining their Internet activity, according to a recent study by the Privacy Foundation, a grassroots public education organization in Denver."** Companies can justify using filtering software for their employees' computers by citing issues of productivity or equipment requirements, and employees may not be aware that they do not have unrestricted access to the World Wide Web.

Similarly, you may want to check if your ISP, such as Earthlink or America Online, is using filtering software. The ISP may argue that it cannot know just who will use its connections, so it wants to set a cautious policy to protect possible younger users. If the ISP normally filters Internet materials, you may be able to turn a filter off to gain unrestricted access—but this may require special action on your part.

If we move beyond the use of filtering software to protect children and job productivity, we will find that there is near-universal agreement regarding the importance of access to materials by adults; at least this appears to be a widely held belief in the United States. When applied to adults on their own time (not at work), the blocking of Internet materials may be viewed as contrary to the United States Bill of Rights. The accompanying sidebar gives the text of a resolution by the American Library Association Council, adopted on July 2, 1997; it overtly protects Internet communications based on the rules set forth in the First Amendment.

The idea that freedom of speech protection laws apply to Web communications raises an interesting and important question. If filtering software is to be used as an aid for parents in supervising their children, how can filtering software be designed and used so it can be effective for children but also provide unrestricted access to adults? To work in both modes, the software must allow adults to bypass filtering, while maintaining controls for children. Often this is done through a password mechanism, although there are conflicting data and arguments about how effective password protection can be. (Recall that we discussed passwords and their effectiveness in some detail in Chapter 10.)

**Karen J. Bannan. "Clean It Up" *PC Magazine*, September 25, 2001. 20(16): 102.

Text of a Resolution by the American Library Association Council, Adopted on July 2, 1997

WHEREAS, On June 26, 1997, the United States Supreme Court issued a sweeping re-affirmation of core First Amendment principles and held that communications over the Internet deserve the highest level of Constitutional protection; and

WHEREAS, The Court's most fundamental holding is that communications on the Internet deserve the same level of Constitutional protection as books, magazines, newspapers, and speakers on a street corner soapbox. The Court found that the Internet "constitutes a vast platform from which to address and hear from a world-wide audience of millions of readers, viewers, researchers, and buyers," and that "any person with a phone line can become a town crier with a voice that resonates farther than it could from any soapbox"; and

WHEREAS, For libraries, the most critical holding of the Supreme Court is that libraries that make content available on the Internet can continue to do so with the same Constitutional protections that apply to the books on libraries' shelves; and

WHEREAS, The Court's conclusion that "the vast democratic fora of the Internet" merit full constitutional protection will also serve to protect libraries that provide their patrons with access to the Internet; and

WHEREAS, The Court recognized the importance of enabling individuals to receive speech from the entire world and to speak to the entire world. Libraries provide those opportunities to many who would not otherwise have them; and

WHEREAS, The Supreme Court's decision will protect that access; and

WHEREAS, The use in libraries of software filters which block Constitutionally protected speech is inconsistent with the United States Constitution and federal law and may lead to legal exposure for the library and its governing authorities; now, therefore, be it

RESOLVED, That the American Library Association affirms that the use of filtering software by libraries to block access to constitutionally protected speech violates the *Library Bill of Rights.*

Let's consider a specific example: the **Children's Internet Protection Act (CIPA)**. As described in the sidebar, CIPA mandates filtering of images in circumstances in which children might be using the Internet, and those filters are required to block specific types of images. Given this law, you should assume that some type of blocking or filtering will be in place when you search the Internet from a public library. If you are an adult, you will not have unrestricted access to the World Wide Web unless you ask for it.

The Children's Internet Protection Act (CIPA)

This extensive bill has the following main points related to our discussion here:

- The law applies to libraries that receive various types of federal funding, including public libraries, school libraries, and museum libraries. The law does not apply to academic and college libraries.
- The law requires use of "specific technology that blocks or filters Internet access to visual depictions that are—(A) obscene . . . ; (B) child pornography . . . ; or (C) harmful to minors." Although specific filtering software or services are not provided, the law requires that schools and libraries certify that they are using technology to block or filter visual depictions as described above.
- The law provides various definitions to clarify specific types of materials, using standards that would arise from "the average person, applying contemporary community standards."
- The law allows adults (17 years of age and older) to request, without explanation, that libraries disable such filters; that is, although libraries must maintain filters for children, the libraries also must disable that software for adults upon request.

The United States Congress passed the Children's Internet Protection Act (CIPA) on December 15, 2000, and this was signed into law in January 2001. A court test was initiated in March 2001, and the Supreme Court upheld the law on June 23, 2003.

Caution: Because this law is complex and legal discussions continue, you should seek legal counsel for handling of any current, specific issues.

As a complication, note that the law applies only to visual materials, not to text or sound. Thus, the filters may or may not restrict your access to nonvisual materials. As a practical matter, however, the determination of content for images is particularly difficult. Thus, at the time this chapter is being written, materials from the American Library Association contain the following passage:

> **Q:** *Is there blocking or filtering technology available that actually filters or blocks access to obscenity, child pornography, and material harmful to minors without also restricting access to constitutionally protected speech falling outside these defined terms?*
>
> **A:** No. At this time we are aware of no filtering technology that will block out illegal content, but allow access to constitutionally protected materials.*

---

*http://www.ala.org/ala/washoff/WOissues/civilliberties/washcipa/qanda/cipaqa0602.pdf

Because the law requires that objectionable materials for images be blocked, one legal approach would be for libraries to block the display of all images and preserve the communication of nonvisual materials. Although this approach seems extreme, it is not at all clear that other approaches are technically viable at the present time. Even for text, the discussion of varying file formats from Chapter 2 and various encryption techniques from Chapter 10 suggests that the identification of "objectionable" materials poses considerable technical difficulty, and our discussions earlier in this chapter indicate that current software filtering programs for text may be only 60% to 80% effective. Because images are more subjective than text, filtering of that medium is particularly difficult. But according to the law, all images (not just 80%) must be blocked for children, and currently this is not attainable in any general way even for text.

Of course, it remains to be seen what other approaches might emerge as a response to this bill.

Summary

Access to computers ranges along a continuous scale, from no access at any time through limited access to full, easy, and ongoing access. Restrictions to access involve such factors as technical considerations, infrastructure, economics, politics, social and cultural matters, and individual traits. Access in specific circumstances may involve subtleties that affect some groups more than others. Generally, policies and practices have affected access for women and ethnic minorities more than other groups.

Software filters restrict access to materials, sometimes by identifying specific materials that can be viewed and sometimes by denying access to specific materials that are identified as objectionable. The first challenge for the developers of filtering software involves identifying what is and what is not objectionable. Another challenge involves determining the level and nature of the screening process. Each area of challenge has numerous pitfalls; objective reviewers report varying levels of effectiveness, but few indicate that software filters provide reasonable access to appropriate materials while blocking inappropriate materials.

The American Library Association (ALA) and others believe adults should have free access to information as part of free speech, and this creates a tension with those who wish to screen information available to children. The Children's Internet Protection Act (CIPA) requires public libraries to provide full screening of objectionable images for children. Currently, the ALA has not found software filters that can adequately meet this standard except by disabling the display of all images. Companies also may install software filters on their computing equipment.

Terminology from This Chapter

Access
Child Internet Protection Act (CIPA)
Direct Subscriber Line (DSL)
Filtering software
Information Technology Association of America (ITAA)

Discussion Questions

1. This chapter identifies five categories of factors for access to computers and the Internet: technological, economic, political, social/cultural/religious, and individual. Review the seven case studies given at the beginning of this chapter. In each case, determine which categories of factors are illustrated by each example.
2. Review the case studies given at the start of this chapter.
   - **a.** Do any of these examples connect with any experiences you or your friends have had?
   - **b.** Identify additional examples from your experience regarding access to computers or limitations to that access.
   - **c.** In each case in a or b where you or a friend have direct experience, how have you felt about the situation, and what have you done in response?
3. Consider the questions raised in this chapter about "effective" software filters.
   - **a.** Can your group agree on a precise definition of "objectionable materials"? If so, present that definition. If not, explain the difficulties your group was having.

b. What are your group's answers to the questions regarding a filter being "effective"? For example, what types of materials should be subject to filtering, what degree of "objectionable" materials could get through an "effective" filter, and to what extent is it acceptable to block "nonobjectionable" material.

4. Consider the following:

> ***Case Study 8***
>
> A retail business used a computer system to keep records on sales, inventory, and the like, and clerks used this system for each sale. When the computer malfunctioned and the clerk was taking appropriate corrective action, a bagger came up, pushed the clerk out of the way, said "I'll handle this; you'll only mess the computer up," and proceeded to make little progress. Although the clerk was supposed to be in charge and the bagger was supposed to be assisting putting goods into bags, the clerk could regain access to the computer only by physically pushing the bagger out of the way and withstanding some verbal abuse.

a. Have you encountered any similar examples in your own experience?

b. How might this experience affect the clerk's views regarding confidence and comfort in accessing computer equipment? Do you think the clerk's response would be different if such unpleasantries occurred several times, rather than just once?

c. Suppose you were the customer working with the clerk when this sequence occurred. What, if anything, would you say to the clerk or to the bagger?

d. Suppose you were the store's manager and observed this exchange. What, if anything, would be your response?

5. Divide the class into teams that will engage in debates on whether filtering software is appropriate for children. As preparation, each team should research its side of its question, identifying outside materials for support. With multiple teams in the class, pairs of teams should be assigned opposite sides of specific issues. Some possible topics follow:

a. Resolved: Parents with children under 12 years old should install filtering software on their home computers.

b. Resolved: Parents with children in high school should install filtering software on their home computers.

c. Resolved: The Children's Internet Protection Act (CIPA) should be repealed.

d. Resolved: Filtering software does not and cannot effectively prevent children from accessing objectionable materials while at the same time allowing access to appropriate materials.

Exercises

1. For each term in the "Terminology from This Chapter" section, write a paragraph explaining the term and indicating its connection to this chapter's theme of access to computers.

2. In each of the seven case studies given at the start of this chapter, access to computing or the Internet is limited in some way. Review each case to determine what might be done to improve the situation. When possible, your discussion should consider both actions that officials might take and approaches that individuals might try on their own.

3. Read an article from the anthology that appears in the "Special Issue on Women and Computing" in the June 2002 *SIGCSE Bulletin Inroads*.

   a. Prepare a report on what issues are identified and what solutions are suggested.

   b. Relate the points presented to your experiences in your own community.

4. Find reviews of current versions of filtering software.

   a. How effective is current software in blocking objectionable material for children?

   b. To what extent does the software also block appropriate material? (And to what extent does this seem to be an issue for software developers or reviewers?)

   c. How easily can an adult disable a software filter for her or his own use, but then re-enable the filter for a child?

   d. To what extent can a child figure out how to disable the filtering software?

5. The American Library Association concluded that "At this time we are aware of no filtering technology that will block out illegal content, but allow access to constitutionally protected materials." Using your understanding of the storage of images from earlier chapters, explain why you think the development of such technology might be so hard. Why do you think vendors have been unable to produce adequate blocking or filtering programs?

Chapter 15

Can I use Web-based materials in the same way as I use printed sources?

Although many of us consider e-mail, FTP, and Web-based information as common forms of communication, the use of the Internet is actually quite a new phenomenon. Until recently, communication depended upon paper-based materials, such as letters, newspapers, published journals, books, photography, painting, and drawing. Sound recordings largely involved phonograph records that depended upon the mechanical pickup of audio signals and tapes that had to physically move over sensors. With either phonograph or tape technology, the quality of sound reproduction deteriorated with use. Within this context, most information for general distribution came from reasonably formal sources, such as newspapers, journals, and books—all of which entail an extensive editorial and production process. In contrast, today's digital technology of CDs and MP3 recordings allows materials to be played as often as desired without any decrease in quality. In many cases, the editorial and production processes also changed.

With the development of the Internet and World Wide Web, authors, musical artists, and anyone who wanted to publish their work found another mechanism to distribute materials. Now they could post materials on a Web site directly, with very little interference or oversight by editors or others. This new outlet allows for remarkable availability of diverse materials, but it also short circuits the traditional process of editing and filtering. Altogether, there are both advantages and drawbacks to using the Web for the distribution of and access to materials, and we will use this chapter to explore these consequences.

Is the content of Web materials as reliable as printed sources?

In most cases, the individual user is responsible for determining the reliability of the Web's abundance of resources. The following fictitious examples illustrate many of the advantages and limitations of the Web as a source of materials.

Example 1: Book Publishing

After a decade of careful research on the dietary preferences of goats, an eccentric combined many notes into a book-length manuscript, entitled "500 Grass-Based Recipes for Goats." When the writing was complete and edited, the eccentric sent the draft to several publishers for consideration. Following the normal process, an editor at each publisher reviewed the manuscript and prospectus. All agreed that the book was beautifully written and wonderfully researched, but various practical considerations, including sales potential and marketing costs, led all publishers to reject the proposal for publication.

With the manuscript rejected by publishers, the author has two main choices: publish the book privately or post the book on the Web. In private publishing, the author would, in effect, set up a small business for the purpose of handling the book. Although this approach is not uncommon, it takes considerable time and expense and may not be feasible.

In contrast, posting the manuscript on the World Wide Web allows immediate and widespread distribution of the material. With the designation of the book as a Web page, anyone can access the book freely and easily. At a more sophisticated level, the author might charge a fee to download the material. This would require use of special software to handle billing and control book access, and such software systems are available at varying prices through several Web-based companies.

As this example illustrates, the World Wide Web gives researchers and authors unrestricted access to a broad audience at very little cost. As a Web user, this means you can obtain vast amounts of high-quality information easily, even if that material has a limited audience and might not be commercially viable as a product.

Example 2: Questionable Research

A student particularly liked a certain deodorant and wanted to convince everyone that this product was better than all others. Toward this end, the student found 10 friends who used the product and 2 that did not. The student wrote these names on pieces of paper, pulled them out of a hat at random, and called each person to ask what deodorant they used. After using this process for all names, the student concluded that, according to a random sample (names pulled randomly out of a hat), 10 of 12 people preferred the certain deodorant. (Although this may seem to be ridiculous research, conflicting advertising statements today suggest that modern claims may indeed depend upon this type of investigation.)

Following this deodorant research, the student wrote a paper describing the experiment, and sent the paper to a research journal for publication. Again an editor considered the article. In this case, the material may have been sufficiently outrageous for the editor to have rejected it out of hand. Alternatively, the editor may have sent the material to experts in the field. With such flawed research methodology, reviewers would certainly have recommended in favor of rejection of the paper, and the general public would be spared having to read such nonsense in a well-respected journal or magazine.

With rejection from the formal research community, the student could have contacted the manufacturer. If the company was not particularly careful in its scrutiny of such results, the company might cite the study in its ads or make the study available in its literature. In such cases, you still might see the student's conclusions or read the article. However, you also would know that the ad or article was sponsored by the manufacturer, and you likely are accustomed to being skeptical about claims in such circumstances.

Alternatively, the student could post the article on the Web in a way that made it look like a legitimate research article. The student could include graphs, colored charts, and other images, and links could be provided to well-respected organizations. Prestigious names could be mentioned—perhaps suggesting some endorsement—but without actually committing libel. With care, such a Web site might look very professional. If the student maintained the page on a Web site at a college, the URL would contain ".edu" to suggest an academic base. With the material available, search engines might find the study and include the findings in indexes.

In this case, the materials presented have no legitimate basis in fact, and if you found this information on the Web you would be on your own to conclude that this research is fatally flawed.

Example 3: Unpopular Perspectives

A faculty member interested in classroom pedagogy conducted a careful study comparing the effectiveness of a lab-based format that encouraged collaboration with a lecture-based class in which the lecturer spoke in a monotone voice. For the sake of this example, suppose that the faculty member concluded that monotone lectures were more effective and wrote the results in a paper entitled *The Effectiveness of the Lecture Method Using a Monotone Voice*. This paper then was submitted to an appropriate educational journal for publication.

As in our previous examples, if the research methodology was flawed, the paper could be rejected (the likely outcome). However, suppose the research was well designed, the statistical analysis compelling, and the write-up convincing. The final paper would include results that were contrary to many other findings and were culturally unpopular. The reviewers and editor might conclude that the paper, although controversial, represents solid research, and the paper might be accepted. Conversely, the reviewers or editor might decide that the paper's conclusions were so unorthodox that the paper should be rejected regardless of its careful methodology. Although we might hope that most research will be accepted or rejected on its objective merits, it is possible that some startling results might not be published because reviewers were not prepared to accept the conclusions.

From a different, but related, perspective, newspapers and magazines typically receive large numbers of stories and articles for possible publication. When the quantity of such submitted materials exceeds space available, the editors must make choices about what will appear. Space limitations imply that some materials must be rejected, but, at the same time, rigorous selection processes can lead to publications of very high quality. On the negative side, selection also may exclude some fine materials that are worthy of general distribution. In this context, the research about monotone lecturing may be considered of high quality, but space constraints may block its publication in favor of other materials that are even better. This situation in publishing is not unlike circumstances regarding college admission, when space constraints sometimes have a significant effect on the numbers admitted. A college may receive applications from many well-qualified candidates, when the school has room for only a relative few. In such cases, the school rejects many candidates, even though they have excellent potential and could make wonderful contributions.

As with the previous examples, if publication in printed forms or presentation at conferences is blocked, the researcher still could publish the findings on the Web.

These examples demonstrate both positive and negative aspects of the comparison between Web-based materials and traditional (printed) sources. Traditional sources often utilize an extensive process of review, selection, and editing. For this reason, readers come to expect and depend on the reliability and accuracy of information provided by printed sources. For various practical reasons, not all legitimate information may be represented in published sources, but reviewing tends to filter out incorrect or misguided research.

In contrast, information posted on the World Wide Web can be posted by anyone and is not subject to filtering or review. This openness allows access to a remarkable diversity of materials, but it also allows questionable information to appear. With such a range of quality and accuracy, you need to be particularly careful to analyze Web-based materials before accepting their statements.

Can Web materials be a source of unbiased information?

As just discussed, the Web contains materials of varying integrity and accuracy, and different factors need to be considered before accepting materials as valid representations of data. One variable that must be taken into consideration is the concept of **bias**. The Random House *College Dictionary, Revised Edition* (1984) defines bias as "a tendency or inclination of outlook; a subjective point of view." Each of us has her or his own perspective, beliefs, and backgrounds; this experience provides a bias. In our writing, we may try to be objective, but we always are making such choices as what to include, what to omit, what words to use, and what style to follow. This is not to suggest that a bias is necessarily bad; rather, we need to recognize that personal elements color our writing, in print and on the Web.

Sometimes an author's biases may be largely tangential to an issue, sometimes the biases may be at only an unconscious level, sometimes the author recognizes the biases and works to set those aside when preparing materials, and sometimes the biases may be a prime motivating factor in the preparation of material. Unfortunately, few Web pages indicate explicitly what these biases might be. It is up to you as reader, therefore, to evaluate each source carefully to identify possible biases and how they might have affected the materials you read.

Of course, over time, each of us typically has come to trust information from some sources. People come to trust specific newspapers, magazines, journals, individuals, organizations, and Web sites as dependable sources of information. Although these sources generally have a reputation of objectivity, even the most well-respected sources are not invariably free of bias. For example, over the years, the *New York Times* and the *Washington Post* built excellent reputations for their objectivity. Many people have relied on information reported in these papers as being beyond question or reproach. Thus, this reputation was a major issue in the scandal at the *New York Times*, when a story reported plagiarism and a subsequent investigation criticized procedures. (See the sidebar for some additional details.) This incident tarnished the image that the *New York Times* worked so hard to earn, and much subsequent effort went to identifying underlying causes and restoring the public's faith in the paper.

The Scandal at the *New York Times*

On April 26, 2003, a story by *New York Times* reporter Jayson Blair contained portions that were largely copied from an April 18, 2003, story that appeared in the *San Antonio Express-News*. A subsequent internal investigation at the *New York Times* found fraud, plagiarism, and inaccuracies in 36 of Blair's 73 articles; Blair resigned on May 1, 2003. On May 23, the *Times* created a review committee to examine newsroom policies. After considerable criticism regarding procedures, two high-level editors resigned on June 5, 2003.

Beyond recognizing that bias is possible, even likely, you should take time to consider various loyalties and possible conflicts of interest. In some cases, loyalties and conflicts of interest may seem reasonably clear. For example, consider corporate Web pages maintained by developers of filtering software (discussed in Chapter 14). As you might expect, these Web sites highlight their effectiveness and ease of use. As a contrast, consider Web sites that contain reports of filtering software, based on tests by outside reviewers. You might expect that the descriptions from the filtering-software companies are more positive than the reports from outside reviewers that have tested several competing products. However, even outsider reviewers can have biases. For example, some testers may have a bias toward using high-tech software and relying upon software to solve various problems, and these reviews may be more positive than reports from individuals or organizations that view filtering software as a threat to free speech.

Although these types of self-promoting biases may be obvious, some may be subtler. For example, when several students were asked to name innovations made by Microsoft, one group went directly to microsoft.com. Another group anticipated that this site might have some biases and went to sites developed by other software companies. In many cases, however, these companies were supplying software applications to run under a Microsoft operating system, so the fortunes of these reviewers depended upon the success of Microsoft—hardly an environment that fosters objectivity regarding possible innovations. A third group wanted to avoid any conflict of interest and sought out reviews by companies involved with the Linux or Unix operating system. However, because Linux and Unix are competitors to Microsoft, these groups also might be considered to have a natural bias. The Web contains a remarkable amount of material on the subject, but sorting out biases can be an enormous task. In many cases, it may be difficult to determine whether the information presented on a site is objective or motive-based.

With the great extent of subtleties and variations in Web materials, you are well advised to check any information you find by an-

Bias through Inclusion, Exclusion, and Emphasis

One subtle type of bias can arise in the selection of material that goes into reports. For example, in the 2003 war with Iraq by the United States and Great Britain, the press in the United States generally highlighted threats posed by Saddam Hussein. Some news organizations covered protests by people around the world, but the time and space devoted to such coverage typically was quite limited. In contrast, the press in New Zealand gave at least as much coverage to the protests as to any potential threats. In hearing reports from both locations, even reports giving multiple perspectives, listeners received very different messages regarding the extent of the threats and the significance of the protests.

In this news coverage, the stories presented various sides of the Iraqi war in objective ways. The amount of space devoted to the varying sides, however, suggested different priorities and perspectives. As this coverage suggests, reports can be biased not only by how a subject is covered, but also by what topics are included, excluded, or emphasized.

alyzing and evaluating the information, as well as locating independent sources. Of course, multiple sources may be subject to similar biases, but independent confirmation of facts can help you weed out blatant problems and provide you with additional assurance that facts and conclusions may be reasonable.

As Science Librarian Kevin Engel notes in *The Strategic Guide to Quality Information in Biology, Chemistry, Computer Science, Medicine, Physics, and Psychology,*

> No, I am not paranoid; I definitely do not think that everyone is out to lie to me or that the world is rife with conspiracies. **There is a very natural tendency, however, for people and organizations to present information in a way that best serves their own self-interests.**
>
> To operate intelligently in our society, to make up your own mind about issues, to be free means that it is essential to critically evaluate the information you gather. What it boils down to is the following:
>
> **Be skeptical about the information you gather. You don't need to be cynical, but a little skepticism is healthy . . . and smart.**

Evaluating an Information Source

The following is taken, with permission of the author, from *The Strategic Guide to Quality Information in Biology, Chemistry, Computer Science, Mathematics, Medicine, Physics, and Psychology*, "Step 4—Evaluate" by Kevin Engel, Science Librarian at Grinnell College. Mr. Engel suggests that you ask yourself these questions in evaluating a source:

Author/Publisher:

- Who is the author/reporter?
    - What expertise does the author or reporter have that lends authority to the information coming from him or her?
- Who is the author or reporter affiliated with?
    - What motive(s) might that organization or the author or reporter have in reporting that information in that particular way?
- Who published the information?
    - What motive(s) might that organization (or person) have in publishing that information in that particular way?

- What review process, if any, does the publisher go through before accepting and printing/reporting/displaying a piece of information?

- Some additional questions to ask if the information appears on an Internet site:
  - Does the page contain one or more *easily found* links for contacting the person or group who put the page together (not just a generic link to a "Webmaster")?
  - And, if you do contact the author of the page, do they respond fairly promptly? Do they respond at all?
  - Does the Web page or site contain *easily found* information about who the author (whether a person or an organization) is and what expertise they may have?

Does the article, book, news program, Internet site, etc. provide any of the above information to you? If not . . . *why not?*

Date of Publication (thanks to Joan Ormondroyd, Michael Engle, and Tony Cosgrave—Cornell University Library):

- When was this information published or last revised?
- Is the publication or revision date of the information appropriate for your topic?
  - Depending on your topic, how current the information is may be of significance. Is a publication/revision date or date of copyright easily findable?

Does the article, book, news program, Internet site, etc. provide any of the above information to you? If not . . . *why not?*

Content:

- Is the information presented in such a way that it is, at least, relatively understandable and easy-to-follow?
- What audience is the information aimed at (scholars, the "average" person on the street, undergraduates, children, etc.)?
- Where did the information come from?
  - Is it original research, a review of research done by others, an overview of a topic based on the work of others, is it strictly someone's opinion, an analysis of current or past events, a mixture, etc.?
- Does the publication contain a bibliography (a listing of articles, books, etc. from which the information presented was partly or wholly derived)? A bibliography that can be checked, if needed or desired?
- If research or survey results are reported, how much information is given about how those results were obtained?
  - Are the methods used to obtain the reported results valid?
  - Have those research or survey results been replicated by others?

An additional question to ask if the information appears on an Internet site:

- Does the Web page or other Internet site appear to be regularly maintained (not all Web pages/sites need frequent updating, but regular periodic maintenance is a good sign that the page/site is still active and that things that don't work will get fixed . . . or, at least, that someone still cares about the site and the information it presents)?

Does the article, book, news program, Internet site, etc. provide any of the above information to you? If not . . . *why not?*

Can all information found in printed sources also be found on the Web?

With the millions of Web pages available, search engines typically find a remarkable number of documents related to subjects we request. This can easily suggest that the Web does indeed have information on anything we might want to know about; however, in practice, the Web does not always have the information we are seeking, whereas published sources might.

The Web cannot provide needed information when:

- The materials you want were published in written sources years ago, but the printed sources have not been converted for viewing on the Web.
- The materials have been published recently and will soon be on the Web, but have not yet been uploaded.
- The information appears in copyrighted materials that are available for sale only. The publisher or owner has decided not to post the information on the World Wide Web, because that would undermine their revenue from sales.
- Materials are available temporarily on the Web, but access is withdrawn after an interval of time elapses.

Many historical sources have never been converted to a format appropriate for display on the Web. As a specific example, in researching materials related to biology, you might come across references suggesting a link between Israil' Iosifovich Agol and stepallelism. A current search of Web materials would find mention of Agol in references, but there is little indication about what he actually did. Consulting the *Dictionary of Scientific Biography*, a standard written source, clarifies that Agol and a group of other relatively young Soviet biologists came up with "a theory of gene structure known as stepallelism" that led to Agol gaining an international reputation for his work on the scute region of the X chromosome in Drosophila melanogaster (*Dictionary of Scientific Biography*, volume 17, page 3). Looking at this example a bit further, it turns out that Agol was a scientist in Russia, fell out of favor with Stalin, and was executed. Subsequent references became scarce—particularly in Russia—and this information has not been placed on the Web. References to Agol's work are available on the Web, but not the work itself.

In a related area, the scanning and indexing of historic documents, newspapers, journals, and books is both time consuming and expensive. For these reasons, the availability of these materials on the Web may be limited.

Electronic storage of materials also can be a factor. Over the years, storage costs continue to decrease as technology improves, and this can help the process. However, machines function only with regular maintenance and oversight, and this work represents an ongoing expense.

If organizations or companies have limited budgets (and they often do), then economic and personnel factors can prevent materials from becoming available on the Web. Such factors are particularly significant if the conversion of old materials to a Web format will generate significant expenses with the anticipation of little or no revenues when the process is completed.

The relationship between the Web and relatively new materials is somewhat more complicated, due to issues of copyright and economics. For example, suppose a professional organization publishes a monthly journal, and one issue each year is devoted to papers presented at a conference. (In practice, this situation is quite common for many professional societies.) For many years prior to the development of the World Wide Web, the journal was made available free to members; libraries and nonmembers could purchase issues at a relatively high subscription rate. This financial arrangement encouraged membership; members received the well-respected journal, but access for nonmembers was either expensive (through subscriptions) or less convenient (through libraries). Also, for the organization, payment from nonmembers provided income to help offset various editorial and production costs.

With this historical background, consider the impact of the Web. The organization still wants to encourage membership, so members should receive free copies. It can choose to mail copies in paper form or provide the material through a password-protected site on the Web. Members, subscribers, and library patrons have access to the material as before, but access is denied to the general public.

As an additional service, the organization can maintain Web-based archives of their past journals, and all of their publications are available to members, subscribers, and paying libraries through well-developed and maintained indexes. Indexing, however, takes some time, and there may be a time interval of a month or two between when an issue appears in paper form and when the issue appears (with indexing) in the online archives.

The circumstances of the organization's conference present special opportunities. As already noted, the proceedings of the conference will eventually appear in the organization's journal, and thus will be available only to members and subscribers. However, the organization has found that publicity can help increase conference attendance. In particular, the organization advertises its conference by making the program available to the world online. Attendance seems to increase further when that online program contains links to the papers that will be presented. (It has been demonstrated that more people attend certain conferences if the full text of the sessions is available in advance.)

With this experience, the organization provides links to all papers to the general public before the conference and for a short time afterwards. However, once the organization's conference issue is mailed to members and subscribers, the online materials are no longer available.

The circumstances described for this professional organization illustrate three common situations in which materials would not be publicly available on the World Wide Web:

- An organization may limit circulation of its materials to paper form or to online subscriptions, because of strategic or financial considerations.
- Even when an organization plans to place materials on the Web, indexing and site preparation can take time. This can cause a delay between when materials might be available in paper form and when they appear on the Web.

- An organization may make some materials available to the general public before an event for publicity, but those materials may be withdrawn from public access afterwards.

The Web is a wonderful place to go for many types of materials, but there are circumstances in which all types of materials, such as historical documents or professional journals, are not accessible on the Web for reasons including time restrictions and financial considerations.

Once you find documents on the World Wide Web, you can read and enjoy them. You may wonder, however, how free you are to use those materials in other contexts.

How do the concepts of intellectual property and academic freedom apply to using materials from the Web?

There seems to be a common belief among users of the Internet that all materials are available for free and unrestricted access, and further, that any downloaded information can be used or posted on the Web without restriction. There are, however, many ethical, economic, and legal reasons that make this untrue. Ethical issues surrounding the use of materials typically relate to a concept called **intellectual property**. To address this concept, let's first examine the nature of ideas and academic exploration.

Ideas, Academic Exploration, and Intellectual Property: Creations of an individual or group are considered to be owned by the creators and are designated *intellectual property*. Ideas and understandings are shaped by many factors, such as time, effort, thought, research, insight, experience, and practice, and the expressions of this work have value. In academia, this perspective has led to the well-established practice that each person gratefully acknowledges the ideas of others. When you write a paper, you may use others' ideas, but you are expected to reference your sources. This is the principle of **academic honesty**. As you likely are aware, academic work requires careful practices of quotation, paraphrasing, and citation. To reinforce this principle, most academic institutions have various rules and policies regarding the copying of materials and the rules of citation.

Such rules and practices are particularly important, because academic work emphasizes ideas. In academia, we study different perspectives of how things are or can be or should be. On one level, we value ideas, and we want to give people credit for the insights they have.

On another level, as we study a topic, we not only want our understandings to evolve, but we also want to know how those ideas evolve. When ideas seem to contradict each other, we want to understand the different perspectives. As we learn a subject, we recognize that different groups or individuals work from different experiences or assumptions, and it is important for us to find connections between those ideas and perspectives. Because various people have particularly insightful or original or biased or peculiar ideas, understanding which ideas came from whom is vital in discovering and investigating those connections.

The opposite of academic honesty is the use of other people's ideas without giving them credit. Sometimes this involves using general ideas, rewording others' writing slightly, or quoting passages word for word. Each of these practices is dishonest and is called **plagiarism**. Academic institutions usually have rules and procedures for handling cases of suspected plagiarism, and penalties may include failure on an exercise, failure in a course, placement on probation, suspension from the school for a period of time, or dismissal.

Academic Freedom: In academia, we frequently hear of the concept of academic freedom, but it is important not to confuse this idea with notions of intellectual property and academic honesty. **Academic freedom** is the principle that intellectual inquiry should allow an individual to pursue ideas, conduct research, and state conclusions based on careful methodology, experimentation, and reasoning. You should not be limited in your opinions because they are unpopular or different. Although academia expects you to be responsible and reasoned, your ideas do not have to conform. Academic freedom allows you to think independently and reach your own conclusions.

In considering this term, however, be careful not to be misled by the word **freedom**. Academic freedom does not mean that you can be irresponsible or careless in your thinking. Thus, in forming your ideas or making your arguments, you are free to draw upon other people's ideas—but academic honesty also means that you need to acknowledge those ideas.

As an extreme example, suppose you were asked to write a paper on whether or not computers could think—the subject of Chapter 16 in this book. From the standpoint of academic honesty, there would be nothing wrong with your simply copying the last chapter of this book, provided you gave a full citation indicating the material was copied. In this case, you would not be dishonest, because you indicated the source of the material; you were open and honest about using the chapter. Of course, the instructor might decide that your copying did not satisfy the assignment, and you might receive a low grade for that reason. However, you could not be cited as being dishonest—you acknowledged the material you used.

On the other hand, if you copied Chapter 16 without indicating the source, then you could not claim you were protected due to academic freedom. Your work was not based on your own inquiry, you did not conduct your research according to your beliefs, and you did not follow an open and responsible methodology. Your work was sloppy and irresponsible; academic freedom does not mean you can do anything you want.

Relating this example to material found on the Internet, exactly the same conclusions would apply if you copied some or all of your paper from a Web site. If you acknowledge the source, you are not being dishonest. Your work may or may not fulfill the terms of an assignment, and you may or may not receive a high grade; however, you have given the source credit for the work, and you are honoring intellectual property. Regardless of your grade, you are not being dishonest. On the other hand, if you do not acknowledge the source, then your methodology is not appropriate, you are not being responsible, and you are being dishonest. None of this behavior is condoned by the principle of academic honesty.

How do copyrights affect the use of Web materials?

Along with the idea of intellectual property, **copyright** also must be considered when gathering information from the World Wide Web. Many people believe that they can

- Use whatever they find on the Web in any way they wish
- E-mail materials from the Web to anyone as they wish
- Incorporate such materials into their own work
- Post this material back on the Web however they wish

Simply stated, *each of these beliefs is contrary to copyright laws.*

What Is Copyright? Copyrights in the United States give authors and artists control over who can use their works. According to copyright law, an author or artist has legal rights to restrict distribution of a work—determining who can be excluded from distribution. Copyright does not promise that a work can be published (for example, other legal limitations apply to libelous or obscene materials, even if they are covered by copyright). However, an author or artist can control whether the person's material can be distributed freely. In short, copyright is a legal right to restrict distribution.

When Do Copyrights Apply? According to U.S. copyright law, the product of an author or artist is covered by copyright automatically when it is stored in a physical medium. Thus, copyright law applies when a work is printed on paper or saved on a disk. Some years ago, an author had to include a copyright notice for legal protections to apply, but that is no longer the case. Copyright law now applies automatically to whatever you create, regardless of whether you state the work is under copyright. When the work is stored, the author or artist is called the **copyright owner**.

To supplement automatic copyright coverage, an author or artist in the United States has the option of registering the work through a simple application form. Although registration is not required for basic copyright protection, copyright owners in the United States must register a work before filing suit regarding a violation. Also, registration of a work within three months of its creation or registration before an infringement occurs may help support a case in court, and such registration allows a copyright owner to seek higher damages.

Similarly, although notices of copyright are not required under U.S. law, the use of such notices can clarify an author's intent and be helpful in court proceedings.

You should always assume that any material is covered by copyright, regardless of whether the work contains a copyright notice or is formally registered.

Do copyrights apply to Web-based and e-mail materials, as well as printed materials?

Copyright law applies to all appropriate materials, in paper form or electronic form, as well as to works of art and music. It does not matter if you find an item written on paper or if you have downloaded it from the World Wide Web. Copyright law applies to any work, regardless of the medium used. Two examples can provide additional insight.

- Although you certainly can look at material posted on the World Wide Web, the presence of the material on the Web does not give you **ownership**. You may have copy permission to download a copy for yourself, but you do not have copyright permission to distribute the materials as you wish.
- Similarly, if you receive material through e-mail, you clearly are allowed to read it. The creator, however, retains copyrights to decide how the material can be distributed; you do not have the legal right to distribute the material (even through e-mail), unless you have permission from the copyright owner.

What's wrong with downloading music or pictures over the Internet to my computer?

From an academic perspective, downloading and using music or pictures for your own use raises the same questions of intellectual property and academic honesty that we just discussed. Also, as we have just established, music and pictures are under copyright.

However, for artists and authors, unauthorized copying has career consequences: These people may depend upon income from their work for all or part of their livelihood, or income from sales may be used to cover the costs of production and recording.

When sales represent the bulk of a musician's livelihood, mechanisms that undercut sales have a direct effect on the person's income and standard of living. For example, if the musician relies on sales of recordings as a primary source of income, then income drops as sales drop. Such a situation might arise if someone posted the music on the Web without the permission of the artist, and you downloaded the music. In a commercial setting where you paid for the songs, all or part of your purchase price would go to the musician, but in this setting the artist receives nothing.

Sometimes folks argue that the downloading of music can generate publicity and increase demand for the artist, thereby having a long-term positive effect on the sales of recordings. However, the relative balance of income lost from downloading individual pieces and possible long-term increased sales can be speculative at best. If the musician decides that free downloading now will generate appropriate sales later, then the musician may post the recordings as part of a publicity campaign. Such an action would be reasonable and proper. Musicians, like other speculators, may gamble on long-term strategies.

Conversely, a musician also may decide that long-term sales are unlikely to cover lost revenue now. If lost current income prevents the musician from paying current bills, the individual cannot devote the time desired to her or his craft, cutting back on performances, practice, or new venues. Over the long term, we all may suffer because the musician cannot continue playing at the same level we enjoyed earlier. From this standpoint, downloading music from sites beyond a musician's or author's control may have a direct effect on the person's financial circumstances and undermine the person's continued work in the field.

Although artists and authors want their materials to be used and enjoyed, they also expect income to offset their expenses and provide a livelihood. You may like to think that information and music are free, but the creators of those materials are rarely in a position to subsidize your enjoyment. From this perspective, when you download music or materials of others without their consent, you are asking the creators of the work to subsidize your habits and behaviors. Such an expectation seems neither fair nor financially viable.

When can I download an article or some music for my own personal use?

This question is somewhat tricky, as different legal issues can come into play. On the one hand, downloading a copy of a work is usually considered as appropriate. However, this normally assumes that the source of the work has been authorized by the author, artist, or musician. For example, Apple has developed an "ITunes Music Store" that allows you to download individual songs as you wish—for a modest price. Although these songs are under copyright protection, Apple has agreements with musicians or their representatives to distribute the materials, and this allows you to download them legally for your own use.

On the other hand, copyright also prevents the widespread copying and distribution of works without permission. For example, court rulings in the Napster case suggest that you cannot download songs for your personal use, if that distribution is being done on a wide scale.

Doesn't fair use give me the freedom to use any materials I wish on my Web pages and in e-mail?

It is a common misconception that *fair use* implies free use; fair use is an imprecise term that depends upon court interpretations in many circumstances. If you need specific legal advice, you will need to consult a lawyer regarding current legislation and case law; this book does not claim to give you direct legal opinions. However, for the most part, **fair use** allows you to make a personal copy of an item for your own use, but you may not distribute the material further. In addition, short parts of a work may be cited for such uses as education, research, criticism, and parody. Thus, you normally may read, print, and enjoy material that you find on the Web or that you obtain via e-mail. You also can include short quotes from a work (appropriately cited) as part of a research paper.

However, material created by others is still owned by its creator. Unless you know you have the permission of the copyright owner, you are not allowed to distribute the information. Because placing material on the Web or sending material through e-mail involves distribution, such actions, without permission, violate copyright laws.

So, how do I know I have permission to distribute materials?

Some materials say explicitly that they may be distributed freely under various circumstances. In such cases, of course, the creator has given you permission. You also may request permission from the author, in which case the author would send you an explicit, written statement that you can distribute the material. Without such explicit permission, you should assume that you are not allowed to distribute materials. Here are a few additional examples that may help clarify what can be distributed legally and what is not legal:

- Suppose an author posts a piece to a listserv, allowing all members of the group to receive the work. By using the listserv, the author has implicitly allowed the listserv to distribute the material to subscribers. However, individuals on the listserv do not have the legal right to forward this material to others, unless the piece explicitly states such a policy for distribution.
- Suppose you find a cartoon or picture on the Web that you particularly enjoy. You likely can make a copy for your own (noncommercial) use, but you do not have the legal right to e-mail the picture to others or to post it on your Web site.

Can I reference Web pages and images from my Web pages if I do not copy the materials to my account?

The allowable use of materials from the Web continues to evolve as laws are passed and revised and as courts hear specific cases. For the most part, it seems likely that you can include links to other sites without trouble. Although your links highlight the work of others, you are not incorporating their work into yours and seeming to claim it for your own.

On the other hand, if you embed the material of others into your page, perhaps as part of a frame or table, then others might claim a misappropriation of their work, and legal discussions could ensue. Although the details might provide interesting new court cases to further clarify the law, you might prefer not to bear the brunt of this legal action.

To clarify this point further, some commercial sites state explicitly that you may make a single copy of their pages for your own noncommercial use, but you are not allowed to distribute the material further. Often, such policies indicate that your storage of material must include all copyright notices, and you are not allowed to change the material in any way. Although such statements may help these companies in legal actions, it is not clear that such statements are strictly necessary to make copyright restrictions apply to their work.

Don't copyright violations arise only if I charge for the materials?

No. Although copyright laws may provide for higher penalties in some cases for commercial violations of copyright materials, the laws regarding copying apply to both noncommercial and commercial uses.

To conclude, copyright laws specify that author, artist, and musician can limit distribution of works as they wish. You normally can download Web pages and receive e-mails without trouble, but copyright laws may limit you from distributing those materials further. It may be that widespread distribution would provide publicity that helps sales of various items, but it is up to the creators of the materials to decide; unless you are the creator, you cannot make that decision.

The distribution of materials, through the Web, e-mail, or printed sources, can be limited by ethical, financial, and legal considerations. Each factor indicates that unrestricted use and distribution of materials is not appropriate. As an individual using the Web, you need to be aware of each of these perspectives as you strive to use the World Wide Web responsibly.

Summary

Although the World Wide Web is a wonderful source of much information, its use has both advantages and limitations.

- Any author can post material on the Web, allowing unrestricted access to ideas without the constraints of sales potential or marketing costs that might concern publishers.
- Publishers often review materials carefully for content and exposition before releasing a work, but readers cannot as-

sume materials found on the Web are correct, unbiased, or well-written.

- With the time and cost associated with scanning and indexing old materials, the Web does not include all historical materials. Also, current materials may not be posted on the World Wide Web due to commercial or timing constraints.

Overall, documents on the Web have mixed quality, and some materials may not be available.

The concepts of intellectual property and copyrights both apply to materials found on the World Wide Web. Although you can read materials you find, only the author and copyright owner can specify the distribution of that material. You should not post material on the Web or send it through e-mail without written permission from the author. Uncontrolled distribution of materials can deprive authors and musicians of the income they need to offset expenses and support their livelihood.

Fair use does not imply free use; rather, distribution of materials has ethical, economic, and legal ramifications.

Terminology from This Chapter

academic honesty	copyright owner	ownership
bias	fair use	plagiarism
copyright	intellectual property	

Discussion Questions

1. To learn about the effectiveness of software filtering products, find some reviews that compare several products, locate statements from Web pages of the developers, and obtain statements about software filters from groups challenging such products as a threat to free speech. What, if any, differences do you find? Do any of the reports seem blatantly incorrect? Are any reports biased? If so, how; if not, how can you tell?
2. One might argue that traditional sources are subject to bias in the same way that Web-based materials may suffer.

a. Do you believe Web-based materials have more, less, or the same level of bias than traditional sources? Explain your answer.

b. In analyzing sources for bias, to what extent should you follow a different approach for Web-based materials than for traditional sources? Justify your conclusions.

3. In recent years, the Recording Industry Association of America (RIAA) has taken a leading role in taking legal actions against those it believes are violating copyright laws.

a. Investigate recent activities of the RIAA to determine current issues and directions related to copying music and the use of the Internet.

b. Some groups oppose the activities of the RIAA for what is seen as the excessive limiting of distribution of materials. Investigate the arguments and actions of the RIAA opponents. What issues are currently being contested, and what arguments are being used?

4. The chapter describes ethical, financial, and legal factors regarding the downloading and use of materials from authors, artists, and musicians. Use the ideas presented to address the question, "What's wrong with downloading and using software from the Internet?"

a. Under what circumstances might such downloading be appropriate?

b. Under what circumstances might such downloading be unethical, financially harmful, or illegal?

c. Based on discussions in other chapters of this book, what additional dangers might you incur by downloading and using such software—beyond the factors identified in parts a and b of this question?

5. This chapter stated that "the scanning and indexing of historical documents, newspapers, journals and books is both time consuming and expensive." This question asks you to estimate these costs.

a. Perform an experiment, during which you scan several pages from each of several magazines into the computer.

Compute the average time required for scanning a page, including your labor in putting the page on the scanner.

b. To be useful, documents should be indexed after they are scanned, with relevant keywords identified. Such index preparation requires careful reading and thoughtful identification of topics. For the pages you scanned in part a, continue the experiment to tabulate an index of topics and keywords for each page. Estimate the average time required to index a scanned page of material.

c. Estimate the average size of a single issue of several magazines, and use your estimates in parts a and b to approximate the cost for placing one back issue of each magazine on the Web with appropriate indexing.

d. Identify the number of issues produced by several magazines in a year, and use your estimates in part c to obtain an approximate cost for placing one year of a back issue of a magazine on the Web with indexing.

Exercises

1. a. Explain each term in the "Terminology from This Chapter" section.

b. If you are a student, relate each word or phrase to any policies or regulations at your school regarding the appropriate use of materials, including rules for citation, quotation, and paraphrasing.

c. To what extent are school policies more or less restrictive than legal copyright requirements?

2. Review the questions cited in this chapter from Kevin Engel on evaluating sources.

a. These questions were developed largely for the review of materials related to the sciences. To what extent do you think these questions apply more generally to all academic disciplines? To sources outside academia?

b. To what extent do these questions apply specifically to Web sources, and to what extent might they apply to information found anywhere?

c. What, if anything, makes evaluation of Web-based sources different from traditional sources?

3. Locate the Web site of a commercial company, perhaps in the news or entertainment industries. For example, you might look at the site of a newspaper, magazine, movie producer, cartoonist, or artist. Determine the company's policy for use of materials found on the site.

   a. Are you allowed to make copies of the materials?

   b. Can you distribute the materials? If so, are there any restrictions? If not, what limitations are specified?

   c. Could you include any of the materials (such as a logo) on your own Web site? Explain.

4. One of the major efforts in the development of software today involves the creation of software libraries to handle various common tasks. The idea is to reuse software, created either by yourself or by others, rather than to start each project from the beginning. After all, if a piece of code worked before and is not changed, then it will likely work the next time—so why bother to rewrite it?

   a. Explain how the ethical, financial, and legal factors of copying or downloading materials might relate to the development of software libraries.

   b. Under what circumstances might it be ethical, financially responsible, and legal to place pieces of software into libraries for common use?

Chapter 16

Can computers think (now or in the future)?

On August 19, 1985, at a meeting of the American Association for Artificial Intelligence (AAAI), Woody Bledsoe, a distinguished researcher and president of the organization, began his address to the group as follows:

> Twenty-five years ago I had a dream, a day dream if you will. A dream shared with many of you. I dreamed of a special kind of computer, which had eyes and ears, and arms and legs, in addition to its "brain."
>
> I did not dream that this new computer friend would be a means of making money for me or my employer, or a help for my country—though I loved my country then and still do, and I have no objection to making money. I did not even dream of such a worthy cause as helping the poor and handicapped of the world using this marvelous new machine.
>
> No, my dream was filled with the wild excitement of seeing a machine act like a human being, at least in many ways.
>
> I wanted it to read printed characters on a page, and handwritten script as well. I could see it, or a part of it, in a small camera which would fit on my glasses, with an attached earplug which would whisper into my ear the names of my friends and acquaintances as I met them on

> the street. Or in a telephone which allowed me to converse with a friend in Germany, he in German and me in English. For you see my computer friend had the ability to recognize faces, synthesize voice, understand spoken sentences, and translate languages, and things like that.*

As this talk by Woody Bledsoe suggests, many researchers have long had the goal of making a machine that has intelligence and can perform in many ways as humans can. So, where do we stand between our goal for simulating intelligence and the reality of the current state-of-the-art technology?

The question of whether a computer can, or will, think can only help us begin a long and exciting inquiry, for even a partial answer must touch such fields as philosophy, religion, biology, psychology, and computing. At the very start, we must consider what we mean by "thought" or intelligence. Before we can know how well computers function, we must consider how we might reasonably know whether something is intelligent or not. From this starting point, we can review how computing has progressed, what computers can do now, and where research might lead in the future.

Our discussion will provide a number of perspectives about the nature of intelligence and the potential for computing. With this information, you can draw your own conclusions about a computer's ability, or potential ability, to think.

 What is intelligence?

Much of the initial trouble in discussing whether computers might be intelligent relates to finding an appropriate definition of intelligence. We want a definition that is general enough to include various forms of thought, but we also want a definition that excludes simple behaviors, such as a doorbell ringing when you push a button. When defining intelligence, the definition should:

- Include rational activities of human beings
- Allow for processes of higher mammals, such as dolphins and chimpanzees, that many people recognize as being intelligent
- Allow for the possibility of different life forms from outer space—perhaps based on quite different chemical systems

*Bledsoe, W.W. "I Had a Dream: AAAI Presidential Address." 19 August 1985. *AI Magazine* 7(1):57–58.

- Take into consideration the possibility of learning from our mistakes
- Exclude simple automatic responses of bacteria and other single-cell organisms
- Exclude mechanical operations, such as are found in the burning of a rocket engine, the running of an internal combustion engine, or the manufacture of pencils

Examples of What Is and Is Not Considered Intelligent

In considering the nature of intelligence, you may want to distinguish between following the steps of a process and understanding those steps. For example, intelligence might be involved in designing rockets, engines, or manufacturing processes, but we likely would not associate intelligence with the actual running of the machinery itself. Similarly, an automobile driver might demonstrate intelligence in driving, but the car is not considered intelligent.

Distinctions involving the performing of music, however, may be more subtle. Consider the playing of a piano. At one level, the production of sound involves using your fingers to hit various piano keys, and this causes the generation of sounds. With today's technology, it is possible to record exactly what notes are pressed, when, and how hard, and this information can be used to have the piano play exactly the same notes in the same way. From the standpoint of tone production, today's equipment can play a piano exactly the same way that a pianist can. Because we likely would not consider the mimicking of piano playing to be intelligent, this suggests that intelligence and artistry have qualities beyond simple tone production on a piano.

Further, experienced listeners to piano music can hear a difference between the playing of music by a virtuoso artist and the playing by a competent, but less sophisticated, player. In these cases, the notes seem to be the same. Even the timing of the notes and shades of intensity may seem the same. However, listeners can recognize inspiration and artistry.

And, in talking to virtuoso players, we may discover that many lose themselves in their playing; they may not be aware of the details of what they are doing when they perform their best work. If this is the case, we may wonder about the role of the rational and conscious in the production of wonderful music.

Altogether, it is interesting to consider what qualities lead to the expert playing of music; what are the roles of artistry and intelligence.

In considering the range of possible forms of intelligence (human beings, higher mammals, possible beings from other solar systems), we must be careful that any definition of thought or intelligence does not unduly prejudge the discussion. For example, if we stated that intelligence was a trait of organic creatures, then we might be ruling out the possibility of intelligent life on other galaxies, where life was not based on carbon molecules (the basis for organic chemistry), but rather on silicon or some other chemical.

This difficulty is compounded in that we do not know how we think or what makes up our intelligence. We have a wide range of thoughts, but we do not know how those come about. At one level, our human behavior is based on our experiences and our system of neurons in the brain and throughout the body. At this level, our bodies have a network of neural cells that collect data and handle basic processing tasks. In our environment, we identify external conditions through our senses of touch, sight, taste, hearing, and smell. Through experience, we learn how to respond to various conditions. When we feel extreme heat, we move away. When we are moving through a building and see a wall and a door, we head for the door rather than try to move through the wall.

Through our experience, we also know how to coordinate the actions of various parts of our body to accomplish a task. To lift a glass, we have learned what muscles to use in what order to move our hand out to the glass, then to grasp it and raise it. In watching the actions of a baby or young child, it is clear that we are not born with knowledge to move away from extreme heat or the skill to lift a glass. These are learned behaviors, based on experience and trial and error. We receive stimuli, and we learn how to respond in various satisfactory ways. Certainly, at one level of our lives, we operate unconsciously, and much of that activity seems to depend on responding to stimuli according to learned behaviors that have become programmed into our system of neural cells.

In recent years, scientific research has identified parts of the brain that process various types of stimuli, and we know that certain areas of the brain are associated with the processing of specific activities and behaviors. For many behaviors, researchers can track how stimuli come into the brain, and what parts of the brain handle the processing that produces the observed response.

Above this stimulus-response level, we identify such processes as thought, decision making, and consciousness. We find ourselves constructing logical arguments, making judgments, and choosing among alternatives. A basic question is whether or not this process involves more than the interactions of neuron cells, already discussed. If our higher-level thinking does require more than electrochemical workings of our neurons, however, then it is reasonable to wonder about the nature of that processing beyond the electrochemical realm. If more is involved, what might that include?

What roles do consciousness and free will play in intelligence?

This question delves into the realms of both philosophy and science, and different people reach various conclusions. Although a full discussion of this question could easily extend to a book by itself, a few observations may suggest that the ability to think is subtle, and some common impressions about thought may break down under close scrutiny.

Regarding the role of consciousness, perhaps you have had the experience of working on a problem during one day, going to sleep, and waking up the next morning knowing the answer or having an important insight. During your initial work on the problem, you considered various approaches, you worked through some possible solutions, but none of these possibilities seemed to work quite right. Then you wake up to become aware of a different idea, and the various pieces fit together nicely. We certainly are not conscious of how we got those ideas. Apparently our minds continue functioning on some level as we sleep, but we are not aware of how the ideas arise.

At a less magical level, consider what you do when you write a paper, compose a song, or create a poem. You may recognize that the result of your energies is creative, but you may not be conscious of the details that led to the conclusion. For example, how did you decide on the words in a particular sentence, or how did you decide to present one idea before another? In some cases, you may have thought through various possibilities carefully and consciously made specific choices. However, often you may find that the words flow from your mind to paper; you cannot describe just what happened to produce the details you see in front of you.

Turning to the topic of free will, Jack Copeland describes a most interesting sequence of events in his book, *Artificial Intelligence: A Philosophical Introduction* (Blackwell Publishers, 1993). The following is an excerpt from Section 7.2, "Is Freedom of the Will an Illusion?"

> Over the next half minute suddenly raise the index finger of your right hand three or four times. Pick your moments spontaneously as you go along. Try to notice whether there is any appreciable time lag in between choosing your moment and your finger beginning to move.
>
> OK. If your subjective experiences were the same as mine, the movement in your finger muscles will have followed on more or less immediately from our conscious decision to initiate the action. The astonishing thing is that a technician equipped with the right instruments would have known you were going to raise your finger about a second before the movement began. H. H. Kornhuber and his associates performed this classic experiment in the seventies, using subjects with a number of electrodes fixed to the scalp and finger. It was discovered that a characteristic pattern of brain activity would begin to build up as much as one and a half seconds before the finger movements commenced. . . . In context, a technician observing the onset of this activity in your brain would know that you are about to raise your finger—and, chillingly, would know this the best part of a second before your subjective experience of freely picking your moment. The implications of this experiment are still the subject of heated debate. However, it has influenced a number of writers in their belief that our subjective experience of free will is an illusion.
>
> Copeland, Jack. Artificial Intelligence. *A Philosophical Introduction.* Blackwell Publishers, 1993, p. 142.

In philosophy, the notion of free will is that intelligent beings are free to make choices. If several alternatives are possible in a situation, then the doctrine of free will states that the individual is free to make any of the choices. In our experience as human beings, we feel that some choices are left completely up to us, and we can do whatever we want arbitrarily. When given a choice of which flavor of ice cream we want at a store, we feel that we are not bound in any way in what we choose; we can make a free and arbitrary choice. On the other hand, in Kornhuber's experiment, we also may think we can make a free and arbitrary choice, but an external observer could learn about our decision before we seem to know about it. In that context, we may wonder how free and arbitrary our choice really was.

Without delving into an in-depth discussion of the notion of free will and intelligence, we can observe that much of our behavior is closely tied to the electrochemical functioning of our brains, neural connections, and muscles. At least a significant part of this behavior is linked to our experiences and learned responses. How all this fits into the realm of intelligence is an open question, but it seems that we may want to investigate some common assumptions before making any final conclusion.

Returning to the realm of computers, observe that computers are electromechanical devices whose behavior depends on programs within memory, the functioning of CPUs, the gathering of data, the processing of the data, and the connections of various components. Because computers are constructed machines, we do not consider them as displaying consciousness or having free will. The discussion in this section, however, suggests that we might consider people as electrochemical beings that may not be fundamentally different from the electromechanical devices known as computers. Computers follow programs, whereas people's behaviors depend upon the functioning of neurons. We do not think of computers as having free will; choices by people similarly seem dependent on underlying electrochemical forces. The connection between intelligence and consciousness is difficult to identify. If people and computers both behave based on internal programming, then it might be plausible that computers might eventually be intelligent, because people are. If, however, intelligence depends upon some other factors, then we may need to probe deeper to determine what those factors might be.

What are some ways that we could determine whether computers can think?

As we have observed, defining the notion of thought or intelligence is difficult. Further, you should observe that common understandings of intelligence have evolved over the years. For example, hundreds of years ago, performing the addition and subtraction of relatively large numbers consistently and correctly was a significant achievement. Fifty years ago, you might have been considered to be particularly intelligent if you could do arithmetic extremely quickly. Adding columns of numbers in just a few seconds was a rare and impressive feat. Similarly, 20 years ago or so, you were considered extremely intelligent if you could play chess at a very high skill level. Only the very best could hope to win a chess tournament over a Grand Master. Of course, as our knowledge has increased, we have learned how to do such things, and now computers can do each of these tasks. The computers may or may not do the work in the same way we would, but they get correct answers reliably—often faster and more consistently than humans. With such advances in technology, we may have higher expectations regarding intelligence now than our ancestors might have had years ago.

How Much Intelligence Is Needed for Addition and Subtraction?

In today's environment, you may think that arithmetic is easy, because you likely learned it in grade school. Much of this ease of computation, however, depends upon our understanding of the decimal system. We learn how to handle the digits 0 through 9, and then we put digits together to form larger numbers. Addition and subtraction proceed in a digit-by-digit fashion, and we do not associate those operations with high intelligence. (To add 14 and 35, we proceed from right to left: First add the 4 and 5 to get 9. Then add the 1 and 3 to get 4. The final answer is 49. The answer is only slightly more complicated if we must carry a result from one digit to another.)

Historically, however, arithmetic has not always been so straightforward. Just consider what result you would get when adding MDCCXLVII to MMCCCLXXIX. When you have that done, subtract the first number from the second. In this notation, addition and subtraction are demanding intellectual challenges.

This development in notation and numeric insight illustrates how new understandings can transform a task from being considered an intellectual feat to a commonplace operation requiring little thought.

With varying subjective views regarding the nature of intelligence, we might look for a more objective approach for determining whether something possesses intelligence. A common approach is to consider developing tests. Rather than prejudge the outcome, we might conclude that something exhibits thought if it passes the test, but does not adequately demonstrate intelligence if it fails. With such an approach, we could objectively conduct a test regarding thinking and reach a conclusion based on our data.

Although many such tests might be contemplated, two general approaches involve **black-box testing** and **white-box testing**. In black-box testing, we give the test subject various problems or inputs, and we examine the results. We do not worry about how the subject determined the answers—we just review the conclusions. A simple example of black-box testing might be a multiple-choice test; questions are given, and the person being tested responds by identifying which answer is correct. In grading the test, we do not consider how the subject came up with the answer; we just mark each answer as right or wrong.

In white-box testing, we examine the results, but we also review the process used for reaching the conclusion. For example, in a long-answer test involving mathematics, a grader may check how a solution was first set up, what approaches were used to solve various equations, what intermediate results were obtained, and how the various pieces led to the conclusion. In white-box testing, the final answer is only one factor among many in determining whether the subject passes the test.

Perhaps the best known proposal for the black-box testing of intelligence is called the **Turing Test**, proposed by Alan Turing in 1950 in the early days of electrical computers. Turing proposed that a (human) investigator be placed in one room, a computer in a second room, and a human respondent in a third room. The investigator would have a teletype (similar to an old typewriter) attached to the computer and another for communication with the human respondent. (See Figure 16.1.) Although the investigator would know that one teletype communicated with a computer and the other corresponded with a human, the investigator would not know which was which. The investigator was charged with asking questions to each party and analyzing the responses in whatever way seemed appropriate. The goal was for the investigator to identify which teletype went to the computer and which to the human. Although the human was to answer questions honestly, the computer was to respond as it wished. If the investigator was able to pick the human only half the time (the same fraction as would be obtained by random guess), then the computer was deemed to have passed this intelligence test.

The rationale for the Turing Test depended on the premise that the human respondent would be intelligent in her or his behavior. If the computer seemed to consistently behave in a similar way, then

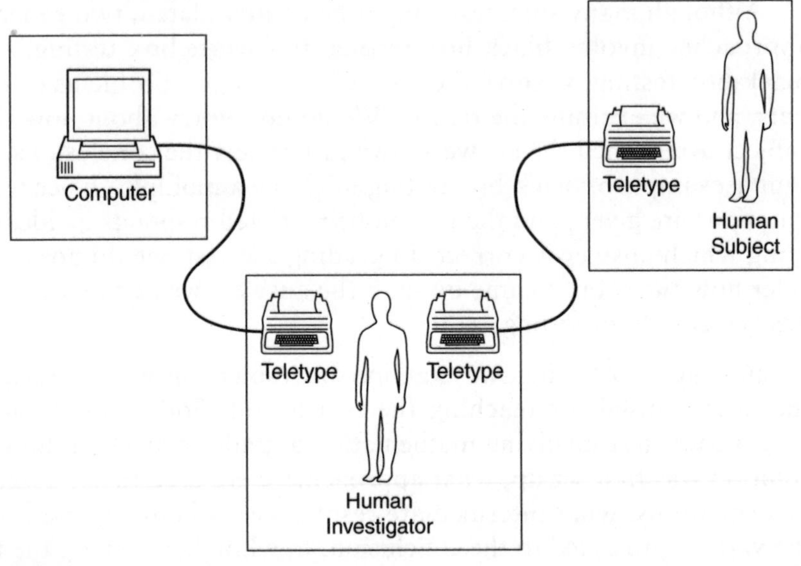

Figure 16.1
Setup for the Turing Test.

the computer would show the same signs of intelligence. Also, because the teletype formed the standard computer interface in 1950, this interface was used for both the computer and the human respondent, so neither party would have an obvious advantage.

With modern technology, we could replace the old teletype with a modern keyboard, screen, and mouse. We also could propose a multimedia workstation with elaborate graphics, sound, mouse or joystick, and other devices. Even with these refinements, the basic Turing Test would be about the same. If a computer can participate in a conversation at the level of a human respondent, supplying answers to questions in whatever field you wish, then the computer would be considered intelligent—or at least as intelligent as the human.

Variations of the Turing Test continue to be discussed in the fields of computer science and philosophy, but the test itself has been subject to at least two types of criticism. The first is that the Turing Test is too restrictive. In particular, earlier in this chapter, we commented that dolphins and chimpanzees are considered to be intelligent. However, neither would be able to pass a test using either a teletype or a multimedia workstation. Similarly, a person who was blind or deaf would not function well with the interface specified, so intelligence clearly is not directly linked to the ability to use a workstation. Overall, various intelligent life forms must allow a more diverse range of interfaces than are typically included in statements of the Turing Test, and this points out some shortcomings.

A second type of criticism suggests that the Turing Test is too inclusive, because it does not consider how the computer or other respondent formulates the answers. Perhaps the most well-known of these critics is philosopher John Searle, who puts forth an objection called the Chinese Room. In this scenario, a person is placed in a room and asked to translate from Chinese to English. This person knows nothing about Chinese, but is given a collection of rules to follow. When this person receives something to translate, the person looks at the characters on the page, identifies the relevant rules, applies the directions given, and produces a translation. Using this method, the person would pass the Turing Test (at least with regard to the translation of Chinese to English) without actually demonstrating any intelligence. Effectively, this objection states that black-box testing cannot provide an adequate mechanism to determine if an entity has intelligence; a similar argument might well apply to any black-box intelligence test.

One counter-argument to the Chinese Room objection analyzes functioning in the human brain—at least as we understand the thought process. Following the scenario for translation from Chinese to English, a person performing translation receives input as Chinese characters and speaks the output in English. To actually receive this input, the human translator reads the characters with her or his eyes, so this information becomes a sequence of impulses that stimulate neurons—first in the translator's eyes, then in the neurons of the brain, and finally in signals to the mouth, tongue, vocal chords, and so on to produce speech. In this process, each neuron gathers electrochemical signals from its neighbors. Then, if conditions are right, a neuron fires, adding further electrochemical signals to the human's system. In this respect, the neuron in the translator's brain has much the same role as the human in Searle's Chinese Room. Neither knows what they are doing; they simply follow rules in their environments. Neither has real knowledge of Chinese or English. From this standpoint, the process for a human translator depends upon basic neurons that respond to electrochemical stimuli, just as the process for the person in the Chinese Room follows another collection of rules. From this perspective, it is difficult to know just what processes we should be examining in identifying intelligence, and black-box testing may seem appropriate after all.

 How do current abilities of computers measure up against these tests for thought?

By most standards, no computer today comes close to passing a Turing Test. Various applications have shown remarkable success in one area or another, but no computer system demonstrates a general knowledge spanning many areas that we might recognize as intelligent. Here are a few examples of success of programs that demonstrate intelligent behavior in a specific context:

- In 1976, Edward Shortliffe published the computer program *Mycin* that captured expertise on the treatment of bacterial blood infections. Based on some 500 rules, Mycin asked a series of questions related to a patient's condition and then recommended an appropriate treatment. Mycin also could provide the chain of reasoning that led to its conclusions—again based on its rules. In this work, Mycin performed as well as specialists in the field and better than most general practitioners.
- By the mid-1990s, computers could transcribe speech as it was said in normal conversation or dictation. For example, Dragon System's NaturallySpeaking and IBM's ViaVoice are reported to work with a 99% accuracy rate. These systems work by dividing speech into sound pieces, called *phonemes*, and then considering how these sounds might fit together to form words. Details include comparing the sound pieces with an extensive database of phonemes through the use of statistical modeling.
- In May 1997, IBM's Deep Blue supercomputer won a six-game chess match against World Champion Garry Kasparov, 3.5–2.5, following standard tournament conditions. To accomplish this level of proficiency, Deep Blue was built upon a reasonably general-purpose, high-performance computing system with many processors. Many details, however, were designed specifically to play chess. For example, the computer contained a database containing details of hundreds of tournament chess matches. Also, the computer could review 100–200 billion positions in the 3 minutes it could take, on average, between moves, according to tournament rules. Before making a move, Deep Blue would consult any relevant

history and also review all possible moves it might make, consider possible responses by its opponent, and so forth, looking a dozen or more moves into the future to determine which current move was most promising.

- In 2000, SpeechWorks was able to extract meanings from speech in certain contexts, in order to allow computer responses to various types of requests. For example, Amtrak uses an automated telephone system by SpeechWorks to allow callers to get train schedules, book reservations, and charge tickets to their credit cards—all based on deciphering a caller's spoken words. After identifying likely words through an analysis of phonemes, it combines the words into phrases and sentences based on both grammatical rules and a vast database of common expressions and sentence fragments.

In each of these cases, computers have performed a task that we might associate with intelligence: medical diagnosis, transcribing speech, winning at chess, and responding to spoken requests regarding trains and reservations. Although each of these applications is a wonderful technical accomplishment, the application has a limited focus, and the computer system does not attempt to respond to more general questions or problems. In each case, the computer might make a credible respondent in some type of Turing Test for the specific area of expertise involved; however, it would have no capacity to work more generally, and the investigator in the Turing Test would have no trouble distinguishing quickly between the computer and the human respondent. The computer would fail the simplest black-box testing of the Turing Test or other test variations.

These applications also would fail white-box testing, as they follow rather different processes than we might expect from people working in similar situations. For example, although Deep Blue reviews roughly 1 billion positions a second, a chess master, such as Garry Kasparov, normally reviews just three positions per second—focusing on which alternatives seem to have the greatest potential. Rather than utilize insight or understanding, Deep Blue proceeds by remarkable computational power. Deep Blue follows a vast array of rules, but it does not comprehend what it is doing.

Interestingly, many popular computer applications have been able to become successful *because* they do not try to seem intelligent. For example, the speech recognition and answering systems do not attempt to analyze what is said or determine its meaning. Rather, they seek to perform useful tasks, based on rules, comparisons with many examples stored in a database, and the use of statistical analysis. The systems do not attempt to summarize words or carry on general conversations. They succeed because they focus on solutions to specific and limited problems, and they utilize mathematical models that take advantage of a computer's ability for the high-speed processing of data. Their methods are often quite different from anything that a human being might be expected to use. Although these applications might pass a black-box Turing Test in a very limited domain, their developers make no attempt to mimic human problem solving or approach something that might pass white-box testing.

Can we expect that future computers might have true intelligence?

Over the years, futurists have established a long tradition of rarely foreseeing the future of technology; for the most part, few people have been able to make reasonable predictions about the long-term future of computing—that is, the nature of computing beyond three to five years. Technology typically evolves differently than futurists predict, or individuals' visions of the future may be shaped too much by their past experiences.

Also, in looking ahead, we need to remember that research normally proceeds incrementally. Although some people theorize about a single breakthrough that will revolutionize technology, the nature of scientific discovery usually is more methodical and evolutionary. Here is another segment from the talk by Woody Bledsoe at the 1985 AAAI meeting:

> First let me express my annoyance with some of our detractors who criticise AI researchers for not "jumping to infinity" in one leap. Somehow to them it is OK to work step-by-step on the dream of obtaining controlled thermonuclear energy or a cure for cancer or a cure for the common cold, but no such step-by-step process is allowed for those trying to (partially) duplicate the intelligent behavior of human beings. To these cynics, a Natural Language system which converses with us in a restricted form of English is somehow

> not a legitimate step toward passing the Turing test. I know of no case in the history of science where such "naysayers" actually helped with a new discovery.**

With the constant evolution of technology, we can be reasonably confident that computers in the future will have significantly greater capabilities than we expect or imagine today. The nature of such capabilities, however, requires speculation. Over the past several decades, the most successful computer applications typically have focused on the solution of specific, narrow problems. When problems are contained, techniques can take advantage of details in the problem, such as limited vocabulary, constrained choices, identifiable algorithms, a wealth or history of examples (perhaps stored in a database), and detailed mathematical models. With this track record, it seems reasonably safe to predict that future computers will be able to solve a wide range of complex problems, well beyond current solutions and applications.

At the same time, past history suggests that applications tend to be less successful when they try to tackle a range of general problems. From this perspective, we might expect computers in a decade or two to show black-box intelligence in significantly more areas, but we would not expect computers to demonstrate the general knowledge needed to handle questions on various subjects as might be given by the human investigator in a general Turing Test. Some current research aims to find methods for general problem solving or conversation, but progress in this area has been slow.

Further, although considerable research is exploring how people function, how the brain works, what electrochemical mechanisms produce what actions, and the like, commercial-level applications seem to be most successful when they do not try to mimic human functioning. Although we can expect many new and spectacular successes from computers, we might be skeptical about whether those successes will come from better understandings of human thought and reasoning. You may or may not believe white-box testing for intelligence is appropriate, but it seems unlikely that computers will satisfy any white-box intelligence tests any time soon.

All of this, however, leaves open the question of whether computers might, someday, be able to think. We may not expect computers to think in the next 10 or 20 years, but is computer intelligence

---

**Bledsoe, W.W. " I Had a Dream: AAAI Presidential Address" 19 August 1985 *AI Magazine* 7(1):58.

even theoretically possible? Details of human thought remain a mystery, so much of the answer to this question depends upon your beliefs regarding the nature of human intelligence. If you believe that humans behave largely based on learned responses to events and stimuli, then you might well believe that research will slowly, but methodically, unpeel the workings of the human brain. Eventually this could lead to understandings of how we think, and such knowledge could lead to various mathematical models and computer applications. From this perspective, computers might eventually be able to think, because we will have learned enough about human thought to model or simulate it.

On the other hand, you may believe that human thought involves something more than electrochemical activities. Until this something more is identified, it would seem that computers might not be able to simulate it for white-box testing of intelligence—although there still might be sufficient technology to handle much black-box intelligence testing. Although this perspective is appealing to many people, it seems to be under constant attack as we learn more about human reactions (as in the experiments of Kornhuber), and as we try to identify what other element(s) might be missing.

Certainly, in the coming years, we all will learn more about the nature of human thought, and many new technologies will emerge to solve problems that we have associated with intelligent behaviors in the past. It will be exciting to observe whether these areas of human thought and computer applications converge, or whether they continue to follow largely separate tracks.

Summary

Consideration of whether computers might one day think begins by investigating what we mean by intelligence. Although some simple definitions can trivially include or exclude the notion that computers could think, these definitions are not very helpful. For example, in a careful analysis of the nature of intelligence, it is not clear that either consciousness or free will is a necessary characteristic.

To avoid biased definitions, objective assessments of intelligence could use either black-box or white-box testing. The Turing Test is the most famous of the black-box testing methods for determining whether or not computers might be able to think. Some criticisms suggest that the Turing Test is too restrictive, whereas others suggest it is too inclusive. Although the Turing Test has its limitations, other testing methodologies also may have shortcomings.

Some current computer systems demonstrate intelligence within a specific area of application. In some areas, computer systems perform as well or better than human experts. The methods used in these computer applications typically take advantage of qualities of computers and may be quite different than methods that humans would use. To date, these application areas are narrow in scope, and modern computers do not demonstrate the breadth of knowledge that we associate with general intelligence.

Woody Bledsoe, a pioneer in the field of artificial intelligence, articulated a vision that one day computers will be able to demonstrate intelligence, acting as a friend and advisor to people, and many researchers in the field today share that vision. Current systems are far from attaining that general vision, and it remains to be seen whether that vision can be obtained.

■ Terminology from This Chapter

black-box testing   Turing Test   white-box testing

■ Discussion Questions

1. The Turing Test is often cited as one mechanism for determining whether an entity is intelligent.

  a. If you needed to update this test to take advantage of modern technology, how would you propose that a current version of the test be run?

  b. To what extent does this test seem adequate or appropriate?

2. The chapter outlines both black-box and white-box testing to determine whether an entity is intelligent. Organize a debate in the class, with one group arguing each of the following positions:

  a. Black-box testing is the appropriate approach for testing intelligence.

  b. White-box testing is the appropriate approach for testing intelligence.

c. No testing strategy can be devised to adequately determine whether an entity is intelligent.

If some members of your group can propose their own approach for determining intelligence, add a fourth team to this debate.

3. Review the description of H. H. Kornhuber's experiment about raising a finger at random.

a. To what extent do you think this supports the notion that free will is an illusion?

b. Organize a class debate, with different teams taking sides on the question of part a.

4. Read the full text of Woody Bledsoe's presidential address to the AAAI, given on August 19, 1985. (This talk, entitled "I Have a Dream," with acknowledgement to Martin Luther King Jr., may be found in *AI Magazine*, volume 7, number 1, pp. 57–61. The reader also might search various online sources for a transcript of the talk.)

a. What is your reaction to the talk?

b. Although the talk was given in 1985, to what extent do you think that its ideas apply today?

c. How might you suggest the talk be updated if it were given again today?

d. The talk was meant to inspire students and potential researchers. Do you think the talk still would accomplish this goal? Explain your answer.

Exercises

1. a. Explain each term in the "Terminology from This Chapter" section.

b. Why do you think the colors "white" and "black" are used in this terminology?

c. Would you consider the Turing Test to be an example of black-box testing, white-box testing, both, or neither? Briefly explain your answer.

2. Read more about IBM's Deep Blue chess-playing computer.
   a. Describe the hardware used for this system. To what extent is this hardware special for this application, and to what extent might the same hardware be used for other applications?
   b. Describe at least five ways in which Deep Blue's approach to playing chess is different from that of a human.
3. Read more about Shortliffe's Mycin program.
   a. Describe precisely what problem Mycin was trying to solve.
   b. Why is this problem considered to be so difficult?
   c. Mycin has been described as being as successful as specialists in the field. How successful is that—about what percentage of the time do specialists in this field typically make exactly the right diagnosis?
   d. Although Mycin has been available for many years, it has not been adopted widely by medical practitioners. Why do you think that Mycin has not been used more?
4. Propose your own definition of "intelligence."
   a. To what extent might dolphins, chimpanzees, or other animals meet your definition—at least in part?
   b. Indicate tests that might be used to determine if a being or computer were intelligent according to your definition.
5. The chapter claims that few, if any, people have been able to make accurate predictions regarding the nature of technology beyond five years or so.
   a. Find some long-term projections made a decade or more ago—perhaps by reading newspaper or magazine articles. Then compare the predictions with what we have actually experienced.
   b. In considering the evolution of technology, identify some factors that might make such predictions difficult.
6. When considering human action, the notion of free will arises when a person must choose among several equally appropriate

choices. If experience or logic dictates one choice over the others, then the alternatives are not equally appropriate, and choice is biased rather than free. For example, in an ice-cream shop where there are dozens of flavors, you know from past experience that you like some flavors better than others, and these preferences likely affect your choice.

a. To what extent do you believe people are in a position to make unbiased choices among equally appropriate choices? That is, can you identify some circumstances for which a person must choose among equally appropriate choices—unbiased by past experience—or can you argue that such circumstances cannot arise?

b. Within computers, programs could make arbitrary choices based on random events, such as the decomposition of radioactive molecules. To what extent could such a choice mechanism be used to simulate the concept of free will?

7. In grade school, I followed the normal process for long division by finding successive digits in the quotient, multiplying a digit by the divisor, subtracting to obtain a new dividend, and continuing until the answer was obtained. For one problem, I was asked to divide a four-digit number by a two-digit number using long division. In this specific case, at one step, I multiplied incorrectly, and I made another error in subtraction. At the end, I got the right answer, but the intermediate steps contained two errors.

a. Would my work on this problem pass black-box testing?

b. Would my work on this problem pass white-box testing?

In each case, justify your conclusion.

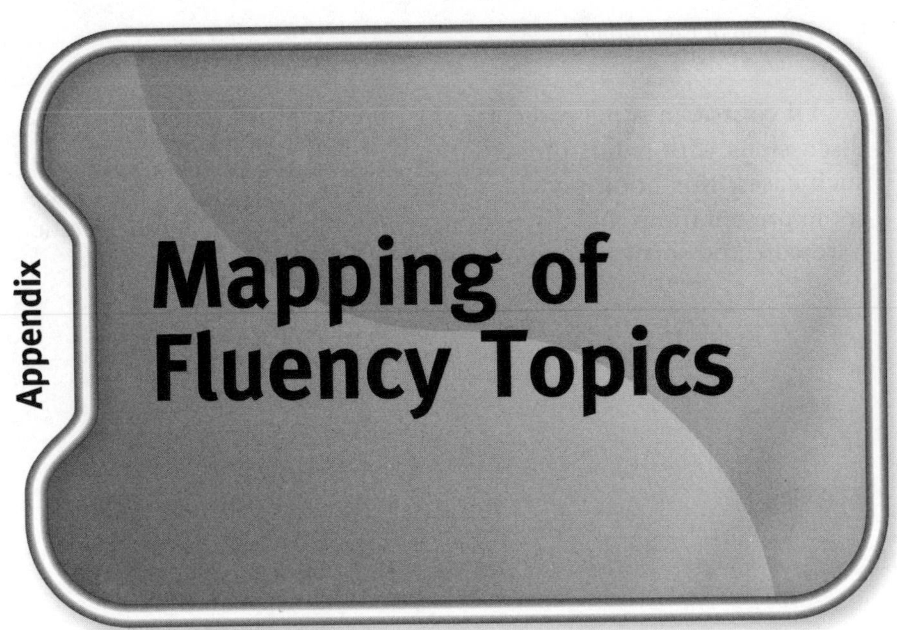

Appendix: Mapping of Fluency Topics

Between 1997 and 1999, the Computer Science and Telecommunications Board of the National Research Council (NRC) considered what computing-related knowledge and skills are vital for general citizens. In 1999, the board's recommendations were published in a booklet, *Being Fluent with Information Technology*. In summary, that report identifies 10 high-level "intellectual capacities," 10 "information technology concepts," and 10 practical "information technology skills" that cover basic computer fluency.

This book has been developed to address each of these capacities, concepts, and skills. More specifically, the following tables provide a general mapping of which of these topics are covered in this book and where. When a chapter discusses a topic, the level of coverage is viewed as "Light," "Moderate," or "Significant." Although these judgments are largely subjective and based on levels appropriate for an introductory audience, they may provide some guidance regarding the organization of topics within this book and extent of topic coverage.

Turning specifically to the coverage of intellectual capacities, the tables that follow highlight discussions within the book. Development of intellectual capacities, however, depends upon practice with exercises as well as understanding of issues and approaches. Thus, in addition to formal discussions, each chapter contains several Discussion Questions and Exercises. These reader-based activities promote many of the identified intellectual capacities throughout the book.

Of course, in some cases, faculty may wish to supplement these discussions with hands-on activities within a laboratory setting. In such cases, this book provides appropriate background for classroom presentations and discussions. A lab might draw upon specific hardware and software manuals and exercises.

Chapter	Intellectual Capacities									
	1. Engage in sustained reasoning	*2. Manage complexity*	*3. Test a solution*	*4. Manage problems in faulty solutions*	*5. Organize, navigate, evaluate information*	*6. Collaborate*	*7. Communi-cate to other audences*	*8. Expect the unexpected*	*9. Anticipate changing technology*	*10. Think about information technology abstractly*
Part I: Low-level Questions										
1. How are computers organized?										
2. How are data represented...?	light								light	
3. Where are programs and data stored?									light	
4. What is an operating system...?		light		moderate						
Part II: Software/Prob.-Solving Questions										
5. How are software packages developed?	significant	moderate	moderate			light		light	moderate	
6. What should I know about sizes/speeds?		moderate				light			moderate	
7. What can computers do for me?	light		light	light				light	moderate	moderate
Part III: Networking/Dist. Sys. Questions										
8. How are computers connected?		light								
9. How do users share computer files?										light
10. When can I consider ... data secure?					light			light		light
Part IV: Web/Internet Questions										
11. How does the Internet work?		light		light	moderate	moderate	light			light
12. How public/private are Web interactions?					light		moderate	light		moderate
13. How do Web applications work?		light		light	moderate		moderate	light		
Part V: Social/Ethical Questions										
14. How universal is access to computers...?								light	moderate	moderate
15. Can I use Web-based materials...?					moderate	light	light			moderate
16. Can computers think...?								light	moderate	moderate

Chapter	Information Technology Concepts									
	1. Computers	*2. Information systems*	*3. Networks*	*4. Digitial represent-ation of information*	*5. Information organization*	*6. Modeling and abstraction*	*7. Algorithmic thinking and prog.*	*8. Univers-ality*	*9. Limitations of information technology*	*10. Societal impact*
Part I: Low-level Questions										
1. How are computers organized?	significant	significant								
2. How are data represented...?				significant					moderate	
3. Where are programs and data stored?	significant									
4. What is an operating system...?	moderate	moderate								
Part II: Software/Prob.-Solving Questions										
5. How are software packages developed?	moderate								moderate	light
6. What should I know about sizes/speeds?								moderate		
7. What can computers do for me?						significant	moderate	significant	significant	
Part III: Networking/Dist. Sys. Questions										
8. How are computers connected?			significant						light	
9. How do users share computer files?			significant						light	light
10. When can I consider ... data secure?	significant	significant	moderate	light					light	moderate
Part IV: Web/Internet Questions										
11. How does the Internet work?			moderate			light	light		light	light
12. How public/private are Web interactions?			moderate				moderate			light
13. How do Web applications work?					significant					moderate
Part V: Social/Ethical Questions										
14. How universal is access to computers...?			light							significant
15. Can I use Web-based materials...?			light		moderate					significant
16. Can computers think...?						moderate			light	moderate

Information Technology Skills

Chapter	*1. Setting up a personal computer*	*2. Using a basic operating system*	*3. Using a word processor*	*4. Using a graphics or artwork package*	*5. Connecting a computer to a network*	*6. Using the Internet to find information*	*7. Using a computer to communicate to others*	*8. Using a spreadsheet to model simple processes*	*9. Using a database system*	*10. Using. instruct. materials to learn new apps.*
Part I: Low-level Questions										
1. How are computers organized?	light									
2. How are data represented...?				light						
3. Where are programs and data stored?										
4. What is an operating system...?	moderate	moderate								
Part II: Software/Prob.-Solving Questions										
5. How are software packages developed?	light									
6. What should I know about sizes/speeds?	moderate									
7. What can computers do for me?	light	moderate	light	light				light	light	
Part III: Networking/Dist. Sys. Questions										
8. How are computers connected?					moderate					
9. How do users share computer files?					moderate		moderate			
10. When can I consider ... data secure?					light	light				
Part IV: Web/Internet Questions										
11. How does the Internet work?						moderate				
12. How public/private are Web interactions?						moderate	moderate			
13. How do Web applications work?						moderate	moderate			moderate
Part V: Social/Ethical Questions										
14. How universal is access to computers...?										
15. Can I use Web-based materials...?						moderate				light
16. Can computers think...?						moderate	light			light

Index

1

8

A

B

C

D

E

F

G

H

I

M

N

O

Q

R

S

T

U

V

W